2014 | THE LITTLE GREEN DATA BOOK

THE WORLD BANK

The Little Green Data Book 2014 is a product of the Development Data Group
of the Development Economics Vice Presidency and the Agriculture and
Environmental Services Department of the World Bank.

Design by Communications Development Incorporated, Washington, D.C.

Contents

Acknowledgments

The Little Green Data Book 2014 is based on *World Development Indicators 2014* and its online database. Defining, gathering, and disseminating international statistics is a collective effort of many people and organizations. The indicators presented in *World Development Indicators* are the fruit of decades of work at many levels, from the field workers who administer censuses and household surveys to the committees and working parties of the national and international statistical agencies that develop the nomenclature, classifications, and standards fundamental to the international statistical system. Nongovernmental organizations have also made important contributions. We are indebted to the *World Development Indicators* partners, as detailed in *World Development Indicators 2014*.

The Little Green Data Book 2014 is the result of close collaboration between the staff of the Development Data Group of the Development Economics Vice Presidency and the Agriculture and Environmental Services Department of the Sustainable Development Vice Presidency. Liu Cui, Mahyar Eshragh-Tabary, Sonu Jain, Esther Naikal, Urvashi Narain, Ulf Narloch, William Prince, and Jomo Tariku contributed to its preparation. Azita Amjadi coordinated the production of the book. Barton Matheson Willse & Worthington typeset the book. The work was carried out under the direction of Haishan Fu and Juergen Voegele. Staff from The World Bank's Publishing and Knowledge Division oversaw publication and dissemination of the book.

Foreword

The goals of the World Bank Group are to eradicate poverty and promote shared prosperity in a manner that ensures environmental, social, and economic sustainability. In a world of finite planetary boundaries and natural resources it is important that any progress made toward these twin goals can be sustained.

To operationalize the twin goals, two indicators—the number of people in extreme poverty and the income growth of the bottom 40 percent—were introduced with the adoption of the goals in April 2013. Yet measuring progress toward these goals requires a better understanding of the sustainability dimensions of progress, with measurable indicators.

Meaningful sustainability indicators are also important for the formulation of the Sustainable Development Goals (SDGs). The importance of putting sustainable development at the core of the post-2015 development framework has been recognized. Yet this will require measurable targets.

Capturing a concept through a few summary indicators is difficult for all fields, but it is doubly complex for sustainability, with its multiple facets, global and local dimensions, long time horizon, and limited data availability.

Accumulation of wealth is at the heart of the issue of determining whether development in a country is sustainable. It is wealth—broadly defined to include produced capital, natural capital (including forests), and human and social capital—that underlies the generation of national income. Gross domestic product (GDP) has conventionally been used to assess economic performance, measuring economic growth from one year to the next. But GDP does not take into account depreciation and depletion of wealth, and therefore does not provide an indication of whether growth is sustainable. An economy could appear to be growing in the near term by running down assets. Assessments of economic performance therefore need to be based on both measures of annual growth (such as GDP) and measures of the comprehensive wealth of a country, which indicate whether that growth is sustainable in the long term.

Touching upon this idea, the World Bank Group's corporate scorecard, result measurement frameworks, and country diagnostics will apply change in wealth per capita as a new sustainability indicator. It is a modified version of the genuine savings or adjusted net savings indicator that measures changes in produced, human, and natural capital, and accounts for the wealth-diluting effects of population growth (Box 1). A country with continuously negative changes in wealth per capita is depleting its wealth and can be said to be on an unsustainable development path.

This metric allows policy makers to identify some of the threats to the sustainability of economic growth and policy solutions to strengthen comprehensive wealth accumulation. Yet we will need complementary indicators to understand all the dimensions of sustainability. *The Little*

Foreword

Box 1. Change in Wealth per Capita: A Framework for Identifying Wealth Depletion

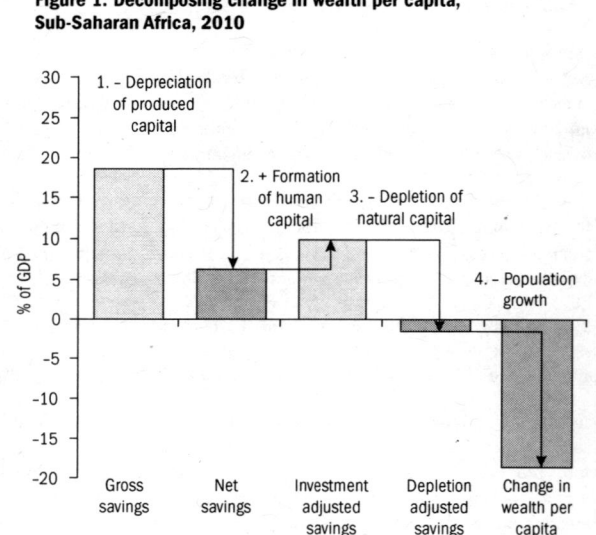

Figure 1: Decomposing change in wealth per capita, Sub-Saharan Africa, 2010

Source: World Bank, *Wealth database*, 2014.

Change in wealth per capita offers a comprehensive framework to look at sustainability threats to the twin goals. It is derived from standard national accounting measures of gross national savings by making four types of adjustments (Figure 1):

(1) Deduction for depreciation of produced capital, measured by capital consumption of produced assets;

(2) Addition from human capital formation, measured by current expenditures on education;

(3) Deduction for depletion of natural capital, including minerals, energy, and forest resources; and

(4) Deduction for wealth-diluting effects of population growth, based on the additional savings needed to keep current tangible wealth per capita constant with a changing population.

As the case of Sub-Saharan Africa in 2010 illustrates, aggregated gross savings and formation of human capital are not sufficient to compensate for depreciation of produced capital, depletion of natural capital, and population growth. The result: the region is wealth depleting (Figure 1).

Furthermore, Sub-Saharan Africa is the region with the poorest record on sustainability. 88 percent of its countries were found to be depleting their wealth in 2010 (Table 1). The share of countries with wealth depletion—globally at about 45 percent—decreases as income levels increase (Table 1), indicating that poorer countries face severe sustainability challenges.

In many resource-rich countries, reinvesting natural resource rents in other forms of productive capital is one important way of avoiding wealth depletion.

Table 1. Overview: Data and Wealth Depletion in 2010

	Number of countries with data	Share of countries with wealth depletion
Global	136	45%
High income countries	41	22%
Upper middle income	35	34%
Lower middle income	33	58%
Low income	24	88%
South Asia	6	17%
Europe & Central Asia	15	27%
East Asia & Pacific	11	36%
Middle East & North Africa	7	43%
Latin America & Caribbean	21	57%
Sub-Saharan Africa	32	88%

Source: World Bank, *Wealth database*, 2014.

Green Data Book offers a starting point for the selection of country-relevant "green" metrics that can provide a comprehensive picture of environmental sustainability challenges.

The *Little Green Data Book* is a result of close collaboration between the Development Data Group of the Development Economics Vice Presidency and the Agriculture and Environmental Services Department of the Sustainable Development Network Vice Presidency. We welcome suggestions on how to improve future editions and make them even more useful.

Juergen Voegle
Director
Agriculture and Environmental Services

Haishan Fu
Director
Development Data Group

Data notes

The data in this book are for the most recent year available as noted in the glossary.

- Growth rates are calculated as annual averages and represented as percentages.

- Regional aggregates include data for low- and middle-income economies only.

- Figures in italics indicate data for years or periods other than those specified in the glossary.

Symbols used:

..	indicates that data are not available or that aggregates cannot be calculated because of missing data.
0 or 0.0	indicates zero or small enough that the number would round to zero at the displayed number of decimal places.
$	indicates current U.S. dollars.

Lettered notes on country tables can be found in the *Notes* page. Data are shown for economies with populations greater than 30,000 or for smaller economies if they are members of the World Bank. The term *country* (used interchangeably with *economy*) does not imply political independence or official recognition by the World Bank but refers to any economy for which the authorities report separate social or economic statistics.

The selection of indicators in these pages includes some of those being used to monitor progress toward the Millennium Development Goals. For more information about the eight goals—halving poverty and increasing well-being by 2015—please see the other books in the *World Development Indicators 2014* family of products.

The cutoff date for data is May 1, 2014.

Regional tables

The country composition of regions is based on the World Bank's analytical regions and may differ from common geographic usage. These regions include low- and middle-income economies only.

East Asia and Pacific

American Samoa, Cambodia, China, Fiji, Indonesia, Kiribati, Democratic People's Republic of Korea, Lao People's Democratic Republic, Malaysia, Marshall Islands, Federated States of Micronesia, Mongolia, Myanmar, Palau, Papua New Guinea, Philippines, Samoa, Solomon Islands, Thailand, Timor-Leste, Tonga, Tuvalu, Vanuatu, Vietnam

Europe and Central Asia

Albania, Armenia, Azerbaijan, Belarus, Bosnia and Herzegovina, Bulgaria, Georgia, Hungary, Kazakhstan, Kosovo, Kyrgyz Republic, Former Yugoslav Republic of Macedonia, Moldova, Montenegro, Romania, Serbia, Tajikistan, Turkey, Turkmenistan, Ukraine, Uzbekistan

Latin America and the Caribbean

Argentina, Belize, Bolivia, Brazil, Colombia, Costa Rica, Cuba, Dominica, Dominican Republic, Ecuador, El Salvador, Grenada, Guatemala, Guyana, Haiti, Honduras, Jamaica, Mexico, Nicaragua, Panama, Paraguay, Peru, St. Lucia, St. Vincent and the Grenadines, Suriname, República Bolivariana de Venezuela

Middle East and North Africa

Algeria, Djibouti, Arab Republic of Egypt, Islamic Republic of Iran, Iraq, Jordan, Lebanon, Libya, Morocco, Syrian Arab Republic, Tunisia, West Bank and Gaza, Republic of Yemen

South Asia

Afghanistan, Bangladesh, Bhutan, India, Maldives, Nepal, Pakistan, Sri Lanka

Sub-Saharan Africa

Angola, Benin, Botswana, Burkina Faso, Burundi, Cabo Verde, Cameroon, Central African Republic, Chad, Comoros, Democratic Republic of Congo, Republic of Congo, Côte d'Ivoire, Eritrea, Ethiopia, Gabon, The Gambia, Ghana, Guinea, Guinea-Bissau, Kenya, Lesotho, Liberia, Madagascar, Malawi, Mali, Mauritania, Mauritius, Mozambique, Namibia, Niger, Nigeria, Rwanda, São Tomé and Príncipe, Senegal, Seychelles, Sierra Leone, Somalia, South Africa, South Sudan, Sudan, Swaziland, Tanzania, Togo, Uganda, Zambia, Zimbabwe

World

Population (millions) **7,043.9** Land area (1,000 sq. km) **129,710** GDP ($ billions) **72,682.0**

GNI per capita, *World Bank Atlas* method ($)	10,212
Adjusted net national income per capita ($)	8,558
Change in wealth per capita (2010 $)	662
Urban population (% of total)	52.5

Agriculture
Agricultural land (% land area)	38
Agricultural irrigated land (% of total agricultural land)	..
Agricultural productivity, value added per worker (2005 $)	1,176
Cereal yield (kg per hectare)	3,622

Forests and biodiversity
Forest area (% land area)	30.9
Deforestation (avg. annual %, 2000–2010)	0.1
Terrestrial protected areas (% of total land area)	14.3
Threatened species, mammals	3,125
Threatened species, birds	3,822
Threatened species, fish	6,404
Threatened species, higher plants	12,670

Oceans
Total fisheries production (thousand metric tons)	182,853
Capture fisheries growth (avg. annual %, 1990–2012)	0.4
Aquaculture growth (avg. annual %, 1990–2012)	7.9
Marine protected areas (% of territorial waters)	*10.0*
Coral reef area (sq. km)	284,300
Mangroves area (sq. km)	150,398

Energy and emissions
Energy use per capita (kg oil equivalent)	1,890
Energy from biomass products and waste (% of total)	9.8
Electric power consumption per capita (kWh)	3,044
Electricity generated using fossil fuel (% of total)	67.0
Electricity generated by hydropower (% of total)	15.6
CO_2 emissions per capita (metric tons)	4.9

Water and sanitation
Internal freshwater resources per capita (cu. m)	6,122
Total freshwater withdrawal (% of internal resources)	9.2
Agriculture (% of total freshwater withdrawal)	70
Access to improved water source (% of total population)	89
Rural (% of rural population)	82
Urban (% of urban population)	96
Access to improved sanitation facilities (% of total population)	64
Rural (% of rural population)	47
Urban (% of urban population)	79

Environment and health
Particulate matter (urban-pop.-weighted avg., μg/cu. m)	61
Acute resp. infection prevalence (% of children under five)	..
Diarrhea prevalence (% of children under five)	..
Under-five mortality rate (per 1,000 live births)	48

National accounting aggregates—savings, depletion and degradation
Gross savings (% of GNI)	24.5
Consumption of fixed capital (% of GNI)	13.6
Education expenditure (% of GNI)	4.3
Energy depletion (% of GNI)	2.4
Mineral depletion (% of GNI)	0.6
Net forest depletion (% of GNI)	0.1
CO_2 damage (% of GNI)	0.5
Particulate emissions damage (% of GNI)	0.6
Adjusted net savings (% of GNI)	11.1

East Asia & Pacific

Population (millions) **1,991.6** Land area (1,000 sq. km) **15,853** GDP ($ billions)**10,329.7**

GNI per capita, *World Bank Atlas* method ($)	4,884
Adjusted net national income per capita ($)	4,305
Change in wealth per capita (2010 $)	1,172
Urban population (% of total)	49.6

Agriculture

Agricultural land (% land area)	48
Agricultural irrigated land (% of total agricultural land)	..
Agricultural productivity, value added per worker (2005 $)	794
Cereal yield (kg per hectare)	5,145

Forests and biodiversity

Forest area (% land area)	29.7
Deforestation (avg. annual %, 2000–2010)	-0.4
Terrestrial protected areas (% of total land area)	15.1
Threatened species, mammals	
Threatened species, birds	
Threatened species, fish	
Threatened species, higher plants	

Oceans

Total fisheries production (thousand metric tons)	108,399
Capture fisheries growth (avg. annual %, 1990–2012)	3.4
Aquaculture growth (avg. annual %, 1990–2012)	9.1
Marine protected areas (% of territorial waters)	1.4
Coral reef area (sq. km)	137,690
Mangroves area (sq. km)	56,537

Energy and emissions

Energy use per capita (kg oil equivalent)	1,671
Energy from biomass products and waste (% of total)	10.1
Electric power consumption per capita (kWh)	2,582
Electricity generated using fossil fuel (% of total)	80.9
Electricity generated by hydropower (% of total)	14.5
CO_2 emissions per capita (metric tons)	4.9

Water and sanitation

Internal freshwater resources per capita (cu. m)	4,438
Total freshwater withdrawal (% of internal resources)	10.9
Agriculture (% of total freshwater withdrawal)	73
Access to improved water source (% of total population)	91
Rural (% of rural population)	85
Urban (% of urban population)	97
Access to improved sanitation facilities (% of total population)	67
Rural (% of rural population)	58
Urban (% of urban population)	76

Environment and health

Particulate matter (urban-pop.-weighted avg., µg/cu. m)	75
Acute resp. infection prevalence (% of children under five)	..
Diarrhea prevalence (% of children under five)	..
Under-five mortality rate (per 1,000 live births)	21

National accounting aggregates—savings, depletion and degradation

Gross savings (% of GNI)	47.6
Consumption of fixed capital (% of GNI)	12.0
Education expenditure (% of GNI)	2.1
Energy depletion (% of GNI)	2.7
Mineral depletion (% of GNI)	1.4
Net forest depletion (% of GNI)	0.1
CO_2 damage (% of GNI)	1.0
Particulate emissions damage (% of GNI)	1.6
Adjusted net savings (% of GNI)	30.9

Europe & Central Asia

Population (millions) **270.8** Land area (1,000 sq. km) **6,337** GDP ($ billions) **1,865.3**

GNI per capita, *World Bank Atlas* method ($)	6,658
Adjusted net national income per capita ($)	5,541
Change in wealth per capita (2010 $)	263
Urban population (% of total)	60.2

Agriculture

Agricultural land (% land area)	66
Agricultural irrigated land (% of total agricultural land)	..
Agricultural productivity, value added per worker (2005 $)	4,866
Cereal yield (kg per hectare)	2,519

Forests and biodiversity

Forest area (% land area)	10.5
Deforestation (avg. annual %, 2000-2010)	-0.5
Terrestrial protected areas (% of total land area)	5.1
Threatened species, mammals	
Threatened species, birds	
Threatened species, fish	
Threatened species, higher plants	

Oceans

Total fisheries production (thousand metric tons)	1,022
Capture fisheries growth (avg. annual %, 1990-2012)	-4.0
Aquaculture growth (avg. annual %, 1990-2012)	1.8
Marine protected areas (% of territorial waters)	10.4
Coral reef area (sq. km)	..
Mangroves area (sq. km)	..

Energy and emissions

Energy use per capita (kg oil equivalent)	2,078
Energy from biomass products and waste (% of total)	2.9
Electric power consumption per capita (kWh)	2,951
Electricity generated using fossil fuel (% of total)	65.8
Electricity generated by hydropower (% of total)	17.9
CO_2 emissions per capita (metric tons)	5.3

Water and sanitation

Internal freshwater resources per capita (cu. m)	2,744
Total freshwater withdrawal (% of internal resources)	34.8
Agriculture (% of total freshwater withdrawal)	70
Access to improved water source (% of total population)	95
Rural (% of rural population)	89
Urban (% of urban population)	99
Access to improved sanitation facilities (% of total population)	94
Rural (% of rural population)	90
Urban (% of urban population)	97

Environment and health

Particulate matter (urban-pop.-weighted avg., µg/cu. m)	48
Acute resp. infection prevalence (% of children under five)	..
Diarrhea prevalence (% of children under five)	..
Under-five mortality rate (per 1,000 live births)	22

National accounting aggregates—savings, depletion and degradation

Gross savings (% of GNI)	18.9
Consumption of fixed capital (% of GNI)	12.4
Education expenditure (% of GNI)	3.8
Energy depletion (% of GNI)	4.4
Mineral depletion (% of GNI)	0.6
Net forest depletion (% of GNI)	0.0
CO_2 damage (% of GNI)	0.8
Particulate emissions damage (% of GNI)	1.8
Adjusted net savings (% of GNI)	2.8

Latin America & Caribbean

Population (millions) **581.4** Land area (1,000 sq. km) **19,197** GDP ($ billions) **5,344.0**

GNI per capita, *World Bank Atlas* method ($)	9,070
Adjusted net national income per capita ($)	7,325
Change in wealth per capita (2010 $)	180
Urban population (% of total)	79.0

Agriculture

Agricultural land (% land area)	37
Agricultural irrigated land (% of total agricultural land)	..
Agricultural productivity, value added per worker (2005 $)	4,135
Cereal yield (kg per hectare)	4,082

Forests and biodiversity

Forest area (% land area)	48.1
Deforestation (avg. annual %, 2000–2010)	0.5
Terrestrial protected areas (% of total land area)	21.4
Threatened species, mammals	
Threatened species, birds	
Threatened species, fish	
Threatened species, higher plants	

Oceans

Total fisheries production (thousand metric tons)	10,964
Capture fisheries growth (avg. annual %, 1990–2012)	-0.6
Aquaculture growth (avg. annual %, 1990–2012)	10.8
Marine protected areas (% of territorial waters)	9.0
Coral reef area (sq. km)	14,860
Mangroves area (sq. km)	39,988

Energy and emissions

Energy use per capita (kg oil equivalent)	1,292
Energy from biomass products and waste (% of total)	16.0
Electric power consumption per capita (kWh)	1,985
Electricity generated using fossil fuel (% of total)	37.3
Electricity generated by hydropower (% of total)	55.1
CO_2 emissions per capita (metric tons)	2.7

Water and sanitation

Internal freshwater resources per capita (cu. m)	21,735
Total freshwater withdrawal (% of internal resources)	2.0
Agriculture (% of total freshwater withdrawal)	68
Access to improved water source (% of total population)	94
Rural (% of rural population)	82
Urban (% of urban population)	97
Access to improved sanitation facilities (% of total population)	81
Rural (% of rural population)	62
Urban (% of urban population)	86

Environment and health

Particulate matter (urban-pop.-weighted avg., μg/cu. m)	43
Acute resp. infection prevalence (% of children under five)	..
Diarrhea prevalence (% of children under five)	..
Under-five mortality rate (per 1,000 live births)	19

National accounting aggregates—savings, depletion and degradation

Gross savings (% of GNI)	19.0
Consumption of fixed capital (% of GNI)	12.2
Education expenditure (% of GNI)	5.1
Energy depletion (% of GNI)	4.7
Mineral depletion (% of GNI)	1.2
Net forest depletion (% of GNI)	0.4
CO_2 damage (% of GNI)	0.3
Particulate emissions damage (% of GNI)	0.8
Adjusted net savings (% of GNI)	4.5

Middle East & North Africa

Population (millions) **339.6**   Land area (1,000 sq. km) **8,641**   GDP ($ billions) **1,662.7**

GNI per capita, *World Bank Atlas* method ($)	3,451
Adjusted net national income per capita ($)	2,602
Change in wealth per capita (2010 $)	101
Urban population (% of total)	59.5

Agriculture

Agricultural land (% land area)	23
Agricultural irrigated land (% of total agricultural land)	..
Agricultural productivity, value added per worker (2005 $)	2,642
Cereal yield (kg per hectare)	2,350

Forests and biodiversity

Forest area (% land area)	2.4
Deforestation (avg. annual %, 2000–2010)	-0.1
Terrestrial protected areas (% of total land area)	6.1
Threatened species, mammals	
Threatened species, birds	
Threatened species, fish	
Threatened species, higher plants	

Oceans

Total fisheries production (thousand metric tons)	3,976
Capture fisheries growth (avg. annual %, 1990–2012)	3.0
Aquaculture growth (avg. annual %, 1990–2012)	12.8
Marine protected areas (% of territorial waters)	9.1
Coral reef area (sq. km)	5,700
Mangroves area (sq. km)	217

Energy and emissions

Energy use per capita (kg oil equivalent)	1,376
Energy from biomass products and waste (% of total)	0.9
Electric power consumption per capita (kWh)	1,696
Electricity generated using fossil fuel (% of total)	91.7
Electricity generated by hydropower (% of total)	5.5
CO_2 emissions per capita (metric tons)	3.9

Water and sanitation

Internal freshwater resources per capita (cu. m)	679
Total freshwater withdrawal (% of internal resources)	122.1
Agriculture (% of total freshwater withdrawal)	86
Access to improved water source (% of total population)	90
Rural (% of rural population)	83
Urban (% of urban population)	95
Access to improved sanitation facilities (% of total population)	88
Rural (% of rural population)	80
Urban (% of urban population)	94

Environment and health

Particulate matter (urban-pop.-weighted avg., µg/cu. m)	79
Acute resp. infection prevalence (% of children under five)	..
Diarrhea prevalence (% of children under five)	..
Under-five mortality rate (per 1,000 live births)	26

National accounting aggregates—savings, depletion and degradation

Gross savings (% of GNI)	25.9
Consumption of fixed capital (% of GNI)	9.9
Education expenditure (% of GNI)	4.5
Energy depletion (% of GNI)	12.9
Mineral depletion (% of GNI)	0.5
Net forest depletion (% of GNI)	0.2
CO_2 damage (% of GNI)	0.7
Particulate emissions damage (% of GNI)	0.9
Adjusted net savings (% of GNI)	5.3

South Asia

Population (millions) **1,649.2**   Land area (1,000 sq. km) **4,771**   GDP ($ billions) **2,303.1**

GNI per capita, *World Bank Atlas* method ($)	1,437
Adjusted net national income per capita ($)	1,168
Change in wealth per capita (2010 $)	158
Urban population (% of total)	31.4

Agriculture

Agricultural land (% land area)	55
Agricultural irrigated land (% of total agricultural land)	..
Agricultural productivity, value added per worker (2005 $)	669
Cereal yield (kg per hectare)	2,925

Forests and biodiversity

Forest area (% land area)	17.1
Deforestation (avg. annual %, 2000–2010)	-0.3
Terrestrial protected areas (% of total land area)	6.2
Threatened species, mammals	
Threatened species, birds	
Threatened species, fish	
Threatened species, higher plants	

Oceans

Total fisheries production (thousand metric tons)	13,613
Capture fisheries growth (avg. annual %, 1990–2012)	2.6
Aquaculture growth (avg. annual %, 1990–2012)	7.6
Marine protected areas (% of territorial waters)	10.7
Coral reef area (sq. km)	15,440
Mangroves area (sq. km)	10,343

Energy and emissions

Energy use per capita (kg oil equivalent)	555
Energy from biomass products and waste (% of total)	26.7
Electric power consumption per capita (kWh)	605
Electricity generated using fossil fuel (% of total)	77.9
Electricity generated by hydropower (% of total)	13.8
CO_2 emissions per capita (metric tons)	1.4

Water and sanitation

Internal freshwater resources per capita (cu. m)	1,217
Total freshwater withdrawal (% of internal resources)	51.6
Agriculture (% of total freshwater withdrawal)	91
Access to improved water source (% of total population)	91
Rural (% of rural population)	89
Urban (% of urban population)	95
Access to improved sanitation facilities (% of total population)	40
Rural (% of rural population)	30
Urban (% of urban population)	61

Environment and health

Particulate matter (urban-pop.-weighted avg., µg/cu. m)	110
Acute resp. infection prevalence (% of children under five)	..
Diarrhea prevalence (% of children under five)	..
Under-five mortality rate (per 1,000 live births)	60

National accounting aggregates—savings, depletion and degradation

Gross savings (% of GNI)	29.3
Consumption of fixed capital (% of GNI)	12.7
Education expenditure (% of GNI)	2.8
Energy depletion (% of GNI)	1.8
Mineral depletion (% of GNI)	0.8
Net forest depletion (% of GNI)	1.1
CO_2 damage (% of GNI)	1.1
Particulate emissions damage (% of GNI)	1.5
Adjusted net savings (% of GNI)	13.1

Sub-Saharan Africa

Population (millions) 911.5 Land area (1,000 sq. km) **23,589** GDP ($ billions) **1,485.0**

GNI per capita, *World Bank Atlas* method ($)	1,547
Adjusted net national income per capita ($)	1,005
Change in wealth per capita (2010 $)	-273
Urban population (% of total)	36.8

Agriculture

Agricultural land (% land area)	44
Agricultural irrigated land (% of total agricultural land)	..
Agricultural productivity, value added per worker (2005 $)	765
Cereal yield (kg per hectare)	1,417

Forests and biodiversity

Forest area (% land area)	27.4
Deforestation (avg. annual %, 2000–2010)	0.5
Terrestrial protected areas (% of total land area)	16.4
Threatened species, mammals	
Threatened species, birds	
Threatened species, fish	
Threatened species, higher plants	

Oceans

Total fisheries production (thousand metric tons)	6,906
Capture fisheries growth (avg. annual %, 1990–2012)	2.1
Aquaculture growth (avg. annual %, 1990–2012)	15.9
Marine protected areas (% of territorial waters)	11.7
Coral reef area (sq. km)	17,980
Mangroves area (sq. km)	27,808

Energy and emissions

Energy use per capita (kg oil equivalent)	681
Energy from biomass products and waste (% of total)	57.6
Electric power consumption per capita (kWh)	535
Electricity generated using fossil fuel (% of total)	65.1
Electricity generated by hydropower (% of total)	20.0
CO_2 emissions per capita (metric tons)	0.8

Water and sanitation

Internal freshwater resources per capita (cu. m)	4,391
Total freshwater withdrawal (% of internal resources)	3.2
Agriculture (% of total freshwater withdrawal)	84
Access to improved water source (% of total population)	64
Rural (% of rural population)	53
Urban (% of urban population)	85
Access to improved sanitation facilities (% of total population)	30
Rural (% of rural population)	23
Urban (% of urban population)	41

Environment and health

Particulate matter (urban-pop.-weighted avg., µg/cu. m)	77
Acute resp. infection prevalence (% of children under five)	5
Diarrhea prevalence (% of children under five)	14
Under-five mortality rate (per 1,000 live births)	98

National accounting aggregates—savings, depletion and degradation

Gross savings (% of GNI)	26.3
Consumption of fixed capital (% of GNI)	13.0
Education expenditure (% of GNI)	3.4
Energy depletion (% of GNI)	10.3
Mineral depletion (% of GNI)	1.8
Net forest depletion (% of GNI)	1.8
CO_2 damage (% of GNI)	0.6
Particulate emissions damage (% of GNI)	1.2
Adjusted net savings (% of GNI)	0.9

Income group tables

For operational and analytical purposes the World Bank's main criterion for classifying economies is gross national income (GNI) per capita. Each economy in *The Little Data Book* is classified as low income, middle income, or high income. Low- and middle-income economies are sometimes referred to as developing economies. The use of the term is convenient; it is not intended to imply that all economies in the group are experiencing similar development or that other economies have reached a preferred or final stage of development. Classification by income does not necessarily reflect development status. Note: Classifications are fixed during the World Bank's fiscal year (ending on June 30), thus countries remain in the categories in which they are classified irrespective of any revisions to their per capita income data.

Low-income economies are those with a GNI per capita of $1,035 or less in 2012.

Middle-income economies are those with a GNI per capita of more than $1,035 but less than $12,616. Lower-middle-income and upper-middle-income economies are separated at a GNI per capita of $4,085.

High-income economies are those with a GNI per capita of $12,616 or more.

Euro area includes the member states of the Economic and Monetary Union of the European Union that have adopted the euro as their currency: Austria, Belgium, Cyprus, Estonia, Finland, France, Germany, Greece, Ireland, Italy, Latvia, Luxembourg, Malta, Netherlands, Portugal, Slovak Republic, Slovenia, and Spain.

Low income

Population (millions) **846.5** Land area (1,000 sq. km) **15,048** GDP ($ billions) **505.8**

GNI per capita, *World Bank Atlas* method ($)	594
Adjusted net national income per capita ($)	495
Change in wealth per capita (2010 $)	–39
Urban population (% of total)	28.2

Agriculture
Agricultural land (% land area)	39
Agricultural irrigated land (% of total agricultural land)	..
Agricultural productivity, value added per worker (2005 $)	367
Cereal yield (kg per hectare)	1,982

Forests and biodiversity
Forest area (% land area)	27.4
Deforestation (avg. annual %, 2000–2010)	0.6
Terrestrial protected areas (% of total land area)	13.7
Threatened species, mammals	
Threatened species, birds	
Threatened species, fish	
Threatened species, higher plants	

Oceans
Total fisheries production (thousand metric tons)	11,789
Capture fisheries growth (avg. annual %, 1990–2012)	3.8
Aquaculture growth (avg. annual %, 1990–2012)	5.1
Marine protected areas (% of territorial waters)	13.1
Coral reef area (sq. km)	15,120
Mangroves area (sq. km)	25,817

Energy and emissions
Energy use per capita (kg oil equivalent)	360
Energy from biomass products and waste (% of total)	66.0
Electric power consumption per capita (kWh)	233
Electricity generated using fossil fuel (% of total)	30.9
Electricity generated by hydropower (% of total)	45.5
CO_2 emissions per capita (metric tons)	0.3

Water and sanitation
Internal freshwater resources per capita (cu. m)	5,121
Total freshwater withdrawal (% of internal resources)	4.4
Agriculture (% of total freshwater withdrawal)	90
Access to improved water source (% of total population)	69
Rural (% of rural population)	61
Urban (% of urban population)	88
Access to improved sanitation facilities (% of total population)	37
Rural (% of rural population)	33
Urban (% of urban population)	46

Environment and health
Particulate matter (urban-pop.-weighted avg., µg/cu. m)	74
Acute resp. infection prevalence (% of children under five)	6
Diarrhea prevalence (% of children under five)	14
Under-five mortality rate (per 1,000 live births)	82

National accounting aggregates—savings, depletion and degradation
Gross savings (% of GNI)	24.6
Consumption of fixed capital (% of GNI)	11.8
Education expenditure (% of GNI)	3.2
Energy depletion (% of GNI)	1.4
Mineral depletion (% of GNI)	1.9
Net forest depletion (% of GNI)	4.4
CO_2 damage (% of GNI)	0.4
Particulate emissions damage (% of GNI)	1.0
Adjusted net savings (% of GNI)	7.0

Middle income

Population (millions) **4,897.6**   Land area (1,000 sq. km) **63,340**   GDP ($ billions) **22,457.2**

GNI per capita, *World Bank Atlas* method ($)	4,408
Adjusted net national income per capita ($)	3,659
Change in wealth per capita (2010 $)	523
Urban population (% of total)	49.5

Agriculture

Agricultural land (% land area)	44
Agricultural irrigated land (% of total agricultural land) .	..
Agricultural productivity, value added per worker (2005 $)	1,045
Cereal yield (kg per hectare)	3,653

Forests and biodiversity

Forest area (% land area)	28.4
Deforestation (avg. annual %, 2000–2010)	0.1
Terrestrial protected areas (% of total land area)	14.9
Threatened species, mammals	
Threatened species, birds	
Threatened species, fish	
Threatened species, higher plants	

Oceans

Total fisheries production (thousand metric tons)	133,091
Capture fisheries growth (avg. annual %, 1990–2012)	1.9
Aquaculture growth (avg. annual %, 1990–2012)	9.3
Marine protected areas (% of territorial waters)	9.4
Coral reef area (sq. km)	176,550
Mangroves area (sq. km)	109,077

Energy and emissions

Energy use per capita (kg oil equivalent)	1,281
Energy from biomass products and waste (% of total)	13.5
Electric power consumption per capita (kWh)	1,816
Electricity generated using fossil fuel (% of total)	74.1
Electricity generated by hydropower (% of total)	19.3
CO_2 emissions per capita (metric tons)	3.5

Water and sanitation

Internal freshwater resources per capita (cu. m)	4,931
Total freshwater withdrawal (% of internal resources)	11.3
Agriculture (% of total freshwater withdrawal)	80
Access to improved water source (% of total population)	90
Rural (% of rural population)	85
Urban (% of urban population)	96
Access to improved sanitation facilities (% of total population)	60
Rural (% of rural population)	46
Urban (% of urban population)	75

Environment and health

Particulate matter (urban-pop.-weighted avg., µg/cu. m)	75
Acute resp. infection prevalence (% of children under five)	..
Diarrhea prevalence (% of children under five)	..
Under-five mortality rate (per 1,000 live births)	45

National accounting aggregates—savings, depletion and degradation

Gross savings (% of GNI)	34.6
Consumption of fixed capital (% of GNI)	12.1
Education expenditure (% of GNI)	3.2
Energy depletion (% of GNI)	4.2
Mineral depletion (% of GNI)	1.2
Net forest depletion (% of GNI)	0.3
CO_2 damage (% of GNI)	0.8
Particulate emissions damage (% of GNI)	1.4
Adjusted net savings (% of GNI)	17.8

Lower middle income

Population (millions) **2,507.0** Land area (1,000 sq. km) **20,594** GDP ($ billions) **5,037.9**

GNI per capita, *World Bank Atlas* method ($)	1,965
Adjusted net national income per capita ($)	1,574
Change in wealth per capita (2010 $)	117
Urban population (% of total)	38.9

Agriculture
Agricultural land (% land area)	46
Agricultural irrigated land (% of total agricultural land)	..
Agricultural productivity, value added per worker (2005 $)	938
Cereal yield (kg per hectare)	3,029

Forests and biodiversity
Forest area (% land area)	26.9
Deforestation (avg. annual %, 2000–2010)	0.3
Terrestrial protected areas (% of total land area)	11.9
Threatened species, mammals	
Threatened species, birds	
Threatened species, fish	
Threatened species, higher plants	

Oceans
Total fisheries production (thousand metric tons)	43,067
Capture fisheries growth (avg. annual %, 1990–2012)	2.6
Aquaculture growth (avg. annual %, 1990–2012)	9.9
Marine protected areas (% of territorial waters)	14.7
Coral reef area (sq. km)	124,480
Mangroves area (sq. km)	58,917

Energy and emissions
Energy use per capita (kg oil equivalent)	687
Energy from biomass products and waste (% of total)	26.8
Electric power consumption per capita (kWh)	734
Electricity generated using fossil fuel (% of total)	72.3
Electricity generated by hydropower (% of total)	16.9
CO_2 emissions per capita (metric tons)	1.6

Water and sanitation
Internal freshwater resources per capita (cu. m)	3,144
Total freshwater withdrawal (% of internal resources)	19.6
Agriculture (% of total freshwater withdrawal)	88
Access to improved water source (% of total population)	88
Rural (% of rural population)	85
Urban (% of urban population)	94
Access to improved sanitation facilities (% of total population)	48
Rural (% of rural population)	36
Urban (% of urban population)	66

Environment and health
Particulate matter (urban-pop.-weighted avg., µg/cu. m)	90
Acute resp. infection prevalence (% of children under five)	..
Diarrhea prevalence (% of children under five)	..
Under-five mortality rate (per 1,000 live births)	61

National accounting aggregates—savings, depletion and degradation
Gross savings (% of GNI)	28.6
Consumption of fixed capital (% of GNI)	11.1
Education expenditure (% of GNI)	3.1
Energy depletion (% of GNI)	4.4
Mineral depletion (% of GNI)	1.1
Net forest depletion (% of GNI)	0.8
CO_2 damage (% of GNI)	0.9
Particulate emissions damage (% of GNI)	1.4
Adjusted net savings (% of GNI)	12.0

Upper middle income

Population (millions) **2,390.6** Land area (1,000 sq. km) **42,746** GDP ($ billions) **17,416.0**

GNI per capita, *World Bank Atlas* method ($)	6,969
Adjusted net national income per capita ($)	5,845
Change in wealth per capita (2010 $)	1,039
Urban population (% of total)	60.7

Agriculture
Agricultural land (% land area)	44
Agricultural irrigated land (% of total agricultural land)	..
Agricultural productivity, value added per worker (2005 $)	1,131
Cereal yield (kg per hectare)	4,255

Forests and biodiversity
Forest area (% land area)	29.1
Deforestation (avg. annual %, 2000–2010)	0.0
Terrestrial protected areas (% of total land area)	16.1
Threatened species, mammals	
Threatened species, birds	
Threatened species, fish	
Threatened species, higher plants	

Oceans
Total fisheries production (thousand metric tons)	90,024
Capture fisheries growth (avg. annual %, 1990–2012)	1.5
Aquaculture growth (avg. annual %, 1990–2012)	9.1
Marine protected areas (% of territorial waters)	7.3
Coral reef area (sq. km)	52,070
Mangroves area (sq. km)	50,160

Energy and emissions
Energy use per capita (kg oil equivalent)	1,893
Energy from biomass products and waste (% of total)	8.5
Electric power consumption per capita (kWh)	2,932
Electricity generated using fossil fuel (% of total)	74.7
Electricity generated by hydropower (% of total)	20.0
CO_2 emissions per capita (metric tons)	5.4

Water and sanitation
Internal freshwater resources per capita (cu. m)	6,791
Total freshwater withdrawal (% of internal resources)	7.4
Agriculture (% of total freshwater withdrawal)	69
Access to improved water source (% of total population)	93
Rural (% of rural population)	85
Urban (% of urban population)	98
Access to improved sanitation facilities (% of total population)	74
Rural (% of rural population)	62
Urban (% of urban population)	82

Environment and health
Particulate matter (urban-pop.-weighted avg., µg/cu. m)	65
Acute resp. infection prevalence (% of children under five)	..
Diarrhea prevalence (% of children under five)	..
Under-five mortality rate (per 1,000 live births)	20

National accounting aggregates—savings, depletion and degradation
Gross savings (% of GNI)	36.4
Consumption of fixed capital (% of GNI)	12.5
Education expenditure (% of GNI)	3.2
Energy depletion (% of GNI)	4.1
Mineral depletion (% of GNI)	1.2
Net forest depletion (% of GNI)	0.2
CO_2 damage (% of GNI)	0.8
Particulate emissions damage (% of GNI)	1.3
Adjusted net savings (% of GNI)	19.5

Low and middle income

Population (millions) **5,744.1** Land area (1,000 sq. km) **78,388** GDP ($ billions) **22,978.0**

GNI per capita, *World Bank Atlas* method ($)	3,848
Adjusted net national income per capita ($)	3,194
Change in wealth per capita (2010 $)	441
Urban population (% of total)	46.4

Agriculture

Agricultural land (% land area)	43
Agricultural irrigated land (% of total agricultural land)	..
Agricultural productivity, value added per worker (2005 $)	941
Cereal yield (kg per hectare)	3,356

Forests and biodiversity

Forest area (% land area)	28.2
Deforestation (avg. annual %, 2000–2010)	0.2
Terrestrial protected areas (% of total land area)	14.6
Threatened species, mammals	
Threatened species, birds	
Threatened species, fish	
Threatened species, higher plants	

Oceans

Total fisheries production (thousand metric tons)	144,880
Capture fisheries growth (avg. annual %, 1990–2012)	2.1
Aquaculture growth (avg. annual %, 1990–2012)	9.0
Marine protected areas (% of territorial waters)	10.2
Coral reef area (sq. km)	191,670
Mangroves area (sq. km)	134,894

Energy and emissions

Energy use per capita (kg oil equivalent)	1,179
Energy from biomass products and waste (% of total)	15.3
Electric power consumption per capita (kWh)	1,646
Electricity generated using fossil fuel (% of total)	73.1
Electricity generated by hydropower (% of total)	19.8
CO_2 emissions per capita (metric tons)	3.0

Water and sanitation

Internal freshwater resources per capita (cu. m)	4,958
Total freshwater withdrawal (% of internal resources)	10.3
Agriculture (% of total freshwater withdrawal)	80
Access to improved water source (% of total population)	87
Rural (% of rural population)	80
Urban (% of urban population)	95
Access to improved sanitation facilities (% of total population)	57
Rural (% of rural population)	43
Urban (% of urban population)	73

Environment and health

Particulate matter (urban-pop.-weighted avg., µg/cu. m)	75
Acute resp. infection prevalence (% of children under five)	..
Diarrhea prevalence (% of children under five)	..
Under-five mortality rate (per 1,000 live births)	53

National accounting aggregates—savings, depletion and degradation

Gross savings (% of GNI)	34.5
Consumption of fixed capital (% of GNI)	12.1
Education expenditure (% of GNI)	3.2
Energy depletion (% of GNI)	4.1
Mineral depletion (% of GNI)	1.2
Net forest depletion (% of GNI)	0.4
CO_2 damage (% of GNI)	0.8
Particulate emissions damage (% of GNI)	1.3
Adjusted net savings (% of GNI)	17.6

High income

Population (millions) **1,299.8** Land area (1,000 sq. km) **51,322** GDP ($ billions) **49,762.8**

GNI per capita, *World Bank Atlas* method ($)	38,444
Adjusted net national income per capita ($)	32,262
Change in wealth per capita (2010 $)	2,210
Urban population (% of total)	80.2

Agriculture

Agricultural land (% land area)	29
Agricultural irrigated land (% of total agricultural land)	..
Agricultural productivity, value added per worker (2005 $)	25,238
Cereal yield (kg per hectare)	4,374

Forests and biodiversity

Forest area (% land area)	35.0
Deforestation (avg. annual %, 2000–2010)	0.0
Terrestrial protected areas (% of total land area)	13.9
Threatened species, mammals	
Threatened species, birds	
Threatened species, fish	
Threatened species, higher plants	

Oceans

Total fisheries production (thousand metric tons)	37,661
Capture fisheries growth (avg. annual %, 1990–2012)	-2.0
Aquaculture growth (avg. annual %, 1990–2012)	2.5
Marine protected areas (% of territorial waters)	14.4
Coral reef area (sq. km)	82,210
Mangroves area (sq. km)	15,504

Energy and emissions

Energy use per capita (kg oil equivalent)	4,872
Energy from biomass products and waste (% of total)	4.3
Electric power consumption per capita (kWh)	8,896
Electricity generated using fossil fuel (% of total)	61.8
Electricity generated by hydropower (% of total)	12.2
CO_2 emissions per capita (metric tons)	11.6

Water and sanitation

Internal freshwater resources per capita (cu. m)	11,335
Total freshwater withdrawal (% of internal resources)	7.0
Agriculture (% of total freshwater withdrawal)	40
Access to improved water source (% of total population)	99
Rural (% of rural population)	98
Urban (% of urban population)	100
Access to improved sanitation facilities (% of total population)	96
Rural (% of rural population)	93
Urban (% of urban population)	97

Environment and health

Particulate matter (urban-pop.-weighted avg., µg/cu. m)	27
Acute resp. infection prevalence (% of children under five)	..
Diarrhea prevalence (% of children under five)	..
Under-five mortality rate (per 1,000 live births)	6

National accounting aggregates—savings, depletion and degradation

Gross savings (% of GNI)	20.1
Consumption of fixed capital (% of GNI)	14.2
Education expenditure (% of GNI)	4.7
Energy depletion (% of GNI)	1.6
Mineral depletion (% of GNI)	0.3
Net forest depletion (% of GNI)	0.0
CO_2 damage (% of GNI)	0.3
Particulate emissions damage (% of GNI)	0.3
Adjusted net savings (% of GNI)	8.1

Euro area

Population (millions) **333.3** Land area (1,000 sq. km) **2,614** GDP ($ billions) **12,213.3**

GNI per capita, *World Bank Atlas* method ($)	38,115
Adjusted net national income per capita ($)	31,497
Change in wealth per capita (2010 $)	2,863
Urban population (% of total)	75.8

Agriculture

Agricultural land (% land area)	45
Agricultural irrigated land (% of total agricultural land)	..
Agricultural productivity, value added per worker (2005 $)	36,135
Cereal yield (kg per hectare)	5,817

Forests and biodiversity

Forest area (% land area)	37.8
Deforestation (avg. annual %, 2000–2010)	-0.3
Terrestrial protected areas (% of total land area)	27.6
Threatened species, mammals	
Threatened species, birds	
Threatened species, fish	
Threatened species, higher plants	

Oceans

Total fisheries production (thousand metric tons)	3,995
Capture fisheries growth (avg. annual %, 1990–2012)	-1.8
Aquaculture growth (avg. annual %, 1990–2012)	0.4
Marine protected areas (% of territorial waters)	15.9
Coral reef area (sq. km)	..
Mangroves area (sq. km)	..

Energy and emissions

Energy use per capita (kg oil equivalent)	3,480
Energy from biomass products and waste (% of total)	7.6
Electric power consumption per capita (kWh)	6,599
Electricity generated using fossil fuel (% of total)	46.6
Electricity generated by hydropower (% of total)	9.1
CO_2 emissions per capita (metric tons)	7.4

Water and sanitation

Internal freshwater resources per capita (cu. m)	2,962
Total freshwater withdrawal (% of internal resources)	19.1
Agriculture (% of total freshwater withdrawal)	32
Access to improved water source (% of total population)	100
Rural (% of rural population)	100
Urban (% of urban population)	100
Access to improved sanitation facilities (% of total population)	100
Rural (% of rural population)	100
Urban (% of urban population)	100

Environment and health

Particulate matter (urban-pop.-weighted avg., µg/cu. m)	27
Acute resp. infection prevalence (% of children under five)	..
Diarrhea prevalence (% of children under five)	..
Under-five mortality rate (per 1,000 live births)	4

National accounting aggregates—savings, depletion and degradation

Gross savings (% of GNI)	20.1
Consumption of fixed capital (% of GNI)	14.3
Education expenditure (% of GNI)	5.0
Energy depletion (% of GNI)	0.1
Mineral depletion (% of GNI)	0.0
Net forest depletion (% of GNI)	0.0
CO_2 damage (% of GNI)	0.2
Particulate emissions damage (% of GNI)	0.4
Adjusted net savings (% of GNI)	10.2

Country tables

Cabo Verde

Cabo Verde is the new name for the country previously listed as Cape Verde.

China

Unless otherwise noted, data for China do not include data for Hong Kong SAR, China; Macao SAR, China; or Taiwan, China.

Cyprus

GNI and GDP data and data calculated using GNI and GDP refer to the area controlled by the government of the Republic of Cyprus.

Georgia

GNI, GDP, and population data and data calculated using GNI, GDP, and population exclude Abkhazia and South Ossetia.

Kosovo, Montenegro, and Serbia

Data for each country are shown separately where available. However, some indicators for Serbia prior to 2006 include data for Montenegro; these data are noted in the tables. Moreover, data for most indicators for Serbia from 1999 onward exclude data for Kosovo, which in 1999 became a territory under international administration pursuant to UN Security Council Resolution 1244 (1999). Kosovo became a member of the World Bank on June 29, 2009, and its data are shown where available.

Moldova

GNI, GDP, and population data and data calculated using GNI, GDP, and population exclude Transnistria.

Morocco

GNI and GDP data and data calculated using GNI and GDP include Former Spanish Sahara.

South Sudan and Sudan

South Sudan declared its independence on July 9, 2011. Data are shown separately for South Sudan where available. However, data reported for Sudan include South Sudan unless otherwise noted.

Tanzania

GNI and GDP data and data calculated using GNI and GDP refer to mainland Tanzania only.

For more information, see *World Development Indicators 2014* or data.worldbank.org.

Afghanistan

Population (millions)	**29.8**	Land area (1,000 sq. km)	**652**	GDP ($ billions)	**20.5**

	Country data	South Asia group	Low-Income group
GNI per capita, *World Bank Atlas* method ($)	680	1,437	594
Adjusted net national income per capita ($)	594	1,168	495
Change in wealth per capita (2010 $)	..	158	-39
Urban population (% of total)	23.9	31.4	28.2
Agriculture			
Agricultural land (% land area)	58	55	39
Agricultural irrigated land (% of total agricultural land)	5.4	..	..
Agricultural productivity, value added per worker (2005 $)	413	669	367
Cereal yield (kg per hectare)	2,072	2,925	1,982
Forests and biodiversity			
Forest area (% land area)	2.1	17.1	27.4
Deforestation (avg. annual %, 2000–2010)	0.0	-0.3	0.6
Terrestrial protected areas (% of total land area)	0.4	6.2	13.7
Threatened species, mammals	11		
Threatened species, birds	14		
Threatened species, fish	5		
Threatened species, higher plants	3		
Oceans			
Total fisheries production (thousand metric tons)	2.1	13,613	11,789
Capture fisheries growth (avg. annual %, 1990–2012)	-0.4	2.6	3.8
Aquaculture growth (avg. annual %, 1990–2012)	5.9	7.6	5.1
Marine protected areas (% of territorial waters)	2.4	10.7	13.1
Coral reef area (sq. km)	..	15,440	15,120
Mangroves area (sq. km)	..	10,343	25,817
Energy and emissions			
Energy use per capita (kg oil equivalent)	..	555	360
Energy from biomass products and waste (% of total)	..	26.7	66.0
Electric power consumption per capita (kWh)	..	605	233
Electricity generated using fossil fuel (% of total)	..	77.9	30.9
Electricity generated by hydropower (% of total)	..	13.8	45.5
CO_2 emissions per capita (metric tons)	0.3	1.4	0.3
Water and sanitation			
Internal freshwater resources per capita (cu. m)	1,620	1,217	5,121
Total freshwater withdrawal (% of internal resources)	43.0	51.6	4.4
Agriculture (% of total freshwater withdrawal)	99	91	90
Access to improved water source (% of total population)	64	91	69
Rural (% of rural population)	56	89	61
Urban (% of urban population)	90	95	88
Access to improved sanitation facilities (% of total population)	29	40	37
Rural (% of rural population)	23	30	33
Urban (% of urban population)	47	61	46
Environment and health			
Particulate matter (urban-pop.-weighted avg., µg/cu. m)	63	110	74
Acute resp. infection prevalence (% of children under five)	..	..	6
Diarrhea prevalence (% of children under five)	..	..	14
Under-five mortality rate (per 1,000 live births)	99	60	82
National accounting aggregates—savings, depletion and degradation			
Gross savings (% of GNI)	-14.9	29.3	24.6
Consumption of fixed capital (% of GNI)	12.4	12.7	11.8
Education expenditure (% of GNI)	..	2.8	3.2
Energy depletion (% of GNI)	0.0	1.8	1.4
Mineral depletion (% of GNI)	0.0	0.8	1.9
Net forest depletion (% of GNI)	1.2	1.1	4.4
CO_2 damage (% of GNI)	0.5	1.1	0.4
Particulate emissions damage (% of GNI)	2.5	1.5	1.0
Adjusted net savings (% of GNI)	..	13.1	7.0

Albania

| Population (millions) | **3.2** | Land area (1,000 sq. km) | **27** | GDP ($ billions) | **12.6** |

	Country data	Europe & Central Asia group	Upper middle-income group
GNI per capita, *World Bank Atlas* method ($)	4,030	6,658	6,969
Adjusted net national income per capita ($)	3,258	5,541	5,845
Change in wealth per capita (2010 $)	39	263	1,039
Urban population (% of total)	54.4	60.2	60.7
Agriculture			
Agricultural land (% land area)	44	66	44
Agricultural irrigated land (% of total agricultural land)	17.0	..	..
Agricultural productivity, value added per worker (2005 $)	3,630	4,866	1,131
Cereal yield (kg per hectare)	4,884	2,519	4,255
Forests and biodiversity			
Forest area (% land area)	28.3	10.5	29.1
Deforestation (avg. annual %, 2000–2010)	–0.1	–0.5	0.0
Terrestrial protected areas (% of total land area)	11.0	5.1	16.1
Threatened species, mammals	3		
Threatened species, birds	6		
Threatened species, fish	39		
Threatened species, higher plants	0		
Oceans			
Total fisheries production (thousand metric tons)	7.3	1,022	90,024
Capture fisheries growth (avg. annual %, 1990–2012)	–2.9	–4.0	1.5
Aquaculture growth (avg. annual %, 1990–2012)	–4.0	1.8	9.1
Marine protected areas (% of territorial waters)	0.36	10.4	7.3
Coral reef area (sq. km)	..	..	52,070
Mangroves area (sq. km)	..	..	50,160
Energy and emissions			
Energy use per capita (kg oil equivalent)	689	2,078	1,893
Energy from biomass products and waste (% of total)	9.6	2.9	8.5
Electric power consumption per capita (kWh)	2,022	2,951	2,932
Electricity generated using fossil fuel (% of total)	0.0	65.8	74.7
Electricity generated by hydropower (% of total)	100.0	17.9	20.0
CO_2 emissions per capita (metric tons)	1.4	5.3	5.4
Water and sanitation			
Internal freshwater resources per capita (cu. m)	8,529	2,744	6,791
Total freshwater withdrawal (% of internal resources)	6.8	34.8	7.4
Agriculture (% of total freshwater withdrawal)	58	70	69
Access to improved water source (% of total population)	96	95	93
Rural (% of rural population)	94	89	85
Urban (% of urban population)	97	99	98
Access to improved sanitation facilities (% of total population)	91	94	74
Rural (% of rural population)	86	90	62
Urban (% of urban population)	95	97	82
Environment and health			
Particulate matter (urban-pop.-weighted avg., µg/cu. m)	43	48	65
Acute resp. infection prevalence (% of children under five)	5	..	..
Diarrhea prevalence (% of children under five)	5	..	..
Under-five mortality rate (per 1,000 live births)	17	22	20
National accounting aggregates—savings, depletion and degradation			
Gross savings (% of GNI)	14.7	18.9	36.4
Consumption of fixed capital (% of GNI)	13.6	12.4	12.5
Education expenditure (% of GNI)	2.8	3.8	3.2
Energy depletion (% of GNI)	3.5	4.4	4.1
Mineral depletion (% of GNI)	0.1	0.6	1.2
Net forest depletion (% of GNI)	0.3	0.0	0.2
CO_2 damage (% of GNI)	0.3	0.8	0.8
Particulate emissions damage (% of GNI)	1.0	1.8	1.3
Adjusted net savings (% of GNI)	–1.3	2.8	19.5

Algeria

	Country data	Middle East & N. Africa group	Upper middle-income group
Population (millions) **38.5** Land area (1,000 sq. km) **2,382** GDP ($ billions) **205.8**			

	Country data	Middle East & N. Africa group	Upper middle-income group
GNI per capita, *World Bank Atlas* method ($)	5,020	3,451	6,969
Adjusted net national income per capita ($)	4,057	2,602	5,845
Change in wealth per capita (2010 $)	467	101	1,039
Urban population (% of total)	73.7	59.5	60.7
Agriculture			
Agricultural land (% land area)	17	23	44
Agricultural irrigated land (% of total agricultural land)	2.1	..	..
Agricultural productivity, value added per worker (2005 $)	3,719	2,642	1,131
Cereal yield (kg per hectare)	1,678	2,350	4,255
Forests and biodiversity			
Forest area (% land area)	0.6	2.4	29.1
Deforestation (avg. annual %, 2000–2010)	0.6	-0.1	0.0
Terrestrial protected areas (% of total land area)	7.5	6.1	16.1
Threatened species, mammals	14		
Threatened species, birds	11		
Threatened species, fish	36		
Threatened species, higher plants	17		
Oceans			
Total fisheries production (thousand metric tons)	108	3,976	90,024
Capture fisheries growth (avg. annual %, 1990–2012)	0.7	3.0	1.5
Aquaculture growth (avg. annual %, 1990–2012)	8.9	12.8	9.1
Marine protected areas (% of territorial waters)	17.1	9.1	7.3
Coral reef area (sq. km)	..	5,700	52,070
Mangroves area (sq. km)	..	217	50,160
Energy and emissions			
Energy use per capita (kg oil equivalent)	1,108	1,376	1,893
Energy from biomass products and waste (% of total)	0.0	0.9	8.5
Electric power consumption per capita (kWh)	1,091	1,696	2,932
Electricity generated using fossil fuel (% of total)	99.0	91.7	74.7
Electricity generated by hydropower (% of total)	1.0	5.5	20.0
CO_2 emissions per capita (metric tons)	3.3	3.9	5.4
Water and sanitation			
Internal freshwater resources per capita (cu. m)	298	679	6,791
Total freshwater withdrawal (% of internal resources)	54.8	122.1	7.4
Agriculture (% of total freshwater withdrawal)	64	86	69
Access to improved water source (% of total population)	84	90	93
Rural (% of rural population)	79	83	85
Urban (% of urban population)	85	95	98
Access to improved sanitation facilities (% of total population)	95	88	74
Rural (% of rural population)	88	80	62
Urban (% of urban population)	98	94	82
Environment and health			
Particulate matter (urban-pop.-weighted avg., μg/cu. m)	34	79	65
Acute resp. infection prevalence (% of children under five)	..	..	..
Diarrhea prevalence (% of children under five)	..	..	..
Under-five mortality rate (per 1,000 live births)	20	26	20

National accounting aggregates—savings, depletion and degradation

	Country data	Middle East & N. Africa group	Upper middle-income group
Gross savings (% of GNI)	48.0	25.9	36.4
Consumption of fixed capital (% of GNI)	7.6	9.9	12.5
Education expenditure (% of GNI)	4.5	4.5	3.2
Energy depletion (% of GNI)	15.3	12.9	4.1
Mineral depletion (% of GNI)	0.1	0.5	1.2
Net forest depletion (% of GNI)	0.3	0.2	0.2
CO_2 damage (% of GNI)	0.7	0.7	0.8
Particulate emissions damage (% of GNI)	0.2	0.9	1.3
Adjusted net savings (% of GNI)	28.2	5.3	19.5

American Samoa

Population (thousands) **55** Land area (sq. km) **200** GDP ($ millions) ..

	Country data	East Asia & Pacific group	Upper middle-income group
GNI per capita, *World Bank Atlas* method ($)	..	4,884	6,969
Adjusted net national income per capita ($)	..	4,305	5,845
Change in wealth per capita (2010 $)	..	1,172	1,039
Urban population (% of total)	93.4	49.6	60.7

Agriculture
Agricultural land (% land area)	25	48	44
Agricultural irrigated land (% of total agricultural land)	..	..	..
Agricultural productivity, value added per worker (2005 $)	..	794	1,131
Cereal yield (kg per hectare)	..	5,145	4,255

Forests and biodiversity
Forest area (% land area)	88.4	29.7	29.1
Deforestation (avg. annual %, 2000–2010)	0.2	-0.4	0.0
Terrestrial protected areas (% of total land area)	2.9	15.1	16.1
Threatened species, mammals	1		
Threatened species, birds	8		
Threatened species, fish	9		
Threatened species, higher plants	1		

Oceans
Total fisheries production (thousand metric tons)	6.1	108,399	90,024
Capture fisheries growth (avg. annual %, 1990–2012)	25.4	3.4	1.5
Aquaculture growth (avg. annual %, 1990–2012)	..	9.1	9.1
Marine protected areas (% of territorial waters)	17.0	1.4	7.3
Coral reef area (sq. km)	220	137,690	52,070
Mangroves area (sq. km)	0.52	56,537	50,160

Energy and emissions
Energy use per capita (kg oil equivalent)	..	1,671	1,893
Energy from biomass products and waste (% of total)	..	10.1	8.5
Electric power consumption per capita (kWh)	..	2,582	2,932
Electricity generated using fossil fuel (% of total)	..	80.9	74.7
Electricity generated by hydropower (% of total)	..	14.5	20.0
CO_2 emissions per capita (metric tons)	..	4.9	5.4

Water and sanitation
Internal freshwater resources per capita (cu. m)	..	4,438	6,791
Total freshwater withdrawal (% of internal resources)	..	10.9	7.4
Agriculture (% of total freshwater withdrawal)	..	73	69
Access to improved water source (% of total population)	100	91	93
Rural (% of rural population)	100	85	85
Urban (% of urban population)	100	97	98
Access to improved sanitation facilities (% of total population)	62	67	74
Rural (% of rural population)	62	58	62
Urban (% of urban population)	62	76	82

Environment and health
Particulate matter (urban-pop.-weighted avg., µg/cu. m)	..	75	65
Acute resp. infection prevalence (% of children under five)	..	..	..
Diarrhea prevalence (% of children under five)	..	..	..
Under-five mortality rate (per 1,000 live births)	..	21	20

National accounting aggregates—savings, depletion and degradation
Gross savings (% of GNI)	..	47.6	36.4
Consumption of fixed capital (% of GNI)	..	12.0	12.5
Education expenditure (% of GNI)	..	2.1	3.2
Energy depletion (% of GNI)	..	2.7	4.1
Mineral depletion (% of GNI)	..	1.4	1.2
Net forest depletion (% of GNI)	..	0.1	0.2
CO_2 damage (% of GNI)	..	1.0	0.8
Particulate emissions damage (% of GNI)	..	1.6	1.3
Adjusted net savings (% of GNI)	..	30.9	19.5

Andorra

| | Population (thousands) **78** Land area (sq. km) | **470** GDP ($ billions) | **3.7** |

	Country data	High-income group
GNI per capita, *World Bank Atlas* method ($)	43,110	38,444
Adjusted net national income per capita ($)	41,147	32,262
Change in wealth per capita (2010 $)	..	2,210
Urban population (% of total)	86.7	80.2
Agriculture		
Agricultural land (% land area)	43	29
Agricultural irrigated land (% of total agricultural land)	..	..
Agricultural productivity, value added per worker (2005 $)	..	25,238
Cereal yield (kg per hectare)	..	4,374
Forests and biodiversity		
Forest area (% land area)	34.0	35.0
Deforestation (avg. annual %, 2000–2010)	0.0	0.0
Terrestrial protected areas (% of total land area)	9.8	13.9
Threatened species, mammals	2	
Threatened species, birds	1	
Threatened species, fish	0	
Threatened species, higher plants	0	
Oceans		
Total fisheries production (thousand metric tons)	..	37,661
Capture fisheries growth (avg. annual %, 1990–2012)	..	-2.0
Aquaculture growth (avg. annual %, 1990–2012)	..	2.5
Marine protected areas (% of territorial waters)	0.07	14.4
Coral reef area (sq. km)	..	82,210
Mangroves area (sq. km)	..	15,504
Energy and emissions		
Energy use per capita (kg oil equivalent)	..	4,872
Energy from biomass products and waste (% of total)	..	4.3
Electric power consumption per capita (kWh)	..	8,896
Electricity generated using fossil fuel (% of total)	..	61.8
Electricity generated by hydropower (% of total)	..	12.2
CO_2 emissions per capita (metric tons)	6.6	11.6
Water and sanitation		
Internal freshwater resources per capita (cu. m)	4,053	11,335
Total freshwater withdrawal (% of internal resources)	..	7.0
Agriculture (% of total freshwater withdrawal)	..	40
Access to improved water source (% of total population)	100	99
Rural (% of rural population)	100	98
Urban (% of urban population)	100	100
Access to improved sanitation facilities (% of total population)	100	96
Rural (% of rural population)	100	93
Urban (% of urban population)	100	97
Environment and health		
Particulate matter (urban-pop.-weighted avg., µg/cu. m)	31	27
Acute resp. infection prevalence (% of children under five)	..	..
Diarrhea prevalence (% of children under five)	..	..
Under-five mortality rate (per 1,000 live births)	3	6
National accounting aggregates—savings, depletion and degradation		
Gross savings (% of GNI)	..	20.1
Consumption of fixed capital (% of GNI)	11.4	14.2
Education expenditure (% of GNI)	3.3	4.7
Energy depletion (% of GNI)	0.0	1.6
Mineral depletion (% of GNI)	0.0	0.3
Net forest depletion (% of GNI)	0.0	0.0
CO_2 damage (% of GNI)	0.1	0.3
Particulate emissions damage (% of GNI)	..	0.3
Adjusted net savings (% of GNI)	..	8.1

Angola

	Population (millions)	**20.8**	Land area (1,000 sq. km)	**1,247**	GDP ($ billions)	**114.1**

	Country data	Sub-Saharan Africa group	Upper middle-income group
GNI per capita, *World Bank Atlas* method ($)	4,580	1,547	6,969
Adjusted net national income per capita ($)	2,585	1,005	5,845
Change in wealth per capita (2010 $)	–1,969	–273	1,039
Urban population (% of total)	59.9	36.8	60.7
Agriculture			
Agricultural land (% of land area)	47	44	44
Agricultural irrigated land (% of total agricultural land)	..	..	..
Agricultural productivity, value added per worker (2005 $)	867	765	1,131
Cereal yield (kg per hectare)	617	1,417	4,255
Forests and biodiversity			
Forest area (% land area)	46.8	27.4	29.1
Deforestation (avg. annual %, 2000–2010)	0.2	0.5	0.0
Terrestrial protected areas (% of total land area)	12.4	16.4	16.1
Threatened species, mammals	15		
Threatened species, birds	25		
Threatened species, fish	40		
Threatened species, higher plants	34		
Oceans			
Total fisheries production (thousand metric tons)	277	6,906	90,024
Capture fisheries growth (avg. annual %, 1990–2012)	3.4	2.1	1.5
Aquaculture growth (avg. annual %, 1990–2012)	..	15.9	9.1
Marine protected areas (% of territorial waters)	7.1	11.7	7.3
Coral reef area (sq. km)	..	17,980	52,070
Mangroves area (sq. km)	312	27,808	50,160
Energy and emissions			
Energy use per capita (kg oil equivalent)	673	681	1,893
Energy from biomass products and waste (% of total)	58.2	57.6	8.5
Electric power consumption per capita (kWh)	248	535	2,932
Electricity generated using fossil fuel (% of total)	29.1	65.1	74.7
Electricity generated by hydropower (% of total)	70.9	20.0	20.0
CO_2 emissions per capita (metric tons)	1.6	0.8	5.4
Water and sanitation			
Internal freshwater resources per capita (cu. m)	7,334	4,391	6,791
Total freshwater withdrawal (% of internal resources)	0.4	3.2	7.4
Agriculture (% of total freshwater withdrawal)	33	84	69
Access to improved water source (% of total population)	54	64	93
Rural (% of rural population)	34	53	85
Urban (% of urban population)	68	85	98
Access to improved sanitation facilities (% of total population)	60	30	74
Rural (% of rural population)	20	23	62
Urban (% of urban population)	87	41	82
Environment and health			
Particulate matter (urban-pop.-weighted avg., µg/cu. m)	21	77	65
Acute resp. infection prevalence (% of children under five)	..	5	..
Diarrhea prevalence (% of children under five)	..	14	..
Under-five mortality rate (per 1,000 live births)	164	98	20
National accounting aggregates—savings, depletion and degradation			
Gross savings (% of GNI)	20.0	26.3	36.4
Consumption of fixed capital (% of GNI)	14.8	13.0	12.5
Education expenditure (% of GNI)	3.6	3.4	3.2
Energy depletion (% of GNI)	32.5	10.3	4.1
Mineral depletion (% of GNI)	0.0	1.8	1.2
Net forest depletion (% of GNI)	0.3	1.8	0.2
CO_2 damage (% of GNI)	0.3	0.6	0.8
Particulate emissions damage (% of GNI)	0.9	1.2	1.3
Adjusted net savings (% of GNI)	–25.2	0.9	19.5

Antigua and Barbuda

Population (thousands)	**89**	Land area (sq. km)	**440**	GDP ($ billions)	**1.1**

	Country data	High-income group
GNI per capita, *World Bank Atlas* method ($)	12,480	38,444
Adjusted net national income per capita ($)	..	32,262
Change in wealth per capita (2010 $)	..	2,210
Urban population (% of total)	29.9	80.2

Agriculture
Agricultural land (% land area)	20	29
Agricultural irrigated land (% of total agricultural land)	..	..
Agricultural productivity, value added per worker (2005 $)	2,097	25,238
Cereal yield (kg per hectare)	2,000	4,374

Forests and biodiversity
Forest area (% land area)	22.3	35.0
Deforestation (avg. annual %, 2000–2010)	0.2	0.0
Terrestrial protected areas (% of total land area)	10.2	13.9
Threatened species, mammals	2	
Threatened species, birds	1	
Threatened species, fish	19	
Threatened species, higher plants	4	

Oceans
Total fisheries production (thousand metric tons)	3.1	37,661
Capture fisheries growth (avg. annual %, 1990–2012)	5.8	-2.0
Aquaculture growth (avg. annual %, 1990–2012)	..	2.5
Marine protected areas (% of territorial waters)	1.6	14.4
Coral reef area (sq. km)	240	82,210
Mangroves area (sq. km)	8.4	15,504

Energy and emissions
Energy use per capita (kg oil equivalent)	1,730	4,872
Energy from biomass products and waste (% of total)	..	4.3
Electric power consumption per capita (kWh)	..	8,896
Electricity generated using fossil fuel (% of total)	..	61.8
Electricity generated by hydropower (% of total)	..	12.2
CO_2 emissions per capita (metric tons)	5.9	11.6

Water and sanitation
Internal freshwater resources per capita (cu. m)	590	11,335
Total freshwater withdrawal (% of internal resources)	9.6	7.0
Agriculture (% of total freshwater withdrawal)	20	40
Access to improved water source (% of total population)	98	99
Rural (% of rural population)	98	98
Urban (% of urban population)	98	100
Access to improved sanitation facilities (% of total population)	91	96
Rural (% of rural population)	91	93
Urban (% of urban population)	91	97

Environment and health
Particulate matter (urban-pop.-weighted avg., μg/cu. m)	9	27
Acute resp. infection prevalence (% of children under five)	..	..
Diarrhea prevalence (% of children under five)	..	..
Under-five mortality rate (per 1,000 live births)	10	6

National accounting aggregates—savings, depletion and degradation
Gross savings (% of GNI)	25.9	20.1
Consumption of fixed capital (% of GNI)	13.0	14.2
Education expenditure (% of GNI)	2.2	4.7
Energy depletion (% of GNI)	0.0	1.6
Mineral depletion (% of GNI)	0.0	0.3
Net forest depletion (% of GNI)	0.0	0.0
CO_2 damage (% of GNI)	0.6	0.3
Particulate emissions damage (% of GNI)	0.0	0.3
Adjusted net savings (% of GNI)	..	8.1

Argentina

Population (millions)	**41.1**	Land area (1,000 sq. km)	**2,737** GDP ($ billions) **475.5**

	Country data	Latin America & Caribbean group	Upper middle-income group
GNI per capita, *World Bank Atlas* method ($)	.. [a]	9,070	6,969
Adjusted net national income per capita ($)	9,416	7,325	5,845
Change in wealth per capita (2010 $)	641	180	1,039
Urban population (% of total)	92.6	79.0	60.7

Agriculture
Agricultural land (% land area)	54	37	44
Agricultural irrigated land (% of total agricultural land)	..	..	..
Agricultural productivity, value added per worker (2005 $)	..	4,135	1,131
Cereal yield (kg per hectare)	4,769	4,082	4,255

Forests and biodiversity
Forest area (% land area)	10.7	48.1	29.1
Deforestation (avg. annual %, 2000–2010)	0.8	0.5	0.0
Terrestrial protected areas (% of total land area)	6.9	21.4	16.1
Threatened species, mammals	39		
Threatened species, birds	50		
Threatened species, fish	37		
Threatened species, higher plants	68		

Oceans
Total fisheries production (thousand metric tons)	741	10,964	90,024
Capture fisheries growth (avg. annual %, 1990–2012)	1.3	-0.6	1.5
Aquaculture growth (avg. annual %, 1990–2012)	11.0	10.8	9.1
Marine protected areas (% of territorial waters)	1.1	9.0	7.3
Coral reef area (sq. km)	..	14,860	52,070
Mangroves area (sq. km)	..	39,988	50,160

Energy and emissions
Energy use per capita (kg oil equivalent)	1,967	1,292	1,893
Energy from biomass products and waste (% of total)	3.8	16.0	8.5
Electric power consumption per capita (kWh)	2,967	1,985	2,932
Electricity generated using fossil fuel (% of total)	69.1	37.3	74.7
Electricity generated by hydropower (% of total)	24.4	55.1	20.0
CO_2 emissions per capita (metric tons)	4.5	2.7	5.4

Water and sanitation
Internal freshwater resources per capita (cu. m)	6,777	21,735	6,791
Total freshwater withdrawal (% of internal resources)	11.8	2.0	7.4
Agriculture (% of total freshwater withdrawal)	66	68	69
Access to improved water source (% of total population)	99	94	93
Rural (% of rural population)	95	82	85
Urban (% of urban population)	99	97	98
Access to improved sanitation facilities (% of total population)	97	81	74
Rural (% of rural population)	99	62	62
Urban (% of urban population)	97	86	82

Environment and health
Particulate matter (urban-pop.-weighted avg., µg/cu. m)	35	43	65
Acute resp. infection prevalence (% of children under five)	..	..	..
Diarrhea prevalence (% of children under five)	..	..	..
Under-five mortality rate (per 1,000 live births)	14	19	20

National accounting aggregates—savings, depletion and degradation
Gross savings (% of GNI)	22.3	19.0	36.4
Consumption of fixed capital (% of GNI)	12.4	12.2	12.5
Education expenditure (% of GNI)	5.7	5.1	3.2
Energy depletion (% of GNI)	3.9	4.7	4.1
Mineral depletion (% of GNI)	0.6	1.2	1.2
Net forest depletion (% of GNI)	0.0	0.4	0.2
CO_2 damage (% of GNI)	0.4	0.3	0.8
Particulate emissions damage (% of GNI)	0.7	0.8	1.3
Adjusted net savings (% of GNI)	10.1	4.5	19.5

Armenia

	Population (millions)	**3.0**	Land area (1,000 sq. km)	**28**	GDP ($ billions)	**10.0**

	Country data	Europe & Central Asia group	Lower middle-income group
GNI per capita, *World Bank Atlas* method ($)	3,720	6,658	1,965
Adjusted net national income per capita ($)	2,930	5,541	1,574
Change in wealth per capita (2010 $)	151	263	117
Urban population (% of total)	64.2	60.2	38.9
Agriculture			
Agricultural land (% land area)	60	66	46
Agricultural irrigated land (% of total agricultural land)	8.9	..	..
Agricultural productivity, value added per worker (2005 $)	8,389	4,866	938
Cereal yield (kg per hectare)	2,649	2,519	3,029
Forests and biodiversity			
Forest area (% land area)	9.1	10.5	26.9
Deforestation (avg. annual %, 2000–2010)	1.5	-0.5	0.3
Terrestrial protected areas (% of total land area)	8.1	5.1	11.9
Threatened species, mammals	9		
Threatened species, birds	13		
Threatened species, fish	3		
Threatened species, higher plants	1		
Oceans			
Total fisheries production (thousand metric tons)	9.7	1,022	43,067
Capture fisheries growth (avg. annual %, 1990–2012)	-5.1	-4.0	2.6
Aquaculture growth (avg. annual %, 1990–2012)	2.6	1.8	9.9
Marine protected areas (% of territorial waters)	..	10.4	14.7
Coral reef area (sq. km)	..	..	124,480
Mangroves area (sq. km)	..	..	58,917
Energy and emissions			
Energy use per capita (kg oil equivalent)	916	2,078	687
Energy from biomass products and waste (% of total)	0.3	2.9	26.8
Electric power consumption per capita (kWh)	1,755	2,951	734
Electricity generated using fossil fuel (% of total)	32.2	65.8	72.3
Electricity generated by hydropower (% of total)	33.5	17.9	16.9
CO_2 emissions per capita (metric tons)	1.4	5.3	1.6
Water and sanitation			
Internal freshwater resources per capita (cu. m)	2,314	2,744	3,144
Total freshwater withdrawal (% of internal resources)	41.2	34.8	19.6
Agriculture (% of total freshwater withdrawal)	66	70	88
Access to improved water source (% of total population)	100	95	88
Rural (% of rural population)	100	89	85
Urban (% of urban population)	100	99	94
Access to improved sanitation facilities (% of total population)	91	94	48
Rural (% of rural population)	81	90	36
Urban (% of urban population)	96	97	66
Environment and health			
Particulate matter (urban-pop.-weighted avg., µg/cu. m)	13	48	90
Acute resp. infection prevalence (% of children under five)	5	..	..
Diarrhea prevalence (% of children under five)	9	..	..
Under-five mortality rate (per 1,000 live births)	16	22	61
National accounting aggregates—savings, depletion and degradation			
Gross savings (% of GNI)	11.1	18.9	28.6
Consumption of fixed capital (% of GNI)	13.2	12.4	11.1
Education expenditure (% of GNI)	2.2	3.8	3.1
Energy depletion (% of GNI)	0.0	4.4	4.4
Mineral depletion (% of GNI)	2.3	0.6	1.1
Net forest depletion (% of GNI)	1.1	0.0	0.8
CO_2 damage (% of GNI)	0.4	0.8	0.9
Particulate emissions damage (% of GNI)	0.0	1.8	1.4
Adjusted net savings (% of GNI)	-3.7	2.8	12.0

Aruba

Population (thousands) **102** Land area (sq. km) **180** GDP ($ billions) **2.6**

	Country data	High-income group
GNI per capita, *World Bank Atlas* method ($)	..	38,444
Adjusted net national income per capita ($)	..	32,262
Change in wealth per capita (2010 $)	..	2,210
Urban population (% of total)	47.0	80.2

Agriculture

Agricultural land (% land area)	11	29
Agricultural irrigated land (% of total agricultural land)	..	..
Agricultural productivity, value added per worker (2005 $)	..	25,238
Cereal yield (kg per hectare)	..	4,374

Forests and biodiversity

Forest area (% land area)	2.3	35.0
Deforestation (avg. annual %, 2000–2010)	0.0	0.0
Terrestrial protected areas (% of total land area)	0.5	13.9
Threatened species, mammals	2	
Threatened species, birds	1	
Threatened species, fish	15	
Threatened species, higher plants	2	

Oceans

Total fisheries production (thousand metric tons)	0.14	37,661
Capture fisheries growth (avg. annual %, 1990–2012)	-4.9	-2.0
Aquaculture growth (avg. annual %, 1990–2012)	..	2.5
Marine protected areas (% of territorial waters)	33.2	14.4
Coral reef area (sq. km)	<50	82,210
Mangroves area (sq. km)	0.71	15,504

Energy and emissions

Energy use per capita (kg oil equivalent)	..	4,872
Energy from biomass products and waste (% of total)	..	4.3
Electric power consumption per capita (kWh)	..	8,896
Electricity generated using fossil fuel (% of total)	..	61.8
Electricity generated by hydropower (% of total)	..	12.2
CO_2 emissions per capita (metric tons)	22.8	11.6

Water and sanitation

Internal freshwater resources per capita (cu. m)	..	11,335
Total freshwater withdrawal (% of internal resources)	..	7.0
Agriculture (% of total freshwater withdrawal)	..	40
Access to improved water source (% of total population)	98	99
Rural (% of rural population)	98	98
Urban (% of urban population)	98	100
Access to improved sanitation facilities (% of total population)	98	96
Rural (% of rural population)	98	93
Urban (% of urban population)	98	97

Environment and health

Particulate matter (urban-pop.-weighted avg., µg/cu. m)	..	27
Acute resp. infection prevalence (% of children under five)	..	..
Diarrhea prevalence (% of children under five)	..	..
Under-five mortality rate (per 1,000 live births)	..	6

National accounting aggregates—savings, depletion and degradation

Gross savings (% of GNI)	..	20.1
Consumption of fixed capital (% of GNI)	..	14.2
Education expenditure (% of GNI)	5.5	4.7
Energy depletion (% of GNI)	..	1.6
Mineral depletion (% of GNI)	..	0.3
Net forest depletion (% of GNI)	..	0.0
CO_2 damage (% of GNI)	..	0.3
Particulate emissions damage (% of GNI)	..	0.3
Adjusted net savings (% of GNI)	..	8.1

Australia

Population (millions) **22.7** Land area (1,000 sq. km) **7,682** GDP ($ billions) **1,532.4**

	Country data	High-income group
GNI per capita, *World Bank Atlas* method ($)	59,260	38,444
Adjusted net national income per capita ($)	50,923	32,262
Change in wealth per capita (2010 $)	-739	2,210
Urban population (% of total)	89.3	80.2
Agriculture		
Agricultural land (% land area)	53	29
Agricultural irrigated land (% of total agricultural land)	0.5	..
Agricultural productivity, value added per worker (2005 $)	53,777	25,238
Cereal yield (kg per hectare)	2,233	4,374
Forests and biodiversity		
Forest area (% land area)	19.3	35.0
Deforestation (avg. annual %, 2000–2010)	0.4	0.0
Terrestrial protected areas (% of total land area)	12.8	13.9
Threatened species, mammals	55	
Threatened species, birds	51	
Threatened species, fish	106	
Threatened species, higher plants	89	
Oceans		
Total fisheries production (thousand metric tons)	240	37,661
Capture fisheries growth (avg. annual %, 1990–2012)	-1.7	-2.0
Aquaculture growth (avg. annual %, 1990–2012)	8.8	2.5
Marine protected areas (% of territorial waters)	28.3	14.4
Coral reef area (sq. km)	48,960	82,210
Mangroves area (sq. km)	9,910	15,504
Energy and emissions		
Energy use per capita (kg oil equivalent)	5,501	4,872
Energy from biomass products and waste (% of total)	3.3	4.3
Electric power consumption per capita (kWh)	10,712	8,896
Electricity generated using fossil fuel (% of total)	89.9	61.8
Electricity generated by hydropower (% of total)	6.6	12.2
CO_2 emissions per capita (metric tons)	16.9	11.6
Water and sanitation		
Internal freshwater resources per capita (cu. m)	22,023	11,335
Total freshwater withdrawal (% of internal resources)	4.6	7.0
Agriculture (% of total freshwater withdrawal)	74	40
Access to improved water source (% of total population)	100	99
Rural (% of rural population)	100	98
Urban (% of urban population)	100	100
Access to improved sanitation facilities (% of total population)	100	96
Rural (% of rural population)	100	93
Urban (% of urban population)	100	97
Environment and health		
Particulate matter (urban-pop.-weighted avg., µg/cu. m)	14	27
Acute resp. infection prevalence (% of children under five)	..	..
Diarrhea prevalence (% of children under five)	..	..
Under-five mortality rate (per 1,000 live births)	5	6
National accounting aggregates—savings, depletion and degradation		
Gross savings (% of GNI)	26.2	20.1
Consumption of fixed capital (% of GNI)	16.5	14.2
Education expenditure (% of GNI)	5.1	4.7
Energy depletion (% of GNI)	1.5	1.6
Mineral depletion (% of GNI)	3.6	0.3
Net forest depletion (% of GNI)	0.0	0.0
CO_2 damage (% of GNI)	0.3	0.3
Particulate emissions damage (% of GNI)	0.0	0.3
Adjusted net savings (% of GNI)	9.4	8.1

Austria

| | Population (millions) | 8.4 | Land area (1,000 sq. km) | 82 | GDP ($ billions) | 394.5 |

	Country data	High-income group
GNI per capita, *World Bank Atlas* method ($)	47,960	38,444
Adjusted net national income per capita ($)	38,755	32,262
Change in wealth per capita (2010 $)	5,884	2,210
Urban population (% of total)	67.9	80.2
Agriculture		
Agricultural land (% land area)	35	29
Agricultural irrigated land (% of total agricultural land)	1.4	..
Agricultural productivity, value added per worker (2005 $)	33,213	25,238
Cereal yield (kg per hectare)	5,999	4,374
Forests and biodiversity		
Forest area (% land area)	47.2	35.0
Deforestation (avg. annual %, 2000-2010)	-0.1	0.0
Terrestrial protected areas (% of total land area)	23.6	13.9
Threatened species, mammals	3	
Threatened species, birds	9	
Threatened species, fish	11	
Threatened species, higher plants	13	
Oceans		
Total fisheries production (thousand metric tons)	3.3	37,661
Capture fisheries growth (avg. annual %, 1990-2012)	-1.9	-2.0
Aquaculture growth (avg. annual %, 1990-2012)	-0.2	2.5
Marine protected areas (% of territorial waters)	..	14.4
Coral reef area (sq. km)	..	82,210
Mangroves area (sq. km)	..	15,504
Energy and emissions		
Energy use per capita (kg oil equivalent)	3,928	4,872
Energy from biomass products and waste (% of total)	19.0	4.3
Electric power consumption per capita (kWh)	8,374	8,896
Electricity generated using fossil fuel (% of total)	33.3	61.8
Electricity generated by hydropower (% of total)	55.0	12.2
CO_2 emissions per capita (metric tons)	8.0	11.6
Water and sanitation		
Internal freshwater resources per capita (cu. m)	6,543	11,335
Total freshwater withdrawal (% of internal resources)	6.6	7.0
Agriculture (% of total freshwater withdrawal)	3	40
Access to improved water source (% of total population)	100	99
Rural (% of rural population)	100	98
Urban (% of urban population)	100	100
Access to improved sanitation facilities (% of total population)	100	96
Rural (% of rural population)	100	93
Urban (% of urban population)	100	97
Environment and health		
Particulate matter (urban-pop.-weighted avg., µg/cu. m)	28	27
Acute resp. infection prevalence (% of children under five)	..	..
Diarrhea prevalence (% of children under five)	..	..
Under-five mortality rate (per 1,000 live births)	4	6
National accounting aggregates—savings, depletion and degradation		
Gross savings (% of GNI)	24.7	20.1
Consumption of fixed capital (% of GNI)	16.5	14.2
Education expenditure (% of GNI)	5.6	4.7
Energy depletion (% of GNI)	0.1	1.6
Mineral depletion (% of GNI)	0.0	0.3
Net forest depletion (% of GNI)	0.0	0.0
CO_2 damage (% of GNI)	0.2	0.3
Particulate emissions damage (% of GNI)	0.3	0.3
Adjusted net savings (% of GNI)	13.1	8.1

Azerbaijan

	Country data	Europe & Central Asia group	Upper middle-income group
Population (millions) **9.3** Land area (1,000 sq. km) **83** GDP ($ billions) **66.6**			
GNI per capita, *World Bank Atlas* method ($)	6,220	6,658	6,969
Adjusted net national income per capita ($)	4,514	5,541	5,845
Change in wealth per capita (2010 $)	18	263	1,039
Urban population (% of total)	53.9	60.2	60.7

Agriculture

Agricultural land (% land area)	58	66	44
Agricultural irrigated land (% of total agricultural land)	29.5	..	..
Agricultural productivity, value added per worker (2005 $)	1,085	4,866	1,131
Cereal yield (kg per hectare)	2,660	2,519	4,255

Forests and biodiversity

Forest area (% land area)	11.3	10.5	29.1
Deforestation (avg. annual %, 2000–2010)	0.0	-0.5	0.0
Terrestrial protected areas (% of total land area)	7.4	5.1	16.1
Threatened species, mammals	7		
Threatened species, birds	15		
Threatened species, fish	10		
Threatened species, higher plants	0		

Oceans

Total fisheries production (thousand metric tons)	1.3	1,022	90,024
Capture fisheries growth (avg. annual %, 1990–2012)	-15.8	-4.0	1.5
Aquaculture growth (avg. annual %, 1990–2012)	-5.3	1.8	9.1
Marine protected areas (% of territorial waters)	0.41	10.4	7.3
Coral reef area (sq. km)	..	..	52,070
Mangroves area (sq. km)	..	..	50,160

Energy and emissions

Energy use per capita (kg oil equivalent)	1,369	2,078	1,893
Energy from biomass products and waste (% of total)	0.8	2.9	8.5
Electric power consumption per capita (kWh)	1,705	2,951	2,932
Electricity generated using fossil fuel (% of total)	86.8	65.8	74.7
Electricity generated by hydropower (% of total)	13.2	17.9	20.0
CO_2 emissions per capita (metric tons)	5.1	5.3	5.4

Water and sanitation

Internal freshwater resources per capita (cu. m)	885	2,744	6,791
Total freshwater withdrawal (% of internal resources)	150.5	34.8	7.4
Agriculture (% of total freshwater withdrawal)	76	70	69
Access to improved water source (% of total population)	80	95	93
Rural (% of rural population)	71	89	85
Urban (% of urban population)	88	99	98
Access to improved sanitation facilities (% of total population)	82	94	74
Rural (% of rural population)	78	90	62
Urban (% of urban population)	86	97	82

Environment and health

Particulate matter (urban-pop.-weighted avg., µg/cu. m)	20	48	65
Acute resp. infection prevalence (% of children under five)	..	..	..
Diarrhea prevalence (% of children under five)	..	..	..
Under-five mortality rate (per 1,000 live births)	35	22	20

National accounting aggregates—savings, depletion and degradation

Gross savings (% of GNI)	45.6	18.9	36.4
Consumption of fixed capital (% of GNI)	3.1	12.4	12.5
Education expenditure (% of GNI)	2.8	3.8	3.2
Energy depletion (% of GNI)	28.2	4.4	4.1
Mineral depletion (% of GNI)	0.1	0.6	1.2
Net forest depletion (% of GNI)	0.0	0.0	0.2
CO_2 damage (% of GNI)	0.7	0.8	0.8
Particulate emissions damage (% of GNI)	0.3	1.8	1.3
Adjusted net savings (% of GNI)	15.9	2.8	19.5

Bahamas, The

| Population (thousands) **372** | Land area (1,000 sq. km) | **10** | GDP ($ billions) | **8.1** |

	Country data	High-Income group
GNI per capita, *World Bank Atlas* method ($)	20,600	38,444
Adjusted net national income per capita ($)	18,602	32,262
Change in wealth per capita (2010 $)	..	2,210
Urban population (% of total)	84.4	80.2
Agriculture		
Agricultural land (% land area)	1	29
Agricultural irrigated land (% of total agricultural land)	..	..
Agricultural productivity, value added per worker (2005 $)	30,915	*25,238*
Cereal yield (kg per hectare)	7,340	4,374
Forests and biodiversity		
Forest area (% land area)	51.4	35.0
Deforestation (avg. annual %, 2000–2010)	0.0	0.0
Terrestrial protected areas (% of total land area)	13.7	13.9
Threatened species, mammals	6	
Threatened species, birds	6	
Threatened species, fish	30	
Threatened species, higher plants	8	
Oceans		
Total fisheries production (thousand metric tons)	19.7	37,661
Capture fisheries growth (avg. annual %, 1990–2012)	3.3	-2.0
Aquaculture growth (avg. annual %, 1990–2012)	..	2.5
Marine protected areas (% of territorial waters)	7.4	*14.4*
Coral reef area (sq. km)	3,150	82,210
Mangroves area (sq. km)	875	15,504
Energy and emissions		
Energy use per capita (kg oil equivalent)	*2,073*	4,872
Energy from biomass products and waste (% of total)	..	4.3
Electric power consumption per capita (kWh)	..	8,896
Electricity generated using fossil fuel (% of total)	..	61.8
Electricity generated by hydropower (% of total)	..	12.2
CO_2 emissions per capita (metric tons)	6.8	11.6
Water and sanitation		
Internal freshwater resources per capita (cu. m)	55	11,335
Total freshwater withdrawal (% of internal resources)	..	7.0
Agriculture (% of total freshwater withdrawal)	..	40
Access to improved water source (% of total population)	98	99
Rural (% of rural population)	98	98
Urban (% of urban population)	98	100
Access to improved sanitation facilities (% of total population)	92	96
Rural (% of rural population)	92	93
Urban (% of urban population)	92	97
Environment and health		
Particulate matter (urban-pop.-weighted avg., µg/cu. m)	..	27
Acute resp. infection prevalence (% of children under five)	..	..
Diarrhea prevalence (% of children under five)	..	..
Under-five mortality rate (per 1,000 live births)	17	6

National accounting aggregates—savings, depletion and degradation

Gross savings (% of GNI)	9.0	20.1
Consumption of fixed capital (% of GNI)	8.9	14.2
Education expenditure (% of GNI)	3.8	4.7
Energy depletion (% of GNI)	0.0	1.6
Mineral depletion (% of GNI)	0.0	0.3
Net forest depletion (% of GNI)	0.0	0.0
CO_2 damage (% of GNI)	0.4	0.3
Particulate emissions damage (% of GNI)	..	0.3
Adjusted net savings (% of GNI)	..	8.1

Bahrain

Population (millions)	**1.3**	Land area (sq. km)	**760**	GDP ($ billions)	**30.4**

	Country data	High-income group
GNI per capita, *World Bank Atlas* method ($)	19,560	38,444
Adjusted net national income per capita ($)	14,985	32,262
Change in wealth per capita (2010 $)	-7,383	2,210
Urban population (% of total)	88.8	80.2
Agriculture		
Agricultural land (% land area)	11	29
Agricultural irrigated land (% of total agricultural land)	..	..
Agricultural productivity, value added per worker (2005 $)	..	25,238
Cereal yield (kg per hectare)	..	4,374
Forests and biodiversity		
Forest area (% land area)	0.7	35.0
Deforestation (avg. annual %, 2000–2010)	-3.6	0.0
Terrestrial protected areas (% of total land area)	2.8	13.9
Threatened species, mammals	3	
Threatened species, birds	3	
Threatened species, fish	9	
Threatened species, higher plants	0	
Oceans		
Total fisheries production (thousand metric tons)	27.1	37,661
Capture fisheries growth (avg. annual %, 1990–2012)	5.6	-2.0
Aquaculture growth (avg. annual %, 1990–2012)	..	2.5
Marine protected areas (% of territorial waters)	2.5	*14.4*
Coral reef area (sq. km)	570	82,210
Mangroves area (sq. km)	0.65	15,504
Energy and emissions		
Energy use per capita (kg oil equivalent)	7,353	4,872
Energy from biomass products and waste (% of total)	0.0	4.3
Electric power consumption per capita (kWh)	10,018	8,896
Electricity generated using fossil fuel (% of total)	100.0	61.8
Electricity generated by hydropower (% of total)	0.0	12.2
CO_2 emissions per capita (metric tons)	19.3	11.6
Water and sanitation		
Internal freshwater resources per capita (cu. m)	3	11,335
Total freshwater withdrawal (% of internal resources)	8,935.0	7.0
Agriculture (% of total freshwater withdrawal)	45	40
Access to improved water source (% of total population)	100	99
Rural (% of rural population)	100	98
Urban (% of urban population)	100	100
Access to improved sanitation facilities (% of total population)	99	96
Rural (% of rural population)	99	93
Urban (% of urban population)	99	97
Environment and health		
Particulate matter (urban-pop.-weighted avg., µg/cu. m)	24	27
Acute resp. infection prevalence (% of children under five)	..	..
Diarrhea prevalence (% of children under five)	..	..
Under-five mortality rate (per 1,000 live births)	10	6
National accounting aggregates—savings, depletion and degradation		
Gross savings (% of GNI)	*21.5*	20.1
Consumption of fixed capital (% of GNI)	7.9	14.2
Education expenditure (% of GNI)	3.0	4.7
Energy depletion (% of GNI)	17.6	1.6
Mineral depletion (% of GNI)	0.0	0.3
Net forest depletion (% of GNI)	0.0	0.0
CO_2 damage (% of GNI)	1.0	0.3
Particulate emissions damage (% of GNI)	0.2	0.3
Adjusted net savings (% of GNI)	-0.8	8.1

Bangladesh

Population (millions) **154.7** Land area (1,000 sq. km) **130** GDP ($ billions) **116.4**

	Country data	South Asia group	Low-income group
GNI per capita, *World Bank Atlas* method ($)	840	1,437	594
Adjusted net national income per capita ($)	703	1,168	495
Change in wealth per capita (2010 $)	113	158	–39
Urban population (% of total)	28.9	31.4	28.2
Agriculture			
Agricultural land (% land area)	70	55	39
Agricultural irrigated land (% of total agricultural land)	52.6	..	..
Agricultural productivity, value added per worker (2005 $)	492	669	367
Cereal yield (kg per hectare)	2,988	2,925	1,982
Forests and biodiversity			
Forest area (% land area)	11.1	17.1	27.4
Deforestation (avg. annual %, 2000–2010)	0.2	–0.3	0.6
Terrestrial protected areas (% of total land area)	4.7	6.2	13.7
Threatened species, mammals	34		
Threatened species, birds	31		
Threatened species, fish	18		
Threatened species, higher plants	17		
Oceans			
Total fisheries production (thousand metric tons)	3,262	13,613	11,789
Capture fisheries growth (avg. annual %, 1990–2012)	4.0	2.6	3.8
Aquaculture growth (avg. annual %, 1990–2012)	10.5	7.6	5.1
Marine protected areas (% of territorial waters)	0.07	10.7	13.1
Coral reef area (sq. km)	<50	15,440	15,120
Mangroves area (sq. km)	4,951	10,343	25,817
Energy and emissions			
Energy use per capita (kg oil equivalent)	205	555	360
Energy from biomass products and waste (% of total)	28.2	26.7	66.0
Electric power consumption per capita (kWh)	259	605	233
Electricity generated using fossil fuel (% of total)	98.0	77.9	30.9
Electricity generated by hydropower (% of total)	2.0	13.8	45.5
CO_2 emissions per capita (metric tons)	0.4	1.4	0.3
Water and sanitation			
Internal freshwater resources per capita (cu. m)	687	1,217	5,121
Total freshwater withdrawal (% of internal resources)	34.2	51.6	4.4
Agriculture (% of total freshwater withdrawal)	88	91	90
Access to improved water source (% of total population)	85	91	69
Rural (% of rural population)	84	89	61
Urban (% of urban population)	86	95	88
Access to improved sanitation facilities (% of total population)	57	40	37
Rural (% of rural population)	58	30	33
Urban (% of urban population)	55	61	46
Environment and health			
Particulate matter (urban-pop.-weighted avg., µg/cu. m)	121	110	74
Acute resp. infection prevalence (% of children under five)	6	..	6
Diarrhea prevalence (% of children under five)	5	..	14
Under-five mortality rate (per 1,000 live births)	41	60	82
National accounting aggregates—savings, depletion and degradation			
Gross savings (% of GNI)	36.2	29.3	24.6
Consumption of fixed capital (% of GNI)	11.5	12.7	11.8
Education expenditure (% of GNI)	1.8	2.8	3.2
Energy depletion (% of GNI)	2.1	1.8	1.4
Mineral depletion (% of GNI)	0.0	0.8	1.9
Net forest depletion (% of GNI)	1.3	1.1	4.4
CO_2 damage (% of GNI)	0.5	1.1	0.4
Particulate emissions damage (% of GNI)	1.4	1.5	1.0
Adjusted net savings (% of GNI)	21.3	13.1	7.0

Barbados

Population (thousands) **283**	Land area (sq. km)	**430** GDP ($ billions)	**4.2**

	Country data	High-income group
GNI per capita, *World Bank Atlas* method ($)	15,080	38,444
Adjusted net national income per capita ($)	12,727	32,262
Change in wealth per capita (2010 $)	..	2,210
Urban population (% of total)	44.9	80.2

Agriculture

Agricultural land (% land area)	35	29
Agricultural irrigated land (% of total agricultural land)	..	..
Agricultural productivity, value added per worker (2005 $)	12,778	25,238
Cereal yield (kg per hectare)	3,200	4,374

Forests and biodiversity

Forest area (% land area)	19.4	35.0
Deforestation (avg. annual %, 2000–2010)	0.0	0.0
Terrestrial protected areas (% of total land area)	0.1	13.9
Threatened species, mammals	3	
Threatened species, birds	2	
Threatened species, fish	21	
Threatened species, higher plants	3	

Oceans

Total fisheries production (thousand metric tons)	1.4	37,661
Capture fisheries growth (avg. annual %, 1990–2012)	-3.6	-2.0
Aquaculture growth (avg. annual %, 1990–2012)	..	2.5
Marine protected areas (% of territorial waters)	0.07	14.4
Coral reef area (sq. km)	<100	82,210
Mangroves area (sq. km)	0.04	15,504

Energy and emissions

Energy use per capita (kg oil equivalent)	1,451	4,872
Energy from biomass products and waste (% of total)	..	4.3
Electric power consumption per capita (kWh)	..	8,896
Electricity generated using fossil fuel (% of total)	..	61.8
Electricity generated by hydropower (% of total)	..	12.2
CO_2 emissions per capita (metric tons)	5.4	11.6

Water and sanitation

Internal freshwater resources per capita (cu. m)	284	11,335
Total freshwater withdrawal (% of internal resources)	76.1	7.0
Agriculture (% of total freshwater withdrawal)	33	40
Access to improved water source (% of total population)	100	99
Rural (% of rural population)	100	98
Urban (% of urban population)	100	100
Access to improved sanitation facilities (% of total population)	..	96
Rural (% of rural population)	..	93
Urban (% of urban population)	..	97

Environment and health

Particulate matter (urban-pop.-weighted avg., µg/cu. m)	11	27
Acute resp. infection prevalence (% of children under five)	..	..
Diarrhea prevalence (% of children under five)	..	..
Under-five mortality rate (per 1,000 live births)	18	6

National accounting aggregates—savings, depletion and degradation

Gross savings (% of GNI)	8.6	20.1
Consumption of fixed capital (% of GNI)	11.9	14.2
Education expenditure (% of GNI)	7.2	4.7
Energy depletion (% of GNI)	0.0	1.6
Mineral depletion (% of GNI)	0.0	0.3
Net forest depletion (% of GNI)	0.0	0.0
CO_2 damage (% of GNI)	0.4	0.3
Particulate emissions damage (% of GNI)	0.0	0.3
Adjusted net savings (% of GNI)	3.6	8.1

Belarus

	Country data	Europe & Central Asia group	Upper middle-income group
Population (millions) **9.5** Land area (1,000 sq. km) **203** GDP ($ billions) **63.3**			

	Country data	Europe & Central Asia group	Upper middle-income group
GNI per capita, *World Bank Atlas* method ($)	6,370	6,658	6,969
Adjusted net national income per capita ($)	5,492	5,541	5,845
Change in wealth per capita (2010 $)	955	263	1,039
Urban population (% of total)	75.4	60.2	60.7
Agriculture			
Agricultural land (% land area)	44	66	44
Agricultural irrigated land (% of total agricultural land)	0.3	..	..
Agricultural productivity, value added per worker (2005 $)	7,845	4,866	1,131
Cereal yield (kg per hectare)	3,486	2,519	4,255
Forests and biodiversity			
Forest area (% land area)	42.7	10.5	29.1
Deforestation (avg. annual %, 2000–2010)	-0.4	-0.5	0.0
Terrestrial protected areas (% of total land area)	8.3	5.1	16.1
Threatened species, mammals	4		
Threatened species, birds	6		
Threatened species, fish	2		
Threatened species, higher plants	1		
Oceans			
Total fisheries production (thousand metric tons)	16.5	1,022	90,024
Capture fisheries growth (avg. annual %, 1990–2012)	-5.0	-4.0	1.5
Aquaculture growth (avg. annual %, 1990–2012)	-0.3	1.8	9.1
Marine protected areas (% of territorial waters)	55.7	10.4	7.3
Coral reef area (sq. km)	..	..	52,070
Mangroves area (sq. km)	..	..	50,160
Energy and emissions			
Energy use per capita (kg oil equivalent)	3,114	2,078	1,893
Energy from biomass products and waste (% of total)	5.9	2.9	8.5
Electric power consumption per capita (kWh)	3,628	2,951	2,932
Electricity generated using fossil fuel (% of total)	99.4	65.8	74.7
Electricity generated by hydropower (% of total)	0.1	17.9	20.0
CO_2 emissions per capita (metric tons)	6.6	5.3	5.4
Water and sanitation			
Internal freshwater resources per capita (cu. m)	3,927	2,744	6,791
Total freshwater withdrawal (% of internal resources)	11.7	34.8	7.4
Agriculture (% of total freshwater withdrawal)	19	70	69
Access to improved water source (% of total population)	100	95	93
Rural (% of rural population)	99	89	85
Urban (% of urban population)	100	99	98
Access to improved sanitation facilities (% of total population)	94	94	74
Rural (% of rural population)	95	90	62
Urban (% of urban population)	94	97	82
Environment and health			
Particulate matter (urban-pop.-weighted avg., µg/cu. m)	20	48	65
Acute resp. infection prevalence (% of children under five)	..	..	..
Diarrhea prevalence (% of children under five)	..	..	..
Under-five mortality rate (per 1,000 live births)	5	22	20
National accounting aggregates—savings, depletion and degradation			
Gross savings (% of GNI)	32.3	18.9	36.4
Consumption of fixed capital (% of GNI)	14.6	12.4	12.5
Education expenditure (% of GNI)	4.8	3.8	3.2
Energy depletion (% of GNI)	1.2	4.4	4.1
Mineral depletion (% of GNI)	0.0	0.6	1.2
Net forest depletion (% of GNI)	0.0	0.0	0.2
CO_2 damage (% of GNI)	1.0	0.8	0.8
Particulate emissions damage (% of GNI)	0.6	1.8	1.3
Adjusted net savings (% of GNI)	19.7	2.8	19.5

Belgium

Population (millions)	**11.1**	Land area (1,000 sq. km)	**30**	GDP ($ billions)	**483.0**

	Country data	High-income group
GNI per capita, *World Bank Atlas* method ($)	44,820	38,444
Adjusted net national income per capita ($)	35,814	32,262
Change in wealth per capita (2010 $)	3,676	2,210
Urban population (% of total)	97.5	80.2
Agriculture		
Agricultural land (% land area)	44	29
Agricultural irrigated land (% of total agricultural land)	0.4	..
Agricultural productivity, value added per worker (2005 $)	56,515	25,238
Cereal yield (kg per hectare)	8,587	4,374
Forests and biodiversity		
Forest area (% land area)	22.4	35.0
Deforestation (avg. annual %, 2000–2010)	-0.2	0.0
Terrestrial protected areas (% of total land area)	23.0	13.9
Threatened species, mammals	2	
Threatened species, birds	4	
Threatened species, fish	11	
Threatened species, higher plants	0	
Oceans		
Total fisheries production (thousand metric tons)	24.7	37,661
Capture fisheries growth (avg. annual %, 1990–2012)	-2.3	-2.0
Aquaculture growth (avg. annual %, 1990–2012)	-11.2	2.5
Marine protected areas (% of territorial waters)	14.2	14.4
Coral reef area (sq. km)	..	82,210
Mangroves area (sq. km)	..	15,504
Energy and emissions		
Energy use per capita (kg oil equivalent)	5,349	4,872
Energy from biomass products and waste (% of total)	8.9	4.3
Electric power consumption per capita (kWh)	8,021	8,896
Electricity generated using fossil fuel (% of total)	34.9	61.8
Electricity generated by hydropower (% of total)	0.2	12.2
CO_2 emissions per capita (metric tons)	10.0	11.6
Water and sanitation		
Internal freshwater resources per capita (cu. m)	1,086	11,335
Total freshwater withdrawal (% of internal resources)	51.8	7.0
Agriculture (% of total freshwater withdrawal)	1	40
Access to improved water source (% of total population)	100	99
Rural (% of rural population)	100	98
Urban (% of urban population)	100	100
Access to improved sanitation facilities (% of total population)	100	96
Rural (% of rural population)	100	93
Urban (% of urban population)	100	97
Environment and health		
Particulate matter (urban-pop.-weighted avg., µg/cu. m)	29	27
Acute resp. infection prevalence (% of children under five)	..	..
Diarrhea prevalence (% of children under five)	..	..
Under-five mortality rate (per 1,000 live births)	4	6
National accounting aggregates—savings, depletion and degradation		
Gross savings (% of GNI)	20.3	20.1
Consumption of fixed capital (% of GNI)	17.7	14.2
Education expenditure (% of GNI)	6.3	4.7
Energy depletion (% of GNI)	0.0	1.6
Mineral depletion (% of GNI)	0.0	0.3
Net forest depletion (% of GNI)	0.0	0.0
CO_2 damage (% of GNI)	0.2	0.3
Particulate emissions damage (% of GNI)	0.6	0.3
Adjusted net savings (% of GNI)	7.9	8.1

Belize

	Country data	Latin America & Caribbean group	Upper middle-income group
Population (thousands) **324**	Land area (1,000 sq. km) **23**	GDP ($ billions)	**1.5**

	Country data	Latin America & Caribbean group	Upper middle-income group
GNI per capita, *World Bank Atlas* method ($)	4,490	9,070	6,969
Adjusted net national income per capita ($)	3,992	7,325	5,845
Change in wealth per capita (2010 $)	–824	180	1,039
Urban population (% of total)	44.6	79.0	60.7
Agriculture			
Agricultural land (% land area)	7	37	44
Agricultural irrigated land (% of total agricultural land)	..	..	..
Agricultural productivity, value added per worker (2005 $)	4,765	4,135	1,131
Cereal yield (kg per hectare)	2,912	4,082	4,255
Forests and biodiversity			
Forest area (% land area)	60.6	48.1	29.1
Deforestation (avg. annual %, 2000–2010)	0.7	0.5	0.0
Terrestrial protected areas (% of total land area)	36.7	21.4	16.1
Threatened species, mammals	9		
Threatened species, birds	5		
Threatened species, fish	31		
Threatened species, higher plants	33		
Oceans			
Total fisheries production (thousand metric tons)	156	10,964	90,024
Capture fisheries growth (avg. annual %, 1990–2012)	21.6	-0.6	1.5
Aquaculture growth (avg. annual %, 1990–2012)	20.4	10.8	9.1
Marine protected areas (% of territorial waters)	11.9	9.0	7.3
Coral reef area (sq. km)	1,330	14,860	52,070
Mangroves area (sq. km)	958	39,988	50,160
Energy and emissions			
Energy use per capita (kg oil equivalent)	622	1,292	1,893
Energy from biomass products and waste (% of total)	..	16.0	8.5
Electric power consumption per capita (kWh)	..	1,985	2,932
Electricity generated using fossil fuel (% of total)	..	37.3	74.7
Electricity generated by hydropower (% of total)	..	55.1	20.0
CO_2 emissions per capita (metric tons)	1.4	2.7	5.4
Water and sanitation			
Internal freshwater resources per capita (cu. m)	50,588	21,735	6,791
Total freshwater withdrawal (% of internal resources)	0.9	2.0	7.4
Agriculture (% of total freshwater withdrawal)	20	68	69
Access to improved water source (% of total population)	99	94	93
Rural (% of rural population)	100	82	85
Urban (% of urban population)	98	97	98
Access to improved sanitation facilities (% of total population)	91	81	74
Rural (% of rural population)	88	62	62
Urban (% of urban population)	94	86	82
Environment and health			
Particulate matter (urban-pop.-weighted avg., µg/cu. m)	18	43	65
Acute resp. infection prevalence (% of children under five)	..	..	..
Diarrhea prevalence (% of children under five)	..	..	..
Under-five mortality rate (per 1,000 live births)	18	19	20
National accounting aggregates—savings, depletion and degradation			
Gross savings (% of GNI)	16.3	19.0	36.4
Consumption of fixed capital (% of GNI)	12.6	12.2	12.5
Education expenditure (% of GNI)	7.2	5.1	3.2
Energy depletion (% of GNI)	0.0	4.7	4.1
Mineral depletion (% of GNI)	0.0	1.2	1.2
Net forest depletion (% of GNI)	0.0	0.4	0.2
CO_2 damage (% of GNI)	0.3	0.3	0.8
Particulate emissions damage (% of GNI)	0.1	0.8	1.3
Adjusted net savings (% of GNI)	10.6	4.5	19.5

Benin

Population (millions)	**10.1**	Land area (1,000 sq. km)	**113**	GDP ($ billions)	**7.6**

	Country data	Sub-Saharan Africa group	Low-Income group
GNI per capita, *World Bank Atlas* method ($)	750	1,547	594
Adjusted net national income per capita ($)	634	1,005	495
Change in wealth per capita (2010 $)	–106	–273	–39
Urban population (% of total)	45.6	36.8	28.2
Agriculture			
Agricultural land (% land area)	30	44	39
Agricultural irrigated land (% of total agricultural land)	..	..	..
Agricultural productivity, value added per worker (2005 $)	*1,041*	765	367
Cereal yield (kg per hectare)	1,478	1,417	1,982
Forests and biodiversity			
Forest area (% land area)	40.0	27.4	27.4
Deforestation (avg. annual %, 2000–2010)	1.0	0.5	0.6
Terrestrial protected areas (% of total land area)	26.1	16.4	13.7
Threatened species, mammals	11		
Threatened species, birds	9		
Threatened species, fish	28		
Threatened species, higher plants	15		
Oceans			
Total fisheries production (thousand metric tons)	40.9	6,906	11,789
Capture fisheries growth (avg. annual %, 1990–2012)	0.2	2.1	3.8
Aquaculture growth (avg. annual %, 1990–2012)	..	15.9	5.1
Marine protected areas (% of territorial waters)	5.0	11.7	13.1
Coral reef area (sq. km)	..	17,980	15,120
Mangroves area (sq. km)	65.7	27,808	25,817
Energy and emissions			
Energy use per capita (kg oil equivalent)	385	681	360
Energy from biomass products and waste (% of total)	56.2	57.6	66.0
Electric power consumption per capita (kWh)	84	535	233
Electricity generated using fossil fuel (% of total)	99.4	65.1	30.9
Electricity generated by hydropower (% of total)	0.0	20.0	45.5
CO_2 emissions per capita (metric tons)	0.5	0.8	0.3
Water and sanitation			
Internal freshwater resources per capita (cu. m)	1,053	4,391	5,121
Total freshwater withdrawal (% of internal resources)	1.3	3.2	4.4
Agriculture (% of total freshwater withdrawal)	45	84	90
Access to improved water source (% of total population)	76	64	69
Rural (% of rural population)	69	53	61
Urban (% of urban population)	85	85	88
Access to improved sanitation facilities (% of total population)	14	30	37
Rural (% of rural population)	5	23	33
Urban (% of urban population)	25	41	46
Environment and health			
Particulate matter (urban-pop.-weighted avg., µg/cu. m)	69	77	74
Acute resp. infection prevalence (% of children under five)	1	5	6
Diarrhea prevalence (% of children under five)	6	14	14
Under-five mortality rate (per 1,000 live births)	90	98	82
National accounting aggregates—savings, depletion and degradation			
Gross savings (% of GNI)	7.2	26.3	24.6
Consumption of fixed capital (% of GNI)	13.6	13.0	11.8
Education expenditure (% of GNI)	4.8	3.4	3.2
Energy depletion (% of GNI)	0.0	10.3	1.4
Mineral depletion (% of GNI)	0.0	1.8	1.9
Net forest depletion (% of GNI)	1.5	1.8	4.4
CO_2 damage (% of GNI)	0.8	0.6	0.4
Particulate emissions damage (% of GNI)	1.3	1.2	1.0
Adjusted net savings (% of GNI)	–5.2	0.9	7.0

Bermuda

Population (thousands)	**65**	Land area (sq. km)	**50**	GDP ($ billions)	**5.5**

	Country data	High-income group
GNI per capita, *World Bank Atlas* method ($)	104,590	38,444
Adjusted net national income per capita ($)	..	32,262
Change in wealth per capita (2010 $)	..	2,210
Urban population (% of total)	100.0	80.2

Agriculture

Agricultural land (% land area)	15	29
Agricultural irrigated land (% of total agricultural land)	..	..
Agricultural productivity, value added per worker (2005 $)	38,510	25,238
Cereal yield (kg per hectare)	..	4,374

Forests and biodiversity

Forest area (% land area)	20.0	35.0
Deforestation (avg. annual %, 2000-2010)	0.0	0.0
Terrestrial protected areas (% of total land area)	5.8	13.9
Threatened species, mammals	4	
Threatened species, birds	1	
Threatened species, fish	16	
Threatened species, higher plants	4	

Oceans

Total fisheries production (thousand metric tons)	0.52	37,661
Capture fisheries growth (avg. annual %, 1990-2012)	0.5	-2.0
Aquaculture growth (avg. annual %, 1990-2012)	..	2.5
Marine protected areas (% of territorial waters)	5.0	14.4
Coral reef area (sq. km)	370	82,210
Mangroves area (sq. km)	0.18	15,504

Energy and emissions

Energy use per capita (kg oil equivalent)	..	4,872
Energy from biomass products and waste (% of total)	..	4.3
Electric power consumption per capita (kWh)	..	8,896
Electricity generated using fossil fuel (% of total)	..	61.8
Electricity generated by hydropower (% of total)	..	12.2
CO_2 emissions per capita (metric tons)	7.3	11.6

Water and sanitation

Internal freshwater resources per capita (cu. m)	..	11,335
Total freshwater withdrawal (% of internal resources)	..	7.0
Agriculture (% of total freshwater withdrawal)	..	40
Access to improved water source (% of total population)	..	99
Rural (% of rural population)	..	98
Urban (% of urban population)	..	100
Access to improved sanitation facilities (% of total population)	..	96
Rural (% of rural population)	..	93
Urban (% of urban population)	..	97

Environment and health

Particulate matter (urban-pop.-weighted avg., µg/cu. m)	..	27
Acute resp. infection prevalence (% of children under five)	..	..
Diarrhea prevalence (% of children under five)	..	..
Under-five mortality rate (per 1,000 live births)	..	6

National accounting aggregates—savings, depletion and degradation

Gross savings (% of GNI)	..	20.1
Consumption of fixed capital (% of GNI)	10.2	14.2
Education expenditure (% of GNI)	2.1	4.7
Energy depletion (% of GNI)	0.0	1.6
Mineral depletion (% of GNI)	0.0	0.3
Net forest depletion (% of GNI)	..	0.0
CO_2 damage (% of GNI)	0.1	0.3
Particulate emissions damage (% of GNI)	..	0.3
Adjusted net savings (% of GNI)	..	8.1

Bhutan

Population (thousands) **742** Land area (1,000 sq. km) **38** GDP ($ billions) **1.8**

	Country data	South Asia group	Lower middle-income group
GNI per capita, *World Bank Atlas* method ($)	2,420	1,437	1,965
Adjusted net national income per capita ($)	1,693	1,168	1,574
Change in wealth per capita (2010 $)	12	158	117
Urban population (% of total)	36.3	31.4	38.9
Agriculture			
Agricultural land (% land area)	14	55	46
Agricultural irrigated land (% of total agricultural land)	6.7	..	..
Agricultural productivity, value added per worker (2005 $)	625	669	938
Cereal yield (kg per hectare)	2,663	2,925	3,029
Forests and biodiversity			
Forest area (% land area)	84.9	17.1	26.9
Deforestation (avg. annual %, 2000–2010)	-0.3	-0.3	0.3
Terrestrial protected areas (% of total land area)	28.4	6.2	11.9
Threatened species, mammals	27		
Threatened species, birds	18		
Threatened species, fish	3		
Threatened species, higher plants	9		
Oceans			
Total fisheries production (thousand metric tons)	0.08	13,613	43,067
Capture fisheries growth (avg. annual %, 1990–2012)	-17.8	2.6	2.6
Aquaculture growth (avg. annual %, 1990–2012)	4.3	7.6	9.9
Marine protected areas (% of territorial waters)	..	10.7	14.7
Coral reef area (sq. km)	..	15,440	124,680
Mangroves area (sq. km)	..	10,343	58,917
Energy and emissions			
Energy use per capita (kg oil equivalent)	*359*	555	687
Energy from biomass products and waste (% of total)	..	26.7	26.8
Electric power consumption per capita (kWh)	..	605	734
Electricity generated using fossil fuel (% of total)	..	77.9	72.3
Electricity generated by hydropower (% of total)	..	13.8	16.9
CO_2 emissions per capita (metric tons)	0.7	1.4	1.6
Water and sanitation			
Internal freshwater resources per capita (cu. m)	106,933	1,217	3,144
Total freshwater withdrawal (% of internal resources)	0.4	51.6	19.6
Agriculture (% of total freshwater withdrawal)	94	91	88
Access to improved water source (% of total population)	98	91	88
Rural (% of rural population)	97	89	85
Urban (% of urban population)	99	95	94
Access to improved sanitation facilities (% of total population)	47	40	48
Rural (% of rural population)	31	30	36
Urban (% of urban population)	75	61	66
Environment and health			
Particulate matter (urban-pop.-weighted avg., μg/cu. m)	16	110	90
Acute resp. infection prevalence (% of children under five)	..	..	..
Diarrhea prevalence (% of children under five)	..	..	..
Under-five mortality rate (per 1,000 live births)	45	60	61
National accounting aggregates—savings, depletion and degradation			
Gross savings (% of GNI)	*47.2*	29.3	28.6
Consumption of fixed capital (% of GNI)	8.5	12.7	11.1
Education expenditure (% of GNI)	3.4	2.8	3.1
Energy depletion (% of GNI)	0.0	1.8	4.4
Mineral depletion (% of GNI)	0.0	0.8	1.1
Net forest depletion (% of GNI)	16.5	1.1	0.8
CO_2 damage (% of GNI)	0.3	1.1	0.9
Particulate emissions damage (% of GNI)	0.0	1.5	1.4
Adjusted net savings (% of GNI)	*23.7*	13.1	12.0

Bolivia

	Country data	Latin America & Caribbean group	Lower middle-income group
Population (millions) **10.5** Land area (1,000 sq. km) **1,083** GDP ($ billions) **27.0**			

	Country data	Latin America & Caribbean group	Lower middle-income group
GNI per capita, World Bank Atlas method ($)	2,220	9,070	1,965
Adjusted net national income per capita ($)	1,782	7,325	1,574
Change in wealth per capita (2010 $)	-207	180	117
Urban population (% of total)	67.2	79.0	38.9
Agriculture			
Agricultural land (% land area)	34	37	46
Agricultural irrigated land (% of total agricultural land)	..	..	..
Agricultural productivity, value added per worker (2005 $)	641	4,135	938
Cereal yield (kg per hectare)	2,463	4,082	3,029
Forests and biodiversity			
Forest area (% land area)	52.5	48.1	26.9
Deforestation (avg. annual %, 2000-2010)	0.5	0.5	0.3
Terrestrial protected areas (% of total land area)	20.8	21.4	11.9
Threatened species, mammals	21		
Threatened species, birds	53		
Threatened species, fish	0		
Threatened species, higher plants	98		
Oceans			
Total fisheries production (thousand metric tons)	7.9	10,964	43,067
Capture fisheries growth (avg. annual %, 1990-2012)	-0.1	-0.6	2.6
Aquaculture growth (avg. annual %, 1990-2012)	3.3	10.8	9.9
Marine protected areas (% of territorial waters)	99.2	9.0	14.7
Coral reef area (sq. km)	..	14,860	124,480
Mangroves area (sq. km)	..	39,988	58,917
Energy and emissions			
Energy use per capita (kg oil equivalent)	746	1,292	687
Energy from biomass products and waste (% of total)	24.6	16.0	26.8
Electric power consumption per capita (kWh)	623	1,985	734
Electricity generated using fossil fuel (% of total)	64.1	37.3	72.3
Electricity generated by hydropower (% of total)	32.5	55.1	16.9
CO_2 emissions per capita (metric tons)	1.5	2.7	1.6
Water and sanitation			
Internal freshwater resources per capita (cu. m)	29,396	21,735	3,144
Total freshwater withdrawal (% of internal resources)	0.7	2.0	19.6
Agriculture (% of total freshwater withdrawal)	57	68	88
Access to improved water source (% of total population)	88	94	88
Rural (% of rural population)	72	82	85
Urban (% of urban population)	96	97	94
Access to improved sanitation facilities (% of total population)	46	81	48
Rural (% of rural population)	24	62	36
Urban (% of urban population)	57	86	66
Environment and health			
Particulate matter (urban-pop.-weighted avg., µg/cu. m)	78	43	90
Acute resp. infection prevalence (% of children under five)	20	..	..
Diarrhea prevalence (% of children under five)	26	..	..
Under-five mortality rate (per 1,000 live births)	41	19	61
National accounting aggregates—savings, depletion and degradation			
Gross savings (% of GNI)	27.4	19.0	28.6
Consumption of fixed capital (% of GNI)	12.5	12.2	11.1
Education expenditure (% of GNI)	6.5	5.1	3.1
Energy depletion (% of GNI)	10.6	4.7	4.4
Mineral depletion (% of GNI)	3.3	1.2	1.1
Net forest depletion (% of GNI)	0.0	0.4	0.8
CO_2 damage (% of GNI)	0.7	0.3	0.9
Particulate emissions damage (% of GNI)	1.5	0.8	1.4
Adjusted net savings (% of GNI)	5.4	4.5	12.0

Bosnia and Herzegovina

Population (millions)	3.8	Land area (1,000 sq. km)	51	GDP ($ billions)	17.5

	Country data	Europe & Central Asia group	Upper middle-income group
GNI per capita, *World Bank Atlas* method ($)	4,750	6,658	6,969
Adjusted net national income per capita ($)	..	5,541	5,845
Change in wealth per capita (2010 $)	..	263	1,039
Urban population (% of total)	48.8	60.2	60.7

Agriculture

Agricultural land (% land area)	42	66	44
Agricultural irrigated land (% of total agricultural land)	..	..	..
Agricultural productivity, value added per worker (2005 $)	28,183	4,866	1,131
Cereal yield (kg per hectare)	3,004	2,519	4,255

Forests and biodiversity

Forest area (% land area)	42.8	10.5	29.1
Deforestation (avg. annual %, 2000–2010)	0.0	-0.5	0.0
Terrestrial protected areas (% of total land area)	1.5	5.1	16.1
Threatened species, mammals	4		
Threatened species, birds	6		
Threatened species, fish	31		
Threatened species, higher plants	1		

Oceans

Total fisheries production (thousand metric tons)	3.9	1,022	90,024
Capture fisheries growth (avg. annual %, 1990–2012)	..	-4.0	1.5
Aquaculture growth (avg. annual %, 1990–2012)	..	1.8	9.1
Marine protected areas (% of territorial waters)	0.71	10.4	7.3
Coral reef area (sq. km)	..	..	52,070
Mangroves area (sq. km)	..	..	50,160

Energy and emissions

Energy use per capita (kg oil equivalent)	1,848	2,078	1,893
Energy from biomass products and waste (% of total)	2.6	2.9	8.5
Electric power consumption per capita (kWh)	3,189	2,951	2,932
Electricity generated using fossil fuel (% of total)	71.3	65.8	74.7
Electricity generated by hydropower (% of total)	28.7	17.9	20.0
CO_2 emissions per capita (metric tons)	8.1	5.3	5.4

Water and sanitation

Internal freshwater resources per capita (cu. m)	9,246	2,744	6,791
Total freshwater withdrawal (% of internal resources)	1.0	34.8	7.4
Agriculture (% of total freshwater withdrawal)	..	70	69
Access to improved water source (% of total population)	100	95	93
Rural (% of rural population)	99	89	85
Urban (% of urban population)	100	99	98
Access to improved sanitation facilities (% of total population)	95	94	74
Rural (% of rural population)	92	90	62
Urban (% of urban population)	99	97	82

Environment and health

Particulate matter (urban-pop.-weighted avg., μg/cu. m)	84	48	65
Acute resp. infection prevalence (% of children under five)	..	..	..
Diarrhea prevalence (% of children under five)	..	..	..
Under-five mortality rate (per 1,000 live births)	7	22	20

National accounting aggregates—savings, depletion and degradation

Gross savings (% of GNI)	14.1	18.9	36.4
Consumption of fixed capital (% of GNI)	11.0	12.4	12.5
Education expenditure (% of GNI)	..	3.8	3.2
Energy depletion (% of GNI)	0.0	4.4	4.1
Mineral depletion (% of GNI)	0.6	0.6	1.2
Net forest depletion (% of GNI)	..	0.0	0.2
CO_2 damage (% of GNI)	1.8	0.8	0.8
Particulate emissions damage (% of GNI)	2.3	1.8	1.3
Adjusted net savings (% of GNI)	..	2.8	19.5

Botswana

	Country data	Sub-Saharan Africa group	Upper middle-income group
GNI per capita, *World Bank Atlas* method ($)	7,650	1,547	6,969
Adjusted net national income per capita ($)	6,118	1,005	5,845
Change in wealth per capita (2010 $)	1,392	-273	1,039
Urban population (% of total)	62.3	36.8	60.7
Agriculture			
Agricultural land (% land area)	46	44	44
Agricultural irrigated land (% of total agricultural land)	0.0	..	..
Agricultural productivity, value added per worker (2005 $)	762	765	1,131
Cereal yield (kg per hectare)	359	1,417	4,255
Forests and biodiversity			
Forest area (% land area)	19.8	27.4	29.1
Deforestation (avg. annual %, 2000-2010)	1.0	0.5	0.0
Terrestrial protected areas (% of total land area)	37.2	16.4	16.1
Threatened species, mammals	7		
Threatened species, birds	10		
Threatened species, fish	2		
Threatened species, higher plants	2		
Oceans			
Total fisheries production (thousand metric tons)	0.38	6,906	90,024
Capture fisheries growth (avg. annual %, 1990-2012)	-5.5	2.1	1.5
Aquaculture growth (avg. annual %, 1990-2012)	..	15.9	9.1
Marine protected areas (% of territorial waters)	16.3	11.7	7.3
Coral reef area (sq. km)	..	17,980	52,070
Mangroves area (sq. km)	..	27,808	50,160
Energy and emissions			
Energy use per capita (kg oil equivalent)	1,115	681	1,893
Energy from biomass products and waste (% of total)	22.3	57.6	8.5
Electric power consumption per capita (kWh)	1,603	535	2,932
Electricity generated using fossil fuel (% of total)	100.0	65.1	74.7
Electricity generated by hydropower (% of total)	0.0	20.0	20.0
CO_2 emissions per capita (metric tons)	2.7	0.8	5.4
Water and sanitation			
Internal freshwater resources per capita (cu. m)	1,208	4,391	6,791
Total freshwater withdrawal (% of internal resources)	8.1	3.2	7.4
Agriculture (% of total freshwater withdrawal)	41	84	69
Access to improved water source (% of total population)	97	64	93
Rural (% of rural population)	93	53	85
Urban (% of urban population)	99	85	98
Access to improved sanitation facilities (% of total population)	64	30	74
Rural (% of rural population)	42	23	62
Urban (% of urban population)	78	41	82
Environment and health			
Particulate matter (urban-pop.-weighted avg., µg/cu. m)	199	77	65
Acute resp. infection prevalence (% of children under five)	..	5	..
Diarrhea prevalence (% of children under five)	..	14	..
Under-five mortality rate (per 1,000 live births)	53	98	20
National accounting aggregates—savings, depletion and degradation			
Gross savings (% of GNI)	40.8	26.3	36.4
Consumption of fixed capital (% of GNI)	12.9	13.0	12.5
Education expenditure (% of GNI)	9.3	3.4	3.2
Energy depletion (% of GNI)	0.2	10.3	4.1
Mineral depletion (% of GNI)	2.1	1.8	1.2
Net forest depletion (% of GNI)	0.0	1.8	0.2
CO_2 damage (% of GNI)	0.4	0.6	0.8
Particulate emissions damage (% of GNI)	1.3	1.2	1.3
Adjusted net savings (% of GNI)	33.2	0.9	19.5

Brazil

Population (millions)	**198.7**	Land area (1,000 sq. km)	**8,459**	GDP ($ billions)	**2,252.7**

	Country data	Latin America & Caribbean group	Upper middle-income group
GNI per capita, *World Bank Atlas* method ($)	11,630	9,070	6,969
Adjusted net national income per capita ($)	9,335	7,325	5,845
Change in wealth per capita (2010 $)	205	180	1,039
Urban population (% of total)	84.9	79.0	60.7
Agriculture			
Agricultural land (% land area)	33	37	44
Agricultural irrigated land (% of total agricultural land)	1.6	..	..
Agricultural productivity, value added per worker (2005 $)	5,035	4,135	1,131
Cereal yield (kg per hectare)	4,599	4,082	4,255
Forests and biodiversity			
Forest area (% land area)	61.2	48.1	29.1
Deforestation (avg. annual %, 2000–2010)	0.5	0.5	0.0
Terrestrial protected areas (% of total land area)	26.3	21.4	16.1
Threatened species, mammals	82		
Threatened species, birds	152		
Threatened species, fish	84		
Threatened species, higher plants	499		
Oceans			
Total fisheries production (thousand metric tons)	1,551	10,964	90,024
Capture fisheries growth (avg. annual %, 1990–2012)	1.4	-0.6	1.5
Aquaculture growth (avg. annual %, 1990–2012)	17.5	10.8	9.1
Marine protected areas (% of territorial waters)	2.0	9.0	7.3
Coral reef area (sq. km)	1,200	14,860	52,070
Mangroves area (sq. km)	12,999	39,988	50,160
Energy and emissions			
Energy use per capita (kg oil equivalent)	1,371	1,292	1,893
Energy from biomass products and waste (% of total)	28.9	16.0	8.5
Electric power consumption per capita (kWh)	2,438	1,985	2,932
Electricity generated using fossil fuel (% of total)	9.8	37.3	74.7
Electricity generated by hydropower (% of total)	80.6	55.1	20.0
CO_2 emissions per capita (metric tons)	2.2	2.7	5.4
Water and sanitation			
Internal freshwater resources per capita (cu. m)	27,512	21,735	6,791
Total freshwater withdrawal (% of internal resources)	1.1	2.0	7.4
Agriculture (% of total freshwater withdrawal)	55	68	69
Access to improved water source (% of total population)	98	94	93
Rural (% of rural population)	85	82	85
Urban (% of urban population)	100	97	98
Access to improved sanitation facilities (% of total population)	81	81	74
Rural (% of rural population)	49	62	62
Urban (% of urban population)	87	86	82
Environment and health			
Particulate matter (urban-pop.-weighted avg., µg/cu. m)	36	43	65
Acute resp. infection prevalence (% of children under five)	..	..	..
Diarrhea prevalence (% of children under five)	..	..	..
Under-five mortality rate (per 1,000 live births)	14	19	20
National accounting aggregates—savings, depletion and degradation			
Gross savings (% of GNI)	15.0	19.0	36.4
Consumption of fixed capital (% of GNI)	12.3	12.2	12.5
Education expenditure (% of GNI)	5.6	5.1	3.2
Energy depletion (% of GNI)	1.9	4.7	4.1
Mineral depletion (% of GNI)	1.4	1.2	1.2
Net forest depletion (% of GNI)	0.7	0.4	0.2
CO_2 damage (% of GNI)	0.2	0.3	0.8
Particulate emissions damage (% of GNI)	1.0	0.8	1.3
Adjusted net savings (% of GNI)	3.1	4.5	19.5

Brunei Darussalam

Population (thousands) **412**	Land area (1,000 sq. km)	**5.3**	GDP ($ billions)	**17.0**

	Country data	High-income group
GNI per capita, *World Bank Atlas* method ($)	31,590	38,444
Adjusted net national income per capita ($)	15,895	32,262
Change in wealth per capita (2010 $)	–7,198	2,210
Urban population (% of total)	76.3	80.2
Agriculture		
Agricultural land (% land area)	2	29
Agricultural irrigated land (% of total agricultural land)	0.9	..
Agricultural productivity, value added per worker (2005 $)	83,867	25,238
Cereal yield (kg per hectare)	632	4,374
Forests and biodiversity		
Forest area (% land area)	71.8	35.0
Deforestation (avg. annual %, 2000–2010)	0.4	0.0
Terrestrial protected areas (% of total land area)	44.0	13.9
Threatened species, mammals	34	
Threatened species, birds	24	
Threatened species, fish	7	
Threatened species, higher plants	104	
Oceans		
Total fisheries production (thousand metric tons)	4.5	37,661
Capture fisheries growth (avg. annual %, 1990–2012)	2.4	–2.0
Aquaculture growth (avg. annual %, 1990–2012)	22.8	2.5
Marine protected areas (% of territorial waters)	15.7	14.4
Coral reef area (sq. km)	210	82,210
Mangroves area (sq. km)	173	15,504
Energy and emissions		
Energy use per capita (kg oil equivalent)	9,427	4,872
Energy from biomass products and waste (% of total)	0.0	4.3
Electric power consumption per capita (kWh)	8,507	8,896
Electricity generated using fossil fuel (% of total)	99.9	61.8
Electricity generated by hydropower (% of total)	0.0	12.2
CO_2 emissions per capita (metric tons)	22.9	11.6
Water and sanitation		
Internal freshwater resources per capita (cu. m)	20,910	11,335
Total freshwater withdrawal (% of internal resources)	1.1	7.0
Agriculture (% of total freshwater withdrawal)	..	40
Access to improved water source (% of total population)	..	99
Rural (% of rural population)	..	98
Urban (% of urban population)	..	100
Access to improved sanitation facilities (% of total population)	..	96
Rural (% of rural population)	..	93
Urban (% of urban population)	..	97
Environment and health		
Particulate matter (urban-pop.-weighted avg., µg/cu. m)	9	27
Acute resp. infection prevalence (% of children under five)	..	..
Diarrhea prevalence (% of children under five)	..	
Under-five mortality rate (per 1,000 live births)	8	6
National accounting aggregates—savings, depletion and degradation		
Gross savings (% of GNI)	50.7	20.1
Consumption of fixed capital (% of GNI)	11.5	14.2
Education expenditure (% of GNI)	2.0	4.7
Energy depletion (% of GNI)	30.4	1.6
Mineral depletion (% of GNI)	0.0	0.3
Net forest depletion (% of GNI)	0.0	0.0
CO_2 damage (% of GNI)	0.8	0.3
Particulate emissions damage (% of GNI)	0.0	0.3
Adjusted net savings (% of GNI)	10.2	8.1

Bulgaria

Population (millions)	7.3	Land area (1,000 sq. km)	109	GDP ($ billions)	51.0

	Country data	Europe & Central Asia group	Upper middle-income group
GNI per capita, *World Bank Atlas* method ($)	6,840	6,658	6,969
Adjusted net national income per capita ($)	5,824	5,541	5,845
Change in wealth per capita (2010 $)	863	263	1,039
Urban population (% of total)	73.6	60.2	60.7
Agriculture			
Agricultural land (% land area)	47	66	44
Agricultural irrigated land (% of total agricultural land)	1.8	..	..
Agricultural productivity, value added per worker (2005 $)	16,101	4,866	1,131
Cereal yield (kg per hectare)	3,798	2,519	4,255
Forests and biodiversity			
Forest area (% land area)	36.7	10.5	29.1
Deforestation (avg. annual %, 2000–2010)	-1.5	-0.5	0.0
Terrestrial protected areas (% of total land area)	36.6	5.1	16.1
Threatened species, mammals	7		
Threatened species, birds	14		
Threatened species, fish	19		
Threatened species, higher plants	6		
Oceans			
Total fisheries production (thousand metric tons)	15.5	1,022	90,024
Capture fisheries growth (avg. annual %, 1990–2012)	-7.2	-4.0	1.5
Aquaculture growth (avg. annual %, 1990–2012)	-1.2	1.8	9.1
Marine protected areas (% of territorial waters)	3.2	10.4	7.3
Coral reef area (sq. km)	..	..	52,070
Mangroves area (sq. km)	..	..	50,160
Energy and emissions			
Energy use per capita (kg oil equivalent)	2,615	2,078	1,893
Energy from biomass products and waste (% of total)	5.1	2.9	8.5
Electric power consumption per capita (kWh)	4,864	2,951	2,932
Electricity generated using fossil fuel (% of total)	59.5	65.8	74.7
Electricity generated by hydropower (% of total)	5.8	17.9	20.0
CO_2 emissions per capita (metric tons)	6.0	5.3	5.4
Water and sanitation			
Internal freshwater resources per capita (cu. m)	2,858	2,744	6,791
Total freshwater withdrawal (% of internal resources)	29.1	34.8	7.4
Agriculture (% of total freshwater withdrawal)	16	70	69
Access to improved water source (% of total population)	99	95	93
Rural (% of rural population)	99	89	85
Urban (% of urban population)	100	99	98
Access to improved sanitation facilities (% of total population)	100	94	74
Rural (% of rural population)	100	90	62
Urban (% of urban population)	100	97	82
Environment and health			
Particulate matter (urban-pop.-weighted avg., µg/cu. m)	41	48	65
Acute resp. infection prevalence (% of children under five)	..	..	..
Diarrhea prevalence (% of children under five)	..	..	..
Under-five mortality rate (per 1,000 live births)	12	22	20
National accounting aggregates—savings, depletion and degradation			
Gross savings (% of GNI)	22.5	18.9	36.4
Consumption of fixed capital (% of GNI)	12.0	12.4	12.5
Education expenditure (% of GNI)	4.1	3.8	3.2
Energy depletion (% of GNI)	0.1	4.4	4.1
Mineral depletion (% of GNI)	1.3	0.6	1.2
Net forest depletion (% of GNI)	0.0	0.0	0.2
CO_2 damage (% of GNI)	0.8	0.8	0.8
Particulate emissions damage (% of GNI)	1.6	1.8	1.3
Adjusted net savings (% of GNI)	10.9	2.8	19.5

Burkina Faso

Population (millions)	**16.5**	Land area (1,000 sq. km)	**274**	GDP ($ billions)	**10.7**

	Country data	Sub-Saharan Africa group	Low-income group
GNI per capita, *World Bank Atlas* method ($)	670	1,547	594
Adjusted net national income per capita ($)	503	1,005	495
Change in wealth per capita (2010 $)	-72	-273	-39
Urban population (% of total)	27.4	36.8	28.2
Agriculture			
Agricultural land (% land area)	43	44	39
Agricultural irrigated land (% of total agricultural land)	..	..	..
Agricultural productivity, value added per worker (2005 $)	361	765	367
Cereal yield (kg per hectare)	1,230	1,417	1,982
Forests and biodiversity			
Forest area (% land area)	20.4	27.4	27.4
Deforestation (avg. annual %, 2000-2010)	1.0	0.5	0.6
Terrestrial protected areas (% of total land area)	15.2	16.4	13.7
Threatened species, mammals	9		
Threatened species, birds	9		
Threatened species, fish	4		
Threatened species, higher plants	3		
Oceans			
Total fisheries production (thousand metric tons)	20.6	6,906	11,789
Capture fisheries growth (avg. annual %, 1990-2012)	5.0	2.1	3.8
Aquaculture growth (avg. annual %, 1990-2012)	18.9	15.9	5.1
Marine protected areas (% of territorial waters)	..	11.7	13.1
Coral reef area (sq. km)	..	17,980	15,120
Mangroves area (sq. km)	..	27,808	25,817
Energy and emissions			
Energy use per capita (kg oil equivalent)	..	681	360
Energy from biomass products and waste (% of total)	..	57.6	66.0
Electric power consumption per capita (kWh)	..	535	233
Electricity generated using fossil fuel (% of total)	..	65.1	30.9
Electricity generated by hydropower (% of total)	..	20.0	45.5
CO_2 emissions per capita (metric tons)	0.1	0.8	0.3
Water and sanitation			
Internal freshwater resources per capita (cu. m)	781	4,391	5,121
Total freshwater withdrawal (% of internal resources)	7.9	3.2	4.4
Agriculture (% of total freshwater withdrawal)	70	84	90
Access to improved water source (% of total population)	82	64	69
Rural (% of rural population)	76	53	61
Urban (% of urban population)	97	85	88
Access to improved sanitation facilities (% of total population)	19	30	37
Rural (% of rural population)	7	23	33
Urban (% of urban population)	50	41	46
Environment and health			
Particulate matter (urban-pop.-weighted avg., µg/cu. m)	51	77	74
Acute resp. infection prevalence (% of children under five)	2	5	6
Diarrhea prevalence (% of children under five)	15	14	14
Under-five mortality rate (per 1,000 live births)	102	98	82
National accounting aggregates—savings, depletion and degradation			
Gross savings (% of GNI)	22.9	26.3	24.6
Consumption of fixed capital (% of GNI)	8.6	13.0	11.8
Education expenditure (% of GNI)	3.1	3.4	3.2
Energy depletion (% of GNI)	0.0	10.3	1.4
Mineral depletion (% of GNI)	10.9	1.8	1.9
Net forest depletion (% of GNI)	3.3	1.8	4.4
CO_2 damage (% of GNI)	0.2	0.6	0.4
Particulate emissions damage (% of GNI)	0.8	1.2	1.0
Adjusted net savings (% of GNI)	8.5	0.9	7.0

Burundi

	Country data	Sub-Saharan Africa group	Low-Income group
Population (millions) **9.8**	Land area (1,000 sq. km)	**26** GDP ($ billions)	**2.5**

	Country data	Sub-Saharan Africa group	Low-Income group
GNI per capita, *World Bank Atlas* method ($)	240	1,547	594
Adjusted net national income per capita ($)	158	1,005	495
Change in wealth per capita (2010 $)	-149	-273	-39
Urban population (% of total)	11.2	36.8	28.2
Agriculture			
Agricultural land (% land area)	86	44	39
Agricultural irrigated land (% of total agricultural land)	..	..	..
Agricultural productivity, value added per worker (2005 $)	129	765	367
Cereal yield (kg per hectare)	1,124	1,417	1,982
Forests and biodiversity			
Forest area (% land area)	6.6	27.4	27.4
Deforestation (avg. annual %, 2000–2010)	1.4	0.5	0.6
Terrestrial protected areas (% of total land area)	4.9	16.4	13.7
Threatened species, mammals	11		
Threatened species, birds	12		
Threatened species, fish	17		
Threatened species, higher plants	4		
Oceans			
Total fisheries production (thousand metric tons)	12.5	6,906	11,789
Capture fisheries growth (avg. annual %, 1990–2012)	-1.6	2.1	3.8
Aquaculture growth (avg. annual %, 1990–2012)	7.9	15.9	5.1
Marine protected areas (% of territorial waters)	0.48	11.7	13.1
Coral reef area (sq. km)	..	17,980	15,120
Mangroves area (sq. km)	..	27,808	25,817
Energy and emissions			
Energy use per capita (kg oil equivalent)	..	681	360
Energy from biomass products and waste (% of total)	..	57.6	66.0
Electric power consumption per capita (kWh)	..	535	233
Electricity generated using fossil fuel (% of total)	..	65.1	30.9
Electricity generated by hydropower (% of total)	..	20.0	45.5
CO_2 emissions per capita (metric tons)	0.0	0.8	0.3
Water and sanitation			
Internal freshwater resources per capita (cu. m)	1,054	4,391	5,121
Total freshwater withdrawal (% of internal resources)	2.9	3.2	4.4
Agriculture (% of total freshwater withdrawal)	77	84	90
Access to improved water source (% of total population)	75	64	69
Rural (% of rural population)	73	53	61
Urban (% of urban population)	92	85	88
Access to improved sanitation facilities (% of total population)	47	30	37
Rural (% of rural population)	48	23	33
Urban (% of urban population)	43	41	46
Environment and health			
Particulate matter (urban-pop.-weighted avg., µg/cu. m)	30	77	74
Acute resp. infection prevalence (% of children under five)	17	5	6
Diarrhea prevalence (% of children under five)	25	14	14
Under-five mortality rate (per 1,000 live births)	104	98	82
National accounting aggregates—savings, depletion and degradation			
Gross savings (% of GNI)	17.6	26.3	24.6
Consumption of fixed capital (% of GNI)	13.6	13.0	11.8
Education expenditure (% of GNI)	5.7	3.4	3.2
Energy depletion (% of GNI)	0.0	10.3	1.4
Mineral depletion (% of GNI)	0.9	1.8	1.9
Net forest depletion (% of GNI)	22.2	1.8	4.4
CO_2 damage (% of GNI)	0.1	0.6	0.4
Particulate emissions damage (% of GNI)	0.2	1.2	1.0
Adjusted net savings (% of GNI)	-13.7	0.9	7.0

Cabo Verde

| Population (thousands) **494** | Land area (1,000 sq. km) | **4.0** | GDP ($ billions) | **1.8** |

	Country data	Sub-Saharan Africa group	Low-Income group
GNI per capita, *World Bank Atlas* method ($)	3,830	1,547	1,965
Adjusted net national income per capita ($)	3,240	1,005	1,574
Change in wealth per capita (2010 $)	803	-273	117
Urban population (% of total)	63.3	36.8	38.9
Agriculture			
Agricultural land (% land area)	19	44	46
Agricultural irrigated land (% of total agricultural land)	..	..	..
Agricultural productivity, value added per worker (2005 $)	*4,015*	765	938
Cereal yield (kg per hectare)	188	1,417	3,029
Forests and biodiversity			
Forest area (% land area)	21.0	27.4	26.9
Deforestation (avg. annual %, 2000–2010)	-0.4	0.5	0.3
Terrestrial protected areas (% of total land area)	2.5	16.4	11.9
Threatened species, mammals	4		
Threatened species, birds	4		
Threatened species, fish	23		
Threatened species, higher plants	3		
Oceans			
Total fisheries production (thousand metric tons)	20.2	6,906	43,067
Capture fisheries growth (avg. annual %, 1990–2012)	5.2	2.1	2.6
Aquaculture growth (avg. annual %, 1990–2012)	..	15.9	9.9
Marine protected areas (% of territorial waters)	1.2	11.7	14.7
Coral reef area (sq. km)	..	17,980	124,480
Mangroves (sq. km)	..	27,808	58,917
Energy and emissions			
Energy use per capita (kg oil equivalent)	*213*	681	687
Energy from biomass products and waste (% of total)	..	57.6	26.8
Electric power consumption per capita (kWh)	..	535	734
Electricity generated using fossil fuel (% of total)	..	65.1	72.3
Electricity generated by hydropower (% of total)	..	20.0	16.9
CO_2 emissions per capita (metric tons)	0.7	0.8	1.6
Water and sanitation			
Internal freshwater resources per capita (cu. m)	612	4,391	3,144
Total freshwater withdrawal (% of internal resources)	7.3	3.2	19.6
Agriculture (% of total freshwater withdrawal)	91	84	88
Access to improved water source (% of total population)	89	64	88
Rural (% of rural population)	86	53	85
Urban (% of urban population)	91	85	94
Access to improved sanitation (% of total population)	65	30	48
Rural (% of rural population)	47	23	36
Urban (% of urban population)	75	41	66
Environment and health			
Particulate matter (urban-pop.-weighted avg., μg/cu. m)	..	77	90
Acute resp. infection prevalence (% of children under five)	..	5	..
Diarrhea prevalence (% of children under five)	..	14	..
Under-five mortality rate (per 1,000 live births)	22	98	61
National accounting aggregates—savings, depletion and degradation			
Gross savings (% of GNI)	*36.1*	26.3	28.6
Consumption of fixed capital (% of GNI)	13.4	13.0	11.1
Education expenditure (% of GNI)	4.9	3.4	3.1
Energy depletion (% of GNI)	0.0	10.3	4.4
Mineral depletion (% of GNI)	0.0	1.8	1.1
Net forest depletion (% of GNI)	0.3	1.8	0.8
CO_2 damage (% of GNI)	0.2	0.6	0.9
Particulate emissions damage (% of GNI)	..	1.2	1.4
Adjusted net savings (% of GNI)	..	0.9	12.0

Cambodia

Population (millions) **14.9** Land area (1,000 sq. km) **177** GDP ($ billions) **14.0**

	Country data	East Asia & Pacific group	Low-income group
GNI per capita, World Bank Atlas method ($)	880	4,884	594
Adjusted net national income per capita ($)	734	4,305	495
Change in wealth per capita (2010 $)	-103	1,172	-39
Urban population (% of total)	20.2	49.6	28.2
Agriculture			
Agricultural land (% land area)	32	48	39
Agricultural irrigated land (% of total agricultural land)	..	..	..
Agricultural productivity, value added per worker (2005 $)	524	794	367
Cereal yield (kg per hectare)	2,942	5,145	1,982
Forests and biodiversity			
Forest area (% land area)	56.5	29.7	27.4
Deforestation (avg. annual %, 2000–2010)	1.3	-0.4	0.6
Terrestrial protected areas (% of total land area)	26.2	15.1	13.7
Threatened species, mammals	37		
Threatened species, birds	26		
Threatened species, fish	40		
Threatened species, higher plants	33		
Oceans			
Total fisheries production (thousand metric tons)	641	108,399	11,789
Capture fisheries growth (avg. annual %, 1990–2012)	8.0	3.4	3.8
Aquaculture growth (avg. annual %, 1990–2012)	11.8	9.1	5.1
Marine protected areas (% of territorial waters)	6.5	1.4	13.1
Coral reef area (sq. km)	<50	137,690	15,120
Mangroves area (sq. km)	728	56,537	25,817
Energy and emissions			
Energy use per capita (kg oil equivalent)	365	1,671	360
Energy from biomass products and waste (% of total)	71.0	10.1	66.0
Electric power consumption per capita (kWh)	164	2,582	233
Electricity generated using fossil fuel (% of total)	93.5	80.9	30.9
Electricity generated by hydropower (% of total)	4.3	14.5	45.5
CO_2 emissions per capita (metric tons)	0.3	4.9	0.3
Water and sanitation			
Internal freshwater resources per capita (cu. m)	8,257	4,438	5,121
Total freshwater withdrawal (% of internal resources)	1.8	10.9	4.4
Agriculture (% of total freshwater withdrawal)	94	73	90
Access to improved water source (% of total population)	71	91	69
Rural (% of rural population)	66	85	61
Urban (% of urban population)	94	97	88
Access to improved sanitation (% of total population)	37	67	37
Rural (% of rural population)	25	58	33
Urban (% of urban population)	82	76	46
Environment and health			
Particulate matter (urban-pop.-weighted avg., μg/cu. m)	89	75	74
Acute resp. infection prevalence (% of children under five)	6	..	6
Diarrhea prevalence (% of children under five)	15	..	14
Under-five mortality rate (per 1,000 live births)	40	21	82
National accounting aggregates—savings, depletion and degradation			
Gross savings (% of GNI)	11.2	47.6	24.6
Consumption of fixed capital (% of GNI)	15.4	12.0	11.8
Education expenditure (% of GNI)	1.6	2.1	3.2
Energy depletion (% of GNI)	0.0	2.7	1.4
Mineral depletion (% of GNI)	0.0	1.4	1.9
Net forest depletion (% of GNI)	2.6	0.1	4.4
CO_2 damage (% of GNI)	0.4	1.0	0.4
Particulate emissions damage (% of GNI)	2.0	1.6	1.0
Adjusted net savings (% of GNI)	-7.5	30.9	7.0

Cameroon

Population (millions)	**21.7**	Land area (1,000 sq. km)	**473**	GDP ($ billions)	**25.3**

	Country data	Sub-Saharan Africa group	Lower middle-income group
GNI per capita, *World Bank Atlas* method ($)	1,170	1,547	1,965
Adjusted net national income per capita ($)	918	1,005	1,574
Change in wealth per capita (2010 $)	-262	-273	117
Urban population (% of total)	52.7	36.8	38.9
Agriculture			
Agricultural land (% land area)	20	44	46
Agricultural irrigated land (% of total agricultural land)	..	..	..
Agricultural productivity, value added per worker (2005 $)	..	765	938
Cereal yield (kg per hectare)	1,720	1,417	3,029
Forests and biodiversity			
Forest area (% land area)	41.7	27.4	26.9
Deforestation (avg. annual %, 2000–2010)	1.0	0.5	0.3
Terrestrial protected areas (% of total land area)	11.0	16.4	11.9
Threatened species, mammals	38		
Threatened species, birds	24		
Threatened species, fish	112		
Threatened species, higher plants	378		
Oceans			
Total fisheries production (thousand metric tons)	141	6,906	43,067
Capture fisheries growth (avg. annual %, 1990–2012)	3.2	2.1	2.6
Aquaculture growth (avg. annual %, 1990–2012)	7.9	15.9	9.9
Marine protected areas (% of territorial waters)	1.3	11.7	14.7
Coral reef area (sq. km)	..	17,980	124,480
Mangroves area (sq. km)	1,962	27,808	58,917
Energy and emissions			
Energy use per capita (kg oil equivalent)	318	681	687
Energy from biomass products and waste (% of total)	67.6	57.6	26.8
Electric power consumption per capita (kWh)	256	535	734
Electricity generated using fossil fuel (% of total)	25.6	65.1	72.3
Electricity generated by hydropower (% of total)	73.3	20.0	16.9
CO_2 emissions per capita (metric tons)	0.4	0.8	1.6
Water and sanitation			
Internal freshwater resources per capita (cu. m)	12,904	4,391	3,144
Total freshwater withdrawal (% of internal resources)	0.4	3.2	19.6
Agriculture (% of total freshwater withdrawal)	76	84	88
Access to improved water source (% of total population)	74	64	88
Rural (% of rural population)	52	53	85
Urban (% of urban population)	94	85	94
Access to improved sanitation (% of total population)	45	30	48
Rural (% of rural population)	27	23	36
Urban (% of urban population)	62	41	66
Environment and health			
Particulate matter (urban-pop.-weighted avg., µg/cu. m)	26	77	90
Acute resp. infection prevalence (% of children under five)	5	5	..
Diarrhea prevalence (% of children under five)	21	14	..
Under-five mortality rate (per 1,000 live births)	95	98	61
National accounting aggregates—savings, depletion and degradation			
Gross savings (% of GNI)	16.1	26.3	28.6
Consumption of fixed capital (% of GNI)	14.4	13.0	11.1
Education expenditure (% of GNI)	2.9	3.4	3.1
Energy depletion (% of GNI)	5.4	10.3	4.4
Mineral depletion (% of GNI)	0.2	1.8	1.1
Net forest depletion (% of GNI)	0.0	1.8	0.8
CO_2 damage (% of GNI)	0.4	0.6	0.9
Particulate emissions damage (% of GNI)	0.3	1.2	1.4
Adjusted net savings (% of GNI)	-1.6	0.9	12.0

Canada

Population (millions) **34.8** Land area (1,000 sq. km) **9,094** GDP ($ billions) **1,779.6**

	Country data	High-Income group
GNI per capita, *World Bank Atlas* method ($)	51,570	38,444
Adjusted net national income per capita ($)	44,536	32,262
Change in wealth per capita (2010 $)	1,113	2,210
Urban population (% of total)	80.8	80.2
Agriculture		
Agricultural land (% land area)	7	29
Agricultural irrigated land (% of total agricultural land)	1.2	..
Agricultural productivity, value added per worker (2005 $)	59,818	25,238
Cereal yield (kg per hectare)	3,540	4,374
Forests and biodiversity		
Forest area (% land area)	34.1	35.0
Deforestation (avg. annual %, 2000–2010)	0.0	0.0
Terrestrial protected areas (% of total land area)	8.6	13.9
Threatened species, mammals	11	
Threatened species, birds	16	
Threatened species, fish	36	
Threatened species, higher plants	2	
Oceans		
Total fisheries production (thousand metric tons)	1,002	37,661
Capture fisheries growth (avg. annual %, 1990–2012)	-3.2	-2.0
Aquaculture growth (avg. annual %, 1990–2012)	6.8	2.5
Marine protected areas (% of territorial waters)	0.0	14.4
Coral reef area (sq. km)	..	82,210
Mangroves area (sq. km)	..	15,504
Energy and emissions		
Energy use per capita (kg oil equivalent)	7,333	4,872
Energy from biomass products and waste (% of total)	4.9	4.3
Electric power consumption per capita (kWh)	16,473	8,896
Electricity generated using fossil fuel (% of total)	22.8	61.8
Electricity generated by hydropower (% of total)	59.0	12.2
CO_2 emissions per capita (metric tons)	14.7	11.6
Water and sanitation		
Internal freshwater resources per capita (cu. m)	82,987	11,335
Total freshwater withdrawal (% of internal resources)	1.6	7.0
Agriculture (% of total freshwater withdrawal)	12	40
Access to improved water source (% of total population)	100	99
Rural (% of rural population)	99	98
Urban (% of urban population)	100	100
Access to improved sanitation (% of total population)	100	96
Rural (% of rural population)	99	93
Urban (% of urban population)	100	97
Environment and health		
Particulate matter (urban-pop.-weighted avg., µg/cu. m)	14	27
Acute resp. infection prevalence (% of children under five)	..	..
Diarrhea prevalence (% of children under five)	..	..
Under-five mortality rate (per 1,000 live births)	5	6
National accounting aggregates—savings, depletion and degradation		
Gross savings (% of GNI)	23.1	20.1
Consumption of fixed capital (% of GNI)	12.4	14.2
Education expenditure (% of GNI)	5.1	4.7
Energy depletion (% of GNI)	2.0	1.6
Mineral depletion (% of GNI)	0.6	0.3
Net forest depletion (% of GNI)	0.0	0.0
CO_2 damage (% of GNI)	0.3	0.3
Particulate emissions damage (% of GNI)	0.0	0.3
Adjusted net savings (% of GNI)	12.9	8.1

Cayman Islands

	Country data	High-income group
Population (thousands) **58** Land area (sq. km) **240** GDP ($ millions) ..		

	Country data	High-income group
GNI per capita, *World Bank Atlas* method ($)	..	38,444
Adjusted net national income per capita ($)	..	32,262
Change in wealth per capita (2010 $)	..	2,210
Urban population (% of total)	100.0	80.2
Agriculture		
Agricultural land (% land area)	11	29
Agricultural irrigated land (% of total agricultural land)	..	
Agricultural productivity, value added per worker (2005 $)	..	25,238
Cereal yield (kg per hectare)	..	4,374
Forests and biodiversity		
Forest area (% land area)	52.9	35.0
Deforestation (avg. annual %, 2000–2010)	0.0	0.0
Terrestrial protected areas (% of total land area)	8.7	13.9
Threatened species, mammals	1	
Threatened species, birds	1	
Threatened species, fish	20	
Threatened species, higher plants	2	
Oceans		
Total fisheries production (thousand metric tons)	0.13	37,661
Capture fisheries growth (avg. annual %, 1990–2012)	-8.3	-2.0
Aquaculture growth (avg. annual %, 1990–2012)	..	2.5
Marine protected areas (% of territorial waters)	1.2	14.4
Coral reef area (sq. km)	230	82,210
Mangroves area (sq. km)	78.3	15,504
Energy and emissions		
Energy use per capita (kg oil equivalent)	..	4,872
Energy from biomass products and waste (% of total)	..	4.3
Electric power consumption per capita (kWh)	..	8,896
Electricity generated using fossil fuel (% of total)	..	61.8
Electricity generated by hydropower (% of total)	..	12.2
CO_2 emissions per capita (metric tons)	10.6	11.6
Water and sanitation		
Internal freshwater resources per capita (cu. m)	..	11,335
Total freshwater withdrawal (% of internal resources)	..	7.0
Agriculture (% of total freshwater withdrawal)	..	40
Access to improved water source (% of total population)	96	99
Rural (% of rural population)	..	98
Urban (% of urban population)	96	100
Access to improved sanitation facilities (% of total population)	96	96
Rural (% of rural population)	..	93
Urban (% of urban population)	96	97
Environment and health		
Particulate matter (urban-pop.-weighted avg., µg/cu. m)	..	27
Acute resp. infection prevalence (% of children under five)	..	..
Diarrhea prevalence (% of children under five)	..	
Under-five mortality rate (per 1,000 live births)	..	6
National accounting aggregates—savings, depletion and degradation		
Gross savings (% of GNI)	..	20.1
Consumption of fixed capital (% of GNI)	..	14.2
Education expenditure (% of GNI)	..	4.7
Energy depletion (% of GNI)	..	1.6
Mineral depletion (% of GNI)	..	0.3
Net forest depletion (% of GNI)	..	0.0
CO_2 damage (% of GNI)	..	0.3
Particulate emissions damage (% of GNI)	..	0.3
Adjusted net savings (% of GNI)	..	8.1

Central African Republic

Population (millions)	**4.5**	Land area (1,000 sq. km)	**623**	GDP ($ billions)	**2.2**

	Country data	Sub-Saharan Africa group	Low-income group
GNI per capita, *World Bank Atlas* method ($)	510	1,547	594
Adjusted net national income per capita ($)	416	1,005	495
Change in wealth per capita (2010 $)	..	-273	-39
Urban population (% of total)	39.4	36.8	28.2

Agriculture

Agricultural land (% land area)	8	44	39
Agricultural irrigated land (% of total agricultural land)	..	..	..
Agricultural productivity, value added per worker (2005 $)	863	765	367
Cereal yield (kg per hectare)	1,684	1,417	1,982

Forests and biodiversity

Forest area (% land area)	36.2	27.4	27.4
Deforestation (avg. annual %, 2000–2010)	0.1	0.5	0.6
Terrestrial protected areas (% of total land area)	18.0	16.4	13.7
Threatened species, mammals	8		
Threatened species, birds	13		
Threatened species, fish	3		
Threatened species, higher plants	18		

Oceans

Total fisheries production (thousand metric tons)	32.2	6,906	11,789
Capture fisheries growth (avg. annual %, 1990–2012)	4.2	2.1	3.8
Aquaculture growth (avg. annual %, 1990–2012)	2.5	15.9	5.1
Marine protected areas (% of territorial waters)	..	11.7	13.1
Coral reef area (sq. km)	..	17,980	15,120
Mangroves area (sq. km)	..	27,808	25,817

Energy and emissions

Energy use per capita (kg oil equivalent)	..	681	360
Energy from biomass products and waste (% of total)	..	57.6	66.0
Electric power consumption per capita (kWh)	..	535	233
Electricity generated using fossil fuel (% of total)	..	65.1	30.9
Electricity generated by hydropower (% of total)	..	20.0	45.5
CO_2 emissions per capita (metric tons)	0.1	0.8	0.3

Water and sanitation

Internal freshwater resources per capita (cu. m)	31,784	4,391	5,121
Total freshwater withdrawal (% of internal resources)	0.0	3.2	4.4
Agriculture (% of total freshwater withdrawal)	1	84	90
Access to improved water source (% of total population)	68	64	69
Rural (% of rural population)	54	53	61
Urban (% of urban population)	90	85	88
Access to improved sanitation facilities (% of total population)	22	30	37
Rural (% of rural population)	7	23	33
Urban (% of urban population)	44	41	46

Environment and health

Particulate matter (urban-pop.-weighted avg., µg/cu. m)	32	77	74
Acute resp. infection prevalence (% of children under five)	..	5	6
Diarrhea prevalence (% of children under five)	..	14	14
Under-five mortality rate (per 1,000 live births)	129	98	82

National accounting aggregates—savings, depletion and degradation

Gross savings (% of GNI)	..	26.3	24.6
Consumption of fixed capital (% of GNI)	13.7	13.0	11.8
Education expenditure (% of GNI)	1.2	3.4	3.2
Energy depletion (% of GNI)	0.0	10.3	1.4
Mineral depletion (% of GNI)	0.2	1.8	1.9
Net forest depletion (% of GNI)	0.0	1.8	4.4
CO_2 damage (% of GNI)	0.1	0.6	0.4
Particulate emissions damage (% of GNI)	0.4	1.2	1.0
Adjusted net savings (% of GNI)	..	0.9	7.0

Chad

	Country data	Sub-Saharan Africa group	Low-Income group
Population (millions) **12.4** Land area (1,000 sq. km) **1,259** GDP ($ billions) **12.9**			

	Country data	Sub-Saharan Africa group	Low-Income group
GNI per capita, *World Bank Atlas* method ($)	970	1,547	594
Adjusted net national income per capita ($)	467	1,005	495
Change in wealth per capita (2010 $)	..	-273	-39
Urban population (% of total)	21.9	36.8	28.2
Agriculture			
Agricultural land (% land area)	40	44	39
Agricultural irrigated land (% of total agricultural land)	..	..	..
Agricultural productivity, value added per worker (2005 $)	1,297	765	367
Cereal yield (kg per hectare)	1,282	1,417	1,982
Forests and biodiversity			
Forest area (% land area)	9.1	27.4	27.4
Deforestation (avg. annual %, 2000–2010)	0.7	0.5	0.6
Terrestrial protected areas (% of total land area)	16.6	16.4	13.7
Threatened species, mammals	13		
Threatened species, birds	11		
Threatened species, fish	1		
Threatened species, higher plants	4		
Oceans			
Total fisheries production (thousand metric tons)	100	6,906	11,789
Capture fisheries growth (avg. annual %, 1990–2012)	1.6	2.1	3.8
Aquaculture growth (avg. annual %, 1990–2012)	..	15.9	5.1
Marine protected areas (% of territorial waters)	4.7	11.7	13.1
Coral reef area (sq. km)	..	17,980	15,120
Mangroves area (sq. km)	..	27,808	25,817
Energy and emissions			
Energy use per capita (kg oil equivalent)	..	681	360
Energy from biomass products and waste (% of total)	..	57.6	66.0
Electric power consumption per capita (kWh)	..	535	233
Electricity generated using fossil fuel (% of total)	..	65.1	30.9
Electricity generated by hydropower (% of total)	..	20.0	45.5
CO_2 emissions per capita (metric tons)	0.0	0.8	0.3
Water and sanitation			
Internal freshwater resources per capita (cu. m)	1,242	4,391	5,121
Total freshwater withdrawal (% of internal resources)	2.4	3.2	4.4
Agriculture (% of total freshwater withdrawal)	52	84	90
Access to improved water source (% of total population)	51	64	69
Rural (% of rural population)	45	53	61
Urban (% of urban population)	72	85	88
Access to improved sanitation facilities (% of total population)	12	30	37
Rural (% of rural population)	6	23	33
Urban (% of urban population)	31	41	46
Environment and health			
Particulate matter (urban-pop.-weighted avg., µg/cu. m)	50	77	74
Acute resp. infection prevalence (% of children under five)	..	5	6
Diarrhea prevalence (% of children under five)	..	14	14
Under-five mortality rate (per 1,000 live births)	150	98	82
National accounting aggregates—savings, depletion and degradation			
Gross savings (% of GNI)	..	26.3	24.6
Consumption of fixed capital (% of GNI)	18.6	13.0	11.8
Education expenditure (% of GNI)	2.0	3.4	3.2
Energy depletion (% of GNI)	21.8	10.3	1.4
Mineral depletion (% of GNI)	0.0	1.8	1.9
Net forest depletion (% of GNI)	0.0	1.8	4.4
CO_2 damage (% of GNI)	0.0	0.6	0.4
Particulate emissions damage (% of GNI)	0.6	1.2	1.0
Adjusted net savings (% of GNI)	..	0.9	7.0

Channel Islands

Population (thousands) **161** Land area (sq. km)   **190** GDP ($ billions) *11.5*

	Country data	High-income group
GNI per capita, *World Bank Atlas* method ($)	*65,440*	38,444
Adjusted net national income per capita ($)	..	32,262
Change in wealth per capita (2010 $)	..	2,210
Urban population (% of total)	31.4	80.2
Agriculture		
Agricultural land (% land area)	51	29
Agricultural irrigated land (% of total agricultural land)	4.3	..
Agricultural productivity, value added per worker (2005 $)	..	25,238
Cereal yield (kg per hectare)	..	4,374
Forests and biodiversity		
Forest area (% land area)	4.2	35.0
Deforestation (avg. annual %, 2000–2010)	..	0.0
Terrestrial protected areas (% of total land area)	*9.3*	13.9
Threatened species, mammals	..	
Threatened species, birds	..	
Threatened species, fish	..	
Threatened species, higher plants	..	
Oceans		
Total fisheries production (thousand metric tons)	3.8	37,661
Capture fisheries growth (avg. annual %, 1990–2012)	-0.1	-2.0
Aquaculture growth (avg. annual %, 1990–2012)	12.4	2.5
Marine protected areas (% of territorial waters)	*0.02*	*14.4*
Coral reef area (sq. km)	..	82,210
Mangroves area (sq. km)	..	15,504
Energy and emissions		
Energy use per capita (kg oil equivalent)	..	4,872
Energy from biomass products and waste (% of total)	..	4.3
Electric power consumption per capita (kWh)	..	8,896
Electricity generated using fossil fuel (% of total)	..	61.8
Electricity generated by hydropower (% of total)	..	12.2
CO_2 emissions per capita (metric tons)	..	11.6
Water and sanitation		
Internal freshwater resources per capita (cu. m)	..	11,335
Total freshwater withdrawal (% of internal resources)	..	7.0
Agriculture (% of total freshwater withdrawal)	..	40
Access to improved water source (% of total population)	..	99
Rural (% of rural population)	..	98
Urban (% of urban population)	..	100
Access to improved sanitation facilities (% of total population)	..	96
Rural (% of rural population)	..	93
Urban (% of urban population)	..	97
Environment and health		
Particulate matter (urban-pop.-weighted avg., µg/cu. m)	..	27
Acute resp. infection prevalence (% of children under five)	..	..
Diarrhea prevalence (% of children under five)	..	..
Under-five mortality rate (per 1,000 live births)	..	6
National accounting aggregates—savings, depletion and degradation		
Gross savings (% of GNI)	..	20.1
Consumption of fixed capital (% of GNI)	*12.0*	14.2
Education expenditure (% of GNI)	..	4.7
Energy depletion (% of GNI)	*0.0*	1.6
Mineral depletion (% of GNI)	*0.0*	0.3
Net forest depletion (% of GNI)	..	0.0
CO_2 damage (% of GNI)	..	0.3
Particulate emissions damage (% of GNI)	..	0.3
Adjusted net savings (% of GNI)	..	8.1

Chile

| | Population (millions) | **17.5** | Land area (1,000 sq. km) | **744** | GDP ($ billions) | **269.9** |

	Country data	High-income group
GNI per capita, *World Bank Atlas* method ($)	14,310	38,444
Adjusted net national income per capita ($)	10,908	32,262
Change in wealth per capita (2010 $)	-534	2,210
Urban population (% of total)	89.3	80.2

Agriculture

Agricultural land (% land area)	21	29
Agricultural irrigated land (% of total agricultural land)	5.6	..
Agricultural productivity, value added per worker (2005 $)	6,548	25,238
Cereal yield (kg per hectare)	6,230	4,374

Forests and biodiversity

Forest area (% land area)	21.9	35.0
Deforestation (avg. annual %, 2000–2010)	-0.2	0.0
Terrestrial protected areas (% of total land area)	18.6	13.9
Threatened species, mammals	20	
Threatened species, birds	33	
Threatened species, fish	20	
Threatened species, higher plants	71	

Oceans

Total fisheries production (thousand metric tons)	4,084	37,661
Capture fisheries growth (avg. annual %, 1990–2012)	-2.6	-2.0
Aquaculture growth (avg. annual %, 1990–2012)	13.2	2.5
Marine protected areas (% of territorial waters)	1.6	14.4
Coral reef area (sq. km)	..	82,210
Mangroves area (sq. km)	..	15,504

Energy and emissions

Energy use per capita (kg oil equivalent)	1,940	4,872
Energy from biomass products and waste (% of total)	17.6	4.3
Electric power consumption per capita (kWh)	3,568	8,896
Electricity generated using fossil fuel (% of total)	60.4	61.8
Electricity generated by hydropower (% of total)	32.0	12.2
CO_2 emissions per capita (metric tons)	4.2	11.6

Water and sanitation

Internal freshwater resources per capita (cu. m)	51,073	11,335
Total freshwater withdrawal (% of internal resources)	1.3	7.0
Agriculture (% of total freshwater withdrawal)	70	40
Access to improved water source (% of total population)	99	99
Rural (% of rural population)	91	98
Urban (% of urban population)	100	100
Access to improved sanitation facilities (% of total population)	99	96
Rural (% of rural population)	89	93
Urban (% of urban population)	100	97

Environment and health

Particulate matter (urban-pop.-weighted avg., µg/cu. m)	60	27
Acute resp. infection prevalence (% of children under five)	..	..
Diarrhea prevalence (% of children under five)	..	..
Under-five mortality rate (per 1,000 live births)	9	6

National accounting aggregates—savings, depletion and degradation

Gross savings (% of GNI)	22.5	20.1
Consumption of fixed capital (% of GNI)	15.8	14.2
Education expenditure (% of GNI)	4.1	4.7
Energy depletion (% of GNI)	0.1	1.6
Mineral depletion (% of GNI)	10.0	0.3
Net forest depletion (% of GNI)	0.0	0.0
CO_2 damage (% of GNI)	0.3	0.3
Particulate emissions damage (% of GNI)	0.9	0.3
Adjusted net savings (% of GNI)	-0.5	8.1

China

Population (millions) **1,350.7** Land area (1,000 sq. km) **9,327** GDP ($ billions) **8,227.1**

	Country data	East Asia & Pacific group	Upper middle-income group
GNI per capita, *World Bank Atlas* method ($)	5,720	4,884	6,969
Adjusted net national income per capita ($)	5,062	4,305	5,845
Change in wealth per capita (2010 $)	1,513	1,172	1,039
Urban population (% of total)	51.8	49.6	60.7
Agriculture			
Agricultural land (% land area)	56	48	44
Agricultural irrigated land (% of total agricultural land)	10.3	..	..
Agricultural productivity, value added per worker (2005 $)	749	794	1,131
Cereal yield (kg per hectare)	5,837	5,145	4,255
Forests and biodiversity			
Forest area (% land area)	22.5	29.7	29.1
Deforestation (avg. annual %, 2000–2010)	-1.6	-0.4	0.0
Terrestrial protected areas (% of total land area)	16.7	15.1	16.1
Threatened species, mammals	75		
Threatened species, birds	87		
Threatened species, fish	121		
Threatened species, higher plants	475		
Oceans			
Total fisheries production (thousand metric tons)	70,368	108,399	90,024
Capture fisheries growth (avg. annual %, 1990–2012)	4.1	3.4	1.5
Aquaculture growth (avg. annual %, 1990–2012)	9.1	9.1	9.1
Marine protected areas (% of territorial waters)	1.3	1.4	7.3
Coral reef area (sq. km)	1,510	137,690	52,070
Mangroves area (sq. km)	208	56,537	50,160
Energy and emissions			
Energy use per capita (kg oil equivalent)	2,029	1,671	1,893
Energy from biomass products and waste (% of total)	7.9	10.1	8.5
Electric power consumption per capita (kWh)	3,298	2,582	2,932
Electricity generated using fossil fuel (% of total)	80.9	80.9	74.7
Electricity generated by hydropower (% of total)	14.8	14.5	20.0
CO_2 emissions per capita (metric tons)	6.2	4.9	5.4
Water and sanitation			
Internal freshwater resources per capita (cu. m)	2,093	4,438	6,791
Total freshwater withdrawal (% of internal resources)	19.7	10.9	7.4
Agriculture (% of total freshwater withdrawal)	65	73	69
Access to improved water source (% of total population)	92	91	93
Rural (% of rural population)	85	85	85
Urban (% of urban population)	98	97	98
Access to improved sanitation facilities (% of total population)	65	67	74
Rural (% of rural population)	56	58	62
Urban (% of urban population)	74	76	82
Environment and health			
Particulate matter (urban-pop.-weighted avg., µg/cu. m)	82	75	65
Acute resp. infection prevalence (% of children under five)	..	..	..
Diarrhea prevalence (% of children under five)	..	..	..
Under-five mortality rate (per 1,000 live births)	14	21	20
National accounting aggregates—savings, depletion and degradation			
Gross savings (% of GNI)	51.4	47.6	36.4
Consumption of fixed capital (% of GNI)	12.5	12.0	12.5
Education expenditure (% of GNI)	1.8	2.1	3.2
Energy depletion (% of GNI)	2.4	2.7	4.1
Mineral depletion (% of GNI)	1.5	1.4	1.2
Net forest depletion (% of GNI)	0.1	0.1	0.2
CO_2 damage (% of GNI)	1.1	1.0	0.8
Particulate emissions damage (% of GNI)	1.8	1.6	1.3
Adjusted net savings (% of GNI)	33.9	30.9	19.5

Colombia

Population (millions)	**47.7** Land area (1,000 sq. km)	**1,110** GDP ($ billions)	**369.6**

	Country data	Latin America & Caribbean group	Upper middle-income group
GNI per capita, *World Bank Atlas* method ($)	7,020	9,070	6,969
Adjusted net national income per capita ($)	5,547	7,325	5,845
Change in wealth per capita (2010 $)	-462	180	1,039
Urban population (% of total)	75.6	79.0	60.7
Agriculture			
Agricultural land (% land area)	39	37	44
Agricultural irrigated land (% of total agricultural land)	..	..	..
Agricultural productivity, value added per worker (2005 $)	3,599	4,135	1,131
Cereal yield (kg per hectare)	3,749	4,082	4,255
Forests and biodiversity			
Forest area (% land area)	54.4	48.1	29.1
Deforestation (avg. annual %, 2000–2010)	0.2	0.5	0.0
Terrestrial protected areas (% of total land area)	21.2	21.4	16.1
Threatened species, mammals	54		
Threatened species, birds	112		
Threatened species, fish	54		
Threatened species, higher plants	238		
Oceans			
Total fisheries production (thousand metric tons)	168	10,964	90,024
Capture fisheries growth (avg. annual %, 1990–2012)	-1.9	-0.6	1.5
Aquaculture growth (avg. annual %, 1990–2012)	10.3	10.8	9.1
Marine protected areas (% of territorial waters)	3.2	9.0	7.3
Coral reef area (sq. km)	940	14,860	52,070
Mangroves area (sq. km)	4,079	39,988	50,160
Energy and emissions			
Energy use per capita (kg oil equivalent)	671	1,292	1,893
Energy from biomass products and waste (% of total)	11.5	16.0	8.5
Electric power consumption per capita (kWh)	1,123	1,985	2,932
Electricity generated using fossil fuel (% of total)	17.6	37.3	74.7
Electricity generated by hydropower (% of total)	79.1	55.1	20.0
CO_2 emissions per capita (metric tons)	1.6	2.7	5.4
Water and sanitation			
Internal freshwater resources per capita (cu. m)	44,861	21,735	6,791
Total freshwater withdrawal (% of internal resources)	0.6	2.0	7.4
Agriculture (% of total freshwater withdrawal)	39	68	69
Access to improved water source (% of total population)	91	94	93
Rural (% of rural population)	74	82	85
Urban (% of urban population)	97	97	98
Access to improved sanitation facilities (% of total population)	80	81	74
Rural (% of rural population)	66	62	62
Urban (% of urban population)	85	86	82
Environment and health			
Particulate matter (urban-pop.-weighted avg., μg/cu. m)	53	43	65
Acute resp. infection prevalence (% of children under five)	6	..	..
Diarrhea prevalence (% of children under five)	13	..	..
Under-five mortality rate (per 1,000 live births)	18	19	20
National accounting aggregates—savings, depletion and degradation			
Gross savings (% of GNI)	19.7	19.0	36.4
Consumption of fixed capital (% of GNI)	16.0	12.2	12.5
Education expenditure (% of GNI)	3.3	5.1	3.2
Energy depletion (% of GNI)	8.3	4.7	4.1
Mineral depletion (% of GNI)	0.8	1.2	1.2
Net forest depletion (% of GNI)	0.0	0.4	0.2
CO_2 damage (% of GNI)	0.2	0.3	0.8
Particulate emissions damage (% of GNI)	0.8	0.8	1.3
Adjusted net savings (% of GNI)	-3.2	4.5	19.5

Comoros

Population (thousands) **718** Land area (1,000 sq. km) **1.9** GDP ($ millions) **595.9**

	Country data	Sub-Saharan Africa group	Low-income group
GNI per capita, *World Bank Atlas* method ($)	840	1,547	594
Adjusted net national income per capita ($)	694	1,005	495
Change in wealth per capita (2010 $)	..	−273	−39
Urban population (% of total)	28.2	36.8	28.2

Agriculture

Agricultural land (% land area)	83	44	39
Agricultural irrigated land (% of total agricultural land)	..	..	..
Agricultural productivity, value added per worker (2005 $)	922	765	367
Cereal yield (kg per hectare)	1,390	1,417	1,982

Forests and biodiversity

Forest area (% land area)	1.4	27.4	27.4
Deforestation (avg. annual %, 2000–2010)	9.3	0.5	0.6
Terrestrial protected areas (% of total land area)	10.1	16.4	13.7
Threatened species, mammals	5		
Threatened species, birds	9		
Threatened species, fish	7		
Threatened species, higher plants	6		

Oceans

Total fisheries production (thousand metric tons)	12.3	6,906	11,789
Capture fisheries growth (avg. annual %, 1990–2012)	0.4	2.1	3.8
Aquaculture growth (avg. annual %, 1990–2012)	..	15.9	5.1
Marine protected areas (% of territorial waters)	33.5	11.7	13.1
Coral reef area (sq. km)	430	17,980	15,120
Mangroves area (sq. km)	1.2	27,808	25,817

Energy and emissions

Energy use per capita (kg oil equivalent)	65	681	360
Energy from biomass products and waste (% of total)	..	57.6	66.0
Electric power consumption per capita (kWh)	..	535	233
Electricity generated using fossil fuel (% of total)	..	65.1	30.9
Electricity generated by hydropower (% of total)	..	20.0	45.5
CO_2 emissions per capita (metric tons)	0.2	0.8	0.3

Water and sanitation

Internal freshwater resources per capita (cu. m)	1,714	4,391	5,121
Total freshwater withdrawal (% of internal resources)	0.8	3.2	4.4
Agriculture (% of total freshwater withdrawal)	47	84	90
Access to improved water source (% of total population)	95	64	69
Rural (% of rural population)	97	53	61
Urban (% of urban population)	91	85	88
Access to improved sanitation facilities (% of total population)	35	30	37
Rural (% of rural population)	30	23	33
Urban (% of urban population)	50	41	46

Environment and health

Particulate matter (urban-pop.-weighted avg., μg/cu. m)	21	77	74
Acute resp. infection prevalence (% of children under five)	..	5	6
Diarrhea prevalence (% of children under five)	..	14	14
Under-five mortality rate (per 1,000 live births)	78	98	82

National accounting aggregates—savings, depletion and degradation

Gross savings (% of GNI)	..	26.3	24.6
Consumption of fixed capital (% of GNI)	13.5	13.0	11.8
Education expenditure (% of GNI)	4.2	3.4	3.2
Energy depletion (% of GNI)	0.0	10.3	1.4
Mineral depletion (% of GNI)	0.0	1.8	1.9
Net forest depletion (% of GNI)	2.8	1.8	4.4
CO_2 damage (% of GNI)	0.3	0.6	0.4
Particulate emissions damage (% of GNI)	0.1	1.2	1.0
Adjusted net savings (% of GNI)	..	0.9	7.0

Congo, Dem. Rep.

Population (millions)	**65.7**	Land area (1,000 sq. km)	**2,267**	GDP ($ billions)	**17.2**

	Country data	Sub-Saharan Africa group	Low-Income group
GNI per capita, *World Bank Atlas* method ($)	230	1,547	594
Adjusted net national income per capita ($)	104	1,005	495
Change in wealth per capita (2010 $)	-121	-273	-39
Urban population (% of total)	34.8	36.8	28.2
Agriculture			
Agricultural land (% of land area)	11	44	39
Agricultural irrigated land (% of total agricultural land)	..	..	..
Agricultural productivity, value added per worker (2005 $)	285	765	367
Cereal yield (kg per hectare)	799	1,417	1,982
Forests and biodiversity			
Forest area (% land area)	67.9	27.4	27.4
Deforestation (avg. annual %, 2000–2010)	0.2	0.5	0.6
Terrestrial protected areas (% of total land area)	12.0	16.4	13.7
Threatened species, mammals	30		
Threatened species, birds	35		
Threatened species, fish	84		
Threatened species, higher plants	93		
Oceans			
Total fisheries production (thousand metric tons)	223	6,906	11,789
Capture fisheries growth (avg. annual %, 1990–2012)	1.4	2.1	3.8
Aquaculture growth (avg. annual %, 1990–2012)	6.6	15.9	5.1
Marine protected areas (% of territorial waters)	29.2	11.7	13.1
Coral reef area (sq. km)	..	17,980	15,120
Mangroves area (sq. km)	193	27,808	25,817
Energy and emissions			
Energy use per capita (kg oil equivalent)	383	681	360
Energy from biomass products and waste (% of total)	93.1	57.6	66.0
Electric power consumption per capita (kWh)	105	535	233
Electricity generated using fossil fuel (% of total)	0.4	65.1	30.9
Electricity generated by hydropower (% of total)	99.6	20.0	45.5
CO_2 emissions per capita (metric tons)	0.0	0.8	0.3
Water and sanitation			
Internal freshwater resources per capita (cu. m)	14,078	4,391	5,121
Total freshwater withdrawal (% of internal resources)	0.1	3.2	4.4
Agriculture (% of total freshwater withdrawal)	18	84	90
Access to improved water source (% of total population)	46	64	69
Rural (% of rural population)	29	53	61
Urban (% of urban population)	79	85	88
Access to improved sanitation facilities (% of total population)	31	30	37
Rural (% of rural population)	33	23	33
Urban (% of urban population)	29	41	46
Environment and health			
Particulate matter (urban-pop.-weighted avg., µg/cu. m)	46	77	74
Acute resp. infection prevalence (% of children under five)	..	5	6
Diarrhea prevalence (% of children under five)	16	14	14
Under-five mortality rate (per 1,000 live births)	146	98	82
National accounting aggregates—savings, depletion and degradation			
Gross savings (% of GNI)	18.9	26.3	24.6
Consumption of fixed capital (% of GNI)	13.2	13.0	11.8
Education expenditure (% of GNI)	2.4	3.4	3.2
Energy depletion (% of GNI)	2.8	10.3	1.4
Mineral depletion (% of GNI)	15.8	1.8	1.9
Net forest depletion (% of GNI)	25.6	1.8	4.4
CO_2 damage (% of GNI)	0.2	0.6	0.4
Particulate emissions damage (% of GNI)	1.0	1.2	1.0
Adjusted net savings (% of GNI)	-29.9	0.9	7.0

Congo, Rep.

Population (millions)	**4.3** Land area (1,000 sq. km)	**342** GDP ($ billions)	**13.7**

	Country data	Sub-Saharan Africa group	Lower middle-income group
GNI per capita, *World Bank Atlas* method ($)	2,550	1,547	1,965
Adjusted net national income per capita ($)	388	1,005	1,574
Change in wealth per capita (2010 $)	–1,981	–273	117
Urban population (% of total)	64.1	36.8	38.9
Agriculture			
Agricultural land (% land area)	31	44	46
Agricultural irrigated land (% of total agricultural land)	..	..	..
Agricultural productivity, value added per worker (2005 $)	685	765	938
Cereal yield (kg per hectare)	848	1,417	3,029
Forests and biodiversity			
Forest area (% land area)	65.6	27.4	26.9
Deforestation (avg. annual %, 2000–2010)	0.1	0.5	0.3
Terrestrial protected areas (% of total land area)	30.4	16.4	11.9
Threatened species, mammals	11		
Threatened species, birds	4		
Threatened species, fish	47		
Threatened species, higher plants	38		
Oceans			
Total fisheries production (thousand metric tons)	81.2	6,906	43,067
Capture fisheries growth (avg. annual %, 1990–2012)	2.4	2.1	2.6
Aquaculture growth (avg. annual %, 1990–2012)	–4.0	15.9	9.9
Marine protected areas (% of territorial waters)	0.05	11.7	14.7
Coral reef area (sq. km)	..	17,980	124,480
Mangroves area (sq. km)	16.7	27,808	58,917
Energy and emissions			
Energy use per capita (kg oil equivalent)	393	681	687
Energy from biomass products and waste (% of total)	46.9	57.6	26.8
Electric power consumption per capita (kWh)	172	535	734
Electricity generated using fossil fuel (% of total)	38.8	65.1	72.3
Electricity generated by hydropower (% of total)	61.2	20.0	16.9
CO_2 emissions per capita (metric tons)	0.5	0.8	1.6
Water and sanitation			
Internal freshwater resources per capita (cu. m)	52,540	4,391	3,144
Total freshwater withdrawal (% of internal resources)	0.0	3.2	19.6
Agriculture (% of total freshwater withdrawal)	9	84	88
Access to improved water source (% of total population)	75	64	88
Rural (% of rural population)	39	53	85
Urban (% of urban population)	96	85	94
Access to improved sanitation facilities (% of total population)	15	30	48
Rural (% of rural population)	6	23	36
Urban (% of urban population)	20	41	66
Environment and health			
Particulate matter (urban-pop.-weighted avg., µg/cu. m)	29	77	90
Acute resp. infection prevalence (% of children under five)	..	5	..
Diarrhea prevalence (% of children under five)	..	14	..
Under-five mortality rate (per 1,000 live births)	96	98	61
National accounting aggregates—savings, depletion and degradation			
Gross savings (% of GNI)	22.0	26.3	28.6
Consumption of fixed capital (% of GNI)	17.7	13.0	11.1
Education expenditure (% of GNI)	2.5	3.4	3.1
Energy depletion (% of GNI)	66.8	10.3	4.4
Mineral depletion (% of GNI)	0.0	1.8	1.1
Net forest depletion (% of GNI)	0.0	1.8	0.8
CO_2 damage (% of GNI)	0.2	0.6	0.9
Particulate emissions damage (% of GNI)	0.2	1.2	1.4
Adjusted net savings (% of GNI)	–56.1	0.9	12.0

Costa Rica

	Country data	Latin America & Caribbean group	Upper middle-income group
Population (millions)	**4.8**	Land area (1,000 sq. km)	**51**

Population (millions) **4.8** Land area (1,000 sq. km) **51** GDP ($ billions) **45.1**			
	Country data	Latin America & Caribbean group	Upper middle-income group
GNI per capita, *World Bank Atlas* method ($)	8,820	9,070	6,969
Adjusted net national income per capita ($)	8,597	7,325	5,845
Change in wealth per capita (2010 $)	773	180	1,039
Urban population (% of total)	65.1	79.0	60.7
Agriculture			
Agricultural land (% land area)	37	37	44
Agricultural irrigated land (% of total agricultural land)	1.5	..	..
Agricultural productivity, value added per worker (2005 $)	6,404	4,135	1,131
Cereal yield (kg per hectare)	2,732	4,082	4,255
Forests and biodiversity			
Forest area (% land area)	51.5	48.1	29.1
Deforestation (avg. annual %, 2000–2010)	-0.9	0.5	0.0
Terrestrial protected areas (% of total land area)	26.9	21.4	16.1
Threatened species, mammals	10		
Threatened species, birds	22		
Threatened species, fish	50		
Threatened species, higher plants	128		
Oceans			
Total fisheries production (thousand metric tons)	47.7	10,964	90,024
Capture fisheries growth (avg. annual %, 1990–2012)	0.5	-0.6	1.5
Aquaculture growth (avg. annual %, 1990–2012)	19.2	10.8	9.1
Marine protected areas (% of territorial waters)	2.0	9.0	7.3
Coral reef area (sq. km)	970	14,860	52,070
Mangroves area (sq. km)	418	39,988	50,160
Energy and emissions			
Energy use per capita (kg oil equivalent)	983	1,292	1,893
Energy from biomass products and waste (% of total)	15.8	16.0	8.5
Electric power consumption per capita (kWh)	1,844	1,985	2,932
Electricity generated using fossil fuel (% of total)	8.8	37.3	74.7
Electricity generated by hydropower (% of total)	72.6	55.1	20.0
CO_2 emissions per capita (metric tons)	1.7	2.7	5.4
Water and sanitation			
Internal freshwater resources per capita (cu. m)	23,725	21,735	6,791
Total freshwater withdrawal (% of internal resources)	2.4	2.0	7.4
Agriculture (% of total freshwater withdrawal)	53	68	69
Access to improved water source (% of total population)	97	94	93
Rural (% of rural population)	91	82	85
Urban (% of urban population)	100	97	98
Access to improved sanitation facilities (% of total population)	94	81	74
Rural (% of rural population)	92	62	62
Urban (% of urban population)	95	86	82
Environment and health			
Particulate matter (urban-pop.-weighted avg., µg/cu. m)	48	43	65
Acute resp. infection prevalence (% of children under five)	..	..	..
Diarrhea prevalence (% of children under five)	..	..	..
Under-five mortality rate (per 1,000 live births)	10	19	20
National accounting aggregates—savings, depletion and degradation			
Gross savings (% of GNI)	16.2	19.0	36.4
Consumption of fixed capital (% of GNI)	6.0	12.2	12.5
Education expenditure (% of GNI)	6.2	5.1	3.2
Energy depletion (% of GNI)	0.0	4.7	4.1
Mineral depletion (% of GNI)	0.0	1.2	1.2
Net forest depletion (% of GNI)	0.7	0.4	0.2
CO_2 damage (% of GNI)	0.2	0.3	0.8
Particulate emissions damage (% of GNI)	0.5	0.8	1.3
Adjusted net savings (% of GNI)	15.1	4.5	19.5

Côte d'Ivoire

Population (millions)	**19.8**	Land area (1,000 sq. km)	**318**	GDP ($ billions)	**24.7**

	Country data	Sub-Saharan Africa group	Lower middle-income group
GNI per capita, *World Bank Atlas* method ($)	1,220	1,547	1,965
Adjusted net national income per capita ($)	961	1,005	1,574
Change in wealth per capita (2010 $)	-146	-273	117
Urban population (% of total)	52.0	36.8	38.9
Agriculture			
Agricultural land (% land area)	64	44	46
Agricultural irrigated land (% of total agricultural land)	..	..	..
Agricultural productivity, value added per worker (2005 $)	*1,369*	765	938
Cereal yield (kg per hectare)	1,723	1,417	3,029
Forests and biodiversity			
Forest area (% land area)	32.7	27.4	26.9
Deforestation (avg. annual %, 2000–2010)	-0.2	0.5	0.3
Terrestrial protected areas (% of total land area)	22.9	16.4	11.9
Threatened species, mammals	23		
Threatened species, birds	20		
Threatened species, fish	46		
Threatened species, higher plants	105		
Oceans			
Total fisheries production (thousand metric tons)	79.3	6,906	43,067
Capture fisheries growth (avg. annual %, 1990–2012)	-1.0	2.1	2.6
Aquaculture growth (avg. annual %, 1990–2012)	17.9	15.9	9.9
Marine protected areas (% of territorial waters)	3.5	11.7	14.7
Coral reef area (sq. km)	..	17,980	124,480
Mangroves area (sq. km)	99.6	27,808	58,917
Energy and emissions			
Energy use per capita (kg oil equivalent)	579	681	687
Energy from biomass products and waste (% of total)	77.6	57.6	26.8
Electric power consumption per capita (kWh)	212	535	734
Electricity generated using fossil fuel (% of total)	69.9	65.1	72.3
Electricity generated by hydropower (% of total)	29.1	20.0	16.9
CO_2 emissions per capita (metric tons)	0.3	0.8	1.6
Water and sanitation			
Internal freshwater resources per capita (cu. m)	3,963	4,391	3,144
Total freshwater withdrawal (% of internal resources)	1.8	3.2	19.6
Agriculture (% of total freshwater withdrawal)	43	84	88
Access to improved water source (% of total population)	80	64	88
Rural (% of rural population)	68	53	85
Urban (% of urban population)	92	85	94
Access to improved sanitation facilities (% of total population)	22	30	48
Rural (% of rural population)	10	23	36
Urban (% of urban population)	33	41	66
Environment and health			
Particulate matter (urban-pop.-weighted avg., µg/cu. m)	21	77	90
Acute resp. infection prevalence (% of children under five)	4	5	..
Diarrhea prevalence (% of children under five)	18	14	..
Under-five mortality rate (per 1,000 live births)	108	98	61
National accounting aggregates—savings, depletion and degradation			
Gross savings (% of GNI)	*12.8*	26.3	28.6
Consumption of fixed capital (% of GNI)	14.7	13.0	11.1
Education expenditure (% of GNI)	4.3	3.4	3.1
Energy depletion (% of GNI)	3.3	10.3	4.4
Mineral depletion (% of GNI)	1.4	1.8	1.1
Net forest depletion (% of GNI)	0.0	1.8	0.8
CO_2 damage (% of GNI)	0.2	0.6	0.9
Particulate emissions damage (% of GNI)	0.2	1.2	1.4
Adjusted net savings (% of GNI)	-3.4	0.9	12.0

Croatia

	Population (millions)	**4.3**	Land area (1,000 sq. km)	**56**	GDP ($ billions)	**59.2**

	Country data	High-income group
GNI per capita, *World Bank Atlas* method ($)	13,490	38,444
Adjusted net national income per capita ($)	11,574	32,262
Change in wealth per capita (2010 $)	1,447	2,210
Urban population (% of total)	58.1	80.2

Agriculture
Agricultural land (% land area)	24	29
Agricultural irrigated land (% of total agricultural land)	1.1	..
Agricultural productivity, value added per worker (2005 $)	23,521	*25,238*
Cereal yield (kg per hectare)	4,578	4,374

Forests and biodiversity
Forest area (% land area)	34.4	35.0
Deforestation (avg. annual %, 2000–2010)	-0.2	0.0
Terrestrial protected areas (% of total land area)	14.1	13.9
Threatened species, mammals	8	
Threatened species, birds	12	
Threatened species, fish	60	
Threatened species, higher plants	7	

Oceans
Total fisheries production (thousand metric tons)	74.7	37,661
Capture fisheries growth (avg. annual %, 1990–2012)	..	-2.0
Aquaculture growth (avg. annual %, 1990–2012)	..	2.5
Marine protected areas (% of territorial waters)	7.6	*14.4*
Coral reef area (sq. km)	..	82,210
Mangroves area (sq. km)	..	15,504

Energy and emissions
Energy use per capita (kg oil equivalent)	1,971	4,872
Energy from biomass products and waste (% of total)	5.6	4.3
Electric power consumption per capita (kWh)	3,901	8,896
Electricity generated using fossil fuel (% of total)	55.6	61.8
Electricity generated by hydropower (% of total)	42.0	12.2
CO_2 emissions per capita (metric tons)	4.7	11.6

Water and sanitation
Internal freshwater resources per capita (cu. m)	8,807	11,335
Total freshwater withdrawal (% of internal resources)	1.7	7.0
Agriculture (% of total freshwater withdrawal)	2	40
Access to improved water source (% of total population)	99	99
Rural (% of rural population)	97	98
Urban (% of urban population)	100	100
Access to improved sanitation facilities (% of total population)	98	96
Rural (% of rural population)	98	93
Urban (% of urban population)	99	97

Environment and health
Particulate matter (urban-pop.-weighted avg., µg/cu. m)	30	27
Acute resp. infection prevalence (% of children under five)	..	..
Diarrhea prevalence (% of children under five)	..	..
Under-five mortality rate (per 1,000 live births)	5	6

National accounting aggregates—savings, depletion and degradation
Gross savings (% of GNI)	19.7	20.1
Consumption of fixed capital (% of GNI)	12.1	14.2
Education expenditure (% of GNI)	4.2	4.7
Energy depletion (% of GNI)	0.6	1.6
Mineral depletion (% of GNI)	0.0	0.3
Net forest depletion (% of GNI)	0.7	0.0
CO_2 damage (% of GNI)	0.3	0.3
Particulate emissions damage (% of GNI)	0.7	0.3
Adjusted net savings (% of GNI)	9.3	8.1

Cuba

Population (millions)	**11.3**	Land area (1,000 sq. km)	**106**	GDP ($ billions)	**68.2**

	Country data	Latin America & Caribbean group	Upper middle-income group
GNI per capita, *World Bank Atlas* method ($)	5,890	9,070	6,969
Adjusted net national income per capita ($)	5,022	7,325	5,845
Change in wealth per capita (2010 $)	..	180	1,039
Urban population (% of total)	75.2	79.0	60.7

Agriculture

Agricultural land (% land area)	62	37	44
Agricultural irrigated land (% of total agricultural land)	..	..	..
Agricultural productivity, value added per worker (2005 $)	4,188	4,135	1,131
Cereal yield (kg per hectare)	2,652	4,082	4,255

Forests and biodiversity

Forest area (% land area)	27.3	48.1	29.1
Deforestation (avg. annual %, 2000–2010)	-1.7	0.5	0.0
Terrestrial protected areas (% of total land area)	12.4	21.4	16.1
Threatened species, mammals	14		
Threatened species, birds	17		
Threatened species, fish	35		
Threatened species, higher plants	176		

Oceans

Total fisheries production (thousand metric tons)	48.5	10,964	90,024
Capture fisheries growth (avg. annual %, 1990–2012)	-9.0	-0.6	1.5
Aquaculture growth (avg. annual %, 1990–2012)	5.4	10.8	9.1
Marine protected areas (% of territorial waters)	1.3	9.0	7.3
Coral reef area (sq. km)	3,020	14,860	52,070
Mangroves area (sq. km)	4,944	39,988	50,160

Energy and emissions

Energy use per capita (kg oil equivalent)	992	1,292	1,893
Energy from biomass products and waste (% of total)	13.2	16.0	8.5
Electric power consumption per capita (kWh)	1,327	1,985	2,932
Electricity generated using fossil fuel (% of total)	54.9	37.3	74.7
Electricity generated by hydropower (% of total)	0.6	55.1	20.0
CO_2 emissions per capita (metric tons)	3.4	2.7	5.4

Water and sanitation

Internal freshwater resources per capita (cu. m)	3,381	21,735	6,791
Total freshwater withdrawal (% of internal resources)	19.8	2.0	7.4
Agriculture (% of total freshwater withdrawal)	75	68	69
Access to improved water source (% of total population)	94	94	93
Rural (% of rural population)	87	82	85
Urban (% of urban population)	96	97	98
Access to improved sanitation facilities (% of total population)	93	81	74
Rural (% of rural population)	88	62	62
Urban (% of urban population)	94	86	82

Environment and health

Particulate matter (urban-pop.-weighted avg., μg/cu. m)	37	43	65
Acute resp. infection prevalence (% of children under five)	..	..	..
Diarrhea prevalence (% of children under five)	..	..	..
Under-five mortality rate (per 1,000 live births)	6	19	20

National accounting aggregates—savings, depletion and degradation

Gross savings (% of GNI)	..	19.0	36.4
Consumption of fixed capital (% of GNI)	11.8	12.2	12.5
Education expenditure (% of GNI)	12.9	5.1	3.2
Energy depletion (% of GNI)	2.6	4.7	4.1
Mineral depletion (% of GNI)	1.4	1.2	1.2
Net forest depletion (% of GNI)	0.0	0.4	0.2
CO_2 damage (% of GNI)	0.6	0.3	0.8
Particulate emissions damage (% of GNI)	0.8	0.8	1.3
Adjusted net savings (% of GNI)	..	4.5	19.5

Curaçao

Population (thousands) **152** Land area (sq. km) **444** GDP ($ millions) ..

	Country data	High-income group
GNI per capita, *World Bank Atlas* method ($)	..	38,444
Adjusted net national income per capita ($)	..	32,262
Change in wealth per capita (2010 $)	..	2,210
Urban population (% of total)	..	80.2
Agriculture		
Agricultural land (% land area)	..	29
Agricultural irrigated land (% of total agricultural land)	..	..
Agricultural productivity, value added per worker (2005 $)	..	25,238
Cereal yield (kg per hectare)	..	4,374
Forests and biodiversity		
Forest area (% land area)	..	35.0
Deforestation (avg. annual %, 2000–2010)	..	0.0
Terrestrial protected areas (% of total land area)	..	13.9
Threatened species, mammals	1	
Threatened species, birds	1	
Threatened species, fish	9	
Threatened species, higher plants	0	
Oceans		
Total fisheries production (thousand metric tons)	23.8	37,661
Capture fisheries growth (avg. annual %, 1990–2012)	..	-2.0
Aquaculture growth (avg. annual %, 1990–2012)	..	2.5
Marine protected areas (% of territorial waters)	..	14.4
Coral reef area (sq. km)	..	82,210
Mangroves area (sq. km)	..	15,504
Energy and emissions		
Energy use per capita (kg oil equivalent)	..	4,872
Energy from biomass products and waste (% of total)	..	4.3
Electric power consumption per capita (kWh)	..	8,896
Electricity generated using fossil fuel (% of total)	..	61.8
Electricity generated by hydropower (% of total)	..	12.2
CO_2 emissions per capita (metric tons)	..	11.6
Water and sanitation		
Internal freshwater resources per capita (cu. m)	..	11,335
Total freshwater withdrawal (% of internal resources)	..	7.0
Agriculture (% of total freshwater withdrawal)	..	40
Access to improved water source (% of total population)	..	99
Rural (% of rural population)	..	98
Urban (% of urban population)	..	100
Access to improved sanitation facilities (% of total population)	..	96
Rural (% of rural population)	..	93
Urban (% of urban population)	..	97
Environment and health		
Particulate matter (urban-pop.-weighted avg., µg/cu. m)	..	27
Acute resp. infection prevalence (% of children under five)	..	..
Diarrhea prevalence (% of children under five)	..	..
Under-five mortality rate (per 1,000 live births)	..	6
National accounting aggregates—savings, depletion and degradation		
Gross savings (% of GNI)	..	20.1
Consumption of fixed capital (% of GNI)	..	14.2
Education expenditure (% of GNI)	..	4.7
Energy depletion (% of GNI)	..	1.6
Mineral depletion (% of GNI)	..	0.3
Net forest depletion (% of GNI)	..	0.0
CO_2 damage (% of GNI)	..	0.3
Particulate emissions damage (% of GNI)	..	0.3
Adjusted net savings (% of GNI)	..	8.1

Cyprus

	Population (millions)	**1.1**	Land area (1,000 sq. km)	**9.2**	GDP ($ billions)	**22.8**

	Country data	High-income group
GNI per capita, *World Bank Atlas* method ($)	26,110	38,444
Adjusted net national income per capita ($)	17,103	32,262
Urban population (% of total)	385	2,210
Urban population growth (avg. annual %, 1990–2011)	70.7	80.2
Agriculture		
Agricultural land (% land area)	13	29
Agricultural irrigated land (% of total agricultural land)	*21.9*	*..*
Agricultural productivity, value added per worker (2000 $)	*11,380*	*25,238*
Cereal yield (kg per hectare)	1,521	4,374
Forests and biodiversity		
Forest area (% land area)	18.8	35.0
Deforestation (avg. annual %, 2000–2010)	-0.1	0.0
Terrestrial protected areas (% of total land area)	40.9	13.9
Threatened species, mammals	5	
Threatened species, birds	5	
Threatened species, fish	19	
Threatened species, higher plants	18	
Oceans		
Total fisheries production (thousand metric tons)	5.7	37,661
Capture fisheries growth (avg. annual %, 1990–2011)	-3.0	-2.0
Aquaculture growth (avg. annual %, 1990–2011)	17.5	2.5
Marine protected areas (% of territorial waters)	*0.56*	*14.4*
Coral reef area (sq. km)	..	82,210
Mangroves area (sq. km)	..	15,504
Energy and emissions		
Energy use per capita (kg oil equivalent)	2,121	4,872
Energy from biomass products and waste (% of total)	2.0	4.3
Electric power consumption per capita (kWh)	4,271	8,896
Electricity generated using fossil fuel (% of total)	96.4	61.8
Electricity generated by hydropower (% of total)	0.0	12.2
CO_2 emissions per capita (metric tons)	7.0	11.6
Water and sanitation		
Internal freshwater resources per capita (cu. m)	699	11,335
Total freshwater withdrawal (% of internal resources)	23.6	7.0
Agriculture (% of total freshwater withdrawal)	86	40
Access to improved water source (% of total population)	100	99
Rural (% of rural population)	100	98
Urban (% of urban population)	100	100
Access to improved sanitation facilities (% of total population)	100	96
Rural (% of rural population)	100	93
Urban (% of urban population)	100	97
Environment and health		
Particulate matter (urban-pop.-weighted avg., µg/cu. m)	42	27
Acute resp. infection prevalence (% of children under five)	..	..
Diarrhea prevalence (% of children under five)	..	..
Under-five mortality rate (per 1,000 live births)	3	6
National accounting aggregates—savings, depletion and degradation		
Gross savings (% of GNI)	*9.0*	20.1
Consumption of fixed capital (% of GNI)	12.5	14.2
Education expenditure (% of GNI)	6.7	4.7
Energy depletion (% of GNI)	0.0	1.6
Mineral depletion (% of GNI)	0.0	0.3
Net forest depletion (% of GNI)	0.0	0.0
CO_2 damage (% of GNI)	0.3	0.3
Particulate emissions damage (% of GNI)	0.6	0.3
Adjusted net savings (% of GNI)	*3.9*	8.1

Czech Republic

Population (millions)	**10.5**	Land area (1,000 sq. km)	**77**	GDP ($ billions)	**196.4**

	Country data	High-income group
GNI per capita, *World Bank Atlas* method ($)	18,130	38,444
Adjusted net national income per capita ($)	13,769	32,262
Urban population (% of total)	698	2,210
Urban population growth (avg. annual %, 1990–2011)	73.4	80.2

Agriculture
Agricultural land (% land area)	55	29
Agricultural irrigated land (% of total agricultural land)	0.4	..
Agricultural productivity, value added per worker (2000 $)	6,680	25,238
Cereal yield (kg per hectare)	4,533	4,374

Forests and biodiversity
Forest area (% land area)	34.4	35.0
Deforestation (avg. annual %, 2000–2010)	-0.1	0.0
Terrestrial protected areas (% of total land area)	22.4	13.9
Threatened species, mammals	2	
Threatened species, birds	7	
Threatened species, fish	2	
Threatened species, higher plants	11	

Oceans
Total fisheries production (thousand metric tons)	24.8	37,661
Capture fisheries growth (avg. annual %, 1990–2011)	..	-2.0
Aquaculture growth (avg. annual %, 1990–2011)	..	2.5
Marine protected areas (% of territorial waters)	4.4	14.4
Coral reef area (sq. km)	..	82,210
Mangroves area (sq. km)	..	15,504

Energy and emissions
Energy use per capita (kg oil equivalent)	4,138	4,872
Energy from biomass products and waste (% of total)	6.5	4.3
Electric power consumption per capita (kWh)	6,289	8,896
Electricity generated using fossil fuel (% of total)	59.0	61.8
Electricity generated by hydropower (% of total)	2.3	12.2
CO_2 emissions per capita (metric tons)	10.7	11.6

Water and sanitation
Internal freshwater resources per capita (cu. m)	1,253	11,335
Total freshwater withdrawal (% of internal resources)	12.9	7.0
Agriculture (% of total freshwater withdrawal)	2	40
Access to improved water source (% of total population)	100	99
Rural (% of rural population)	100	98
Urban (% of urban population)	100	100
Access to improved sanitation facilities (% of total population)	100	96
Rural (% of rural population)	100	93
Urban (% of urban population)	100	97

Environment and health
Particulate matter (urban-pop.-weighted avg., µg/cu. m)	29	27
Acute resp. infection prevalence (% of children under five)	..	..
Diarrhea prevalence (% of children under five)	..	..
Under-five mortality rate (per 1,000 live births)	4	6

National accounting aggregates—savings, depletion and degradation
Gross savings (% of GNI)	22.7	20.1
Consumption of fixed capital (% of GNI)	20.1	14.2
Education expenditure (% of GNI)	4.1	4.7
Energy depletion (% of GNI)	0.3	1.6
Mineral depletion (% of GNI)	0.0	0.3
Net forest depletion (% of GNI)	0.0	0.0
CO_2 damage (% of GNI)	0.6	0.3
Particulate emissions damage (% of GNI)	0.7	0.3
Adjusted net savings (% of GNI)	5.1	8.1

Denmark

Population (millions)	**5.6**	Land area (1,000 sq. km)	**42**	GDP ($ billions)	**315.2**

	Country data	High-income group
GNI per capita, *World Bank Atlas* method ($)	59,870	38,444
Adjusted net national income per capita ($)	49,489	32,262
Urban population (% of total)	6,423	2,210
Urban population growth (avg. annual %, 1990–2011)	87.1	80.2
Agriculture		
Agricultural land (% land area)	63	29
Agricultural irrigated land (% of total agricultural land)	*12.1*	..
Agricultural productivity, value added per worker (2000 $)	31,885	*25,238*
Cereal yield (kg per hectare)	6,314	4,374
Forests and biodiversity		
Forest area (% land area)	12.9	35.0
Deforestation (avg. annual %, 2000–2010)	-1.1	0.0
Terrestrial protected areas (% of total land area)	18.4	13.9
Threatened species, mammals	2	
Threatened species, birds	4	
Threatened species, fish	15	
Threatened species, higher plants	2	
Oceans		
Total fisheries production (thousand metric tons)	541	37,661
Capture fisheries growth (avg. annual %, 1990–2011)	-4.8	-2.0
Aquaculture growth (avg. annual %, 1990–2011)	-0.4	2.5
Marine protected areas (% of territorial waters)	0.49	*14.4*
Coral reef area (sq. km)	..	82,210
Mangroves area (sq. km)	..	15,504
Energy and emissions		
Energy use per capita (kg oil equivalent)	3,231	4,872
Energy from biomass products and waste (% of total)	19.7	4.3
Electric power consumption per capita (kWh)	6,122	8,896
Electricity generated using fossil fuel (% of total)	57.5	61.8
Electricity generated by hydropower (% of total)	0.0	12.2
CO_2 emissions per capita (metric tons)	8.3	11.6
Water and sanitation		
Internal freshwater resources per capita (cu. m)	1,077	11,335
Total freshwater withdrawal (% of internal resources)	11.0	7.0
Agriculture (% of total freshwater withdrawal)	36	40
Access to improved water source (% of total population)	100	99
Rural (% of rural population)	100	98
Urban (% of urban population)	100	100
Access to improved sanitation facilities (% of total population)	100	96
Rural (% of rural population)	100	93
Urban (% of urban population)	100	97
Environment and health		
Particulate matter (urban-pop.-weighted avg., µg/cu. m)	25	27
Acute resp. infection prevalence (% of children under five)	..	..
Diarrhea prevalence (% of children under five)	..	..
Under-five mortality rate (per 1,000 live births)	4	6
National accounting aggregates—savings, depletion and degradation		
Gross savings (% of GNI)	22.9	20.1
Consumption of fixed capital (% of GNI)	13.0	14.2
Education expenditure (% of GNI)	8.1	4.7
Energy depletion (% of GNI)	1.7	1.6
Mineral depletion (% of GNI)	0.0	0.3
Net forest depletion (% of GNI)	0.0	0.0
CO_2 damage (% of GNI)	0.1	0.3
Particulate emissions damage (% of GNI)	0.5	0.3
Adjusted net savings (% of GNI)	15.7	8.1

Djibouti

Population (thousands) **860** Land area (1,000 sq. km) **23** GDP ($ millions) *847.9*

	Country data	Middle East & N. Africa group	Lower middle-income group
GNI per capita, *World Bank Atlas* method ($)	..	*3,451*	1,965
Adjusted net national income per capita ($)	..	*2,602*	1,574
Urban population (% of total)	..	101	117
Urban population growth (avg. annual %, 1990–2011)	77.2	59.5	38.9
Agriculture			
Agricultural land (% land area)	73	23	46
Agricultural irrigated land (% of total agricultural land)	..	..	..
Agricultural productivity, value added per worker (2000 $)	..	*2,642*	938
Cereal yield (kg per hectare)	2,000	2,350	3,029
Forests and biodiversity			
Forest area (% land area)	0.2	2.4	26.9
Deforestation (avg. annual %, 2000–2010)	0.0	-0.1	0.3
Terrestrial protected areas (% of total land area)	0.1	6.1	11.9
Threatened species, mammals	7		
Threatened species, birds	9		
Threatened species, fish	17		
Threatened species, higher plants	2		
Oceans			
Total fisheries production (thousand metric tons)	2.2	3,976	43,067
Capture fisheries growth (avg. annual %, 1990–2011)	8.5	3.0	2.6
Aquaculture growth (avg. annual %, 1990–2011)	..	12.8	9.9
Marine protected areas (% of territorial waters)	0.13	9.1	14.7
Coral reef area (sq. km)	450	5,700	124,480
Mangroves area (sq. km)	10.0	217	58,917
Energy and emissions			
Energy use per capita (kg oil equivalent)	*179*	1,376	687
Energy from biomass products and waste (% of total)	..	0.9	26.8
Electric power consumption per capita (kWh)	..	1,696	734
Electricity generated using fossil fuel (% of total)	..	91.7	72.3
Electricity generated by hydropower (% of total)	..	5.5	16.9
CO_2 emissions per capita (metric tons)	0.6	3.9	1.6
Water and sanitation			
Internal freshwater resources per capita (cu. m)	354	679	3,144
Total freshwater withdrawal (% of internal resources)	6.3	122.1	19.6
Agriculture (% of total freshwater withdrawal)	16	86	88
Access to improved water source (% of total population)	92	90	88
Rural (% of rural population)	65	83	85
Urban (% of urban population)	100	95	94
Access to improved sanitation facilities (% of total population)	61	88	48
Rural (% of rural population)	22	80	36
Urban (% of urban population)	73	94	66
Environment and health			
Particulate matter (urban-pop.-weighted avg., μg/cu. m)	40	79	90
Acute resp. infection prevalence (% of children under five)	..	..	..
Diarrhea prevalence (% of children under five)	..	..	..
Under-five mortality rate (per 1,000 live births)	81	26	61
National accounting aggregates—savings, depletion and degradation			
Gross savings (% of GNI)	..	25.9	28.6
Consumption of fixed capital (% of GNI)	..	9.9	11.1
Education expenditure (% of GNI)	..	4.5	3.1
Energy depletion (% of GNI)	..	12.9	4.4
Mineral depletion (% of GNI)	..	0.5	1.1
Net forest depletion (% of GNI)	..	0.2	0.8
CO_2 damage (% of GNI)	..	0.7	0.9
Particulate emissions damage (% of GNI)	1.0	0.9	1.4
Adjusted net savings (% of GNI)	..	5.3	12.0

Dominica

Population (thousands)	72	Land area (sq. km)		750	GDP ($ millions)	479.7

	Country data	Latin America & Caribbean group	Upper middle-income group
GNI per capita, *World Bank Atlas* method ($)	6,440	9,070	6,969
Adjusted net national income per capita ($)	5,640	7,325	5,845
Change in wealth per capita (2010 $)	-265	180	1,039
Urban population (% of total)	67.3	79.0	60.7
Agriculture			
Agricultural land (% land area)	35	37	44
Agricultural irrigated land (% of total agricultural land)	..	..	..
Agricultural productivity, value added per worker (2005 $)	7,141	4,135	1,131
Cereal yield (kg per hectare)	2,222	4,082	4,255
Forests and biodiversity			
Forest area (% land area)	59.2	48.1	29.1
Deforestation (avg. annual %, 2000–2010)	0.6	0.5	0.0
Terrestrial protected areas (% of total land area)	21.7	21.4	16.1
Threatened species, mammals	3		
Threatened species, birds	3		
Threatened species, fish	20		
Threatened species, higher plants	10		
Oceans			
Total fisheries production (thousand metric tons)	0.60	10,964	90,024
Capture fisheries growth (avg. annual %, 1990–2012)	0.9	-0.6	1.5
Aquaculture growth (avg. annual %, 1990–2012)	..	10.8	9.1
Marine protected areas (% of territorial waters)	28.6	9.0	7.3
Coral reef area (sq. km)	<100	14,860	52,070
Mangroves area (sq. km)	0.10	39,988	50,160
Energy and emissions			
Energy use per capita (kg oil equivalent)	607	1,292	1,893
Energy from biomass products and waste (% of total)	..	16.0	8.5
Electric power consumption per capita (kWh)	..	1,985	2,932
Electricity generated using fossil fuel (% of total)	..	37.3	74.7
Electricity generated by hydropower (% of total)	..	55.1	20.0
CO_2 emissions per capita (metric tons)	1.9	2.7	5.4
Water and sanitation			
Internal freshwater resources per capita (cu. m)	..	21,735	6,791
Total freshwater withdrawal (% of internal resources)	..	2.0	7.4
Agriculture (% of total freshwater withdrawal)	..	68	69
Access to improved water source (% of total population)	..	94	93
Rural (% of rural population)	..	82	85
Urban (% of urban population)	96	97	98
Access to improved sanitation facilities (% of total population)	..	81	74
Rural (% of rural population)	..	62	62
Urban (% of urban population)	..	86	82
Environment and health			
Particulate matter (urban-pop.-weighted avg., µg/cu. m)	15	43	65
Acute resp. infection prevalence (% of children under five)	..	..	..
Diarrhea prevalence (% of children under five)	..	..	..
Under-five mortality rate (per 1,000 live births)	13	19	20
National accounting aggregates—savings, depletion and degradation			
Gross savings (% of GNI)	11.2	19.0	36.4
Consumption of fixed capital (% of GNI)	12.5	12.2	12.5
Education expenditure (% of GNI)	5.0	5.1	3.2
Energy depletion (% of GNI)	0.0	4.7	4.1
Mineral depletion (% of GNI)	0.0	1.2	1.2
Net forest depletion (% of GNI)	0.1	0.4	0.2
CO_2 damage (% of GNI)	0.3	0.3	0.8
Particulate emissions damage (% of GNI)	..	0.8	1.3
Adjusted net savings (% of GNI)	..	4.5	19.5

Dominican Republic

	Country data	Latin America & Caribbean group	Upper middle-income group
Population (millions) **10.3** Land area (1,000 sq. km) **48** GDP ($ billions) **59.0**			

	Country data	Latin America & Caribbean group	Upper middle-income group
GNI per capita, *World Bank Atlas* method ($)	5,470	9,070	6,969
Adjusted net national income per capita ($)	4,768	7,325	5,845
Change in wealth per capita (2010 $)	-361	180	1,039
Urban population (% of total)	70.2	79.0	60.7

Agriculture

Agricultural land (% land area)	51	37	44
Agricultural irrigated land (% of total agricultural land)	..	..	..
Agricultural productivity, value added per worker (2005 $)	7,369	4,135	1,131
Cereal yield (kg per hectare)	4,375	4,082	4,255

Forests and biodiversity

Forest area (% land area)	40.8	48.1	29.1
Deforestation (avg. annual %, 2000–2010)	0.0	0.5	0.0
Terrestrial protected areas (% of total land area)	18.6	21.4	16.1
Threatened species, mammals	6		
Threatened species, birds	14		
Threatened species, fish	22		
Threatened species, higher plants	38		

Oceans

Total fisheries production (thousand metric tons)	14.7	10,964	90,024
Capture fisheries growth (avg. annual %, 1990–2012)	-1.6	-0.6	1.5
Aquaculture growth (avg. annual %, 1990–2012)	6.1	10.8	9.1
Marine protected areas (% of territorial waters)	75.7	9.0	7.3
Coral reef area (sq. km)	610	14,860	52,070
Mangroves area (sq. km)	212	39,988	50,160

Energy and emissions

Energy use per capita (kg oil equivalent)	727	1,292	1,893
Energy from biomass products and waste (% of total)	8.9	16.0	8.5
Electric power consumption per capita (kWh)	893	1,985	2,932
Electricity generated using fossil fuel (% of total)	88.0	37.3	74.7
Electricity generated by hydropower (% of total)	11.8	55.1	20.0
CO_2 emissions per capita (metric tons)	2.1	2.7	5.4

Water and sanitation

Internal freshwater resources per capita (cu. m)	2,069	21,735	6,791
Total freshwater withdrawal (% of internal resources)	16.6	2.0	7.4
Agriculture (% of total freshwater withdrawal)	64	68	69
Access to improved water source (% of total population)	81	94	93
Rural (% of rural population)	77	82	85
Urban (% of urban population)	82	97	98
Access to improved sanitation facilities (% of total population)	82	81	74
Rural (% of rural population)	74	62	62
Urban (% of urban population)	86	86	82

Environment and health

Particulate matter (urban-pop.-weighted avg., µg/cu. m)	31	43	65
Acute resp. infection prevalence (% of children under five)	7	..	..
Diarrhea prevalence (% of children under five)	15	..	..
Under-five mortality rate (per 1,000 live births)	27	19	20

National accounting aggregates—savings, depletion and degradation

Gross savings (% of GNI)	9.6	19.0	36.4
Consumption of fixed capital (% of GNI)	13.3	12.2	12.5
Education expenditure (% of GNI)	1.9	5.1	3.2
Energy depletion (% of GNI)	0.0	4.7	4.1
Mineral depletion (% of GNI)	0.5	1.2	1.2
Net forest depletion (% of GNI)	0.0	0.4	0.2
CO_2 damage (% of GNI)	0.4	0.3	0.8
Particulate emissions damage (% of GNI)	0.6	0.8	1.3
Adjusted net savings (% of GNI)	-3.2	4.5	19.5

Ecuador

| Population (millions) | **15.5** | Land area (1,000 sq. km) | **248** | GDP ($ billions) | **84.0** |

	Country data	Latin America & Caribbean group	Upper middle-income group
GNI per capita, *World Bank Atlas* method ($)	5,170	9,070	6,969
Adjusted net national income per capita ($)	4,024	7,325	5,845
Change in wealth per capita (2010 $)	-395	180	1,039
Urban population (% of total)	68.0	79.0	60.7
Agriculture			
Agricultural land (% land area)	30	37	44
Agricultural irrigated land (% of total agricultural land)	12.6	..	..
Agricultural productivity, value added per worker (2005 $)	3,899	4,135	1,131
Cereal yield (kg per hectare)	3,511	4,082	4,255
Forests and biodiversity			
Forest area (% land area)	38.9	48.1	29.1
Deforestation (avg. annual %, 2000–2010)	1.8	0.5	0.0
Terrestrial protected areas (% of total land area)	23.7	21.4	16.1
Threatened species, mammals	45		
Threatened species, birds	94		
Threatened species, fish	52		
Threatened species, higher plants	1,842		
Oceans			
Total fisheries production (thousand metric tons)	835	10,964	90,024
Capture fisheries growth (avg. annual %, 1990–2012)	2.6	-0.6	1.5
Aquaculture growth (avg. annual %, 1990–2012)	6.7	10.8	9.1
Marine protected areas (% of territorial waters)	13.1	9.0	7.3
Coral reef area (sq. km)	<50	14,860	52,070
Mangroves area (sq. km)	1,583	39,988	50,160
Energy and emissions			
Energy use per capita (kg oil equivalent)	849	1,292	1,893
Energy from biomass products and waste (% of total)	5.4	16.0	8.5
Electric power consumption per capita (kWh)	1,192	1,985	2,932
Electricity generated using fossil fuel (% of total)	42.3	37.3	74.7
Electricity generated by hydropower (% of total)	54.9	55.1	20.0
CO_2 emissions per capita (metric tons)	2.2	2.7	5.4
Water and sanitation			
Internal freshwater resources per capita (cu. m)	28,334	21,735	6,791
Total freshwater withdrawal (% of internal resources)	3.5	2.0	7.4
Agriculture (% of total freshwater withdrawal)	92	68	69
Access to improved water source (% of total population)	86	94	93
Rural (% of rural population)	75	82	85
Urban (% of urban population)	92	97	98
Access to improved sanitation facilities (% of total population)	83	81	74
Rural (% of rural population)	76	62	62
Urban (% of urban population)	86	86	82
Environment and health			
Particulate matter (urban-pop.-weighted avg., µg/cu. m)	32	43	65
Acute resp. infection prevalence (% of children under five)	..	..	..
Diarrhea prevalence (% of children under five)	..	..	..
Under-five mortality rate (per 1,000 live births)	23	19	20
National accounting aggregates—savings, depletion and degradation			
Gross savings (% of GNI)	27.3	19.0	36.4
Consumption of fixed capital (% of GNI)	12.0	12.2	12.5
Education expenditure (% of GNI)	4.1	5.1	3.2
Energy depletion (% of GNI)	12.2	4.7	4.1
Mineral depletion (% of GNI)	0.1	1.2	1.2
Net forest depletion (% of GNI)	0.4	0.4	0.2
CO_2 damage (% of GNI)	0.4	0.3	0.8
Particulate emissions damage (% of GNI)	0.2	0.8	1.3
Adjusted net savings (% of GNI)	6.1	4.5	19.5

Egypt, Arab Rep.

Population (millions)	**80.7**	Land area (1,000 sq. km)	**995**	GDP ($ billions)	**262.8**

	Country data	Middle East & N. Africa group	Lower middle-income group
GNI per capita, *World Bank Atlas* method ($)	2,980	3,451	1,965
Adjusted net national income per capita ($)	2,675	2,602	1,574
Change in wealth per capita (2010 $)	-63	101	117
Urban population (% of total)	43.7	59.5	38.9

Agriculture

Agricultural land (% land area)	4	23	46
Agricultural irrigated land (% of total agricultural land)	..	..	..
Agricultural productivity, value added per worker (2005 $)	2,408	2,642	938
Cereal yield (kg per hectare)	7,693	2,350	3,029

Forests and biodiversity

Forest area (% land area)	0.1	2.4	26.9
Deforestation (avg. annual %, 2000-2010)	-1.7	-0.1	0.3
Terrestrial protected areas (% of total land area)	11.2	6.1	11.9
Threatened species, mammals	18		
Threatened species, birds	10		
Threatened species, fish	40		
Threatened species, higher plants	2		

Oceans

Total fisheries production (thousand metric tons)	1,372	3,976	43,067
Capture fisheries growth (avg. annual %, 1990-2012)	1.6	3.0	2.6
Aquaculture growth (avg. annual %, 1990-2012)	13.6	12.8	9.9
Marine protected areas (% of territorial waters)	9.5	9.1	14.7
Coral reef area (sq. km)	3,800	5,700	124,480
Mangroves area (sq. km)	5.1	217	58,917

Energy and emissions

Energy use per capita (kg oil equivalent)	978	1,376	687
Energy from biomass products and waste (% of total)	2.1	0.9	26.8
Electric power consumption per capita (kWh)	1,743	1,696	734
Electricity generated using fossil fuel (% of total)	90.5	91.7	72.3
Electricity generated by hydropower (% of total)	8.3	5.5	16.9
CO_2 emissions per capita (metric tons)	2.6	3.9	1.6

Water and sanitation

Internal freshwater resources per capita (cu. m)	23	679	3,144
Total freshwater withdrawal (% of internal resources)	3,794.4	122.1	19.6
Agriculture (% of total freshwater withdrawal)	86	86	88
Access to improved water source (% of total population)	99	90	88
Rural (% of rural population)	99	83	85
Urban (% of urban population)	100	95	94
Access to improved sanitation facilities (% of total population)	96	88	48
Rural (% of rural population)	94	80	36
Urban (% of urban population)	98	94	66

Environment and health

Particulate matter (urban-pop.-weighted avg., µg/cu. m)	120	79	90
Acute resp. infection prevalence (% of children under five)	8	..	..
Diarrhea prevalence (% of children under five)	9	..	..
Under-five mortality rate (per 1,000 live births)	21	26	61

National accounting aggregates—savings, depletion and degradation

Gross savings (% of GNI)	13.4	25.9	28.6
Consumption of fixed capital (% of GNI)	7.2	9.9	11.1
Education expenditure (% of GNI)	4.4	4.5	3.1
Energy depletion (% of GNI)	8.0	12.9	4.4
Mineral depletion (% of GNI)	0.1	0.5	1.1
Net forest depletion (% of GNI)	0.5	0.2	0.8
CO_2 damage (% of GNI)	0.8	0.7	0.9
Particulate emissions damage (% of GNI)	1.2	0.9	1.4
Adjusted net savings (% of GNI)	0.0	5.3	12.0

El Salvador

	Country data	Latin America & Caribbean group	Lower middle-income group
Population (millions) **6.3** Land area (1,000 sq. km) **21** GDP ($ billions) **23.9**			

	Country data	Latin America & Caribbean group	Lower middle-income group
GNI per capita, *World Bank Atlas* method ($)	3,590	9,070	1,965
Adjusted net national income per capita ($)	3,461	7,325	1,574
Change in wealth per capita (2010 $)	221	180	117
Urban population (% of total)	65.2	79.0	38.9
Agriculture			
Agricultural land (% land area)	74	37	46
Agricultural irrigated land (% of total agricultural land)	2.1	..	..
Agricultural productivity, value added per worker (2005 $)	3,437	4,135	938
Cereal yield (kg per hectare)	2,782	4,082	3,029
Forests and biodiversity			
Forest area (% land area)	13.6	48.1	26.9
Deforestation (avg. annual %, 2000–2010)	1.5	0.5	0.3
Terrestrial protected areas (% of total land area)	8.4	21.4	11.9
Threatened species, mammals	6		
Threatened species, birds	6		
Threatened species, fish	14		
Threatened species, higher plants	29		
Oceans			
Total fisheries production (thousand metric tons)	57.3	10,964	43,067
Capture fisheries growth (avg. annual %, 1990–2012)	8.6	-0.6	2.6
Aquaculture growth (avg. annual %, 1990–2012)	10.2	10.8	9.9
Marine protected areas (% of territorial waters)	2.8	9.0	14.7
Coral reef area (sq. km)	..	14,860	124,480
Mangroves area (sq. km)	252	39,988	58,917
Energy and emissions			
Energy use per capita (kg oil equivalent)	690	1,292	687
Energy from biomass products and waste (% of total)	17.4	16.0	26.8
Electric power consumption per capita (kWh)	830	1,985	734
Electricity generated using fossil fuel (% of total)	34.1	37.3	72.3
Electricity generated by hydropower (% of total)	34.6	55.1	16.9
CO_2 emissions per capita (metric tons)	1.0	2.7	1.6
Water and sanitation			
Internal freshwater resources per capita (cu. m)	2,837	21,735	3,144
Total freshwater withdrawal (% of internal resources)	7.8	2.0	19.6
Agriculture (% of total freshwater withdrawal)	55	68	88
Access to improved water source (% of total population)	90	94	88
Rural (% of rural population)	81	82	85
Urban (% of urban population)	95	97	94
Access to improved sanitation facilities (% of total population)	70	81	48
Rural (% of rural population)	53	62	36
Urban (% of urban population)	80	86	66
Environment and health			
Particulate matter (urban-pop.-weighted avg., µg/cu. m)	46	43	90
Acute resp. infection prevalence (% of children under five)	..	..	..
Diarrhea prevalence (% of children under five)	..	..	..
Under-five mortality rate (per 1,000 live births)	16	19	61
National accounting aggregates—savings, depletion and degradation			
Gross savings (% of GNI)	9.3	19.0	28.6
Consumption of fixed capital (% of GNI)	3.5	12.2	11.1
Education expenditure (% of GNI)	3.2	5.1	3.1
Energy depletion (% of GNI)	0.0	4.7	4.4
Mineral depletion (% of GNI)	0.0	1.2	1.1
Net forest depletion (% of GNI)	1.5	0.4	0.8
CO_2 damage (% of GNI)	0.3	0.3	0.9
Particulate emissions damage (% of GNI)	0.6	0.8	1.4
Adjusted net savings (% of GNI)	6.6	4.5	12.0

Equatorial Guinea

Population (thousands) **736**	Land area (1,000 sq. km) **28**	GDP ($ billions) **17.7**

	Country data	High-Income group
GNI per capita, *World Bank Atlas* method ($)	13,560	38,444
Adjusted net national income per capita ($)	3,070	32,262
Change in wealth per capita (2010 $)	..	2,210
Urban population (% of total)	39.7	80.2

Agriculture
Agricultural land (% of land area)	11	29
Agricultural irrigated land (% of total agricultural land)	..	..
Agricultural productivity, value added per worker (2005 $)	2,024	25,238
Cereal yield (kg per hectare)	..	4,374

Forests and biodiversity
Forest area (% land area)	57.5	35.0
Deforestation (avg. annual %, 2000–2010)	0.7	0.0
Terrestrial protected areas (% of total land area)	20.6	13.9
Threatened species, mammals	19	
Threatened species, birds	6	
Threatened species, fish	29	
Threatened species, higher plants	68	

Oceans
Total fisheries production (thousand metric tons)	10.8	37,661
Capture fisheries growth (avg. annual %, 1990–2012)	5.0	-2.0
Aquaculture growth (avg. annual %, 1990–2012)	..	2.5
Marine protected areas (% of territorial waters)	2.6	14.4
Coral reef area (sq. km)	..	82,210
Mangroves area (sq. km)	253	15,504

Energy and emissions
Energy use per capita (kg oil equivalent)	2,750	4,872
Energy from biomass products and waste (% of total)	..	4.3
Electric power consumption per capita (kWh)	..	8,896
Electricity generated using fossil fuel (% of total)	..	61.8
Electricity generated by hydropower (% of total)	..	12.2
CO_2 emissions per capita (metric tons)	6.7	11.6

Water and sanitation
Internal freshwater resources per capita (cu. m)	36,313	11,335
Total freshwater withdrawal (% of internal resources)	0.1	7.0
Agriculture (% of total freshwater withdrawal)	6	40
Access to improved water source (% of total population)	..	99
Rural (% of rural population)	..	98
Urban (% of urban population)	..	100
Access to improved sanitation facilities (% of total population)	..	96
Rural (% of rural population)	..	93
Urban (% of urban population)	..	97

Environment and health
Particulate matter (urban-pop.-weighted avg., μg/cu. m)	21	27
Acute resp. infection prevalence (% of children under five)	..	..
Diarrhea prevalence (% of children under five)	..	
Under-five mortality rate (per 1,000 live births)	100	6

National accounting aggregates—savings, depletion and degradation
Gross savings (% of GNI)	..	20.1
Consumption of fixed capital (% of GNI)	24.2	14.2
Education expenditure (% of GNI)	1.0	4.7
Energy depletion (% of GNI)	55.4	1.6
Mineral depletion (% of GNI)	0.0	0.3
Net forest depletion (% of GNI)	0.0	0.0
CO_2 damage (% of GNI)	0.4	0.3
Particulate emissions damage (% of GNI)	0.1	0.3
Adjusted net savings (% of GNI)	..	8.1

Eritrea

Population (millions)	**6.1**	Land area (1,000 sq. km)	**101**	GDP ($ billions)	**3.1**

	Country data	Sub-Saharan Africa group	Low-Income group
GNI per capita, *World Bank Atlas* method ($)	450	1,547	594
Adjusted net national income per capita ($)	382	1,005	495
Change in wealth per capita (2010 $)	..	–273	–39
Urban population (% of total)	21.8	36.8	28.2

Agriculture

	Country data	Sub-Saharan Africa group	Low-Income group
Agricultural land (% land area)	75	44	39
Agricultural irrigated land (% of total agricultural land)	..	..	..
Agricultural productivity, value added per worker (2005 $)	106	765	367
Cereal yield (kg per hectare)	605	1,417	1,982

Forests and biodiversity

	Country data	Sub-Saharan Africa group	Low-Income group
Forest area (% land area)	15.1	27.4	27.4
Deforestation (avg. annual %, 2000–2010)	0.3	0.5	0.6
Terrestrial protected areas (% of total land area)	5.0	16.4	13.7
Threatened species, mammals	10		
Threatened species, birds	14		
Threatened species, fish	20		
Threatened species, higher plants	4		

Oceans

	Country data	Sub-Saharan Africa group	Low-Income group
Total fisheries production (thousand metric tons)	4.2	6,906	11,789
Capture fisheries growth (avg. annual %, 1990-2012)	..	2.1	3.8
Aquaculture growth (avg. annual %, 1990-2012)	..	15.9	5.1
Marine protected areas (% of territorial waters)	27.5	11.7	13.1
Coral reef area (sq. km)	3,260	17,980	15,120
Mangroves area (sq. km)	102	27,808	25,817

Energy and emissions

	Country data	Sub-Saharan Africa group	Low-Income group
Energy use per capita (kg oil equivalent)	129	681	360
Energy from biomass products and waste (% of total)	78.2	57.6	66.0
Electric power consumption per capita (kWh)	49	535	233
Electricity generated using fossil fuel (% of total)	99.4	65.1	30.9
Electricity generated by hydropower (% of total)	0.0	20.0	45.5
CO_2 emissions per capita (metric tons)	0.1	0.8	0.3

Water and sanitation

	Country data	Sub-Saharan Africa group	Low-Income group
Internal freshwater resources per capita (cu. m)	472	4,391	5,121
Total freshwater withdrawal (% of internal resources)	20.8	3.2	4.4
Agriculture (% of total freshwater withdrawal)	95	84	90
Access to improved water source (% of total population)	..	64	69
Rural (% of rural population)	..	53	61
Urban (% of urban population)	..	85	88
Access to improved sanitation facilities (% of total population)	..	30	37
Rural (% of rural population)	4	23	33
Urban (% of urban population)	..	41	46

Environment and health

	Country data	Sub-Saharan Africa group	Low-Income group
Particulate matter (urban-pop.-weighted avg., µg/cu. m)	77	77	74
Acute resp. infection prevalence (% of children under five)	..	5	6
Diarrhea prevalence (% of children under five)	..	14	14
Under-five mortality rate (per 1,000 live births)	52	98	82

National accounting aggregates—savings, depletion and degradation

	Country data	Sub-Saharan Africa group	Low-Income group
Gross savings (% of GNI)	..	26.3	24.6
Consumption of fixed capital (% of GNI)	11.6	13.0	11.8
Education expenditure (% of GNI)	1.7	3.4	3.2
Energy depletion (% of GNI)	0.0	10.3	1.4
Mineral depletion (% of GNI)	10.0	1.8	1.9
Net forest depletion (% of GNI)	2.0	1.8	4.4
CO_2 damage (% of GNI)	0.2	0.6	0.4
Particulate emissions damage (% of GNI)	0.4	1.2	1.0
Adjusted net savings (% of GNI)	..	0.9	7.0

Estonia

	Country data	High-Income group
Population (millions) 1.3	Land area (1,000 sq. km) 42	GDP ($ billions) 22.4

	Country data	High-Income group
GNI per capita, *World Bank Atlas* method ($)	16,310	38,444
Adjusted net national income per capita ($)	13,111	32,262
Change in wealth per capita (2010 $)	..	2,210
Urban population (% of total)	69.6	80.2
Agriculture		
Agricultural land (% land area)	22	29
Agricultural irrigated land (% of total agricultural land)	..	..
Agricultural productivity, value added per worker (2005 $)	9,771	*25,238*
Cereal yield (kg per hectare)	3,357	4,374
Forests and biodiversity		
Forest area (% land area)	52.1	35.0
Deforestation (avg. annual %, 2000–2010)	0.1	0.0
Terrestrial protected areas (% of total land area)	20.9	13.9
Threatened species, mammals	1	
Threatened species, birds	5	
Threatened species, fish	5	
Threatened species, higher plants	0	
Oceans		
Total fisheries production (thousand metric tons)	68.0	37,661
Capture fisheries growth (avg. annual %, 1990–2012)	-7.1	-2.0
Aquaculture growth (avg. annual %, 1990–2012)	-4.1	2.5
Marine protected areas (% of territorial waters)	*26.5*	*14.4*
Coral reef area (sq. km)	..	82,210
Mangroves area (sq. km)	..	15,504
Energy and emissions		
Energy use per capita (kg oil equivalent)	4,197	4,872
Energy from biomass products and waste (% of total)	14.2	4.3
Electric power consumption per capita (kWh)	6,279	8,896
Electricity generated using fossil fuel (% of total)	90.2	61.8
Electricity generated by hydropower (% of total)	0.2	12.2
CO_2 emissions per capita (metric tons)	13.7	11.6
Water and sanitation		
Internal freshwater resources per capita (cu. m)	9,521	11,335
Total freshwater withdrawal (% of internal resources)	14.1	7.0
Agriculture (% of total freshwater withdrawal)	0	40
Access to improved water source (% of total population)	99	99
Rural (% of rural population)	98	98
Urban (% of urban population)	100	100
Access to improved sanitation facilities (% of total population)	95	96
Rural (% of rural population)	94	93
Urban (% of urban population)	96	97
Environment and health		
Particulate matter (urban-pop.-weighted avg., µg/cu. m)	17	27
Acute resp. infection prevalence (% of children under five)	..	..
Diarrhea prevalence (% of children under five)	..	..
Under-five mortality rate (per 1,000 live births)	4	6
National accounting aggregates—savings, depletion and degradation		
Gross savings (% of GNI)	26.3	20.1
Consumption of fixed capital (% of GNI)	17.3	14.2
Education expenditure (% of GNI)	5.6	4.7
Energy depletion (% of GNI)	0.3	1.6
Mineral depletion (% of GNI)	0.0	0.3
Net forest depletion (% of GNI)	0.6	0.0
CO_2 damage (% of GNI)	1.0	0.3
Particulate emissions damage (% of GNI)	0.1	0.3
Adjusted net savings (% of GNI)	12.5	8.1

Ethiopia

	Country data	Sub-Saharan Africa group	Low-income group
Population (millions)	**91.7**		
Land area (1,000 sq. km)	**1,000**		
GDP ($ billions)	**41.7**		

	Country data	Sub-Saharan Africa group	Low-income group
GNI per capita, *World Bank Atlas* method ($)	380	1,547	594
Adjusted net national income per capita ($)	341	1,005	495
Urban population (% of total)	-67	-273	-39
Urban population growth (avg. annual %, 1990–2011)	17.3	36.8	28.2
Agriculture			
Agricultural land (% land area)	36	44	39
Agricultural irrigated land (% of total agricultural land)	0.5	..	..
Agricultural productivity, value added per worker (2000 $)	257	765	367
Cereal yield (kg per hectare)	1,970	1,417	1,982
Forests and biodiversity			
Forest area (% land area)	12.2	27.4	27.4
Deforestation (avg. annual %, 2000–2010)	1.1	0.5	0.6
Terrestrial protected areas (% of total land area)	18.4	16.4	13.7
Threatened species, mammals	33		
Threatened species, birds	26		
Threatened species, fish	14		
Threatened species, higher plants	28		
Oceans			
Total fisheries production (thousand metric tons)	29.0	6,906	11,789
Capture fisheries growth (avg. annual %, 1990–2011)	8.4	2.1	3.8
Aquaculture growth (avg. annual %, 1990–2011)	0.2	15.9	5.1
Marine protected areas (% of territorial waters)	0.76	11.7	13.1
Coral reef area (sq. km)	..	17,980	15,120
Mangroves area (sq. km)	..	27,808	25,817
Energy and emissions			
Energy use per capita (kg oil equivalent)	381	681	360
Energy from biomass products and waste (% of total)	92.9	57.6	66.0
Electric power consumption per capita (kWh)	52	535	233
Electricity generated using fossil fuel (% of total)	0.6	65.1	30.9
Electricity generated by hydropower (% of total)	99.0	20.0	45.5
CO_2 emissions per capita (metric tons)	0.1	0.8	0.3
Water and sanitation			
Internal freshwater resources per capita (cu. m)	1,365	4,391	5,121
Total freshwater withdrawal (% of internal resources)	4.6	3.2	4.4
Agriculture (% of total freshwater withdrawal)	94	84	90
Access to improved water source (% of total population)	52	64	69
Rural (% of rural population)	42	53	61
Urban (% of urban population)	97	85	88
Access to improved sanitation facilities (% of total population)	24	30	37
Rural (% of rural population)	23	23	33
Urban (% of urban population)	27	41	46
Environment and health			
Particulate matter (urban-pop.-weighted avg., µg/cu. m)	86	77	74
Acute resp. infection prevalence (% of children under five)	7	5	6
Diarrhea prevalence (% of children under five)	13	14	14
Under-five mortality rate (per 1,000 live births)	68	98	82
National accounting aggregates—savings, depletion and degradation			
Gross savings (% of GNI)	28.9	26.3	24.6
Consumption of fixed capital (% of GNI)	12.2	13.0	11.8
Education expenditure (% of GNI)	2.9	3.4	3.2
Energy depletion (% of GNI)	0.0	10.3	1.4
Mineral depletion (% of GNI)	0.8	1.8	1.9
Net forest depletion (% of GNI)	11.7	1.8	4.4
CO_2 damage (% of GNI)	0.2	0.6	0.4
Particulate emissions damage (% of GNI)	0.9	1.2	1.0
Adjusted net savings (% of GNI)	6.1	0.9	7.0

Faeroe Islands

Population (thousands)	**50**	Land area (1,000 sq. km)	**1.4**	GDP ($ billions)	**2.2**

	Country data	High-income group
GNI per capita, *World Bank Atlas* method ($)	..	38,444
Adjusted net national income per capita ($)	..	32,262
Urban population (% of total)	..	2,210
Urban population growth (avg. annual %, 1990–2011)	41.4	80.2

Agriculture

Agricultural land (% land area)	2	29
Agricultural irrigated land (% of total agricultural land)	..	..
Agricultural productivity, value added per worker (2000 $)	..	25,238
Cereal yield (kg per hectare)	..	4,374

Forests and biodiversity

Forest area (% land area)	0.1	35.0
Deforestation (avg. annual %, 2000–2010)	0.0	0.0
Terrestrial protected areas (% of total land area)	1.7	13.9
Threatened species, mammals	4	
Threatened species, birds	1	
Threatened species, fish	8	
Threatened species, higher plants	0	

Oceans

Total fisheries production (thousand metric tons)	437	37,661
Capture fisheries growth (avg. annual %, 1990–2011)	1.3	-2.0
Aquaculture growth (avg. annual %, 1990–2011)	8.4	2.5
Marine protected areas (% of territorial waters)	0.30	14.4
Coral reef area (sq. km)	..	82,210
Mangroves area (sq. km)	..	15,504

Energy and emissions

Energy use per capita (kg oil equivalent)	..	4,872
Energy from biomass products and waste (% of total)	..	4.3
Electric power consumption per capita (kWh)	..	8,896
Electricity generated using fossil fuel (% of total)	..	61.8
Electricity generated by hydropower (% of total)	..	12.2
CO_2 emissions per capita (metric tons)	14.3	11.6

Water and sanitation

Internal freshwater resources per capita (cu. m)	..	11,335
Total freshwater withdrawal (% of internal resources)	..	7.0
Agriculture (% of total freshwater withdrawal)	..	40
Access to improved water source (% of total population)	..	99
Rural (% of rural population)	..	98
Urban (% of urban population)	..	100
Access to improved sanitation facilities (% of total population)	..	96
Rural (% of rural population)	..	93
Urban (% of urban population)	..	97

Environment and health

Particulate matter (urban-pop.-weighted avg., µg/cu. m)	21	27
Acute resp. infection prevalence (% of children under five)	..	..
Diarrhea prevalence (% of children under five)	..	..
Under-five mortality rate (per 1,000 live births)	..	6

National accounting aggregates—savings, depletion and degradation

Gross savings (% of GNI)	..	20.1
Consumption of fixed capital (% of GNI)	..	14.2
Education expenditure (% of GNI)	..	4.7
Energy depletion (% of GNI)	0.0	1.6
Mineral depletion (% of GNI)	0.0	0.3
Net forest depletion (% of GNI)	0.0	0.0
CO_2 damage (% of GNI)	0.3	0.3
Particulate emissions damage (% of GNI)	..	0.3
Adjusted net savings (% of GNI)	..	8.1

Fiji

Population (thousands) **875** Land area (1,000 sq. km) **18** GDP ($ billions) **3.9**

	Country data	East Asia & Pacific group	Upper middle-income group
GNI per capita, *World Bank Atlas* method ($)	4,110	4,884	6,969
Adjusted net national income per capita ($)	3,688	4,305	5,845
Change in wealth per capita (2010 $)	–96	1,172	1,039
Urban population (% of total)	52.6	49.6	60.7
Agriculture			
Agricultural land (% land area)	23	48	44
Agricultural irrigated land (% of total agricultural land)	..	..	..
Agricultural productivity, value added per worker (2005 $)	2,778	794	1,131
Cereal yield (kg per hectare)	3,160	5,145	4,255
Forests and biodiversity			
Forest area (% land area)	55.7	29.7	29.1
Deforestation (avg. annual %, 2000–2010)	–0.3	–0.4	0.0
Terrestrial protected areas (% of total land area)	4.3	15.1	16.1
Threatened species, mammals	6		
Threatened species, birds	14		
Threatened species, fish	13		
Threatened species, higher plants	65		
Oceans			
Total fisheries production (thousand metric tons)	46.0	108,399	90,024
Capture fisheries growth (avg. annual %, 1990–2012)	1.4	3.4	1.5
Aquaculture growth (avg. annual %, 1990–2012)	–9.5	9.1	9.1
Marine protected areas (% of territorial waters)	15.6	1.4	7.3
Coral reef area (sq. km)	10,020	137,690	52,070
Mangroves area (sq. km)	425	56,537	50,160
Energy and emissions			
Energy use per capita (kg oil equivalent)	627	1,671	1,893
Energy from biomass products and waste (% of total)	..	10.1	8.5
Electric power consumption per capita (kWh)	..	2,582	2,932
Electricity generated using fossil fuel (% of total)	..	80.9	74.7
Electricity generated by hydropower (% of total)	..	14.5	20.0
CO_2 emissions per capita (metric tons)	1.5	4.9	5.4
Water and sanitation			
Internal freshwater resources per capita (cu. m)	32,895	4,438	6,791
Total freshwater withdrawal (% of internal resources)	0.3	10.9	7.4
Agriculture (% of total freshwater withdrawal)	61	73	69
Access to improved water source (% of total population)	96	91	93
Rural (% of rural population)	92	85	85
Urban (% of urban population)	100	97	98
Access to improved sanitation facilities (% of total population)	87	67	74
Rural (% of rural population)	82	58	62
Urban (% of urban population)	92	76	82
Environment and health			
Particulate matter (urban-pop.-weighted avg., µg/cu. m)	27	75	65
Acute resp. infection prevalence (% of children under five)	..	..	..
Diarrhea prevalence (% of children under five)	..	..	..
Under-five mortality rate (per 1,000 live births)	22	21	20
National accounting aggregates—savings, depletion and degradation			
Gross savings (% of GNI)	10.1	47.6	36.4
Consumption of fixed capital (% of GNI)	12.3	12.0	12.5
Education expenditure (% of GNI)	4.2	2.1	3.2
Energy depletion (% of GNI)	0.0	2.7	4.1
Mineral depletion (% of GNI)	1.8	1.4	1.2
Net forest depletion (% of GNI)	0.0	0.1	0.2
CO_2 damage (% of GNI)	0.4	1.0	0.8
Particulate emissions damage (% of GNI)	0.4	1.6	1.3
Adjusted net savings (% of GNI)	3.1	30.9	19.5

Finland

Population (millions)	**5.4**	Land area (1,000 sq. km)	**304**	GDP ($ billions)	**247.4**

	Country data	High-income group
GNI per capita, *World Bank Atlas* method ($)	46,590	38,444
Adjusted net national income per capita ($)	38,100	32,262
Change in wealth per capita (2010 $)	3,926	2,210
Urban population (% of total)	83.8	80.2

Agriculture

Agricultural land (% land area)	8	29
Agricultural irrigated land (% of total agricultural land)	0.6	..
Agricultural productivity, value added per worker (2005 $)	56,998	*25,238*
Cereal yield (kg per hectare)	3,533	4,374

Forests and biodiversity

Forest area (% land area)	72.9	35.0
Deforestation (avg. annual %, 2000–2010)	0.1	0.0
Terrestrial protected areas (% of total land area)	15.1	13.9
Threatened species, mammals	1	
Threatened species, birds	6	
Threatened species, fish	6	
Threatened species, higher plants	2	

Oceans

Total fisheries production (thousand metric tons)	180	37,661
Capture fisheries growth (avg. annual %, 1990–2012)	1.0	-2.0
Aquaculture growth (avg. annual %, 1990–2012)	-1.7	2.5
Marine protected areas (% of territorial waters)	58.5	*14.4*
Coral reef area (sq. km)	..	82,210
Mangroves area (sq. km)	..	15,504

Energy and emissions

Energy use per capita (kg oil equivalent)	6,449	4,872
Energy from biomass products and waste (% of total)	23.3	4.3
Electric power consumption per capita (kWh)	15,738	8,896
Electricity generated using fossil fuel (% of total)	27.4	61.8
Electricity generated by hydropower (% of total)	16.9	12.2
CO_2 emissions per capita (metric tons)	11.5	11.6

Water and sanitation

Internal freshwater resources per capita (cu. m)	19,858	11,335
Total freshwater withdrawal (% of internal resources)	1.5	7.0
Agriculture (% of total freshwater withdrawal)	3	40
Access to improved water source (% of total population)	100	99
Rural (% of rural population)	100	98
Urban (% of urban population)	100	100
Access to improved sanitation facilities (% of total population)	100	96
Rural (% of rural population)	100	93
Urban (% of urban population)	100	97

Environment and health

Particulate matter (urban-pop.-weighted avg., µg/cu. m)	16	27
Acute resp. infection prevalence (% of children under five)	..	..
Diarrhea prevalence (% of children under five)	..	..
Under-five mortality rate (per 1,000 live births)	3	6

National accounting aggregates—savings, depletion and degradation

Gross savings (% of GNI)	18.1	20.1
Consumption of fixed capital (% of GNI)	16.4	14.2
Education expenditure (% of GNI)	6.3	4.7
Energy depletion (% of GNI)	0.0	1.6
Mineral depletion (% of GNI)	0.2	0.3
Net forest depletion (% of GNI)	0.0	0.0
CO_2 damage (% of GNI)	0.2	0.3
Particulate emissions damage (% of GNI)	0.0	0.3
Adjusted net savings (% of GNI)	7.6	8.1

France

	Population (millions) **65.7**	Land area (1,000 sq. km)	**548** GDP ($ billions) **2,611.2**

	Country data	High-income group
GNI per capita, *World Bank Atlas* method ($)	41,850	38,444
Adjusted net national income per capita ($)	35,517	32,262
Change in wealth per capita (2010 $)	2,943	2,210
Urban population (% of total)	86.3	80.2

Agriculture
Agricultural land (% land area)	53	29
Agricultural irrigated land (% of total agricultural land)	5.1	..
Agricultural productivity, value added per worker (2005 $)	75,178	25,238
Cereal yield (kg per hectare)	7,524	4,374

Forests and biodiversity
Forest area (% land area)	29.2	35.0
Deforestation (avg. annual %, 2000–2010)	-0.4	0.0
Terrestrial protected areas (% of total land area)	24.7	13.9
Threatened species, mammals	8	
Threatened species, birds	9	
Threatened species, fish	46	
Threatened species, higher plants	32	

Oceans
Total fisheries production (thousand metric tons)	673	37,661
Capture fisheries growth (avg. annual %, 1990–2012)	-1.8	-2.0
Aquaculture growth (avg. annual %, 1990–2012)	-1.0	2.5
Marine protected areas (% of territorial waters)	12.1	14.4
Coral reef area (sq. km)	..	82,210
Mangroves area (sq. km)	..	15,504

Energy and emissions
Energy use per capita (kg oil equivalent)	3,868	4,872
Energy from biomass products and waste (% of total)	5.6	4.3
Electric power consumption per capita (kWh)	7,289	8,896
Electricity generated using fossil fuel (% of total)	8.5	61.8
Electricity generated by hydropower (% of total)	8.0	12.2
CO_2 emissions per capita (metric tons)	5.6	11.6

Water and sanitation
Internal freshwater resources per capita (cu. m)	3,059	11,335
Total freshwater withdrawal (% of internal resources)	15.8	7.0
Agriculture (% of total freshwater withdrawal)	12	40
Access to improved water source (% of total population)	100	99
Rural (% of rural population)	100	98
Urban (% of urban population)	100	100
Access to improved sanitation facilities (% of total population)	100	96
Rural (% of rural population)	100	93
Urban (% of urban population)	100	97

Environment and health
Particulate matter (urban-pop.-weighted avg., µg/cu. m)	24	27
Acute resp. infection prevalence (% of children under five)	..	..
Diarrhea prevalence (% of children under five)	..	..
Under-five mortality rate (per 1,000 live births)	4	6

National accounting aggregates—savings, depletion and degradation
Gross savings (% of GNI)	17.2	20.1
Consumption of fixed capital (% of GNI)	12.2	14.2
Education expenditure (% of GNI)	5.3	4.7
Energy depletion (% of GNI)	0.0	1.6
Mineral depletion (% of GNI)	0.0	0.3
Net forest depletion (% of GNI)	0.0	0.0
CO_2 damage (% of GNI)	0.1	0.3
Particulate emissions damage (% of GNI)	0.2	0.3
Adjusted net savings (% of GNI)	9.9	8.1

French Polynesia

Population (thousands) **274**   Land area (1,000 sq. km)   **3.7** GDP ($ millions)   ..

	Country data	High-income group
GNI per capita, *World Bank Atlas* method ($)	..	38,444
Adjusted net national income per capita ($)	..	32,262
Change in wealth per capita (2010 $)	..	2,210
Urban population (% of total)	51.4	80.2

Agriculture
Agricultural land (% land area)	12	29
Agricultural irrigated land (% of total agricultural land)	..	..
Agricultural productivity, value added per worker (2005 $)	..	*25,238*
Cereal yield (kg per hectare)	..	4,374

Forests and biodiversity
Forest area (% land area)	43.7	35.0
Deforestation (avg. annual %, 2000–2010)	-4.0	0.0
Terrestrial protected areas (% of total land area)	2.0	13.9
Threatened species, mammals	0	
Threatened species, birds	33	
Threatened species, fish	27	
Threatened species, higher plants	47	

Oceans
Total fisheries production (thousand metric tons)	16.8	37,661
Capture fisheries growth (avg. annual %, 1990–2012)	5.7	-2.0
Aquaculture growth (avg. annual %, 1990–2012)	16.7	2.5
Marine protected areas (% of territorial waters)	8.9	*14.4*
Coral reef area (sq. km)	6,000	82,210
Mangroves area (sq. km)	..	15,504

Energy and emissions
Energy use per capita (kg oil equivalent)	..	4,872
Energy from biomass products and waste (% of total)	..	4.3
Electric power consumption per capita (kWh)	..	8,896
Electricity generated using fossil fuel (% of total)	..	61.8
Electricity generated by hydropower (% of total)	..	12.2
CO_2 emissions per capita (metric tons)	3.3	11.6

Water and sanitation
Internal freshwater resources per capita (cu. m)	*38,408*	11,335
Total freshwater withdrawal (% of internal resources)	..	7.0
Agriculture (% of total freshwater withdrawal)	..	40
Access to improved water source (% of total population)	100	99
Rural (% of rural population)	100	98
Urban (% of urban population)	100	100
Access to improved sanitation facilities (% of total population)	97	96
Rural (% of rural population)	97	93
Urban (% of urban population)	97	97

Environment and health
Particulate matter (urban-pop.-weighted avg., μg/cu. m)	..	27
Acute resp. infection prevalence (% of children under five)	..	..
Diarrhea prevalence (% of children under five)	..	..
Under-five mortality rate (per 1,000 live births)	..	6

National accounting aggregates—savings, depletion and degradation
Gross savings (% of GNI)	..	20.1
Consumption of fixed capital (% of GNI)	..	14.2
Education expenditure (% of GNI)	..	4.7
Energy depletion (% of GNI)	..	1.6
Mineral depletion (% of GNI)	..	0.3
Net forest depletion (% of GNI)	..	0.0
CO_2 damage (% of GNI)	..	0.3
Particulate emissions damage (% of GNI)	..	0.3
Adjusted net savings (% of GNI)	..	8.1

Gabon

| Population (millions) | **1.6** | Land area (1,000 sq. km) | **258** | GDP ($ billions) | **18.4** |

	Country data	Sub-Saharan Africa group	Upper middle-income group
GNI per capita, *World Bank Atlas* method ($)	10,040	1,547	6,969
Adjusted net national income per capita ($)	5,266	1,005	5,845
Change in wealth per capita (2010 $)	-2,726	-273	1,039
Urban population (% of total)	86.5	36.8	60.7
Agriculture			
Agricultural land (% land area)	20	44	44
Agricultural irrigated land (% of total agricultural land)	..	..	..
Agricultural productivity, value added per worker (2005 $)	2,577	765	1,131
Cereal yield (kg per hectare)	1,685	1,417	4,255
Forests and biodiversity			
Forest area (% land area)	85.4	27.4	29.1
Deforestation (avg. annual %, 2000–2010)	0.0	0.5	0.0
Terrestrial protected areas (% of total land area)	19.9	16.4	16.1
Threatened species, mammals	15		
Threatened species, birds	5		
Threatened species, fish	62		
Threatened species, higher plants	120		
Oceans			
Total fisheries production (thousand metric tons)	32.2	6,906	90,024
Capture fisheries growth (avg. annual %, 1990–2012)	2.2	2.1	1.5
Aquaculture growth (avg. annual %, 1990–2012)	22.0	15.9	9.1
Marine protected areas (% of territorial waters)	2.4	11.7	7.3
Coral reef area (sq. km)	..	17,980	52,070
Mangroves area (sq. km)	1,598	27,808	50,160
Energy and emissions			
Energy use per capita (kg oil equivalent)	1,253	681	1,893
Energy from biomass products and waste (% of total)	57.7	57.6	8.5
Electric power consumption per capita (kWh)	907	535	2,932
Electricity generated using fossil fuel (% of total)	53.8	65.1	74.7
Electricity generated by hydropower (% of total)	45.7	20.0	20.0
CO_2 emissions per capita (metric tons)	1.7	0.8	5.4
Water and sanitation			
Internal freshwater resources per capita (cu. m)	102,884	4,391	6,791
Total freshwater withdrawal (% of internal resources)	0.1	3.2	7.4
Agriculture (% of total freshwater withdrawal)	38	84	69
Access to improved water source (% of total population)	92	64	93
Rural (% of rural population)	63	53	85
Urban (% of urban population)	97	85	98
Access to improved sanitation facilities (% of total population)	41	30	74
Rural (% of rural population)	32	23	62
Urban (% of urban population)	43	41	82
Environment and health			
Particulate matter (urban-pop.-weighted avg., µg/cu. m)	12	77	65
Acute resp. infection prevalence (% of children under five)	8	5	..
Diarrhea prevalence (% of children under five)	16	14	..
Under-five mortality rate (per 1,000 live births)	62	98	20
National accounting aggregates—savings, depletion and degradation			
Gross savings (% of GNI)	..	26.3	36.4
Consumption of fixed capital (% of GNI)	16.3	13.0	12.5
Education expenditure (% of GNI)	3.1	3.4	3.2
Energy depletion (% of GNI)	31.3	10.3	4.1
Mineral depletion (% of GNI)	0.1	1.8	1.2
Net forest depletion (% of GNI)	0.0	1.8	0.2
CO_2 damage (% of GNI)	0.2	0.6	0.8
Particulate emissions damage (% of GNI)	0.0	1.2	1.3
Adjusted net savings (% of GNI)	..	0.9	19.5

Gambia, The

| Population (millions) | 1.8 | Land area (1,000 sq. km) | 10 | GDP ($ millions) | 907.4 |

	Country data	Sub-Saharan Africa group	Low-Income group
GNI per capita, *World Bank Atlas* method ($)	.510	1,547	594
Adjusted net national income per capita ($)	398	1,005	495
Change in wealth per capita (2010 $)	-69	-273	-39
Urban population (% of total)	57.8	36.8	28.2
Agriculture			
Agricultural land (% land area)	61	44	39
Agricultural irrigated land (% of total agricultural land)	..	..	..
Agricultural productivity, value added per worker (2005 $)	249	765	367
Cereal yield (kg per hectare)	1,024	1,417	1,982
Forests and biodiversity			
Forest area (% land area)	47.6	27.4	27.4
Deforestation (avg. annual %, 2000-2010)	-0.4	0.5	0.6
Terrestrial protected areas (% of total land area)	4.8	16.4	13.7
Threatened species, mammals	10		
Threatened species, birds	10		
Threatened species, fish	24		
Threatened species, higher plants	5		
Oceans			
Total fisheries production (thousand metric tons)	36.1	6,906	11,789
Capture fisheries growth (avg. annual %, 1990-2012)	2.4	2.1	3.8
Aquaculture growth (avg. annual %, 1990-2012)	-2.7	15.9	5.1
Marine protected areas (% of territorial waters)	0.89	11.7	13.1
Coral reef area (sq. km)	..	17,980	15,120
Mangroves area (sq. km)	581	27,808	25,817
Energy and emissions			
Energy use per capita (kg oil equivalent)	87	681	360
Energy from biomass products and waste (% of total)	..	57.6	66.0
Electric power consumption per capita (kWh)	..	535	233
Electricity generated using fossil fuel (% of total)	..	65.1	30.9
Electricity generated by hydropower (% of total)	..	20.0	45.5
CO_2 emissions per capita (metric tons)	0.3	0.8	0.3
Water and sanitation			
Internal freshwater resources per capita (cu. m)	1,729	4,391	5,121
Total freshwater withdrawal (% of internal resources)	2.4	3.2	4.4
Agriculture (% of total freshwater withdrawal)	28	84	90
Access to improved water source (% of total population)	90	64	69
Rural (% of rural population)	84	53	61
Urban (% of urban population)	94	85	88
Access to improved sanitation facilities (% of total population)	60	30	37
Rural (% of rural population)	55	23	33
Urban (% of urban population)	64	41	46
Environment and health			
Particulate matter (urban-pop.-weighted avg., µg/cu. m)	39	77	74
Acute resp. infection prevalence (% of children under five)	..	5	6
Diarrhea prevalence (% of children under five)	..	14	14
Under-five mortality rate (per 1,000 live births)	73	98	82
National accounting aggregates—savings, depletion and degradation			
Gross savings (% of GNI)	17.8	26.3	24.6
Consumption of fixed capital (% of GNI)	13.1	13.0	11.8
Education expenditure (% of GNI)	2.5	3.4	3.2
Energy depletion (% of GNI)	0.0	10.3	1.4
Mineral depletion (% of GNI)	0.0	1.8	1.9
Net forest depletion (% of GNI)	5.2	1.8	4.4
CO_2 damage (% of GNI)	0.6	0.6	0.4
Particulate emissions damage (% of GNI)	0.6	1.2	1.0
Adjusted net savings (% of GNI)	0.9	0.9	7.0

Georgia

	Country data	Europe & Central Asia group	Lower middle-income group
Population (millions) **4.5**	Land area (1,000 sq. km) **69**	GDP ($ billions) **15.7**	
GNI per capita, *World Bank Atlas* method ($)	3,290	6,658	1,965
Adjusted net national income per capita ($)	3,065	5,541	1,574
Change in wealth per capita (2010 $)	-13	263	117
Urban population (% of total)	53.0	60.2	38.9

Agriculture

Agricultural land (% land area)	36	66	46
Agricultural irrigated land (% of total agricultural land)	4.0	..	..
Agricultural productivity, value added per worker (2005 $)	2,512	4,866	938
Cereal yield (kg per hectare)	2,195	2,519	3,029

Forests and biodiversity

Forest area (% land area)	39.4	10.5	26.9
Deforestation (avg. annual %, 2000-2010)	0.1	-0.5	0.3
Terrestrial protected areas (% of total land area)	3.9	5.1	11.9
Threatened species, mammals	10		
Threatened species, birds	11		
Threatened species, fish	9		
Threatened species, higher plants	0		

Oceans

Total fisheries production (thousand metric tons)	12.7	1,022	43,067
Capture fisheries growth (avg. annual %, 1990-2012)	-9.3	-4.0	2.6
Aquaculture growth (avg. annual %, 1990-2012)	0.3	1.8	9.9
Marine protected areas (% of territorial waters)	64.5	10.4	14.7
Coral reef area (sq. km)	..	..	124,480
Mangroves area (sq. km)	..	..	58,917

Energy and emissions

Energy use per capita (kg oil equivalent)	790	2,078	687
Energy from biomass products and waste (% of total)	8.9	2.9	26.8
Electric power consumption per capita (kWh)	1,918	2,951	734
Electricity generated using fossil fuel (% of total)	22.6	65.8	72.3
Electricity generated by hydropower (% of total)	77.4	17.9	16.9
CO_2 emissions per capita (metric tons)	1.4	5.3	1.6

Water and sanitation

Internal freshwater resources per capita (cu. m)	12,966	2,744	3,144
Total freshwater withdrawal (% of internal resources)	3.1	34.8	19.6
Agriculture (% of total freshwater withdrawal)	58	70	88
Access to improved water source (% of total population)	99	95	88
Rural (% of rural population)	97	89	85
Urban (% of urban population)	100	99	94
Access to improved sanitation facilities (% of total population)	93	94	48
Rural (% of rural population)	91	90	36
Urban (% of urban population)	96	97	66

Environment and health

Particulate matter (urban-pop.-weighted avg., µg/cu. m)	35	48	90
Acute resp. infection prevalence (% of children under five)	..	..	..
Diarrhea prevalence (% of children under five)	..	..	..
Under-five mortality rate (per 1,000 live births)	20	22	61

National accounting aggregates—savings, depletion and degradation

Gross savings (% of GNI)	18.5	18.9	28.6
Consumption of fixed capital (% of GNI)	11.3	12.4	11.1
Education expenditure (% of GNI)	1.8	3.8	3.1
Energy depletion (% of GNI)	0.1	4.4	4.4
Mineral depletion (% of GNI)	0.2	0.6	1.1
Net forest depletion (% of GNI)	0.4	0.0	0.8
CO_2 damage (% of GNI)	0.4	0.8	0.9
Particulate emissions damage (% of GNI)	0.8	1.8	1.4
Adjusted net savings (% of GNI)	7.0	2.8	12.0

Germany

Population (millions)	**80.4**	Land area (1,000 sq. km)	**349**	GDP ($ billions) **3,425.9**

	Country data	High-income group
GNI per capita, *World Bank Atlas* method ($)	45,170	38,444
Adjusted net national income per capita ($)	38,343	32,262
Change in wealth per capita (2010 $)	5,510	2,210
Urban population (% of total)	74.1	80.2

Agriculture

Agricultural land (% land area)	48	29
Agricultural irrigated land (% of total agricultural land)	2.2	..
Agricultural productivity, value added per worker (2005 $)	31,641	*25,238*
Cereal yield (kg per hectare)	6,900	4,374

Forests and biodiversity

Forest area (% land area)	31.8	35.0
Deforestation (avg. annual %, 2000–2010)	0.0	0.0
Terrestrial protected areas (% of total land area)	48.0	13.9
Threatened species, mammals	5	
Threatened species, birds	7	
Threatened species, fish	23	
Threatened species, higher plants	17	

Oceans

Total fisheries production (thousand metric tons)	234	37,661
Capture fisheries growth (avg. annual %, 1990–2012)	–2.0	–2.0
Aquaculture growth (avg. annual %, 1990–2012)	–4.0	2.5
Marine protected areas (% of territorial waters)	1.7	*14.4*
Coral reef area (sq. km)	..	82,210
Mangroves area (sq. km)	..	15,504

Energy and emissions

Energy use per capita (kg oil equivalent)	3,811	4,872
Energy from biomass products and waste (% of total)	8.5	4.3
Electric power consumption per capita (kWh)	7,081	8,896
Electricity generated using fossil fuel (% of total)	60.1	61.8
Electricity generated by hydropower (% of total)	2.9	12.2
CO_2 emissions per capita (metric tons)	9.1	11.6

Water and sanitation

Internal freshwater resources per capita (cu. m)	1,308	11,335
Total freshwater withdrawal (% of internal resources)	30.2	7.0
Agriculture (% of total freshwater withdrawal)	0	40
Access to improved water source (% of total population)	100	99
Rural (% of rural population)	100	98
Urban (% of urban population)	100	100
Access to improved sanitation facilities (% of total population)	100	96
Rural (% of rural population)	100	93
Urban (% of urban population)	100	97

Environment and health

Particulate matter (urban-pop.-weighted avg., µg/cu. m)	24	27
Acute resp. infection prevalence (% of children under five)	..	..
Diarrhea prevalence (% of children under five)	..	..
Under-five mortality rate (per 1,000 live births)	4	6

National accounting aggregates—savings, depletion and degradation

Gross savings (% of GNI)	23.6	20.1
Consumption of fixed capital (% of GNI)	12.1	14.2
Education expenditure (% of GNI)	4.8	4.7
Energy depletion (% of GNI)	0.1	1.6
Mineral depletion (% of GNI)	0.0	0.3
Net forest depletion (% of GNI)	0.0	0.0
CO_2 damage (% of GNI)	0.2	0.3
Particulate emissions damage (% of GNI)	0.3	0.3
Adjusted net savings (% of GNI)	15.8	8.1

Ghana

Population (millions)	**25.4**	Land area (1,000 sq. km)	**228**	GDP ($ billions)	**40.7**

	Country data	Sub-Saharan Africa group	Lower-Income group
GNI per capita, *World Bank Atlas* method ($)	1,550	1,547	1,965
Adjusted net national income per capita ($)	1,110	1,005	1,574
Change in wealth per capita (2010 $)	-196	-273	117
Urban population (% of total)	52.5	36.8	38.9
Agriculture			
Agricultural land (% land area)	70	44	46
Agricultural irrigated land (% of total agricultural land)	0.2	..	..
Agricultural productivity, value added per worker (2005 $)	..	765	938
Cereal yield (kg per hectare)	1,768	1,417	3,029
Forests and biodiversity			
Forest area (% land area)	21.2	27.4	26.9
Deforestation (avg. annual %, 2000–2010)	2.1	0.5	0.3
Terrestrial protected areas (% of total land area)	15.1	16.4	11.9
Threatened species, mammals	16		
Threatened species, birds	17		
Threatened species, fish	45		
Threatened species, higher plants	117		
Oceans			
Total fisheries production (thousand metric tons)	392	6,906	43,067
Capture fisheries growth (avg. annual %, 1990–2012)	-0.4	2.1	2.6
Aquaculture growth (avg. annual %, 1990–2012)	21.8	15.9	9.9
Marine protected areas (% of territorial waters)	54.3	11.7	14.7
Coral reef area (sq. km)	..	17,980	124,480
Mangroves area (sq. km)	137	27,808	58,917
Energy and emissions			
Energy use per capita (kg oil equivalent)	425	681	687
Energy from biomass products and waste (% of total)	57.0	57.6	26.8
Electric power consumption per capita (kWh)	344	535	734
Electricity generated using fossil fuel (% of total)	24.3	65.1	72.3
Electricity generated by hydropower (% of total)	67.5	20.0	16.9
CO_2 emissions per capita (metric tons)	0.4	0.8	1.6
Water and sanitation			
Internal freshwater resources per capita (cu. m)	1,221	4,391	3,144
Total freshwater withdrawal (% of internal resources)	3.2	3.2	19.6
Agriculture (% of total freshwater withdrawal)	66	84	88
Access to improved water source (% of total population)	87	64	88
Rural (% of rural population)	81	53	85
Urban (% of urban population)	93	85	94
Access to improved sanitation facilities (% of total population)	14	30	48
Rural (% of rural population)	8	23	36
Urban (% of urban population)	20	41	66
Environment and health			
Particulate matter (urban-pop.-weighted avg., µg/cu. m)	82	77	90
Acute resp. infection prevalence (% of children under five)	6	5	..
Diarrhea prevalence (% of children under five)	20	14	..
Under-five mortality rate (per 1,000 live births)	72	98	61
National accounting aggregates—savings, depletion and degradation			
Gross savings (% of GNI)	22.7	26.3	28.6
Consumption of fixed capital (% of GNI)	12.0	13.0	11.1
Education expenditure (% of GNI)	8.2	3.4	3.1
Energy depletion (% of GNI)	3.7	10.3	4.4
Mineral depletion (% of GNI)	6.0	1.8	1.1
Net forest depletion (% of GNI)	5.3	1.8	0.8
CO_2 damage (% of GNI)	0.3	0.6	0.9
Particulate emissions damage (% of GNI)	1.0	1.2	1.4
Adjusted net savings (% of GNI)	2.7	0.9	12.0

Greece

| | Population (millions) | **11.1** | Land area (1,000 sq. km) | **129** | GDP ($ billions) | **248.9** |

	Country data	High-income group
GNI per capita, World Bank Atlas method ($)	23,710	38,444
Adjusted net national income per capita ($)	18,878	32,262
Change in wealth per capita (2010 $)	-2,005	2,210
Urban population (% of total)	61.7	80.2
Agriculture		
Agricultural land (% land area)	63	29
Agricultural irrigated land (% of total agricultural land)	16.9	..
Agricultural productivity, value added per worker (2005 $)	14,169	25,238
Cereal yield (kg per hectare)	4,668	4,374
Forests and biodiversity		
Forest area (% land area)	30.5	35.0
Deforestation (avg. annual %, 2000-2010)	-0.8	0.0
Terrestrial protected areas (% of total land area)	34.7	13.9
Threatened species, mammals	10	
Threatened species, birds	12	
Threatened species, fish	75	
Threatened species, higher plants	57	
Oceans		
Total fisheries production (thousand metric tons)	198	37,661
Capture fisheries growth (avg. annual %, 1990-2012)	-3.5	-2.0
Aquaculture growth (avg. annual %, 1990-2012)	12.9	2.5
Marine protected areas (% of territorial waters)	36.7	14.4
Coral reef area (sq. km)	..	82,210
Mangroves area (sq. km)	..	15,504
Energy and emissions		
Energy use per capita (kg oil equivalent)	2,402	4,872
Energy from biomass products and waste (% of total)	4.7	4.3
Electric power consumption per capita (kWh)	5,380	8,896
Electricity generated using fossil fuel (% of total)	86.0	61.8
Electricity generated by hydropower (% of total)	6.8	12.2
CO_2 emissions per capita (metric tons)	7.7	11.6
Water and sanitation		
Internal freshwater resources per capita (cu. m)	5,214	11,335
Total freshwater withdrawal (% of internal resources)	16.3	7.0
Agriculture (% of total freshwater withdrawal)	89	40
Access to improved water source (% of total population)	100	99
Rural (% of rural population)	99	98
Urban (% of urban population)	100	100
Access to improved sanitation facilities (% of total population)	99	96
Rural (% of rural population)	97	93
Urban (% of urban population)	99	97
Environment and health		
Particulate matter (urban-pop.-weighted avg., µg/cu. m)	35	27
Acute resp. infection prevalence (% of children under five)	..	..
Diarrhea prevalence (% of children under five)	..	..
Under-five mortality rate (per 1,000 live births)	5	6
National accounting aggregates—savings, depletion and degradation		
Gross savings (% of GNI)	9.8	20.1
Consumption of fixed capital (% of GNI)	16.2	14.2
Education expenditure (% of GNI)	3.2	4.7
Energy depletion (% of GNI)	0.0	1.6
Mineral depletion (% of GNI)	0.1	0.3
Net forest depletion (% of GNI)	0.0	0.0
CO_2 damage (% of GNI)	0.3	0.3
Particulate emissions damage (% of GNI)	0.7	0.3
Adjusted net savings (% of GNI)	-4.4	8.1

Greenland

Population (thousands) **57** Land area (1,000 sq. km) **410ᵇ** GDP ($ billions) *1.3*

	Country data	High-income group
GNI per capita, *World Bank Atlas* method ($)	*26,020*	38,444
Adjusted net national income per capita ($)	*17,691*	32,262
Change in wealth per capita (2010 $)	..	2,210
Urban population (% of total)	84.9	80.2
Agriculture		
Agricultural land (% land area)	1	29
Agricultural irrigated land (% of total agricultural land)	..	..
Agricultural productivity, value added per worker (2005 $)	..	*25,238*
Cereal yield (kg per hectare)	..	4,374
Forests and biodiversity		
Forest area (% land area)	0.0	35.0
Deforestation (avg. annual %, 2000–2010)	0.0	0.0
Terrestrial protected areas (% of total land area)	41.1	13.9
Threatened species, mammals	7	
Threatened species, birds	1	
Threatened species, fish	7	
Threatened species, higher plants	1	
Oceans		
Total fisheries production (thousand metric tons)	223	37,661
Capture fisheries growth (avg. annual %, 1990–2012)	2.0	-2.0
Aquaculture growth (avg. annual %, 1990–2012)	..	2.5
Marine protected areas (% of territorial waters)	0.09	*14.4*
Coral reef area (sq. km)	..	82,210
Mangroves area (sq. km)	..	15,504
Energy and emissions		
Energy use per capita (kg oil equivalent)	..	4,872
Energy from biomass products and waste (% of total)	..	4.3
Electric power consumption per capita (kWh)	..	8,896
Electricity generated using fossil fuel (% of total)	..	61.8
Electricity generated by hydropower (% of total)	..	12.2
CO_2 emissions per capita (metric tons)	11.1	11.6
Water and sanitation		
Internal freshwater resources per capita (cu. m)	*10,662,187*	11,335
Total freshwater withdrawal (% of internal resources)	..	7.0
Agriculture (% of total freshwater withdrawal)	..	40
Access to improved water source (% of total population)	100	99
Rural (% of rural population)	100	98
Urban (% of urban population)	100	100
Access to improved sanitation facilities (% of total population)	100	96
Rural (% of rural population)	100	93
Urban (% of urban population)	100	97
Environment and health		
Particulate matter (urban-pop.-weighted avg., µg/cu. m)	..	27
Acute resp. infection prevalence (% of children under five)	..	..
Diarrhea prevalence (% of children under five)	..	..
Under-five mortality rate (per 1,000 live births)	..	6
National accounting aggregates—savings, depletion and degradation		
Gross savings (% of GNI)	..	20.1
Consumption of fixed capital (% of GNI)	13.0	14.2
Education expenditure (% of GNI)	..	4.7
Energy depletion (% of GNI)	0.0	1.6
Mineral depletion (% of GNI)	0.0	0.3
Net forest depletion (% of GNI)	0.0	0.0
CO_2 damage (% of GNI)	0.5	0.3
Particulate emissions damage (% of GNI)	..	0.3
Adjusted net savings (% of GNI)	..	8.1

Grenada

	Country data	Latin America & Caribbean group	Upper middle-income group
Population (thousands) **105**	Land area (sq. km)	**340** GDP ($ millions)	**766.5**

	Country data	Latin America & Caribbean group	Upper middle-income group
GNI per capita, *World Bank Atlas* method ($)	7,220	9,070	6,969
Adjusted net national income per capita ($)	..	7,325	5,845
Change in wealth per capita (2010 $)	..	180	1,039
Urban population (% of total)	39.5	79.0	60.7
Agriculture			
Agricultural land (% land area)	32	37	44
Agricultural irrigated land (% of total agricultural land)	2.0	..	..
Agricultural productivity, value added per worker (2005 $)	3,776	4,135	1,131
Cereal yield (kg per hectare)	1,029	4,082	4,255
Forests and biodiversity			
Forest area (% land area)	50.0	48.1	29.1
Deforestation (avg. annual %, 2000–2010)	0.0	0.5	0.0
Terrestrial protected areas (% of total land area)	2.2	21.4	16.1
Threatened species, mammals	3		
Threatened species, birds	1		
Threatened species, fish	20		
Threatened species, higher plants	3		
Oceans			
Total fisheries production (thousand metric tons)	2.3	10,964	90,024
Capture fisheries growth (avg. annual %, 1990–2012)	0.8	-0.6	1.5
Aquaculture growth (avg. annual %, 1990–2012)	..	10.8	9.1
Marine protected areas (% of territorial waters)	11.6	9.0	7.3
Coral reef area (sq. km)	150	14,860	52,070
Mangroves area (sq. km)	1.4	39,988	50,160
Energy and emissions			
Energy use per capita (kg oil equivalent)	782	1,292	1,893
Energy from biomass products and waste (% of total)	..	16.0	8.5
Electric power consumption per capita (kWh)	..	1,985	2,932
Electricity generated using fossil fuel (% of total)	..	37.3	74.7
Electricity generated by hydropower (% of total)	..	55.1	20.0
CO_2 emissions per capita (metric tons)	2.5	2.7	5.4
Water and sanitation			
Internal freshwater resources per capita (cu. m)	..	21,735	6,791
Total freshwater withdrawal (% of internal resources)	..	2.0	7.4
Agriculture (% of total freshwater withdrawal)	..	68	69
Access to improved water source (% of total population)	97	94	93
Rural (% of rural population)	95	82	85
Urban (% of urban population)	99	97	98
Access to improved sanitation facilities (% of total population)	98	81	74
Rural (% of rural population)	98	62	62
Urban (% of urban population)	98	86	82
Environment and health			
Particulate matter (urban-pop.-weighted avg., µg/cu. m)	9	43	65
Acute resp. infection prevalence (% of children under five)	..	..	..
Diarrhea prevalence (% of children under five)	..	..	..
Under-five mortality rate (per 1,000 live births)	14	19	20
National accounting aggregates—savings, depletion and degradation			
Gross savings (% of GNI)	-10.7	19.0	36.4
Consumption of fixed capital (% of GNI)	12.8	12.2	12.5
Education expenditure (% of GNI)	3.7	5.1	3.2
Energy depletion (% of GNI)	0.0	4.7	4.1
Mineral depletion (% of GNI)	0.0	1.2	1.2
Net forest depletion (% of GNI)	..	0.4	0.2
CO_2 damage (% of GNI)	0.4	0.3	0.8
Particulate emissions damage (% of GNI)	0.0	0.8	1.3
Adjusted net savings (% of GNI)	..	4.5	19.5

Guam

Population (thousands) **163** Land area (sq. km)   **540** GDP ($ millions)   ..

	Country data	High-Income group
GNI per capita, *World Bank Atlas* method ($)	..	38,444
Adjusted net national income per capita ($)	..	32,262
Change in wealth per capita (2010 $)	..	2,210
Urban population (% of total)	93.2	80.2

Agriculture
Agricultural land (% land area)	33	29
Agricultural irrigated land (% of total agricultural land)	..	..
Agricultural productivity, value added per worker (2005 $)	..	25,238
Cereal yield (kg per hectare)	2,421	4,374

Forests and biodiversity
Forest area (% land area)	47.9	35.0
Deforestation (avg. annual %, 2000–2010)	0.0	0.0
Terrestrial protected areas (% of total land area)	26.8	13.9
Threatened species, mammals	2	
Threatened species, birds	14	
Threatened species, fish	9	
Threatened species, higher plants	4	

Oceans
Total fisheries production (thousand metric tons)	0.46	37,661
Capture fisheries growth (avg. annual %, 1990–2012)	-1.5	-2.0
Aquaculture growth (avg. annual %, 1990–2012)	-2.9	2.5
Marine protected areas (% of territorial waters)	13.0	14.4
Coral reef area (sq. km)	220	82,210
Mangroves area (sq. km)	0.97	15,504

Energy and emissions
Energy use per capita (kg oil equivalent)	..	4,872
Energy from biomass products and waste (% of total)	..	4.3
Electric power consumption per capita (kWh)	..	8,896
Electricity generated using fossil fuel (% of total)	..	61.8
Electricity generated by hydropower (% of total)	..	12.2
CO_2 emissions per capita (metric tons)	..	11.6

Water and sanitation
Internal freshwater resources per capita (cu. m)	..	11,335
Total freshwater withdrawal (% of internal resources)	..	7.0
Agriculture (% of total freshwater withdrawal)	..	40
Access to improved water source (% of total population)	100	99
Rural (% of rural population)	100	98
Urban (% of urban population)	100	100
Access to improved sanitation facilities (% of total population)	90	96
Rural (% of rural population)	90	93
Urban (% of urban population)	90	97

Environment and health
Particulate matter (urban-pop.-weighted avg., µg/cu. m)	..	27
Acute resp. infection prevalence (% of children under five)	..	..
Diarrhea prevalence (% of children under five)	..	..
Under-five mortality rate (per 1,000 live births)	..	6

National accounting aggregates—savings, depletion and degradation
Gross savings (% of GNI)	..	20.1
Consumption of fixed capital (% of GNI)	..	14.2
Education expenditure (% of GNI)	..	4.7
Energy depletion (% of GNI)	..	1.6
Mineral depletion (% of GNI)	..	0.3
Net forest depletion (% of GNI)	..	0.0
CO_2 damage (% of GNI)	..	0.3
Particulate emissions damage (% of GNI)	..	0.3
Adjusted net savings (% of GNI)	..	8.1

Guatemala

	Country data	Latin America & Caribbean group	Lower middle-income group
Population (millions) **15.1** Land area (1,000 sq. km) **107** GDP ($ billions) **50.2**			

	Country data	Latin America & Caribbean group	Lower middle-income group
GNI per capita, *World Bank Atlas* method ($)	3,120	9,070	1,965
Adjusted net national income per capita ($)	2,703	7,325	1,574
Change in wealth per capita (2010 $)	-853	180	117
Urban population (% of total)	50.2	79.0	38.9
Agriculture			
Agricultural land (% land area)	41	37	46
Agricultural irrigated land (% of total agricultural land)	..	..	..
Agricultural productivity, value added per worker (2005 $)	1,935	4,135	938
Cereal yield (kg per hectare)	2,000	4,082	3,029
Forests and biodiversity			
Forest area (% land area)	33.6	48.1	26.9
Deforestation (avg. annual %, 2000–2010)	1.4	0.5	0.3
Terrestrial protected areas (% of total land area)	30.9	21.4	11.9
Threatened species, mammals	17		
Threatened species, birds	14		
Threatened species, fish	26		
Threatened species, higher plants	93	.	
Oceans			
Total fisheries production (thousand metric tons)	37.3	10,964	43,067
Capture fisheries growth (avg. annual %, 1990–2012)	4.9	-0.6	2.6
Aquaculture growth (avg. annual %, 1990–2012)	14.5	10.8	9.9
Marine protected areas (% of territorial waters)	4.2	9.0	14.7
Coral reef area (sq. km)	..	14,860	124,480
Mangroves area (sq. km)	177	39,988	58,917
Energy and emissions			
Energy use per capita (kg oil equivalent)	691	1,292	687
Energy from biomass products and waste (% of total)	62.2	16.0	26.8
Electric power consumption per capita (kWh)	539	1,985	734
Electricity generated using fossil fuel (% of total)	33.1	37.3	72.3
Electricity generated by hydropower (% of total)	39.8	55.1	16.9
CO_2 emissions per capita (metric tons)	0.8	2.7	1.6
Water and sanitation			
Internal freshwater resources per capita (cu. m)	7,425	21,735	3,144
Total freshwater withdrawal (% of internal resources)	2.7	2.0	19.6
Agriculture (% of total freshwater withdrawal)	55	68	88
Access to improved water source (% of total population)	94	94	88
Rural (% of rural population)	89	82	85
Urban (% of urban population)	99	97	94
Access to improved sanitation facilities (% of total population)	80	81	48
Rural (% of rural population)	72	62	36
Urban (% of urban population)	88	86	66
Environment and health			
Particulate matter (urban-pop.-weighted avg., µg/cu. m)	75	43	90
Acute resp. infection prevalence (% of children under five)	..	..	..
Diarrhea prevalence (% of children under five)	..	..	..
Under-five mortality rate (per 1,000 live births)	32	19	61
National accounting aggregates—savings, depletion and degradation			
Gross savings (% of GNI)	12.3	19.0	28.6
Consumption of fixed capital (% of GNI)	12.8	12.2	11.1
Education expenditure (% of GNI)	2.9	5.1	3.1
Energy depletion (% of GNI)	0.6	4.7	4.4
Mineral depletion (% of GNI)	0.9	1.2	1.1
Net forest depletion (% of GNI)	2.3	0.4	0.8
CO_2 damage (% of GNI)	0.2	0.3	0.9
Particulate emissions damage (% of GNI)	0.8	0.8	1.4
Adjusted net savings (% of GNI)	-2.3	4.5	12.0

Guinea

	Country data	Sub-Saharan Africa group	Low-Income group
Population (millions)	**11.5**	Land area (1,000 sq. km) **246**	GDP ($ billions) **5.6**

	Country data	Sub-Saharan Africa group	Low-Income group
GNI per capita, *World Bank Atlas* method ($)	440	1,547	594
Adjusted net national income per capita ($)	296	1,005	495
Change in wealth per capita (2010 $)	–258	–273	–39
Urban population (% of total)	35.9	36.8	28.2
Agriculture			
Agricultural land (% land area)	58	44	39
Agricultural irrigated land (% of total agricultural land)	..	..	..
Agricultural productivity, value added per worker (2005 $)	206	765	367
Cereal yield (kg per hectare)	1,522	1,417	1,982
Forests and biodiversity			
Forest area (% land area)	26.5	27.4	27.4
Deforestation (avg. annual %, 2000–2010)	0.5	0.5	0.6
Terrestrial protected areas (% of total land area)	28.1	16.4	13.7
Threatened species, mammals	21		
Threatened species, birds	17		
Threatened species, fish	67		
Threatened species, higher plants	28		
Oceans			
Total fisheries production (thousand metric tons)	132	6,906	11,789
Capture fisheries growth (avg. annual %, 1990–2012)	5.1	2.1	3.8
Aquaculture growth (avg. annual %, 1990–2012)	28.5	15.9	5.1
Marine protected areas (% of territorial waters)	45.9	11.7	13.1
Coral reef area (sq. km)	..	17,980	15,120
Mangroves area (sq. km)	2,033	27,808	25,817
Energy and emissions			
Energy use per capita (kg oil equivalent)	..	681	360
Energy from biomass products and waste (% of total)	..	57.6	66.0
Electric power consumption per capita (kWh)	..	535	233
Electricity generated using fossil fuel (% of total)	..	65.1	30.9
Electricity generated by hydropower (% of total)	..	20.0	45.5
CO_2 emissions per capita (metric tons)	0.1	0.8	0.3
Water and sanitation			
Internal freshwater resources per capita (cu. m)	20,248	4,391	5,121
Total freshwater withdrawal (% of internal resources)	0.7	3.2	4.4
Agriculture (% of total freshwater withdrawal)	84	84	90
Access to improved water source (% of total population)	75	64	69
Rural (% of rural population)	65	53	61
Urban (% of urban population)	92	85	88
Access to improved sanitation facilities (% of total population)	19	30	37
Rural (% of rural population)	11	23	33
Urban (% of urban population)	33	41	46
Environment and health			
Particulate matter (urban-pop.-weighted avg., µg/cu. m)	37	77	74
Acute resp. infection prevalence (% of children under five)	6	5	6
Diarrhea prevalence (% of children under five)	16	14	14
Under-five mortality rate (per 1,000 live births)	101	98	82
National accounting aggregates—savings, depletion and degradation			
Gross savings (% of GNI)	–6.8	26.3	24.6
Consumption of fixed capital (% of GNI)	9.0	13.0	11.8
Education expenditure (% of GNI)	2.6	3.4	3.2
Energy depletion (% of GNI)	0.0	10.3	1.4
Mineral depletion (% of GNI)	13.8	1.8	1.9
Net forest depletion (% of GNI)	12.1	1.8	4.4
CO_2 damage (% of GNI)	0.3	0.6	0.4
Particulate emissions damage (% of GNI)	0.4	1.2	1.0
Adjusted net savings (% of GNI)	–42.8	0.9	7.0

Guinea-Bissau

	Country data	Sub-Saharan Africa group	Low-Income group
Population (millions) **1.7** Land area (1,000 sq. km) **28** GDP ($ millions) **822.3**			

	Country data	Sub-Saharan Africa group	Low-Income group
GNI per capita, World Bank Atlas method ($)	510	1,547	594
Adjusted net national income per capita ($)	362	1,005	495
Change in wealth per capita (2010 $)	-217	-273	-39
Urban population (% of total)	44.6	36.8	28.2
Agriculture			
Agricultural land (% land area)	58	44	39
Agricultural irrigated land (% of total agricultural land)	..	..	..
Agricultural productivity, value added per worker (2005 $)	..	765	367
Cereal yield (kg per hectare)	1,510	1,417	1,982
Forests and biodiversity			
Forest area (% land area)	71.6	27.4	27.4
Deforestation (avg. annual %, 2000-2010)	0.5	0.5	0.6
Terrestrial protected areas (% of total land area)	16.3	16.4	13.7
Threatened species, mammals	12		
Threatened species, birds	9		
Threatened species, fish	31		
Threatened species, higher plants	5		
Oceans			
Total fisheries production (thousand metric tons)	6.6	6,906	11,789
Capture fisheries growth (avg. annual %, 1990-2012)	0.9	2.1	3.8
Aquaculture growth (avg. annual %, 1990-2012)	..	15.9	5.1
Marine protected areas (% of territorial waters)	45.8	11.7	13.1
Coral reef area (sq. km)	..	17,980	15,120
Mangroves area (sq. km)	2,982	27,808	25,817
Energy and emissions			
Energy use per capita (kg oil equivalent)	64	681	360
Energy from biomass products and waste (% of total)	..	57.6	66.0
Electric power consumption per capita (kWh)	..	535	233
Electricity generated using fossil fuel (% of total)	..	65.1	30.9
Electricity generated by hydropower (% of total)	..	20.0	45.5
CO_2 emissions per capita (metric tons)	0.2	0.8	0.3
Water and sanitation			
Internal freshwater resources per capita (cu. m)	9,851	4,391	5,121
Total freshwater withdrawal (% of internal resources)	1.1	3.2	4.4
Agriculture (% of total freshwater withdrawal)	82	84	90
Access to improved water source (% of total population)	74	64	69
Rural (% of rural population)	56	53	61
Urban (% of urban population)	96	85	88
Access to improved sanitation facilities (% of total population)	20	30	37
Rural (% of rural population)	8	23	33
Urban (% of urban population)	34	41	46
Environment and health			
Particulate matter (urban-pop.-weighted avg., µg/cu. m)	34	77	74
Acute resp. infection prevalence (% of children under five)	..	5	6
Diarrhea prevalence (% of children under five)	..	14	14
Under-five mortality rate (per 1,000 live births)	129	98	82
National accounting aggregates—savings, depletion and degradation			
Gross savings (% of GNI)	1.5	26.3	24.6
Consumption of fixed capital (% of GNI)	13.6	13.0	11.8
Education expenditure (% of GNI)	2.3	3.4	3.2
Energy depletion (% of GNI)	0.0	10.3	1.4
Mineral depletion (% of GNI)	0.0	1.8	1.9
Net forest depletion (% of GNI)	13.1	1.8	4.4
CO_2 damage (% of GNI)	0.3	0.6	0.4
Particulate emissions damage (% of GNI)	0.8	1.2	1.0
Adjusted net savings (% of GNI)	-22.4	0.9	7.0

Guyana

Population (thousands) **795** Land area (1,000 sq. km) **197** GDP ($ billions) **2.9**

	Country data	Latin America & Caribbean group	Lower middle-income group
GNI per capita, *World Bank Atlas* method ($)	3,410	9,070	1,965
Adjusted net national income per capita ($)	2,681	7,325	1,574
Change in wealth per capita (2010 $)	–409	180	117
Urban population (% of total)	28.5	79.0	38.9
Agriculture			
Agricultural land (% land area)	9	37	46
Agricultural irrigated land (% of total agricultural land)	..	..	..
Agricultural productivity, value added per worker (2005 $)	4,856	4,135	938
Cereal yield (kg per hectare)	4,432	4,082	3,029
Forests and biodiversity			
Forest area (% land area)	77.2	48.1	26.9
Deforestation (avg. annual %, 2000–2010)	0.0	0.5	0.3
Terrestrial protected areas (% of total land area)	5.2	21.4	11.9
Threatened species, mammals	11		
Threatened species, birds	13		
Threatened species, fish	28		
Threatened species, higher plants	23		
Oceans			
Total fisheries production (thousand metric tons)	54.1	10,964	43,067
Capture fisheries growth (avg. annual %, 1990–2012)	1.7	-0.6	2.6
Aquaculture growth (avg. annual %, 1990–2012)	7.8	10.8	9.9
Marine protected areas (% of territorial waters)	0.0	9.0	14 7
Coral reef area (sq. km)	..	14,860	124,480
Mangroves area (sq. km)	396	39,988	58,917
Energy and emissions			
Energy use per capita (kg oil equivalent)	649	1,292	687
Energy from biomass products and waste (% of total)	..	16.0	26.8
Electric power consumption per capita (kWh)	..	1,985	734
Electricity generated using fossil fuel (% of total)	..	37.3	72.3
Electricity generated by hydropower (% of total)	..	55.1	16.9
CO_2 emissions per capita (metric tons)	2.2	2.7	1.6
Water and sanitation			
Internal freshwater resources per capita (cu. m)	304,723	21,735	3,144
Total freshwater withdrawal (% of internal resources)	0.7	2.0	19.6
Agriculture (% of total freshwater withdrawal)	98	68	88
Access to improved water source (% of total population)	98	94	88
Rural (% of rural population)	98	82	85
Urban (% of urban population)	97	97	94
Access to improved sanitation facilities (% of total population)	84	81	48
Rural (% of rural population)	82	62	36
Urban (% of urban population)	88	86	66
Environment and health			
Particulate matter (urban-pop.-weighted avg., µg/cu. m)	17	43	90
Acute resp. infection prevalence (% of children under five)	5	..	..
Diarrhea prevalence (% of children under five)	10	..	..
Under-five mortality rate (per 1,000 live births)	35	19	61
National accounting aggregates—savings, depletion and degradation			
Gross savings (% of GNI)	11.1	19.0	28.6
Consumption of fixed capital (% of GNI)	13.6	12.2	11.1
Education expenditure (% of GNI)	3.0	5.1	3.1
Energy depletion (% of GNI)	0.0	4.7	4.4
Mineral depletion (% of GNI)	11.6	1.2	1.1
Net forest depletion (% of GNI)	0.0	0.4	0.8
CO_2 damage (% of GNI)	0.7	0.3	0.9
Particulate emissions damage (% of GNI)	0.0	0.8	1.4
Adjusted net savings (% of GNI)	–11.8	4.5	12.0

Haiti

	Country data	Latin America & Caribbean group	Low-Income group
Population (millions) **10.2** Land area (1,000 sq. km) **28** GDP ($ billions) **7.8**			

	Country data	Latin America & Caribbean group	Low-Income group
GNI per capita, *World Bank Atlas* method ($)	760	9,070	594
Adjusted net national income per capita ($)	677	7,325	495
Change in wealth per capita (2010 $)	4	180	-39
Urban population (% of total)	54.6	79.0	28.2
Agriculture			
Agricultural land (% land area)	64	37	39
Agricultural irrigated land (% of total agricultural land)	5.4	..	..
Agricultural productivity, value added per worker (2005 $)	..	4,135	367
Cereal yield (kg per hectare)	766	4,082	1,982
Forests and biodiversity			
Forest area (% land area)	3.6	48.1	27.4
Deforestation (avg. annual %, 2000–2010)	0.8	-0.5	0.6
Terrestrial protected areas (% of total land area)	0.3	21.4	13.7
Threatened species, mammals	5		
Threatened species, birds	13		
Threatened species, fish	21		
Threatened species, higher plants	38		
Oceans			
Total fisheries production (thousand metric tons)	17.2	10,964	11,789
Capture fisheries growth (avg. annual %, 1990–2012)	5.4	-0.6	3.8
Aquaculture growth (avg. annual %, 1990–2012)	..	10.8	5.1
Marine protected areas (% of territorial waters)	2.7	9.0	13.1
Coral reef area (sq. km)	450	14,860	15,120
Mangroves area (sq. km)	136	39,988	25,817
Energy and emissions			
Energy use per capita (kg oil equivalent)	320	1,292	360
Energy from biomass products and waste (% of total)	77.7	16.0	66.0
Electric power consumption per capita (kWh)	32	1,985	233
Electricity generated using fossil fuel (% of total)	79.0	37.3	30.9
Electricity generated by hydropower (% of total)	16.7	55.1	45.5
CO_2 emissions per capita (metric tons)	0.2	2.7	0.3
Water and sanitation			
Internal freshwater resources per capita (cu. m)	1,297	21,735	5,121
Total freshwater withdrawal (% of internal resources)	9.2	2.0	4.4
Agriculture (% of total freshwater withdrawal)	78	68	90
Access to improved water source (% of total population)	62	94	69
Rural (% of rural population)	47	82	61
Urban (% of urban population)	75	97	88
Access to improved sanitation facilities (% of total population)	24	81	37
Rural (% of rural population)	16	62	33
Urban (% of urban population)	31	86	46
Environment and health			
Particulate matter (urban-pop.-weighted avg., µg/cu. m)	56	43	74
Acute resp. infection prevalence (% of children under five)	14	..	6
Diarrhea prevalence (% of children under five)	21	..	14
Under-five mortality rate (per 1,000 live births)	76	19	82
National accounting aggregates—savings, depletion and degradation			
Gross savings (% of GNI)	25.4	19.0	24.6
Consumption of fixed capital (% of GNI)	11.2	12.2	11.8
Education expenditure (% of GNI)	1.5	5.1	3.2
Energy depletion (% of GNI)	0.0	4.7	1.4
Mineral depletion (% of GNI)	0.0	1.2	1.9
Net forest depletion (% of GNI)	1.8	0.4	4.4
CO_2 damage (% of GNI)	0.3	0.3	0.4
Particulate emissions damage (% of GNI)	0.9	0.8	1.0
Adjusted net savings (% of GNI)	12.7	4.5	7.0

Honduras

| Population (millions) | **7.9** | Land area (1,000 sq. km) | **112** | GDP ($ billions) | **18.4** |

	Country data	Latin America & Caribbean group	Lower middle-income group
GNI per capita, *World Bank Atlas* method ($)	2,120	9,070	1,965
Adjusted net national income per capita ($)	1,982	7,325	1,574
Change in wealth per capita (2010 $)	–69	180	117
Urban population (% of total)	52.7	79.0	38.9
Agriculture			
Agricultural land (% land area)	29	37	46
Agricultural irrigated land (% of total agricultural land)	..	..	..
Agricultural productivity, value added per worker (2005 $)	2,463	4,135	938
Cereal yield (kg per hectare)	1,224	4,082	3,029
Forests and biodiversity			
Forest area (% land area)	45.3	48.1	26.9
Deforestation (avg. annual %, 2000–2010)	2.1	0.5	0.3
Terrestrial protected areas (% of total land area)	21.1	21.4	11.9
Threatened species, mammals	8		
Threatened species, birds	11		
Threatened species, fish	30		
Threatened species, higher plants	118		
Oceans			
Total fisheries production (thousand metric tons)	43.3	10,964	43,067
Capture fisheries growth (avg. annual %, 1990–2012)	-2.9	-0.6	2.6
Aquaculture growth (avg. annual %, 1990–2012)	11.2	10.8	9.9
Marine protected areas (% of territorial waters)	1.9	9.0	14.7
Coral reef area (sq. km)	810	14,860	124,480
Mangroves area (sq. km)	628	39,988	58,917
Energy and emissions			
Energy use per capita (kg oil equivalent)	609	1,292	687
Energy from biomass products and waste (% of total)	43.7	16.0	26.8
Electric power consumption per capita (kWh)	708	1,985	734
Electricity generated using fossil fuel (% of total)	56.5	37.3	72.3
Electricity generated by hydropower (% of total)	39.5	55.1	16.9
CO_2 emissions per capita (metric tons)	1.1	2.7	1.6
Water and sanitation			
Internal freshwater resources per capita (cu. m)	12,336	21,735	3,144
Total freshwater withdrawal (% of internal resources)	1.2	2.0	19.6
Agriculture (% of total freshwater withdrawal)	58	68	88
Access to improved water source (% of total population)	90	94	88
Rural (% of rural population)	82	82	85
Urban (% of urban population)	97	97	94
Access to improved sanitation facilities (% of total population)	80	81	48
Rural (% of rural population)	74	62	36
Urban (% of urban population)	85	86	66
Environment and health			
Particulate matter (urban-pop.-weighted avg., µg/cu. m)	84	43	90
Acute resp. infection prevalence (% of children under five)	13	..	..
Diarrhea prevalence (% of children under five)	18	..	..
Under-five mortality rate (per 1,000 live births)	23	19	61
National accounting aggregates—savings, depletion and degradation			
Gross savings (% of GNI)	17.8	19.0	28.6
Consumption of fixed capital (% of GNI)	5.5	12.2	11.1
Education expenditure (% of GNI)	3.5	5.1	3.1
Energy depletion (% of GNI)	0.0	4.7	4.4
Mineral depletion (% of GNI)	0.6	1.2	1.1
Net forest depletion (% of GNI)	2.0	0.4	0.8
CO_2 damage (% of GNI)	0.5	0.3	0.9
Particulate emissions damage (% of GNI)	1.3	0.8	1.4
Adjusted net savings (% of GNI)	11.4	4.5	12.0

Hong Kong SAR, China

| Population (millions) | **7.2** | Land area (1,000 sq. km) | **1.0** | GDP ($ billions) | **263.3** |

	Country data	High-income group
GNI per capita, *World Bank Atlas* method ($)	36,560	38,444
Adjusted net national income per capita ($)	..	32,262
Change in wealth per capita (2010 $)	..	2,210
Urban population (% of total)	100.0	80.2

Agriculture

Agricultural land (% of land area)	..	29
Agricultural irrigated land (% of total agricultural land)	..	..
Agricultural productivity, value added per worker (2005 $)	..	25,238
Cereal yield (kg per hectare)	..	4,374

Forests and biodiversity

Forest area (% land area)	..	35.0
Deforestation (avg. annual %, 2000–2010)	..	0.0
Terrestrial protected areas (% of total land area)	41.9	13.9
Threatened species, mammals	2	
Threatened species, birds	20	
Threatened species, fish	13	
Threatened species, higher plants	6	

Oceans

Total fisheries production (thousand metric tons)	159	37,661
Capture fisheries growth (avg. annual %, 1990–2012)	-1.7	-2.0
Aquaculture growth (avg. annual %, 1990–2012)	-4.1	2.5
Marine protected areas (% of territorial waters)	..	14.4
Coral reef area (sq. km)	..	82,210
Mangroves area (sq. km)	..	15,504

Energy and emissions

Energy use per capita (kg oil equivalent)	2,106	4,872
Energy from biomass products and waste (% of total)	0.4	4.3
Electric power consumption per capita (kWh)	5,949	8,896
Electricity generated using fossil fuel (% of total)	100.0	61.8
Electricity generated by hydropower (% of total)	0.0	12.2
CO_2 emissions per capita (metric tons)	5.2	11.6

Water and sanitation

Internal freshwater resources per capita (cu. m)	..	11,335
Total freshwater withdrawal (% of internal resources)	..	7.0
Agriculture (% of total freshwater withdrawal)	..	40
Access to improved water source (% of total population)	..	99
Rural (% of rural population)	..	98
Urban (% of urban population)	..	100
Access to improved sanitation facilities (% of total population)	..	96
Rural (% of rural population)	..	93
Urban (% of urban population)	..	97

Environment and health

Particulate matter (urban-pop.-weighted avg., µg/cu. m)	30	27
Acute resp. infection prevalence (% of children under five)	..	..
Diarrhea prevalence (% of children under five)	..	..
Under-five mortality rate (per 1,000 live births)	..	6

National accounting aggregates—savings, depletion and degradation

Gross savings (% of GNI)	27.7	20.1
Consumption of fixed capital (% of GNI)	13.3	14.2
Education expenditure (% of GNI)	2.8	4.7
Energy depletion (% of GNI)	0.0	1.6
Mineral depletion (% of GNI)	0.0	0.3
Net forest depletion (% of GNI)	..	0.0
CO_2 damage (% of GNI)	0.1	0.3
Particulate emissions damage (% of GNI)	..	0.3
Adjusted net savings (% of GNI)	..	8.1

Hungary

	Country data	Europe & Central Asia group	Upper middle-income group
Population (millions) **9.9** Land area (1,000 sq. km)		**91** GDP ($ billions)	**124.6**

	Country data	Europe & Central Asia group	Upper middle-income group
GNI per capita, *World Bank Atlas* method ($)	12,410	6,658	6,969
Adjusted net national income per capita ($)	10,012	5,541	5,845
Change in wealth per capita (2010 $)	1,255	263	1,039
Urban population (% of total)	69.9	60.2	60.7
Agriculture			
Agricultural land (% land area)	59	66	44
Agricultural irrigated land (% of total agricultural land)	1.8	..	..
Agricultural productivity, value added per worker (2005 $)	9,964	4,866	1,131
Cereal yield (kg per hectare)	3,662	2,519	4,255
Forests and biodiversity			
Forest area (% land area)	22.5	10.5	29.1
Deforestation (avg. annual %, 2000–2010)	-0.6	-0.5	0.0
Terrestrial protected areas (% of total land area)	23.1	5.1	16.1
Threatened species, mammals	2		
Threatened species, birds	10		
Threatened species, fish	9		
Threatened species, higher plants	9		
Oceans			
Total fisheries production (thousand metric tons)	21.9	1,022	90,024
Capture fisheries growth (avg. annual %, 1990–2012)	-3.9	-4.0	1.5
Aquaculture growth (avg. annual %, 1990–2012)	-0.7	1.8	9.1
Marine protected areas (% of territorial waters)	3.9	10.4	7.3
Coral reef area (sq. km)	..	..	52,070
Mangroves area (sq. km)	..	..	50,160
Energy and emissions			
Energy use per capita (kg oil equivalent)	2,503	2,078	1,893
Energy from biomass products and waste (% of total)	7.2	2.9	8.5
Electric power consumption per capita (kWh)	3,895	2,951	2,932
Electricity generated using fossil fuel (% of total)	48.5	65.8	74.7
Electricity generated by hydropower (% of total)	0.6	17.9	20.0
CO_2 emissions per capita (metric tons)	5.1	5.3	5.4
Water and sanitation			
Internal freshwater resources per capita (cu. m)	602	2,744	6,791
Total freshwater withdrawal (% of internal resources)	93.2	34.8	7.4
Agriculture (% of total freshwater withdrawal)	6	70	69
Access to improved water source (% of total population)	100	95	93
Rural (% of rural population)	100	89	85
Urban (% of urban population)	100	99	98
Access to improved sanitation facilities (% of total population)	100	94	74
Rural (% of rural population)	100	90	62
Urban (% of urban population)	100	97	82
Environment and health			
Particulate matter (urban-pop.-weighted avg., µg/cu. m)	32	48	65
Acute resp. infection prevalence (% of children under five)	..	..	..
Diarrhea prevalence (% of children under five)	..	..	..
Under-five mortality rate (per 1,000 live births)	6	22	20
National accounting aggregates—savings, depletion and degradation			
Gross savings (% of GNI)	24.4	18.9	36.4
Consumption of fixed capital (% of GNI)	15.1	12.4	12.5
Education expenditure (% of GNI)	4.6	3.8	3.2
Energy depletion (% of GNI)	0.3	4.4	4.1
Mineral depletion (% of GNI)	0.0	0.6	1.2
Net forest depletion (% of GNI)	0.0	0.0	0.2
CO_2 damage (% of GNI)	0.4	0.8	0.8
Particulate emissions damage (% of GNI)	0.9	1.8	1.3
Adjusted net savings (% of GNI)	12.4	2.8	19.5

Iceland

Population (thousands)	**321**	Land area (1,000 sq. km)	**100**	GDP ($ billions)	**13.6**

	Country data	High-income group
GNI per capita, *World Bank Atlas* method ($)	38,270	38,444
Adjusted net national income per capita ($)	31,440	32,262
Change in wealth per capita (2010 $)	–1,366	2,210
Urban population (% of total)	93.8	80.2
Agriculture		
Agricultural land (% land area)	16	29
Agricultural irrigated land (% of total agricultural land)	..	..
Agricultural productivity, value added per worker (2005 $)	*68,013*	*25,238*
Cereal yield (kg per hectare)	..	4,374
Forests and biodiversity		
Forest area (% land area)	0.3	35.0
Deforestation (avg. annual %, 2000–2010)	–5.0	0.0
Terrestrial protected areas (% of total land area)	19.9	13.9
Threatened species, mammals	6	
Threatened species, birds	1	
Threatened species, fish	12	
Threatened species, higher plants	0	
Oceans		
Total fisheries production (thousand metric tons)	1,475	37,661
Capture fisheries growth (avg. annual %, 1990–2012)	–0.2	–2.0
Aquaculture growth (avg. annual %, 1990–2012)	4.5	2.5
Marine protected areas (% of territorial waters)	1.6	*14.4*
Coral reef area (sq. km)	..	82,210
Mangroves area (sq. km)	..	15,504
Energy and emissions		
Energy use per capita (kg oil equivalent)	17,964	4,872
Energy from biomass products and waste (% of total)	0.0	4.3
Electric power consumption per capita (kWh)	52,374	8,896
Electricity generated using fossil fuel (% of total)	0.0	61.8
Electricity generated by hydropower (% of total)	72.7	12.2
CO_2 emissions per capita (metric tons)	6.2	11.6
Water and sanitation		
Internal freshwater resources per capita (cu. m)	532,892	11,335
Total freshwater withdrawal (% of internal resources)	0.1	7.0
Agriculture (% of total freshwater withdrawal)	42	40
Access to improved water source (% of total population)	100	99
Rural (% of rural population)	100	98
Urban (% of urban population)	100	100
Access to improved sanitation facilities (% of total population)	100	96
Rural (% of rural population)	100	93
Urban (% of urban population)	100	97
Environment and health		
Particulate matter (urban-pop.-weighted avg., µg/cu. m)	18	27
Acute resp. infection prevalence (% of children under five)	..	..
Diarrhea prevalence (% of children under five)	..	..
Under-five mortality rate (per 1,000 live births)	2	6
National accounting aggregates—savings, depletion and degradation		
Gross savings (% of GNI)	10.4	20.1
Consumption of fixed capital (% of GNI)	16.5	14.2
Education expenditure (% of GNI)	8.6	4.7
Energy depletion (% of GNI)	0.0	1.6
Mineral depletion (% of GNI)	0.0	0.3
Net forest depletion (% of GNI)	0.0	0.0
CO_2 damage (% of GNI)	0.2	0.3
Particulate emissions damage (% of GNI)	0.1	0.3
Adjusted net savings (% of GNI)	2.3	8.1

India

Population (millions) **1,236.7** Land area (1,000 sq. km) **2,973** GDP ($ billions) **1,858.7**

	Country data	South Asia group	Lower middle-income group
GNI per capita, *World Bank Atlas* method ($)	1,550	1,437	1,965
Adjusted net national income per capita ($)	1,233	1,168	1,574
Change in wealth per capita (2010 $)	196	158	117
Urban population (% of total)	31.7	31.4	38.9
Agriculture			
Agricultural land (% land area)	60	55	46
Agricultural irrigated land (% of total agricultural land)	35.2	..	..
Agricultural productivity, value added per worker (2005 $)	672	669	938
Cereal yield (kg per hectare)	2,954	2,925	3,029
Forests and biodiversity			
Forest area (% land area)	23.1	17.1	26.9
Deforestation (avg. annual %, 2000–2010)	-0.5	-0.3	0.3
Terrestrial protected areas (% of total land area)	5.2	6.2	11.9
Threatened species, mammals	95		
Threatened species, birds	80		
Threatened species, fish	213		
Threatened species, higher plants	326		
Oceans			
Total fisheries production (thousand metric tons)	9,077	13,613	43,067
Capture fisheries growth (avg. annual %, 1990–2012)	2.4	2.6	2.6
Aquaculture growth (avg. annual %, 1990–2012)	6.7	7.6	9.9
Marine protected areas (% of territorial waters)	5.8	10.7	14.7
Coral reef area (sq. km)	5,790	15,440	124,480
Mangroves area (sq. km)	4,326	10,343	58,917
Energy and emissions			
Energy use per capita (kg oil equivalent)	614	555	687
Energy from biomass products and waste (% of total)	24.7	26.7	26.8
Electric power consumption per capita (kWh)	684	605	734
Electricity generated using fossil fuel (% of total)	79.4	77.9	72.3
Electricity generated by hydropower (% of total)	12.4	13.8	16.9
CO_2 emissions per capita (metric tons)	1.7	1.4	1.6
Water and sanitation			
Internal freshwater resources per capita (cu. m)	1,184	1,217	3,144
Total freshwater withdrawal (% of internal resources)	52.6	51.6	19.6
Agriculture (% of total freshwater withdrawal)	90	91	88
Access to improved water source (% of total population)	93	91	88
Rural (% of rural population)	91	89	85
Urban (% of urban population)	97	95	94
Access to improved sanitation facilities (% of total population)	36	40	48
Rural (% of rural population)	25	30	36
Urban (% of urban population)	60	61	66
Environment and health			
Particulate matter (urban-pop.-weighted avg., µg/cu. m)	100	110	90
Acute resp. infection prevalence (% of children under five)	..	..	..
Diarrhea prevalence (% of children under five)	..	..	..
Under-five mortality rate (per 1,000 live births)	56	60	61
National accounting aggregates—savings, depletion and degradation			
Gross savings (% of GNI)	30.7	29.3	28.6
Consumption of fixed capital (% of GNI)	13.1	12.7	11.1
Education expenditure (% of GNI)	3.1	2.8	3.1
Energy depletion (% of GNI)	1.9	1.8	4.4
Mineral depletion (% of GNI)	1.0	0.8	1.1
Net forest depletion (% of GNI)	1.1	1.1	0.8
CO_2 damage (% of GNI)	1.3	1.1	0.9
Particulate emissions damage (% of GNI)	1.6	1.5	1.4
Adjusted net savings (% of GNI)	13.8	13.1	12.0

Indonesia

Population (millions) **246.9**	Land area (1,000 sq. km)	**1,812** GDP ($ billions)	**878.0**

	Country data	East Asia & Pacific group	Lower middle-income group
GNI per capita, *World Bank Atlas* method ($)	3,420	4,884	1,965
Adjusted net national income per capita ($)	3,116	4,305	1,574
Change in wealth per capita (2010 $)	498	1,172	117
Urban population (% of total)	51.4	49.6	38.9
Agriculture			
Agricultural land (% of land area)	30	48	46
Agricultural irrigated land (% of total agricultural land)	..	..	..
Agricultural productivity, value added per worker (2005 $)	979	794	938
Cereal yield (kg per hectare)	5,081	5,145	3,029
Forests and biodiversity			
Forest area (% land area)	51.7	29.7	26.9
Deforestation (avg. annual %, 2000–2010)	0.5	-0.4	0.3
Terrestrial protected areas (% of total land area)	14.7	15.1	11.9
Threatened species, mammals	185		
Threatened species, birds	122		
Threatened species, fish	145		
Threatened species, higher plants	404		
Oceans			
Total fisheries production (thousand metric tons)	15,422	108,399	43,067
Capture fisheries growth (avg. annual %, 1990–2012)	3.7	3.4	2.6
Aquaculture growth (avg. annual %, 1990–2012)	13.4	9.1	9.9
Marine protected areas (% of territorial waters)	2.2	1.4	14.7
Coral reef area (sq. km)	51,020	137,690	124,480
Mangroves area (sq. km)	31,894	56,537	58,917
Energy and emissions			
Energy use per capita (kg oil equivalent)	857	1,671	687
Energy from biomass products and waste (% of total)	25.4	10.1	26.8
Electric power consumption per capita (kWh)	680	2,582	734
Electricity generated using fossil fuel (% of total)	87.9	80.9	72.3
Electricity generated by hydropower (% of total)	6.8	14.5	16.9
CO_2 emissions per capita (metric tons)	1.8	4.9	1.6
Water and sanitation			
Internal freshwater resources per capita (cu. m)	8,281	4,438	3,144
Total freshwater withdrawal (% of internal resources)	5.6	10.9	19.6
Agriculture (% of total freshwater withdrawal)	82	73	88
Access to improved water source (% of total population)	85	91	88
Rural (% of rural population)	76	85	85
Urban (% of urban population)	93	97	94
Access to improved sanitation facilities (% of total population)	59	67	48
Rural (% of rural population)	46	58	36
Urban (% of urban population)	71	76	66
Environment and health			
Particulate matter (urban-pop.-weighted avg., µg/cu. m)	47	75	90
Acute resp. infection prevalence (% of children under five)	5	..	..
Diarrhea prevalence (% of children under five)	14	..	..
Under-five mortality rate (per 1,000 live births)	31	21	61
National accounting aggregates—savings, depletion and degradation			
Gross savings (% of GNI)	33.0	47.6	28.6
Consumption of fixed capital (% of GNI)	5.1	12.0	11.1
Education expenditure (% of GNI)	2.5	2.1	3.1
Energy depletion (% of GNI)	3.4	2.7	4.4
Mineral depletion (% of GNI)	1.0	1.4	1.1
Net forest depletion (% of GNI)	0.2	0.1	0.8
CO_2 damage (% of GNI)	0.6	1.0	0.9
Particulate emissions damage (% of GNI)	0.9	1.6	1.4
Adjusted net savings (% of GNI)			

Iran, Islamic Rep.

Population (millions)	**76.4**	Land area (1,000 sq. km)	**1,629**	GDP ($ billions)	**552.4**

	Country data	Middle East & N. Africa group	Upper middle-income group
GNI per capita, *World Bank Atlas* method ($)	4,330	3,451	6,969
Adjusted net national income per capita ($)	3,236	2,602	5,845
Change in wealth per capita (2010 $)	..	101	1,039
Urban population (% of total)	69.2	59.5	60.7
Agriculture			
Agricultural land (% land area)	30	23	44
Agricultural irrigated land (% of total agricultural land)	19.0	..	..
Agricultural productivity, value added per worker (2005 $)	3,313	2,642	1,131
Cereal yield (kg per hectare)	2,228	2,350	4,255
Forests and biodiversity			
Forest area (% land area)	6.8	2.4	29.1
Deforestation (avg. annual %, 2000–2010)	0.0	-0.1	0.0
Terrestrial protected areas (% of total land area)	7.2	6.1	16.1
Threatened species, mammals	17		
Threatened species, birds	22		
Threatened species, fish	31		
Threatened species, higher plants	2		
Oceans			
Total fisheries production (thousand metric tons)	839	3,976	90,024
Capture fisheries growth (avg. annual %, 1990–2012)	3.7	3.0	1.5
Aquaculture growth (avg. annual %, 1990–2012)	11.5	12.8	9.1
Marine protected areas (% of territorial waters)	0.0	9.1	7.3
Coral reef area (sq. km)	700	5,700	52,070
Mangroves area (sq. km)	192	217	50,160
Energy and emissions			
Energy use per capita (kg oil equivalent)	2,813	1,376	1,893
Energy from biomass products and waste (% of total)	0.1	0.9	8.5
Electric power consumption per capita (kWh)	2,649	1,696	2,932
Electricity generated using fossil fuel (% of total)	94.7	91.7	74.7
Electricity generated by hydropower (% of total)	5.0	5.5	20.0
CO_2 emissions per capita (metric tons)	7.7	3.9	5.4
Water and sanitation			
Internal freshwater resources per capita (cu. m)	1,704	679	6,791
Total freshwater withdrawal (% of internal resources)	72.6	122.1	7.4
Agriculture (% of total freshwater withdrawal)	92	86	69
Access to improved water source (% of total population)	96	90	93
Rural (% of rural population)	92	83	85
Urban (% of urban population)	98	95	98
Access to improved sanitation facilities (% of total population)	89	88	74
Rural (% of rural population)	82	80	62
Urban (% of urban population)	93	94	82
Environment and health			
Particulate matter (urban-pop.-weighted avg., µg/cu. m)	115	79	65
Acute resp. infection prevalence (% of children under five)	..	..	..
Diarrhea prevalence (% of children under five)	..	..	..
Under-five mortality rate (per 1,000 live births)	18	26	20
National accounting aggregates—savings, depletion and degradation			
Gross savings (% of GNI)	..	25.9	36.4
Consumption of fixed capital (% of GNI)	7.9	9.9	12.5
Education expenditure (% of GNI)	4.1	4.5	3.2
Energy depletion (% of GNI)	19.2	12.9	4.1
Mineral depletion (% of GNI)	0.4	0.5	1.2
Net forest depletion (% of GNI)	0.0	0.2	0.2
CO_2 damage (% of GNI)	1.6	0.7	0.8
Particulate emissions damage (% of GNI)	2.1	0.9	1.3
Adjusted net savings (% of GNI)	..	5.3	19.5

| Population (millions) | **32.6** | Land area (1,000 sq. km) | **434** | GDP ($ billions) | **215.8** |

	Country data	Middle East & N. Africa group	Upper middle-income group
GNI per capita, *World Bank Atlas* method ($)	6,130	*3,451*	6,969
Adjusted net national income per capita ($)	3,968	*2,602*	5,845
Change in wealth per capita (2010 $)	..	101	1,039
Urban population (% of total)	66.5	59.5	60.7

Agriculture

Agricultural land (% land area)	19	23	44
Agricultural irrigated land (% of total agricultural land)	..	..	..
Agricultural productivity, value added per worker (2005 $)	6,734	2,642	1,131
Cereal yield (kg per hectare)	1,742	2,350	4,255

Forests and biodiversity

Forest area (% land area)	1.9	2.4	29.1
Deforestation (avg. annual %, 2000–2010)	-0.1	-0.1	0.0
Terrestrial protected areas (% of total land area)	0.4	6.1	16.1
Threatened species, mammals	14		
Threatened species, birds	16		
Threatened species, fish	11		
Threatened species, higher plants	1		

Oceans

Total fisheries production (thousand metric tons)	76.1	3,976	90,024
Capture fisheries growth (avg. annual %, 1990–2012)	3.8	3.0	1.5
Aquaculture growth (avg. annual %, 1990–2012)	13.3	12.8	9.1
Marine protected areas (% of territorial waters)	10.2	9.1	7.3
Coral reef area (sq. km)	..	5,700	52,070
Mangroves area (sq. km)	..	217	50,160

Energy and emissions

Energy use per capita (kg oil equivalent)	1,266	1,376	1,893
Energy from biomass products and waste (% of total)	0.1	0.9	8.5
Electric power consumption per capita (kWh)	1,343	1,696	2,932
Electricity generated using fossil fuel (% of total)	74.9	91.7	74.7
Electricity generated by hydropower (% of total)	7.6	5.5	20.0
CO_2 emissions per capita (metric tons)	3.7	3.9	5.4

Water and sanitation

Internal freshwater resources per capita (cu. m)	1,108	679	6,791
Total freshwater withdrawal (% of internal resources)	187.5	122.1	7.4
Agriculture (% of total freshwater withdrawal)	79	86	69
Access to improved water source (% of total population)	85	90	93
Rural (% of rural population)	69	83	85
Urban (% of urban population)	94	95	98
Access to improved sanitation facilities (% of total population)	85	88	74
Rural (% of rural population)	82	80	62
Urban (% of urban population)	86	94	82

Environment and health

Particulate matter (urban-pop.-weighted avg., µg/cu. m)	36	79	65
Acute resp. infection prevalence (% of children under five)	..	..	..
Diarrhea prevalence (% of children under five)	..	..	..
Under-five mortality rate (per 1,000 live births)	34	26	20

National accounting aggregates—savings, depletion and degradation

Gross savings (% of GNI)	26.6	25.9	36.4
Consumption of fixed capital (% of GNI)	11.6	9.9	12.5
Education expenditure (% of GNI)	..	4.5	3.2
Energy depletion (% of GNI)	28.6	12.9	4.1
Mineral depletion (% of GNI)	0.0	0.5	1.2
Net forest depletion (% of GNI)	0.0	0.2	0.2
CO_2 damage (% of GNI)	0.6	0.7	0.8
Particulate emissions damage (% of GNI)	1.0	0.9	1.3
Adjusted net savings (% of GNI)	..	5.3	19.5

Ireland

| | Population (millions) | **4.6** | Land area (1,000 sq. km) | **69** | GDP ($ billions) | **210.6** |

	Country data	High-income group
GNI per capita, *World Bank Atlas* method ($)	39,110	38,444
Adjusted net national income per capita ($)	31,687	32,262
Change in wealth per capita (2010 $)	3,619	2,210
Urban population (% of total)	62.5	80.2
Agriculture		
Agricultural land (% land area)	66	29
Agricultural irrigated land (% of total agricultural land)	..	..
Agricultural productivity, value added per worker (2005 $)	..	*25,238*
Cereal yield (kg per hectare)	6,076	4,374
Forests and biodiversity		
Forest area (% land area)	10.9	35.0
Deforestation (avg. annual %, 2000–2010)	-1.5	0.0
Terrestrial protected areas (% of total land area)	14.3	13.9
Threatened species, mammals	5	
Threatened species, birds	3	
Threatened species, fish	21	
Threatened species, higher plants	1	
Oceans		
Total fisheries production (thousand metric tons)	342	37,661
Capture fisheries growth (avg. annual %, 1990–2012)	0.9	-2.0
Aquaculture growth (avg. annual %, 1990–2012)	1.4	2.5
Marine protected areas (% of territorial waters)	0.45	*14.4*
Coral reef area (sq. km)	..	82,210
Mangroves area (sq. km)	..	15,504
Energy and emissions		
Energy use per capita (kg oil equivalent)	2,888	4,872
Energy from biomass products and waste (% of total)	2.9	4.3
Electric power consumption per capita (kWh)	5,701	8,896
Electricity generated using fossil fuel (% of total)	72.3	61.8
Electricity generated by hydropower (% of total)	2.6	12.2
CO_2 emissions per capita (metric tons)	8.8	11.6
Water and sanitation		
Internal freshwater resources per capita (cu. m)	10,706	11,335
Total freshwater withdrawal (% of internal resources)	1.6	7.0
Agriculture (% of total freshwater withdrawal)	10	40
Access to improved water source (% of total population)	100	99
Rural (% of rural population)	100	98
Urban (% of urban population)	100	100
Access to improved sanitation facilities (% of total population)	99	96
Rural (% of rural population)	98	93
Urban (% of urban population)	100	97
Environment and health		
Particulate matter (urban-pop.-weighted avg., µg/cu. m)	18	27
Acute resp. infection prevalence (% of children under five)	..	..
Diarrhea prevalence (% of children under five)	..	..
Under-five mortality rate (per 1,000 live births)	4	6
National accounting aggregates—savings, depletion and degradation		
Gross savings (% of GNI)	19.6	20.1
Consumption of fixed capital (% of GNI)	15.5	14.2
Education expenditure (% of GNI)	7.1	4.7
Energy depletion (% of GNI)	0.0	1.6
Mineral depletion (% of GNI)	0.1	0.3
Net forest depletion (% of GNI)	0.0	0.0
CO_2 damage (% of GNI)	0.2	0.3
Particulate emissions damage (% of GNI)	0.1	0.3
Adjusted net savings (% of GNI)	10.9	8.1

Isle of Man

Population (thousands)	**85**	Land area (sq. km)	**570**	GDP ($ billions)	*4.1*

	Country data	High-income group
GNI per capita, *World Bank Atlas* method ($)	*48,550*	38,444
Adjusted net national income per capita ($)	..	32,262
Change in wealth per capita (2010 $)	..	2,210
Urban population (% of total)	50.5	80.2

Agriculture
Agricultural land (% land area)	75	29
Agricultural irrigated land (% of total agricultural land)	..	..
Agricultural productivity, value added per worker (2005 $)	..	*25,238*
Cereal yield (kg per hectare)	..	4,374

Forests and biodiversity
Forest area (% land area)	6.1	35.0
Deforestation (avg. annual %, 2000–2010)	0.0	0.0
Terrestrial protected areas (% of total land area)	..	13.9
Threatened species, mammals	1	
Threatened species, birds	0	
Threatened species, fish	2	
Threatened species, higher plants	0	

Oceans
Total fisheries production (thousand metric tons)	6.2	37,661
Capture fisheries growth (avg. annual %, 1990–2012)	1.9	-2.0
Aquaculture growth (avg. annual %, 1990–2012)	..	2.5
Marine protected areas (% of territorial waters)	..	*14.4*
Coral reef area (sq. km)	..	82,210
Mangroves area (sq. km)	..	15,504

Energy and emissions
Energy use per capita (kg oil equivalent)	..	4,872
Energy from biomass products and waste (% of total)	..	4.3
Electric power consumption per capita (kWh)	..	8,896
Electricity generated using fossil fuel (% of total)	..	61.8
Electricity generated by hydropower (% of total)	..	12.2
CO_2 emissions per capita (metric tons)	..	11.6

Water and sanitation
Internal freshwater resources per capita (cu. m)	..	11,335
Total freshwater withdrawal (% of internal resources)	..	7.0
Agriculture (% of total freshwater withdrawal)	..	40
Access to improved water source (% of total population)	..	99
Rural (% of rural population)	..	98
Urban (% of urban population)	..	100
Access to improved sanitation facilities (% of total population)	..	96
Rural (% of rural population)	..	93
Urban (% of urban population)	..	97

Environment and health
Particulate matter (urban-pop.-weighted avg., µg/cu. m)	..	27
Acute resp. infection prevalence (% of children under five)	..	..
Diarrhea prevalence (% of children under five)	..	..
Under-five mortality rate (per 1,000 live births)	..	6

National accounting aggregates—savings, depletion and degradation
Gross savings (% of GNI)	..	20.1
Consumption of fixed capital (% of GNI)	10.7	14.2
Education expenditure (% of GNI)	..	4.7
Energy depletion (% of GNI)	*0.0*	1.6
Mineral depletion (% of GNI)	*0.0*	0.3
Net forest depletion (% of GNI)	..	0.0
CO_2 damage (% of GNI)	..	0.3
Particulate emissions damage (% of GNI)	..	0.3
Adjusted net savings (% of GNI)	..	8.1

Israel

Population (millions)	**7.9**	Land area (1,000 sq. km)	**22**	GDP ($ billions)	**257.6**

	Country data	High-income group
GNI per capita, *World Bank Atlas* method ($)	32,030	38,444
Adjusted net national income per capita ($)	27,149	32,262
Change in wealth per capita (2010 $)	2,841	2,210
Urban population (% of total)	91.9	80.2
Agriculture		
Agricultural land (% land area)	24	29
Agricultural irrigated land (% of total agricultural land)	31.8	..
Agricultural productivity, value added per worker (2005 $)	..	25,238
Cereal yield (kg per hectare)	3,862	4,374
Forests and biodiversity		
Forest area (% land area)	7.1	35.0
Deforestation (avg. annual %, 2000–2010)	-0.1	0.0
Terrestrial protected areas (% of total land area)	17.4	13.9
Threatened species, mammals	15	
Threatened species, birds	14	
Threatened species, fish	35	
Threatened species, higher plants	0	
Oceans		
Total fisheries production (thousand metric tons)	22.4	37,661
Capture fisheries growth (avg. annual %, 1990–2012)	-5.4	-2.0
Aquaculture growth (avg. annual %, 1990–2012)	1.4	2.5
Marine protected areas (% of territorial waters)	19.9	14.4
Coral reef area (sq. km)	<10	82,210
Mangroves area (sq. km)	..	15,504
Energy and emissions		
Energy use per capita (kg oil equivalent)	2,994	4,872
Energy from biomass products and waste (% of total)	0.1	4.3
Electric power consumption per capita (kWh)	6,926	8,896
Electricity generated using fossil fuel (% of total)	99.4	61.8
Electricity generated by hydropower (% of total)	0.0	12.2
CO_2 emissions per capita (metric tons)	9.3	11.6
Water and sanitation		
Internal freshwater resources per capita (cu. m)	97	11,335
Total freshwater withdrawal (% of internal resources)	260.5	7.0
Agriculture (% of total freshwater withdrawal)	58	40
Access to improved water source (% of total population)	100	99
Rural (% of rural population)	100	98
Urban (% of urban population)	100	100
Access to improved sanitation facilities (% of total population)	100	96
Rural (% of rural population)	100	93
Urban (% of urban population)	100	97
Environment and health		
Particulate matter (urban-pop.-weighted avg., µg/cu. m)	47	27
Acute resp. infection prevalence (% of children under five)	..	..
Diarrhea prevalence (% of children under five)	..	..
Under-five mortality rate (per 1,000 live births)	4	6
National accounting aggregates—savings, depletion and degradation		
Gross savings (% of GNI)	21.7	20.1
Consumption of fixed capital (% of GNI)	13.8	14.2
Education expenditure (% of GNI)	5.8	4.7
Energy depletion (% of GNI)	0.1	1.6
Mineral depletion (% of GNI)	0.1	0.3
Net forest depletion (% of GNI)	0.0	0.0
CO_2 damage (% of GNI)	0.3	0.3
Particulate emissions damage (% of GNI)	0.8	0.3
Adjusted net savings (% of GNI)	12.4	8.1

Italy

Population (millions)	**59.5**	Land area (1,000 sq. km)	**294**	GDP ($ billions)	**2,013.4**

	Country data	High-income group
GNI per capita, *World Bank Atlas* method ($)	34,720	38,444
Adjusted net national income per capita ($)	27,648	32,262
Change in wealth per capita (2010 $)	726	2,210
Urban population (% of total)	68.6	80.2

Agriculture

Agricultural land (% land area)	47	29
Agricultural irrigated land (% of total agricultural land)	16.9	..
Agricultural productivity, value added per worker (2005 $)	43,151	25,238
Cereal yield (kg per hectare)	5,328	4,374

Forests and biodiversity

Forest area (% land area)	31.4	35.0
Deforestation (avg. annual %, 2000-2010)	-0.9	0.0
Terrestrial protected areas (% of total land area)	21.6	13.9
Threatened species, mammals	7	
Threatened species, birds	10	
Threatened species, fish	·47	
Threatened species, higher plants	66	

Oceans

Total fisheries production (thousand metric tons)	365	37,661
Capture fisheries growth (avg. annual %, 1990-2012)	-2.8	-2.0
Aquaculture growth (avg. annual %, 1990-2012)	0.3	2.5
Marine protected areas (% of territorial waters)	4.6	14.4
Coral reef area (sq. km)	..	82,210
Mangroves area (sq. km)	..	15,504

Energy and emissions

Energy use per capita (kg oil equivalent)	2,757	4,872
Energy from biomass products and waste (% of total)	6.1	4.3
Electric power consumption per capita (kWh)	5,393	8,896
Electricity generated using fossil fuel (% of total)	71.4	61.8
Electricity generated by hydropower (% of total)	15.2	12.2
CO_2 emissions per capita (metric tons)	6.7	11.6

Water and sanitation

Internal freshwater resources per capita (cu. m)	3,005	11,335
Total freshwater withdrawal (% of internal resources)	24.9	7.0
Agriculture (% of total freshwater withdrawal)	44	40
Access to improved water source (% of total population)	100	99
Rural (% of rural population)	100	98
Urban (% of urban population)	100	100
Access to improved sanitation facilities (% of total population)	..	96
Rural (% of rural population)	..	93
Urban (% of urban population)	..	97

Environment and health

Particulate matter (urban-pop.-weighted avg., μg/cu. m)	34	27
Acute resp. infection prevalence (% of children under five)	..	..
Diarrhea prevalence (% of children under five)	..	..
Under-five mortality rate (per 1,000 live births)	4	6

National accounting aggregates—savings, depletion and degradation

Gross savings (% of GNI)	17.5	20.1
Consumption of fixed capital (% of GNI)	17.6	14.2
Education expenditure (% of GNI)	4.3	4.7
Energy depletion (% of GNI)	0.1	1.6
Mineral depletion (% of GNI)	0.0	0.3
Net forest depletion (% of GNI)	0.0	0.0
CO_2 damage (% of GNI)	0.2	0.3
Particulate emissions damage (% of GNI)	0.5	0.3
Adjusted net savings (% of GNI)	3.3	8.1

Jamaica

Population (millions)	**2.7**	Land area (1,000 sq. km) **11**	GDP ($ billions) **14.8**

	Country data	Latin America & Caribbean group	Upper middle-income group
GNI per capita, *World Bank Atlas* method ($)	5,130	9,070	6,969
Adjusted net national income per capita ($)	4,748	7,325	5,845
Change in wealth per capita (2010 $)	..	180	1,039
Urban population (% of total)	52.2	79.0	60.7
Agriculture			
Agricultural land (% land area)	41	37	44
Agricultural irrigated land (% of total agricultural land)	..	..	..
Agricultural productivity, value added per worker (2005 $)	3,659	4,135	1,131
Cereal yield (kg per hectare)	1,283	4,082	4,255
Forests and biodiversity			
Forest area (% land area)	31.1	48.1	29.1
Deforestation (avg. annual %, 2000–2010)	0.1	0.5	0.0
Terrestrial protected areas (% of total land area)	15.9	21.4	16.1
Threatened species, mammals	5		
Threatened species, birds	10		
Threatened species, fish	22		
Threatened species, higher plants	212		
Oceans			
Total fisheries production (thousand metric tons)	15.6	10,964	90,024
Capture fisheries growth (avg. annual %, 1990–2012)	0.4	-0.6	1.5
Aquaculture growth (avg. annual %, 1990–2012)	-7.3	10.8	9.1
Marine protected areas (% of territorial waters)	5.6	9.0	7.3
Coral reef area (sq. km)	1,240	14,860	52,070
Mangroves area (sq. km)	97.5	39,988	50,160
Energy and emissions			
Energy use per capita (kg oil equivalent)	1,135	1,292	1,893
Energy from biomass products and waste (% of total)	17.2	16.0	8.5
Electric power consumption per capita (kWh)	1,553	1,985	2,932
Electricity generated using fossil fuel (% of total)	91.8	37.3	74.7
Electricity generated by hydropower (% of total)	2.0	55.1	20.0
CO_2 emissions per capita (metric tons)	2.7	2.7	5.4
Water and sanitation			
Internal freshwater resources per capita (cu. m)	3,483	21,735	6,791
Total freshwater withdrawal (% of internal resources)	6.2	2.0	7.4
Agriculture (% of total freshwater withdrawal)	34	68	69
Access to improved water source (% of total population)	93	94	93
Rural (% of rural population)	89	82	85
Urban (% of urban population)	97	97	98
Access to improved sanitation facilities (% of total population)	80	81	74
Rural (% of rural population)	82	62	62
Urban (% of urban population)	78	86	82
Environment and health			
Particulate matter (urban-pop.-weighted avg., µg/cu. m)	41	43	65
Acute resp. infection prevalence (% of children under five)	..	..	..
Diarrhea prevalence (% of children under five)	..	..	..
Under-five mortality rate (per 1,000 live births)	17	19	20
National accounting aggregates—savings, depletion and degradation			
Gross savings (% of GNI)	8.5	19.0	36.4
Consumption of fixed capital (% of GNI)	8.4	12.2	12.5
Education expenditure (% of GNI)	6.0	5.1	3.2
Energy depletion (% of GNI)	0.0	4.7	4.1
Mineral depletion (% of GNI)	1.6	1.2	1.2
Net forest depletion (% of GNI)	0.3	0.4	0.2
CO_2 damage (% of GNI)	0.4	0.3	0.8
Particulate emissions damage (% of GNI)	0.5	0.8	1.3
Adjusted net savings (% of GNI)	3.5	4.5	19.5

Japan

Population (millions) **127.6** Land area (1,000 sq. km) **365** GDP ($ billions) **5,961.1**

	Country data	High-income group
GNI per capita, *World Bank Atlas* method ($)	47,870	38,444
Adjusted net national income per capita ($)	37,487	32,262
Change in wealth per capita (2010 $)	2,023	2,210
Urban population (% of total)	91.7	80.2

Agriculture

Agricultural land (% land area)	13	29
Agricultural irrigated land (% of total agricultural land)	34.5	..
Agricultural productivity, value added per worker (2005 $)	*42,943*	*25,238*
Cereal yield (kg per hectare)	5,020	4,374

Forests and biodiversity

Forest area (% land area)	68.6	35.0
Deforestation (avg. annual %, 2000–2010)	0.0	0.0
Terrestrial protected areas (% of total land area)	16.5	13.9
Threatened species, mammals	27	
Threatened species, birds	40	
Threatened species, fish	66	
Threatened species, higher plants	17	

Oceans

Total fisheries production (thousand metric tons)	4,817	37,661
Capture fisheries growth (avg. annual %, 1990–2012)	-4.3	-2.0
Aquaculture growth (avg. annual %, 1990–2012)	-1.1	2.5
Marine protected areas (% of territorial waters)	30.0	*14.4*
Coral reef area (sq. km)	2,900	82,210
Mangroves area (sq. km)	7.4	15,504

Energy and emissions

Energy use per capita (kg oil equivalent)	3,610	4,872
Energy from biomass products and waste (% of total)	2.3	4.3
Electric power consumption per capita (kWh)	7,848	8,896
Electricity generated using fossil fuel (% of total)	72.9	61.8
Electricity generated by hydropower (% of total)	8.0	12.2
CO_2 emissions per capita (metric tons)	9.2	11.6

Water and sanitation

Internal freshwater resources per capita (cu. m)	3,364	11,335
Total freshwater withdrawal (% of internal resources)	20.9	7.0
Agriculture (% of total freshwater withdrawal)	63	40
Access to improved water source (% of total population)	100	99
Rural (% of rural population)	100	98
Urban (% of urban population)	100	100
Access to improved sanitation facilities (% of total population)	100	96
Rural (% of rural population)	100	93
Urban (% of urban population)	100	97

Environment and health

Particulate matter (urban-pop.-weighted avg., µg/cu. m)	19	27
Acute resp. infection prevalence (% of children under five)	..	..
Diarrhea prevalence (% of children under five)	..	..
Under-five mortality rate (per 1,000 live births)	3	6

National accounting aggregates—savings, depletion and degradation

Gross savings (% of GNI)	20.9	20.1
Consumption of fixed capital (% of GNI)	22.2	14.2
Education expenditure (% of GNI)	3.2	4.7
Energy depletion (% of GNI)	0.0	1.6
Mineral depletion (% of GNI)	0.0	0.3
Net forest depletion (% of GNI)	0.0	0.0
CO_2 damage (% of GNI)	0.2	0.3
Particulate emissions damage (% of GNI)	0.1	0.3
Adjusted net savings (% of GNI)	1.5	8.1

Jordan

| Population (millions) | **6.3** Land area (1,000 sq. km) | **89** | GDP ($ billions) | **31.0** |

	Country data	Middle East & N. Africa group	Upper middle-income group
GNI per capita, *World Bank Atlas* method ($)	4,670	3,451	6,969
Adjusted net national income per capita ($)	4,201	2,602	5,845
Change in wealth per capita (2010 $)	93	101	1,039
Urban population (% of total)	83.0	59.5	60.7
Agriculture			
Agricultural land (% land area)	11	23	44
Agricultural irrigated land (% of total agricultural land)	9.6	..	..
Agricultural productivity, value added per worker (2005 $)	4,461	2,642	1,131
Cereal yield (kg per hectare)	1,556	2,350	4,255
Forests and biodiversity			
Forest area (% land area)	1.1	2.4	29.1
Deforestation (avg. annual %, 2000–2010)	0.0	-0.1	0.0
Terrestrial protected areas (% of total land area)	1.9	6.1	16.1
Threatened species, mammals	13		
Threatened species, birds	10		
Threatened species, fish	13		
Threatened species, higher plants	1		
Oceans			
Total fisheries production (thousand metric tons)	1.1	3,976	90,024
Capture fisheries growth (avg. annual %, 1990–2012)	1.6	3.0	1.5
Aquaculture growth (avg. annual %, 1990–2012)	10.9	12.8	9.1
Marine protected areas (% of territorial waters)	30.0	9.1	7.3
Coral reef area (sq. km)	<50	5,700	52,070
Mangroves area (sq. km)	..	217	50,160
Energy and emissions			
Energy use per capita (kg oil equivalent)	1,143	1,376	1,893
Energy from biomass products and waste (% of total)	0.1	0.9	8.5
Electric power consumption per capita (kWh)	2,289	1,696	2,932
Electricity generated using fossil fuel (% of total)	99.5	91.7	74.7
Electricity generated by hydropower (% of total)	0.4	5.5	20.0
CO_2 emissions per capita (metric tons)	3.4	3.9	5.4
Water and sanitation			
Internal freshwater resources per capita (cu. m)	110	679	6,791
Total freshwater withdrawal (% of internal resources)	138.0	122.1	7.4
Agriculture (% of total freshwater withdrawal)	65	86	69
Access to improved water source (% of total population)	96	90	93
Rural (% of rural population)	90	83	85
Urban (% of urban population)	97	95	98
Access to improved sanitation facilities (% of total population)	98	88	74
Rural (% of rural population)	98	80	62
Urban (% of urban population)	98	94	82
Environment and health			
Particulate matter (urban-pop.-weighted avg., μg/cu. m)	38	79	65
Acute resp. infection prevalence (% of children under five)	7	..	..
Diarrhea prevalence (% of children under five)	16	..	..
Under-five mortality rate (per 1,000 live births)	19	26	20
National accounting aggregates—savings, depletion and degradation			
Gross savings (% of GNI)	8.5	25.9	36.4
Consumption of fixed capital (% of GNI)	11.8	9.9	12.5
Education expenditure (% of GNI)	5.6	4.5	3.2
Energy depletion (% of GNI)	0.0	12.9	4.1
Mineral depletion (% of GNI)	1.7	0.5	1.2
Net forest depletion (% of GNI)	0.1	0.2	0.2
CO_2 damage (% of GNI)	0.6	0.7	0.8
Particulate emissions damage (% of GNI)	0.7	0.9	1.3
Adjusted net savings (% of GNI)	-0.7	5.3	19.5

Kazakhstan

Population (millions)	**16.8**	Land area (1,000 sq. km)	**2,700**	GDP ($ billions)	**203.5**

	Country data	Europe & Central Asia group	Upper middle-income group
GNI per capita, *World Bank Atlas* method ($)	9,780	6,658	6,969
Adjusted net national income per capita ($)	6,340	5,541	5,845
Change in wealth per capita (2010 $)	-1,655	263	1,039
Urban population (% of total)	53.5	60.2	60.7
Agriculture			
Agricultural land (% land area)	77	66	44
Agricultural irrigated land (% of total agricultural land)	..	..	..
Agricultural productivity, value added per worker (2005 $)	3,533	4,866	1,131
Cereal yield (kg per hectare)	950	2,519	4,255
Forests and biodiversity			
Forest area (% land area)	1.2	10.5	29.1
Deforestation (avg. annual %, 2000-2010)	0.2	-0.5	0.0
Terrestrial protected areas (% of total land area)	3.3	5.1	16.1
Threatened species, mammals	16		
Threatened species, birds	22		
Threatened species, fish	15		
Threatened species, higher plants	17		
Oceans			
Total fisheries production (thousand metric tons)	43.3	1,022	90,024
Capture fisheries growth (avg. annual %, 1990-2012)	-2.6	-4.0	1.5
Aquaculture growth (avg. annual %, 1990-2012)	-15.2	1.8	9.1
Marine protected areas (% of territorial waters)	10.5	10.4	7.3
Coral reef area (sq. km)	..	..	52,070
Mangroves area (sq. km)	..	..	50,160
Energy and emissions			
Energy use per capita (kg oil equivalent)	4,717	2,078	1,893
Energy from biomass products and waste (% of total)	0.1	2.9	8.5
Electric power consumption per capita (kWh)	4,893	2,951	2,932
Electricity generated using fossil fuel (% of total)	90.9	65.8	74.7
Electricity generated by hydropower (% of total)	9.1	17.9	20.0
CO_2 emissions per capita (metric tons)	15.2	5.3	5.4
Water and sanitation			
Internal freshwater resources per capita (cu. m)	3,887	2,744	6,791
Total freshwater withdrawal (% of internal resources)	32.9	34.8	7.4
Agriculture (% of total freshwater withdrawal)	66	70	69
Access to improved water source (% of total population)	93	95	93
Rural (% of rural population)	86	89	85
Urban (% of urban population)	99	99	98
Access to improved sanitation facilities (% of total population)	97	94	74
Rural (% of rural population)	98	90	62
Urban (% of urban population)	97	97	82
Environment and health			
Particulate matter (urban-pop.-weighted avg., µg/cu. m)	47	48	65
Acute resp. infection prevalence (% of children under five)	..	..	..
Diarrhea prevalence (% of children under five)	..	..	..
Under-five mortality rate (per 1,000 live births)	19	22	20
National accounting aggregates—savings, depletion and degradation			
Gross savings (% of GNI)	30.4	18.9	36.4
Consumption of fixed capital (% of GNI)	15.8	12.4	12.5
Education expenditure (% of GNI)	4.4	3.8	3.2
Energy depletion (% of GNI)	21.5	4.4	4.1
Mineral depletion (% of GNI)	2.1	0.6	1.2
Net forest depletion (% of GNI)	0.0	0.0	0.2
CO_2 damage (% of GNI)	1.6	0.8	0.8
Particulate emissions damage (% of GNI)	1.9	1.8	1.3
Adjusted net savings (% of GNI)	-8.0	2.8	19.5

Kenya

	Country data	Sub-Saharan Africa group	Low-Income group
Population (millions) **43.2** Land area (1,000 sq. km)	**569** GDP ($ billions)		**40.7**

	Country data	Sub-Saharan Africa group	Low-Income group
GNI per capita, *World Bank Atlas* method ($)	860	1,547	594
Adjusted net national income per capita ($)	847	1,005	495
Change in wealth per capita (2010 $)	-76	-273	-39
Urban population (% of total)	24.4	36.8	28.2
Agriculture			
Agricultural land (% land area)	48	44	39
Agricultural irrigated land (% of total agricultural land)	0.0	..	..
Agricultural productivity, value added per worker (2005 $)	369	765	367
Cereal yield (kg per hectare)	1,660	1,417	1,982
Forests and biodiversity			
Forest area (% land area)	6.1	27.4	27.4
Deforestation (avg. annual %, 2000–2010)	0.3	0.5	0.6
Terrestrial protected areas (% of total land area)	11.6	16.4	13.7
Threatened species, mammals	28		
Threatened species, birds	34		
Threatened species, fish	69		
Threatened species, higher plants	132		
Oceans			
Total fisheries production (thousand metric tons)	179	6,906	11,789
Capture fisheries growth (avg. annual %, 1990–2012)	-1.1	2.1	3.8
Aquaculture growth (avg. annual %, 1990–2012)	13.9	15.9	5.1
Marine protected areas (% of territorial waters)	20.2	11.7	13.1
Coral reef area (sq. km)	630	17,980	15,120
Mangroves area (sq. km)	610	27,808	25,817
Energy and emissions			
Energy use per capita (kg oil equivalent)	480	681	360
Energy from biomass products and waste (% of total)	72.4	57.6	66.0
Electric power consumption per capita (kWh)	155	535	233
Electricity generated using fossil fuel (% of total)	32.7	65.1	30.9
Electricity generated by hydropower (% of total)	44.0	20.0	45.5
CO_2 emissions per capita (metric tons)	0.3	0.8	0.3
Water and sanitation			
Internal freshwater resources per capita (cu. m)	493	4,391	5,121
Total freshwater withdrawal (% of internal resources)	13.2	3.2	4.4
Agriculture (% of total freshwater withdrawal)	79	84	90
Access to improved water source (% of total population)	62	64	69
Rural (% of rural population)	55	53	61
Urban (% of urban population)	82	85	88
Access to improved sanitation facilities (% of total population)	30	30	37
Rural (% of rural population)	29	23	33
Urban (% of urban population)	31	41	46
Environment and health			
Particulate matter (urban-pop.-weighted avg., µg/cu. m)	66	77	74
Acute resp. infection prevalence (% of children under five)	8	5	6
Diarrhea prevalence (% of children under five)	17	14	14
Under-five mortality rate (per 1,000 live births)	73	98	82
National accounting aggregates—savings, depletion and degradation			
Gross savings (% of GNI)	9.4	26.3	24.6
Consumption of fixed capital (% of GNI)	6.3	13.0	11.8
Education expenditure (% of GNI)	5.9	3.4	3.2
Energy depletion (% of GNI)	0.0	10.3	1.4
Mineral depletion (% of GNI)	0.1	1.8	1.9
Net forest depletion (% of GNI)	3.3	1.8	4.4
CO_2 damage (% of GNI)	0.4	0.6	0.4
Particulate emissions damage (% of GNI)	0.5	1.2	1.0
Adjusted net savings (% of GNI)	4.7	0.9	7.0

Kiribati

| Population (thousands) **101** | Land area (sq. km) | **810** | GDP ($ millions) | **175.0** |

	Country data	East Asia & Pacific group	Lower middle-income group
GNI per capita, *World Bank Atlas* method ($)	2,520	4,884	1,965
Adjusted net national income per capita ($)	2,364	4,305	1,574
Change in wealth per capita (2010 $)	..	1,172	117
Urban population (% of total)	44.1	49.6	38.9
Agriculture			
Agricultural land (% land area)	42	48	46
Agricultural irrigated land (% of total agricultural land)	..	..	..
Agricultural productivity, value added per worker (2005 $)	2,382	794	938
Cereal yield (kg per hectare)	..	5,145	3,029
Forests and biodiversity			
Forest area (% land area)	15.0	29.7	26.9
Deforestation (avg. annual %, 2000–2010)	0.0	-0.4	0.3
Terrestrial protected areas (% of total land area)	22.0	15.1	11.9
Threatened species, mammals	1		
Threatened species, birds	6		
Threatened species, fish	11		
Threatened species, higher plants	0		
Oceans			
Total fisheries production (thousand metric tons)	90.8	108,399	43,067
Capture fisheries growth (avg. annual %, 1990–2012)	5.2	3.4	2.6
Aquaculture growth (avg. annual %, 1990–2012)	2.2	9.1	9.9
Marine protected areas (% of territorial waters)	0.11	1.4	14.7
Coral reef area (sq. km)	2,940	137,690	124,480
Mangroves area (sq. km)	2.6	56,537	58,917
Energy and emissions			
Energy use per capita (kg oil equivalent)	118	1,671	687
Energy from biomass products and waste (% of total)	..	10.1	26.8
Electric power consumption per capita (kWh)	..	2,582	734
Electricity generated using fossil fuel (% of total)	..	80.9	72.3
Electricity generated by hydropower (% of total)	..	14.5	16.9
CO_2 emissions per capita (metric tons)	0.6	4.9	1.6
Water and sanitation			
Internal freshwater resources per capita (cu. m)	..	4,438	3,144
Total freshwater withdrawal (% of internal resources)	..	10.9	19.6
Agriculture (% of total freshwater withdrawal)	..	73	88
Access to improved water source (% of total population)	67	91	88
Rural (% of rural population)	51	85	85
Urban (% of urban population)	87	97	94
Access to improved sanitation facilities (% of total population)	40	67	48
Rural (% of rural population)	31	58	36
Urban (% of urban population)	51	76	66
Environment and health			
Particulate matter (urban-pop.-weighted avg., µg/cu. m)	..	75	90
Acute resp. infection prevalence (% of children under five)	..	..	..
Diarrhea prevalence (% of children under five)	..	..	..
Under-five mortality rate (per 1,000 live births)	60	21	61
National accounting aggregates—savings, depletion and degradation			
Gross savings (% of GNI)	..	47.6	28.6
Consumption of fixed capital (% of GNI)	7.7	12.0	11.1
Education expenditure (% of GNI)	..	2.1	3.1
Energy depletion (% of GNI)	0.0	2.7	4.4
Mineral depletion (% of GNI)	0.0	1.4	1.1
Net forest depletion (% of GNI)	0.1	0.1	0.8
CO_2 damage (% of GNI)	0.2	1.0	0.9
Particulate emissions damage (% of GNI)	..	1.6	1.4
Adjusted net savings (% of GNI)	..	30.9	12.0

Korea, Dem. People's Rep.

Population (millions)	**24.8**	Land area (1,000 sq. km)	**120**	GDP ($ millions)	..

	Country data	East Asia & Pacific group	Low-Income group
GNI per capita, *World Bank Atlas* method ($)	..	4,884	594
Adjusted net national income per capita ($)	..	4,305	495
Change in wealth per capita (2010 $)	..	1,172	-39
Urban population (% of total)	60.5	49.6	28.2
Agriculture			
Agricultural land (% land area)	21	48	39
Agricultural irrigated land (% of total agricultural land)	..	..	..
Agricultural productivity, value added per worker (2005 $)	..	794	367
Cereal yield (kg per hectare)	3,128	5,145	1,982
Forests and biodiversity			
Forest area (% land area)	46.0	29.7	27.4
Deforestation (avg. annual %, 2000–2010)	2.0	-0.4	0.6
Terrestrial protected areas (% of total land area)	2.3	15.1	13.7
Threatened species, mammals	9		
Threatened species, birds	25		
Threatened species, fish	14		
Threatened species, higher plants	8		
Oceans			
Total fisheries production (thousand metric tons)	720	108,399	11,789
Capture fisheries growth (avg. annual %, 1990–2012)	-3.6	3.4	3.8
Aquaculture growth (avg. annual %, 1990–2012)	-2.6	9.1	5.1
Marine protected areas (% of territorial waters)	3.9	1.4	13.1
Coral reef area (sq. km)	..	137,690	15,120
Mangroves area (sq. km)	..	56,537	25,817
Energy and emissions			
Energy use per capita (kg oil equivalent)	773	1,671	360
Energy from biomass products and waste (% of total)	5.6	10.1	66.0
Electric power consumption per capita (kWh)	739	2,582	233
Electricity generated using fossil fuel (% of total)	39.0	80.9	30.9
Electricity generated by hydropower (% of total)	61.0	14.5	45.5
CO_2 emissions per capita (metric tons)	2.9	4.9	0.3
Water and sanitation			
Internal freshwater resources per capita (cu. m)	2,720	4,438	5,121
Total freshwater withdrawal (% of internal resources)	12.9	10.9	4.4
Agriculture (% of total freshwater withdrawal)	76	73	90
Access to improved water source (% of total population)	98	91	69
Rural (% of rural population)	97	85	61
Urban (% of urban population)	99	97	88
Access to improved sanitation facilities (% of total population)	82	67	37
Rural (% of rural population)	73	58	33
Urban (% of urban population)	88	76	46
Environment and health			
Particulate matter (urban-pop.-weighted avg., μg/cu. m)	124	75	74
Acute resp. infection prevalence (% of children under five)	..	..	6
Diarrhea prevalence (% of children under five)	..	..	14
Under-five mortality rate (per 1,000 live births)	29	21	82
National accounting aggregates—savings, depletion and degradation			
Gross savings (% of GNI)	..	47.6	24.6
Consumption of fixed capital (% of GNI)	..	12.0	11.8
Education expenditure (% of GNI)	..	2.1	3.2
Energy depletion (% of GNI)	..	2.7	1.4
Mineral depletion (% of GNI)	..	1.4	1.9
Net forest depletion (% of GNI)	..	0.1	4.4
CO_2 damage (% of GNI)	..	1.0	0.4
Particulate emissions damage (% of GNI)	3.1	1.6	1.0
Adjusted net savings (% of GNI)	..	30.9	7.0

Korea, Rep.

Population (millions) **50.0** Land area (1,000 sq. km) **97** GDP ($ billions) **1,129.6**

	Country data	High-income group
GNI per capita, *World Bank Atlas* method ($)	22,670	38,444
Adjusted net national income per capita ($)	19,201	32,262
Change in wealth per capita (2010 $)	4,427	2,210
Urban population (% of total)	83.5	80.2

Agriculture
Agricultural land (% land area)	18	29
Agricultural irrigated land (% of total agricultural land)	51.6	..
Agricultural productivity, value added per worker (2005 $)	23,882	25,238
Cereal yield (kg per hectare)	7,114	4,374

Forests and biodiversity
Forest area (% land area)	64.0	35.0
Deforestation (avg. annual %, 2000–2010)	0.1	0.0
Terrestrial protected areas (% of total land area)	6.3	13.9
Threatened species, mammals	9	
Threatened species, birds	29	
Threatened species, fish	18	
Threatened species, higher plants	6	

Oceans
Total fisheries production (thousand metric tons)	3,187	37,661
Capture fisheries growth (avg. annual %, 1990–2012)	-1.8	-2.0
Aquaculture growth (avg. annual %, 1990–2012)	3.0	2.5
Marine protected areas (% of territorial waters)	0.17	14.4
Coral reef area (sq. km)	..	82,210
Mangroves area (sq. km)	..	15,504

Energy and emissions
Energy use per capita (kg oil equivalent)	5,232	4,872
Energy from biomass products and waste (% of total)	1.5	4.3
Electric power consumption per capita (kWh)	10,162	8,896
Electricity generated using fossil fuel (% of total)	68.6	61.8
Electricity generated by hydropower (% of total)	0.9	12.2
CO_2 emissions per capita (metric tons)	11.5	11.6

Water and sanitation
Internal freshwater resources per capita (cu. m)	1,303	11,335
Total freshwater withdrawal (% of internal resources)	39.3	7.0
Agriculture (% of total freshwater withdrawal)	62	40
Access to improved water source (% of total population)	98	99
Rural (% of rural population)	88	98
Urban (% of urban population)	100	100
Access to improved sanitation facilities (% of total population)	100	96
Rural (% of rural population)	100	93
Urban (% of urban population)	100	97

Environment and health
Particulate matter (urban-pop.-weighted avg., µg/cu. m)	46	27
Acute resp. infection prevalence (% of children under five)	..	..
Diarrhea prevalence (% of children under five)	..	..
Under-five mortality rate (per 1,000 live births)	4	6

National accounting aggregates—savings, depletion and degradation
Gross savings (% of GNI)	30.8	20.1
Consumption of fixed capital (% of GNI)	15.5	14.2
Education expenditure (% of GNI)	4.2	4.7
Energy depletion (% of GNI)	0.0	1.6
Mineral depletion (% of GNI)	0.0	0.3
Net forest depletion (% of GNI)	0.0	0.0
CO_2 damage (% of GNI)	0.5	0.3
Particulate emissions damage (% of GNI)	0.8	0.3
Adjusted net savings (% of GNI)	18.1	8.1

Kosovo

Population (millions) **1.8** Land area (1,000 sq. km) **11** GDP ($ billions) **6.4**

	Country data	Europe & Central Asia group	Lower middle-income group
GNI per capita, *World Bank Atlas* method ($)	3,600	6,658	1,965
Adjusted net national income per capita ($)	..	5,541	1,574
Change in wealth per capita (2010 $)	..	263	117
Urban population (% of total)	..	60.2	38.9
Agriculture			
Agricultural land (% land area)	52	66	46
Agricultural irrigated land (% of total agricultural land)	..	..	..
Agricultural productivity, value added per worker (2005 $)	..	4,866	938
Cereal yield (kg per hectare)	..	2,519	3,029
Forests and biodiversity			
Forest area (% land area)	..	10.5	26.9
Deforestation (avg. annual %, 2000–2010)	..	-0.5	0.3
Terrestrial protected areas (% of total land area)	..	5.1	11.9
Threatened species, mammals	..		
Threatened species, birds	..		
Threatened species, fish	..		
Threatened species, higher plants	..		
Oceans			
Total fisheries production (thousand metric tons)	..	1,022	43,067
Capture fisheries growth (avg. annual %, 1990–2012)	..	-4.0	2.6
Aquaculture growth (avg. annual %, 1990–2012)	..	1.8	9.9
Marine protected areas (% of territorial waters)	..	10.4	14.7
Coral reef area (sq. km)	..	..	124,480
Mangroves area (sq. km)	..	..	58,917
Energy and emissions			
Energy use per capita (kg oil equivalent)	1,411	2,078	687
Energy from biomass products and waste (% of total)	9.6	2.9	26.8
Electric power consumption per capita (kWh)	2,947	2,951	734
Electricity generated using fossil fuel (% of total)	98.2	65.8	72.3
Electricity generated by hydropower (% of total)	1.8	17.9	16.9
CO_2 emissions per capita (metric tons)	..	5.3	1.6
Water and sanitation			
Internal freshwater resources per capita (cu. m)	..	2,744	3,144
Total freshwater withdrawal (% of internal resources)	..	34.8	19.6
Agriculture (% of total freshwater withdrawal)	..	70	88
Access to improved water source (% of total population)	..	95	88
Rural (% of rural population)	..	89	85
Urban (% of urban population)	..	99	94
Access to improved sanitation facilities (% of total population)	..	94	48
Rural (% of rural population)	..	90	36
Urban (% of urban population)	..	97	66
Environment and health			
Particulate matter (urban-pop.-weighted avg., µg/cu. m)	48	48	90
Acute resp. infection prevalence (% of children under five)	..	..	..
Diarrhea prevalence (% of children under five)	..	..	..
Under-five mortality rate (per 1,000 live births)	..	22	61
National accounting aggregates—savings, depletion and degradation			
Gross savings (% of GNI)	18.5	18.9	28.6
Consumption of fixed capital (% of GNI)	11.4	12.4	11.1
Education expenditure (% of GNI)	..	3.8	3.1
Energy depletion (% of GNI)	0.3	4.4	4.4
Mineral depletion (% of GNI)	1.2	0.6	1.1
Net forest depletion (% of GNI)	..	0.0	0.8
CO_2 damage (% of GNI)	..	0.8	0.9
Particulate emissions damage (% of GNI)	..	1.8	1.4
Adjusted net savings (% of GNI)	..	2.8	12.0

Kuwait

| Population (millions) | **3.3** | Land area (1,000 sq. km) | **18** | GDP ($ billions) | **183.2** |

	Country data	High-income group
GNI per capita, *World Bank Atlas* method ($)	44,880	38,444
Adjusted net national income per capita ($)	32,643	32,262
Change in wealth per capita (2010 $)	-22,542	2,210
Urban population (% of total)	98.3	80.2
Agriculture		
Agricultural land (% land area)	9	29
Agricultural irrigated land (% of total agricultural land)	..	..
Agricultural productivity, value added per worker (2005 $)	..	25,238
Cereal yield (kg per hectare)	8,804	4,374
Forests and biodiversity		
Forest area (% land area)	0.4	35.0
Deforestation (avg. annual %, 2000–2010)	-2.6	0.0
Terrestrial protected areas (% of total land area)	18.4	13.9
Threatened species, mammals	6	
Threatened species, birds	8	
Threatened species, fish	11	
Threatened species, higher plants	0	
Oceans		
Total fisheries production (thousand metric tons)	4.8	37,661
Capture fisheries growth (avg. annual %, 1990–2012)	0.0	-2.0
Aquaculture growth (avg. annual %, 1990–2012)	..	2.5
Marine protected areas (% of territorial waters)	0.01	14.4
Coral reef area (sq. km)	110	82,210
Mangroves area (sq. km)	0.05	15,504
Energy and emissions		
Energy use per capita (kg oil equivalent)	10,408	4,872
Energy from biomass products and waste (% of total)	0.0	4.3
Electric power consumption per capita (kWh)	16,122	8,896
Electricity generated using fossil fuel (% of total)	100.0	61.8
Electricity generated by hydropower (% of total)	0.0	12.2
CO_2 emissions per capita (metric tons)	31.3	11.6
Water and sanitation		
Internal freshwater resources per capita (cu. m)	0	11,335
Total freshwater withdrawal (% of internal resources)	..	7.0
Agriculture (% of total freshwater withdrawal)	54	40
Access to improved water source (% of total population)	99	99
Rural (% of rural population)	99	98
Urban (% of urban population)	99	100
Access to improved sanitation facilities (% of total population)	100	96
Rural (% of rural population)	100	93
Urban (% of urban population)	100	97
Environment and health		
Particulate matter (urban-pop.-weighted avg., µg/cu. m)	89	27
Acute resp. infection prevalence (% of children under five)	..	..
Diarrhea prevalence (% of children under five)	..	..
Under-five mortality rate (per 1,000 live births)	11	6
National accounting aggregates—savings, depletion and degradation		
Gross savings (% of GNI)	55.7	20.1
Consumption of fixed capital (% of GNI)	6.2	14.2
Education expenditure (% of GNI)	3.2	4.7
Energy depletion (% of GNI)	34.4	1.6
Mineral depletion (% of GNI)	0.0	0.3
Net forest depletion (% of GNI)	0.0	0.0
CO_2 damage (% of GNI)	0.6	0.3
Particulate emissions damage (% of GNI)	1.3	0.3
Adjusted net savings (% of GNI)	16.4	8.1

Kyrgyz Republic

Population (millions)	**5.6** Land area (1,000 sq. km)	**192** GDP ($ billions)	**6.5**

	Country data	Europe & Central Asia group	Low-income group
GNI per capita, *World Bank Atlas* method ($)	990	6,658	594
Adjusted net national income per capita ($)	822	5,541	495
Change in wealth per capita (2010 $)	-23	263	-39
Urban population (% of total)	35.5	60.2	28.2
Agriculture			
Agricultural land (% land area)	55	66	39
Agricultural irrigated land (% of total agricultural land)	9.4	..	..
Agricultural productivity, value added per worker (2005 $)	1,367	4,866	367
Cereal yield (kg per hectare)	2,367	2,519	1,982
Forests and biodiversity			
Forest area (% land area)	5.1	10.5	27.4
Deforestation (avg. annual %, 2000–2010)	-1.1	-0.5	0.6
Terrestrial protected areas (% of total land area)	6.3	5.1	13.7
Threatened species, mammals	6		
Threatened species, birds	12		
Threatened species, fish	3		
Threatened species, higher plants	14		
Oceans			
Total fisheries production (thousand metric tons)	0.32	1,022	11,789
Capture fisheries growth (avg. annual %, 1990–2012)	-10.7	-4.0	3.8
Aquaculture growth (avg. annual %, 1990–2012)	-5.3	1.8	5.1
Marine protected areas (% of territorial waters)	..	10.4	13.1
Coral reef area (sq. km)	..	..	15,120
Mangroves area (sq. km)	..	..	25,817
Energy and emissions			
Energy use per capita (kg oil equivalent)	562	2,078	360
Energy from biomass products and waste (% of total)	0.1	2.9	66.0
Electric power consumption per capita (kWh)	1,642	2,951	233
Electricity generated using fossil fuel (% of total)	6.7	65.8	30.9
Electricity generated by hydropower (% of total)	93.3	17.9	45.5
CO_2 emissions per capita (metric tons)	1.2	5.3	0.3
Water and sanitation			
Internal freshwater resources per capita (cu. m)	8,873	2,744	5,121
Total freshwater withdrawal (% of internal resources)	20.6	34.8	4.4
Agriculture (% of total freshwater withdrawal)	94	70	90
Access to improved water source (% of total population)	88	95	69
Rural (% of rural population)	82	89	61
Urban (% of urban population)	97	99	88
Access to improved sanitation facilities (% of total population)	92	94	37
Rural (% of rural population)	92	90	33
Urban (% of urban population)	92	97	46
Environment and health			
Particulate matter (urban-pop.-weighted avg., µg/cu. m)	50	48	74
Acute resp. infection prevalence (% of children under five)	1	..	6
Diarrhea prevalence (% of children under five)	5	..	14
Under-five mortality rate (per 1,000 live births)	27	22	82
National accounting aggregates—savings, depletion and degradation			
Gross savings (% of GNI)	31.5	18.9	24.6
Consumption of fixed capital (% of GNI)	12.6	12.4	11.8
Education expenditure (% of GNI)	7.0	3.8	3.2
Energy depletion (% of GNI)	0.8	4.4	1.4
Mineral depletion (% of GNI)	10.9	0.6	1.9
Net forest depletion (% of GNI)	0.0	0.0	4.4
CO_2 damage (% of GNI)	1.1	0.8	0.4
Particulate emissions damage (% of GNI)	1.0	1.8	1.0
Adjusted net savings (% of GNI)	12.1	2.8	7.0

Lao PDR

	Country data	East Asia & Pacific group	Lower middle-income group
Population (millions) **6.6** Land area (1,000 sq. km) **231** GDP ($ billions) **9.4**			

	Country data	East Asia & Pacific group	Lower middle-income group
GNI per capita, *World Bank Atlas* method ($)	1,270	4,884	1,965
Adjusted net national income per capita ($)	946	4,305	1,574
Change in wealth per capita (2010 $)	-297	1,172	117
Urban population (% of total)	35.3	49.6	38.9
Agriculture			
Agricultural land (% land area)	10	48	46
Agricultural irrigated land (% of total agricultural land)	..	..	..
Agricultural productivity, value added per worker (2005 $)	476	794	938
Cereal yield (kg per hectare)	4,082	5,145	3,029
Forests and biodiversity			
Forest area (% land area)	67.9	29.7	26.9
Deforestation (avg. annual %, 2000–2010)	0.5	-0.4	0.3
Terrestrial protected areas (% of total land area)	16.7	15.1	11.9
Threatened species, mammals	45		
Threatened species, birds	24		
Threatened species, fish	55		
Threatened species, higher plants	32		
Oceans			
Total fisheries production (thousand metric tons)	136	108,399	43,067
Capture fisheries growth (avg. annual %, 1990–2012)	2.9	3.4	2.6
Aquaculture growth (avg. annual %, 1990–2012)	11.1	9.1	9.9
Marine protected areas (% of territorial waters)	11.5	1.4	14.7
Coral reef area (sq. km)	..	137,690	124,480
Mangroves area (sq. km)	..	56,537	58,917
Energy and emissions			
Energy use per capita (kg oil equivalent)	..	1,671	687
Energy from biomass products and waste (% of total)	..	10.1	26.8
Electric power consumption per capita (kWh)	..	2,582	734
Electricity generated using fossil fuel (% of total)	..	80.9	72.3
Electricity generated by hydropower (% of total)	..	14.5	16.9
CO_2 emissions per capita (metric tons)	0.3	4.9	1.6
Water and sanitation			
Internal freshwater resources per capita (cu. m)	29,197	4,438	3,144
Total freshwater withdrawal (% of internal resources)	2.2	10.9	19.6
Agriculture (% of total freshwater withdrawal)	93	73	88
Access to improved water source (% of total population)	72	91	88
Rural (% of rural population)	65	85	85
Urban (% of urban population)	84	97	94
Access to improved sanitation facilities (% of total population)	65	67	48
Rural (% of rural population)	50	58	36
Urban (% of urban population)	90	76	66
Environment and health			
Particulate matter (urban-pop.-weighted avg., μg/cu. m)	46	75	90
Acute resp. infection prevalence (% of children under five)	..	..	..
Diarrhea prevalence (% of children under five)	..	..	..
Under-five mortality rate (per 1,000 live births)	72	21	61
National accounting aggregates—savings, depletion and degradation			
Gross savings (% of GNI)	16.8	47.6	28.6
Consumption of fixed capital (% of GNI)	16.2	12.0	11.1
Education expenditure (% of GNI)	1.1	2.1	3.1
Energy depletion (% of GNI)	0.0	2.7	4.4
Mineral depletion (% of GNI)	9.3	1.4	1.1
Net forest depletion (% of GNI)	2.9	0.1	0.8
CO_2 damage (% of GNI)	0.2	1.0	0.9
Particulate emissions damage (% of GNI)	0.8	1.6	1.4
Adjusted net savings (% of GNI)	-11.6	30.9	12.0

Latvia

	Population (millions)	**2.0**	Land area (1,000 sq. km)	**62**	GDP ($ billions)	**28.4**

	Country data	High-income group
GNI per capita, *World Bank Atlas* method ($)	14,060	38,444
Adjusted net national income per capita ($)	11,448	32,262
Change in wealth per capita (2010 $)	2,463	2,210
Urban population (% of total)	67.7	80.2
Agriculture		
Agricultural land (% land area)	29	29
Agricultural irrigated land (% of total agricultural land)	0.1	..
Agricultural productivity, value added per worker (2005 $)	5,467	25,238
Cereal yield (kg per hectare)	3,720	4,374
Forests and biodiversity		
Forest area (% land area)	54.1	35.0
Deforestation (avg. annual %, 2000–2010)	-0.3	0.0
Terrestrial protected areas (% of total land area)	18.6	13.9
Threatened species, mammals	1	
Threatened species, birds	6	
Threatened species, fish	6	
Threatened species, higher plants	0	
Oceans		
Total fisheries production (thousand metric tons)	95.1	37,661
Capture fisheries growth (avg. annual %, 1990–2012)	-6.9	-2.0
Aquaculture growth (avg. annual %, 1990–2012)	-6.0	2.5
Marine protected areas (% of territorial waters)	0.24	14.4
Coral reef area (sq. km)	..	82,210
Mangroves area (sq. km)	..	15,504
Energy and emissions		
Energy use per capita (kg oil equivalent)	2,122	4,872
Energy from biomass products and waste (% of total)	28.0	4.3
Electric power consumption per capita (kWh)	3,264	8,896
Electricity generated using fossil fuel (% of total)	49.5	61.8
Electricity generated by hydropower (% of total)	47.4	12.2
CO_2 emissions per capita (metric tons)	3.6	11.6
Water and sanitation		
Internal freshwater resources per capita (cu. m)	8,127	11,335
Total freshwater withdrawal (% of internal resources)	2.5	7.0
Agriculture (% of total freshwater withdrawal)	12	40
Access to improved water source (% of total population)	98	99
Rural (% of rural population)	96	98
Urban (% of urban population)	100	100
Access to improved sanitation facilities (% of total population)	..	96
Rural (% of rural population)	..	93
Urban (% of urban population)	..	97
Environment and health		
Particulate matter (urban-pop.-weighted avg., µg/cu. m)	39	27
Acute resp. infection prevalence (% of children under five)	..	..
Diarrhea prevalence (% of children under five)	..	..
Under-five mortality rate (per 1,000 live births)	9	6
National accounting aggregates—savings, depletion and degradation		
Gross savings (% of GNI)	25.6	20.1
Consumption of fixed capital (% of GNI)	17.0	14.2
Education expenditure (% of GNI)	5.6	4.7
Energy depletion (% of GNI)	0.0	1.6
Mineral depletion (% of GNI)	0.0	0.3
Net forest depletion (% of GNI)	0.9	0.0
CO_2 damage (% of GNI)	0.3	0.3
Particulate emissions damage (% of GNI)	1.7	0.3
Adjusted net savings (% of GNI)	11.0	8.1

2014 The Little Green Data Book

Lebanon

	Population (millions)	**4.4**	Land area (1,000 sq. km)	**10**	GDP ($ billions)	**42.9**

	Country data	Middle East & N. Africa group	Upper middle-income group
GNI per capita, *World Bank Atlas* method ($)	9,190	3,451	6,969
Adjusted net national income per capita ($)	8,082	2,602	5,845
Change in wealth per capita (2010 $)	-667	101	1,039
Urban population (% of total)	87.4	59.5	60.7
Agriculture			
Agricultural land (% land area)	62	23	44
Agricultural irrigated land (% of total agricultural land)	20.2	..	..
Agricultural productivity, value added per worker (2005 $)	49,689	2,642	1,131
Cereal yield (kg per hectare)	3,476	2,350	4,255
Forests and biodiversity			
Forest area (% land area)	13.4	2.4	29.1
Deforestation (avg. annual %, 2000–2010)	-0.4	-0.1	0.0
Terrestrial protected areas (% of total land area)	0.6	6.1	16.1
Threatened species, mammals	10		
Threatened species, birds	9		
Threatened species, fish	21		
Threatened species, higher plants	2		
Oceans			
Total fisheries production (thousand metric tons)	5.1	3,976	90,024
Capture fisheries growth (avg. annual %, 1990–2012)	4.6	3.0	1.5
Aquaculture growth (avg. annual %, 1990–2012)	13.4	12.8	9.1
Marine protected areas (% of territorial waters)	0.11	9.1	7.3
Coral reef area (sq. km)	..	5,700	52,070
Mangroves area (sq. km)	..	217	50,160
Energy and emissions			
Energy use per capita (kg oil equivalent)	1,449	1,376	1,893
Energy from biomass products and waste (% of total)	2.0	0.9	8.5
Electric power consumption per capita (kWh)	3,499	1,696	2,932
Electricity generated using fossil fuel (% of total)	95.1	91.7	74.7
Electricity generated by hydropower (% of total)	4.9	5.5	20.0
CO_2 emissions per capita (metric tons)	4.7	3.9	5.4
Water and sanitation			
Internal freshwater resources per capita (cu. m)	1,095	679	6,791
Total freshwater withdrawal (% of internal resources)	27.3	122.1	7.4
Agriculture (% of total freshwater withdrawal)	60	86	69
Access to improved water source (% of total population)	100	90	93
Rural (% of rural population)	100	83	85
Urban (% of urban population)	100	95	98
Access to improved sanitation facilities (% of total population)	..	88	74
Rural (% of rural population)	..	80	62
Urban (% of urban population)	100	94	82
Environment and health			
Particulate matter (urban-pop.-weighted avg., µg/cu. m)	43	79	65
Acute resp. infection prevalence (% of children under five)	..	..	..
Diarrhea prevalence (% of children under five)	..	..	..
Under-five mortality rate (per 1,000 live births)	9	26	20
National accounting aggregates—savings, depletion and degradation			
Gross savings (% of GNI)	13.8	25.9	36.4
Consumption of fixed capital (% of GNI)	15.5	9.9	12.5
Education expenditure (% of GNI)	1.4	4.5	3.2
Energy depletion (% of GNI)	0.0	12.9	4.1
Mineral depletion (% of GNI)	0.0	0.5	1.2
Net forest depletion (% of GNI)	0.0	0.2	0.2
CO_2 damage (% of GNI)	0.6	0.7	0.8
Particulate emissions damage (% of GNI)	1.4	0.9	1.3
Adjusted net savings (% of GNI)	-2.2	5.3	19.5

Lesotho

| | Population (millions) | 2.1 | Land area (1,000 sq. km) | 30 | GDP ($ billions) | 2.4 |

	Country data	Sub-Saharan Africa group	Lower middle-income group
GNI per capita, *World Bank Atlas* method ($)	1,380	1,547	1,965
Adjusted net national income per capita ($)	1,150	1,005	1,574
Change in wealth per capita (2010 $)	24	-273	117
Urban population (% of total)	28.3	36.8	38.9
Agriculture			
Agricultural land (% land area)	76	44	46
Agricultural irrigated land (% of total agricultural land)	..	..	..
Agricultural productivity, value added per worker (2005 $)	321	765	938
Cereal yield (kg per hectare)	603	1,417	3,029
Forests and biodiversity			
Forest area (% land area)	1.5	27.4	26.9
Deforestation (avg. annual %, 2000–2010)	-0.5	0.5	0.3
Terrestrial protected areas (% of total land area)	0.5	16.4	11.9
Threatened species, mammals	2		
Threatened species, birds	7		
Threatened species, fish	1		
Threatened species, higher plants	4		
Oceans			
Total fisheries production (thousand metric tons)	0.45	6,906	43,067
Capture fisheries growth (avg. annual %, 1990–2012)	7.6	2.1	2.6
Aquaculture growth (avg. annual %, 1990–2012)	14.6	15.9	9.9
Marine protected areas (% of territorial waters)	1.8	11.7	14.7
Coral reef area (sq. km)	..	17,980	124,480
Mangroves area (sq. km)	..	27,808	58,917
Energy and emissions			
Energy use per capita (kg oil equivalent)	10	681	687
Energy from biomass products and waste (% of total)	..	57.6	26.8
Electric power consumption per capita (kWh)	..	535	734
Electricity generated using fossil fuel (% of total)	..	65.1	72.3
Electricity generated by hydropower (% of total)	..	20.0	16.9
CO_2 emissions per capita (metric tons)	0.0	0.8	1.6
Water and sanitation			
Internal freshwater resources per capita (cu. m)	2,577	4,391	3,144
Total freshwater withdrawal (% of internal resources)	1.0	3.2	19.6
Agriculture (% of total freshwater withdrawal)	20	84	88
Access to improved water source (% of total population)	81	64	88
Rural (% of rural population)	77	53	85
Urban (% of urban population)	93	85	94
Access to improved sanitation facilities (% of total population)	30	30	48
Rural (% of rural population)	27	23	36
Urban (% of urban population)	37	41	66
Environment and health			
Particulate matter (urban-pop.-weighted avg., µg/cu. m)	42	77	90
Acute resp. infection prevalence (% of children under five)	6	5	..
Diarrhea prevalence (% of children under five)	11	14	..
Under-five mortality rate (per 1,000 live births)	100	98	61
National accounting aggregates—savings, depletion and degradation			
Gross savings (% of GNI)	16.1	26.3	28.6
Consumption of fixed capital (% of GNI)	10.6	13.0	11.1
Education expenditure (% of GNI)	9.8	3.4	3.1
Energy depletion (% of GNI)	0.0	10.3	4.4
Mineral depletion (% of GNI)	0.0	1.8	1.1
Net forest depletion (% of GNI)	3.7	1.8	0.8
CO_2 damage (% of GNI)	0.0	0.6	0.9
Particulate emissions damage (% of GNI)	0.1	1.2	1.4
Adjusted net savings (% of GNI)	11.5	0.9	12.0

Liberia

	Country data	Sub-Saharan Africa group	Low-Income group
Population (millions) 4.2	Land area (1,000 sq. km) 96	GDP ($ billions)	1.7

	Country data	Sub-Saharan Africa group	Low-Income group
GNI per capita, World Bank Atlas method ($)	370	1,547	594
Adjusted net national income per capita ($)	218	1,005	495
Change in wealth per capita (2010 $)	-148	-273	-39
Urban population (% of total)	48.6	36.8	28.2

Agriculture

Agricultural land (% land area)	27	44	39
Agricultural irrigated land (% of total agricultural land)	..	..	
Agricultural productivity, value added per worker (2005 $)	700	765	367
Cereal yield (kg per hectare)	1,210	1,417	1,982

Forests and biodiversity

Forest area (% land area)	44.6	27.4	27.4
Deforestation (avg. annual %, 2000-2010)	0.7	0.5	0.6
Terrestrial protected areas (% of total land area)	2.5	16.4	13.7
Threatened species, mammals	18		
Threatened species, birds	13		
Threatened species, fish	54		
Threatened species, higher plants	47		

Oceans

Total fisheries production (thousand metric tons)	9.5	6,906	11,789
Capture fisheries growth (avg. annual %, 1990-2012)	1.8	2.1	3.8
Aquaculture growth (avg. annual %, 1990-2012)	..	15.9	5.1
Marine protected areas (% of territorial waters)	0.05	11.7	13.1
Coral reef area (sq. km)	..	17,980	15,120
Mangroves area (sq. km)	109	27,808	25,817

Energy and emissions

Energy use per capita (kg oil equivalent)	..	681	360
Energy from biomass products and waste (% of total)	..	57.6	66.0
Electric power consumption per capita (kWh)	..	535	233
Electricity generated using fossil fuel (% of total)	..	65.1	30.9
Electricity generated by hydropower (% of total)	..	20.0	45.5
CO$_2$ emissions per capita (metric tons)	0.2	0.8	0.3

Water and sanitation

Internal freshwater resources per capita (cu. m)	49,023	4,391	5,121
Total freshwater withdrawal (% of internal resources)	0.1	3.2	4.4
Agriculture (% of total freshwater withdrawal)	34	84	90
Access to improved water source (% of total population)	75	64	69
Rural (% of rural population)	63	53	61
Urban (% of urban population)	87	85	88
Access to improved sanitation facilities (% of total population)	17	30	37
Rural (% of rural population)	6	23	33
Urban (% of urban population)	28	41	46

Environment and health

Particulate matter (urban-pop.-weighted avg., µg/cu. m)	25	77	74
Acute resp. infection prevalence (% of children under five)	9	5	6
Diarrhea prevalence (% of children under five)	20	14	14
Under-five mortality rate (per 1,000 live births)	75	98	82

National accounting aggregates—savings, depletion and degradation

Gross savings (% of GNI)	34.0	26.3	24.6
Consumption of fixed capital (% of GNI)	13.6	13.0	11.8
Education expenditure (% of GNI)	3.7	3.4	3.2
Energy depletion (% of GNI)	0.0	10.3	1.4
Mineral depletion (% of GNI)	1.2	1.8	1.9
Net forest depletion (% of GNI)	27.3	1.8	4.4
CO$_2$ damage (% of GNI)	0.6	0.6	0.4
Particulate emissions damage (% of GNI)	0.5	1.2	1.0
Adjusted net savings (% of GNI)	-6.0	0.9	7.0

Libya

Population (millions)	**6.2**	Land area (1,000 sq. km)	**1,760**	GDP ($ billions)	**62.4**

	Country data	Middle East & N. Africa group	Upper middle-income group
GNI per capita, *World Bank Atlas* method ($)	12,930	3,451	6,969
Adjusted net national income per capita ($)	6,239	2,602	5,845
Change in wealth per capita (2010 $)	..	101	1,039
Urban population (% of total)	77.9	59.5	60.7

Agriculture

Agricultural land (% land area)	9	23	44
Agricultural irrigated land (% of total agricultural land)	..	..	..
Agricultural productivity, value added per worker (2005 $)	..	2,642	1,131
Cereal yield (kg per hectare)	815	2,350	4,255

Forests and biodiversity

Forest area (% land area)	0.1	2.4	29.1
Deforestation (avg. annual %, 2000–2010)	0.0	-0.1	0.0
Terrestrial protected areas (% of total land area)	0.1	6.1	16.1
Threatened species, mammals	12		
Threatened species, birds	4		
Threatened species, fish	24		
Threatened species, higher plants	3		

Oceans

Total fisheries production (thousand metric tons)	35.2	3,976	90,024
Capture fisheries growth (avg. annual %, 1990–2012)	1.6	3.0	1.5
Aquaculture growth (avg. annual %, 1990–2012)	5.8	12.8	9.1
Marine protected areas (% of territorial waters)	0.05	9.1	7.3
Coral reef area (sq. km)	..	5,700	52,070
Mangroves area (sq. km)	..	217	50,160

Energy and emissions

Energy use per capita (kg oil equivalent)	2,186	1,376	1,893
Energy from biomass products and waste (% of total)	1.3	0.9	8.5
Electric power consumption per capita (kWh)	3,926	1,696	2,932
Electricity generated using fossil fuel (% of total)	100.0	91.7	74.7
Electricity generated by hydropower (% of total)	0.0	5.5	20.0
CO_2 emissions per capita (metric tons)	9.8	3.9	5.4

Water and sanitation

Internal freshwater resources per capita (cu. m)	115	679	6,791
Total freshwater withdrawal (% of internal resources)	618.0	122.1	7.4
Agriculture (% of total freshwater withdrawal)	83	86	69
Access to improved water source (% of total population)	..	90	93
Rural (% of rural population)	..	83	85
Urban (% of urban population)	..	95	98
Access to improved sanitation facilities (% of total population)	97	88	74
Rural (% of rural population)	96	80	62
Urban (% of urban population)	97	94	82

Environment and health

Particulate matter (urban-pop.-weighted avg., µg/cu. m)	74	79	65
Acute resp. infection prevalence (% of children under five)	..	..	..
Diarrhea prevalence (% of children under five)	..	..	..
Under-five mortality rate (per 1,000 live births)	15	26	20

National accounting aggregates—savings, depletion and degradation

Gross savings (% of GNI)	66.8	25.9	36.4
Consumption of fixed capital (% of GNI)	10.8	9.9	12.5
Education expenditure (% of GNI)	..	4.5	3.2
Energy depletion (% of GNI)	29.1	12.9	4.1
Mineral depletion (% of GNI)	0.0	0.5	1.2
Net forest depletion (% of GNI)	0.1	0.2	0.2
CO_2 damage (% of GNI)	1.0	0.7	0.8
Particulate emissions damage (% of GNI)	1.5	0.9	1.3
Adjusted net savings (% of GNI)	..	5.3	19.5

Liechtenstein

	Population (thousands) **37**	Land area (sq. km) **160**	GDP ($ billions) ***4.8***

	Country data	High-Income group
GNI per capita, *World Bank Atlas* method ($)	*136,770*	38,444
Adjusted net national income per capita ($)	..	32,262
Change in wealth per capita (2010 $)	..	2,210
Urban population (% of total)	14.4	80.2

Agriculture

Agricultural land (% land area)	41	29
Agricultural irrigated land (% of total agricultural land)	..	..
Agricultural productivity, value added per worker (2005 $)	..	25,238
Cereal yield (kg per hectare)	..	4,374

Forests and biodiversity

Forest area (% land area)	43.1	35.0
Deforestation (avg. annual %, 2000–2010)	0.0	0.0
Terrestrial protected areas (% of total land area)	43.1	13.9
Threatened species, mammals	0	
Threatened species, birds	0	
Threatened species, fish	0	
Threatened species, higher plants	0	

Oceans

Total fisheries production (thousand metric tons)	..	37,661
Capture fisheries growth (avg. annual %, 1990–2012)	..	-2.0
Aquaculture growth (avg. annual %, 1990–2012)	..	2.5
Marine protected areas (% of territorial waters)	30.7	14.4
Coral reef area (sq. km)	..	82,210
Mangroves area (sq. km)	..	15,504

Energy and emissions

Energy use per capita (kg oil equivalent)	..	4,872
Energy from biomass products and waste (% of total)	..	4.3
Electric power consumption per capita (kWh)	..	8,896
Electricity generated using fossil fuel (% of total)	..	61.8
Electricity generated by hydropower (% of total)	..	12.2
CO_2 emissions per capita (metric tons)	..	11.6

Water and sanitation

Internal freshwater resources per capita (cu. m)	..	11,335
Total freshwater withdrawal (% of internal resources)	..	7.0
Agriculture (% of total freshwater withdrawal)	..	40
Access to improved water source (% of total population)	..	99
Rural (% of rural population)	..	98
Urban (% of urban population)	..	100
Access to improved sanitation facilities (% of total population)	..	96
Rural (% of rural population)	..	93
Urban (% of urban population)	..	97

Environment and health

Particulate matter (urban-pop.-weighted avg., µg/cu. m)	30	27
Acute resp. infection prevalence (% of children under five)	..	..
Diarrhea prevalence (% of children under five)	..	..
Under-five mortality rate (per 1,000 live births)	..	6

National accounting aggregates—savings, depletion and degradation

Gross savings (% of GNI)	..	20.1
Consumption of fixed capital (% of GNI)	*14.3*	14.2
Education expenditure (% of GNI)	2.4	4.7
Energy depletion (% of GNI)	*0.0*	1.6
Mineral depletion (% of GNI)	*0.0*	0.3
Net forest depletion (% of GNI)	..	0.0
CO_2 damage (% of GNI)	..	0.3
Particulate emissions damage (% of GNI)	..	0.3
Adjusted net savings (% of GNI)	..	8.1

Lithuania

Population (millions)	**3.0**	Land area (1,000 sq. km)	**63**	GDP ($ billions)	**42.3**

	Country data	High-Income group
GNI per capita, *World Bank Atlas* method ($)	13,820	38,444
Adjusted net national income per capita ($)	11,918	32,262
Change in wealth per capita (2010 $)	1,924	2,210
Urban population (% of total)	67.2	80.2
Agriculture		
Agricultural land (% land area)	45	29
Agricultural irrigated land (% of total agricultural land)	..	..
Agricultural productivity, value added per worker (2005 $)	9,369	25,238
Cereal yield (kg per hectare)	3,990	4,374
Forests and biodiversity		
Forest area (% land area)	34.6	35.0
Deforestation (avg. annual %, 2000–2010)	-0.7	0.0
Terrestrial protected areas (% of total land area)	16.8	13.9
Threatened species, mammals	3	
Threatened species, birds	6	
Threatened species, fish	6	
Threatened species, higher plants	1	
Oceans		
Total fisheries production (thousand metric tons)	70.5	37,661
Capture fisheries growth (avg. annual %, 1990–2012)	-7.1	-2.0
Aquaculture growth (avg. annual %, 1990–2012)	-1.2	2.5
Marine protected areas (% of territorial waters)	10.7	14.4
Coral reef area (sq. km)	..	82,210
Mangroves area (sq. km)	..	15,504
Energy and emissions		
Energy use per capita (kg oil equivalent)	2,406	4,872
Energy from biomass products and waste (% of total)	13.3	4.3
Electric power consumption per capita (kWh)	3,530	8,896
Electricity generated using fossil fuel (% of total)	67.7	61.8
Electricity generated by hydropower (% of total)	11.3	12.2
CO_2 emissions per capita (metric tons)	4.4	11.6
Water and sanitation		
Internal freshwater resources per capita (cu. m)	5,139	11,335
Total freshwater withdrawal (% of internal resources)	15.3	7.0
Agriculture (% of total freshwater withdrawal)	3	40
Access to improved water source (% of total population)	96	99
Rural (% of rural population)	89	98
Urban (% of urban population)	99	100
Access to improved sanitation facilities (% of total population)	94	96
Rural (% of rural population)	85	93
Urban (% of urban population)	99	97
Environment and health		
Particulate matter (urban-pop.-weighted avg., µg/cu. m)	32	27
Acute resp. infection prevalence (% of children under five)	..	..
Diarrhea prevalence (% of children under five)	..	..
Under-five mortality rate (per 1,000 live births)	5	6
National accounting aggregates—savings, depletion and degradation		
Gross savings (% of GNI)	17.7	20.1
Consumption of fixed capital (% of GNI)	12.7	14.2
Education expenditure (% of GNI)	5.2	4.7
Energy depletion (% of GNI)	0.1	1.6
Mineral depletion (% of GNI)	0.0	0.3
Net forest depletion (% of GNI)	0.2	0.0
CO_2 damage (% of GNI)	0.4	0.3
Particulate emissions damage (% of GNI)	0.5	0.3
Adjusted net savings (% of GNI)	9.1	8.1

Luxembourg

Population (thousands) **531**	Land area (1,000 sq. km) **2.6**	GDP ($ billions) **55.1**

	Country data	High-income group
GNI per capita, *World Bank Atlas* method ($)	71,810	38,444
Adjusted net national income per capita ($)	57,322	32,262
Change in wealth per capita (2010 $)	756	2,210
Urban population (% of total)	85.6	80.2
Agriculture		
Agricultural land (% land area)	51	29
Agricultural irrigated land (% of total agricultural land)	..	..
Agricultural productivity, value added per worker (2005 $)	36,230	25,238
Cereal yield (kg per hectare)	5,331	4,374
Forests and biodiversity		
Forest area (% land area)	33.5	35.0
Deforestation (avg. annual %, 2000–2010)	0.0	0.0
Terrestrial protected areas (% of total land area)	39.7	13.9
Threatened species, mammals	0	
Threatened species, birds	1	
Threatened species, fish	1	
Threatened species, higher plants	0	
Oceans		
Total fisheries production (thousand metric tons)	..	37,661
Capture fisheries growth (avg. annual %, 1990–2012)	..	-2.0
Aquaculture growth (avg. annual %, 1990–2012)	..	2.5
Marine protected areas (% of territorial waters)	3.5	14.4
Coral reef area (sq. km)	..	82,210
Mangroves area (sq. km)	..	15,504
Energy and emissions		
Energy use per capita (kg oil equivalent)	8,046	4,872
Energy from biomass products and waste (% of total)	3.4	4.3
Electric power consumption per capita (kWh)	15,530	8,896
Electricity generated using fossil fuel (% of total)	88.5	61.8
Electricity generated by hydropower (% of total)	2.2	12.2
CO_2 emissions per capita (metric tons)	21.4	11.6
Water and sanitation		
Internal freshwater resources per capita (cu. m)	1,929	11,335
Total freshwater withdrawal (% of internal resources)	6.0	7.0
Agriculture (% of total freshwater withdrawal)	0	40
Access to improved water source (% of total population)	100	99
Rural (% of rural population)	100	98
Urban (% of urban population)	100	100
Access to improved sanitation facilities (% of total population)	100	96
Rural (% of rural population)	100	93
Urban (% of urban population)	100	97
Environment and health		
Particulate matter (urban-pop.-weighted avg., µg/cu. m)	17	27
Acute resp. infection prevalence (% of children under five)	..	..
Diarrhea prevalence (% of children under five)	..	..
Under-five mortality rate (per 1,000 live births)	2	6
National accounting aggregates—savings, depletion and degradation		
Gross savings (% of GNI)	24.1	20.1
Consumption of fixed capital (% of GNI)	18.9	14.2
Education expenditure (% of GNI)	3.5	4.7
Energy depletion (% of GNI)	0.0	1.6
Mineral depletion (% of GNI)	0.1	0.3
Net forest depletion (% of GNI)	0.0	0.0
CO_2 damage (% of GNI)	0.3	0.3
Particulate emissions damage (% of GNI)	0.1	0.3
Adjusted net savings (% of GNI)	8.3	8.1

Macao SAR, China

Population (thousands) **557** Land area (sq. km) **28** GDP ($ billions) **43.6**

	Country data	High-income group
GNI per capita, *World Bank Atlas* method ($)	55,720	38,444
Adjusted net national income per capita ($)	..	32,262
Change in wealth per capita (2010 $)	..	2,210
Urban population (% of total)	100.0	80.2

Agriculture

Agricultural land (% land area)	..	29
Agricultural irrigated land (% of total agricultural land)	..	..
Agricultural productivity, value added per worker (2005 $)	..	25,238
Cereal yield (kg per hectare)	..	4,374

Forests and biodiversity

Forest area (% land area)	..	35.0
Deforestation (avg. annual %, 2000–2010)	..	0.0
Terrestrial protected areas (% of total land area)	..	13.9
Threatened species, mammals	0	
Threatened species, birds	4	
Threatened species, fish	5	
Threatened species, higher plants	0	

Oceans

Total fisheries production (thousand metric tons)	1.5	37,661
Capture fisheries growth (avg. annual %, 1990–2012)	-2.4	-2.0
Aquaculture growth (avg. annual %, 1990–2012)	..	2.5
Marine protected areas (% of territorial waters)	16.1	14.4
Coral reef area (sq. km)	..	82,210
Mangroves area (sq. km)	..	15,504

Energy and emissions

Energy use per capita (kg oil equivalent)	..	4,872
Energy from biomass products and waste (% of total)	..	4.3
Electric power consumption per capita (kWh)	..	8,896
Electricity generated using fossil fuel (% of total)	..	61.8
Electricity generated by hydropower (% of total)	..	12.2
CO_2 emissions per capita (metric tons)	1.9	11.6

Water and sanitation

Internal freshwater resources per capita (cu. m)	..	11,335
Total freshwater withdrawal (% of internal resources)	..	7.0
Agriculture (% of total freshwater withdrawal)	..	40
Access to improved water source (% of total population)	..	99
Rural (% of rural population)	..	98
Urban (% of urban population)	..	100
Access to improved sanitation facilities (% of total population)	..	96
Rural (% of rural population)	..	93
Urban (% of urban population)	..	97

Environment and health

Particulate matter (urban-pop.-weighted avg., µg/cu. m)	33	27
Acute resp. infection prevalence (% of children under five)	..	..
Diarrhea prevalence (% of children under five)	..	..
Under-five mortality rate (per 1,000 live births)	..	6

National accounting aggregates—savings, depletion and degradation

Gross savings (% of GNI)	66.4	20.1
Consumption of fixed capital (% of GNI)	1.9	14.2
Education expenditure (% of GNI)	1.9	4.7
Energy depletion (% of GNI)	0.0	1.6
Mineral depletion (% of GNI)	0.0	0.3
Net forest depletion (% of GNI)	..	0.0
CO_2 damage (% of GNI)	0.0	0.3
Particulate emissions damage (% of GNI)	..	0.3
Adjusted net savings (% of GNI)	..	8.1

Macedonia, FYR

Population (millions)	**2.1** Land area (1,000 sq. km)	**25** GDP ($ billions)	**9.6**

	Country data	Europe & Central Asia group	Upper middle-income group
GNI per capita, *World Bank Atlas* method ($)	4,620	6,658	6,969
Adjusted net national income per capita ($)	3,520	5,541	5,845
Change in wealth per capita (2010 $)	403	263	1,039
Urban population (% of total)	59.4	60.2	60.7
Agriculture			
Agricultural land (% land area)	44	66	44
Agricultural irrigated land (% of total agricultural land)	7.4	..	..
Agricultural productivity, value added per worker (2005 $)	12,397	4,866	1,131
Cereal yield (kg per hectare)	2,839	2,519	4,255
Forests and biodiversity			
Forest area (% land area)	39.8	10.5	29.1
Deforestation (avg. annual %, 2000–2010)	-0.4	-0.5	0.0
Terrestrial protected areas (% of total land area)	7.3	5.1	16.1
Threatened species, mammals	5		
Threatened species, birds	11		
Threatened species, fish	13		
Threatened species, higher plants	0		
Oceans			
Total fisheries production (thousand metric tons)	1.6	1,022	90,024
Capture fisheries growth (avg. annual %, 1990–2012)	..	-4.0	1.5
Aquaculture growth (avg. annual %, 1990–2012)	..	1.8	9.1
Marine protected areas (% of territorial waters)	3.8	10.4	7.3
Coral reef area (sq. km)	..	..	52,070
Mangroves area (sq. km)	..	..	50,160
Energy and emissions			
Energy use per capita (kg oil equivalent)	1,484	2,078	1,893
Energy from biomass products and waste (% of total)	6.1	2.9	8.5
Electric power consumption per capita (kWh)	3,881	2,951	2,932
Electricity generated using fossil fuel (% of total)	79.1	65.8	74.7
Electricity generated by hydropower (% of total)	20.8	17.9	20.0
CO_2 emissions per capita (metric tons)	5.2	5.3	5.4
Water and sanitation			
Internal freshwater resources per capita (cu. m)	2,567	2,744	6,791
Total freshwater withdrawal (% of internal resources)	19.0	34.8	7.4
Agriculture (% of total freshwater withdrawal)	12	70	69
Access to improved water source (% of total population)	99	95	93
Rural (% of rural population)	99	89	85
Urban (% of urban population)	100	99	98
Access to improved sanitation facilities (% of total population)	91	94	74
Rural (% of rural population)	83	90	62
Urban (% of urban population)	97	97	82
Environment and health			
Particulate matter (urban-pop.-weighted avg., μg/cu. m)	82	48	65
Acute resp. infection prevalence (% of children under five)	..	..	..
Diarrhea prevalence (% of children under five)	..	..	..
Under-five mortality rate (per 1,000 live births)	7	22	20
National accounting aggregates—savings, depletion and degradation			
Gross savings (% of GNI)	26.2	18.9	36.4
Consumption of fixed capital (% of GNI)	18.1	12.4	12.5
Education expenditure (% of GNI)	4.9	3.8	3.2
Energy depletion (% of GNI)	0.2	4.4	4.1
Mineral depletion (% of GNI)	2.1	0.6	1.2
Net forest depletion (% of GNI)	0.4	0.0	0.2
CO_2 damage (% of GNI)	1.1	0.8	0.8
Particulate emissions damage (% of GNI)	3.0	1.8	1.3
Adjusted net savings (% of GNI)	6.0	2.8	19.5

Madagascar

| | Population (millions) | **22.3** | Land area (1,000 sq. km) | **582** | GDP ($ billions) | **10.0** |

	Country data	Sub-Saharan Africa group	Low-Income group
GNI per capita, *World Bank Atlas* method ($)	430	1,547	594
Adjusted net national income per capita ($)	361	1,005	495
Change in wealth per capita (2010 $)	–118	–273	–39
Urban population (% of total)	33.2	36.8	28.2
Agriculture			
Agricultural land (% land area)	71	44	39
Agricultural irrigated land (% of total agricultural land)	2.2	..	..
Agricultural productivity, value added per worker (2005 $)	215	765	367
Cereal yield (kg per hectare)	2,663	1,417	1,982
Forests and biodiversity			
Forest area (% land area)	21.5	27.4	27.4
Deforestation (avg. annual %, 2000–2010)	0.4	0.5	0.6
Terrestrial protected areas (% of total land area)	5.0	16.4	13.7
Threatened species, mammals	65		
Threatened species, birds	35		
Threatened species, fish	87		
Threatened species, higher plants	369		
Oceans			
Total fisheries production (thousand metric tons)	116	6,906	11,789
Capture fisheries growth (avg. annual %, 1990–2012)	0.1	2.1	3.8
Aquaculture growth (avg. annual %, 1990–2012)	17.6	15.9	5.1
Marine protected areas (% of territorial waters)	0.12	11.7	13.1
Coral reef area (sq. km)	2,230	17,980	15,120
Mangroves area (sq. km)	2,991	27,808	25,817
Energy and emissions			
Energy use per capita (kg oil equivalent)	..	681	360
Energy from biomass products and waste (% of total)	..	57.6	66.0
Electric power consumption per capita (kWh)	..	535	233
Electricity generated using fossil fuel (% of total)	..	65.1	30.9
Electricity generated by hydropower (% of total)	..	20.0	45.5
CO_2 emissions per capita (metric tons)	0.1	0.8	0.3
Water and sanitation			
Internal freshwater resources per capita (cu. m)	15,545	4,391	5,121
Total freshwater withdrawal (% of internal resources)	4.4	3.2	4.4
Agriculture (% of total freshwater withdrawal)	97	84	90
Access to improved water source (% of total population)	50	64	69
Rural (% of rural population)	35	53	61
Urban (% of urban population)	78	85	88
Access to improved sanitation facilities (% of total population)	14	30	37
Rural (% of rural population)	11	23	33
Urban (% of urban population)	19	41	46
Environment and health			
Particulate matter (urban-pop.-weighted avg., µg/cu. m)	48	77	74
Acute resp. infection prevalence (% of children under five)	3	5	6
Diarrhea prevalence (% of children under five)	8	14	14
Under-five mortality rate (per 1,000 live births)	58	98	82
National accounting aggregates—savings, depletion and degradation			
Gross savings (% of GNI)	..	26.3	24.6
Consumption of fixed capital (% of GNI)	13.2	13.0	11.8
Education expenditure (% of GNI)	2.7	3.4	3.2
Energy depletion (% of GNI)	0.0	10.3	1.4
Mineral depletion (% of GNI)	1.4	1.8	1.9
Net forest depletion (% of GNI)	2.2	1.8	4.4
CO_2 damage (% of GNI)	0.2	0.6	0.4
Particulate emissions damage (% of GNI)	0.6	1.2	1.0
Adjusted net savings (% of GNI)	..	0.9	7.0

Malawi

	Country data	Sub-Saharan Africa group	Low-Income group
Population (millions) **15.9** Land area (1,000 sq. km) **94** GDP ($ billions) **4.3**			

	Country data	Sub-Saharan Africa group	Low-Income group
GNI per capita, *World Bank Atlas* method ($)	320	1,547	594
Adjusted net national income per capita ($)	204	1,005	495
Change in wealth per capita (2010 $)	-145	-273	-39
Urban population (% of total)	15.8	36.8	28.2
Agriculture			
Agricultural land (% land area)	59	44	39
Agricultural irrigated land (% of total agricultural land)	0.5	..	..
Agricultural productivity, value added per worker (2005 $)	193	765	367
Cereal yield (kg per hectare)	2,087	1,417	1,982
Forests and biodiversity			
Forest area (% land area)	34.0	27.4	27.4
Deforestation (avg. annual %, 2000-2010)	1.0	0.5	0.6
Terrestrial protected areas (% of total land area)	18.3	16.4	13.7
Threatened species, mammals	7		
Threatened species, birds	15		
Threatened species, fish	101		
Threatened species, higher plants	20		
Oceans			
Total fisheries production (thousand metric tons)	124	6,906	11,789
Capture fisheries growth (avg. annual %, 1990-2012)	2.2	2.1	3.8
Aquaculture growth (avg. annual %, 1990-2012)	13.6	15.9	5.1
Marine protected areas (% of territorial waters)	2.3	11.7	13.1
Coral reef area (sq. km)	..	17,980	15,120
Mangroves area (sq. km)	..	27,808	25,817
Energy and emissions			
Energy use per capita (kg oil equivalent)	..	681	360
Energy from biomass products and waste (% of total)	..	57.6	66.0
Electric power consumption per capita (kWh)	..	535	233
Electricity generated using fossil fuel (% of total)	..	65.1	30.9
Electricity generated by hydropower (% of total)	..	20.0	45.5
CO_2 emissions per capita (metric tons)	0.1	0.8	0.3
Water and sanitation			
Internal freshwater resources per capita (cu. m)	1,044	4,391	5,121
Total freshwater withdrawal (% of internal resources)	6.0	3.2	4.4
Agriculture (% of total freshwater withdrawal)	84	84	90
Access to improved water source (% of total population)	85	64	69
Rural (% of rural population)	83	53	61
Urban (% of urban population)	95	85	88
Access to improved sanitation facilities (% of total population)	10	30	37
Rural (% of rural population)	8	23	33
Urban (% of urban population)	22	41	46
Environment and health			
Particulate matter (urban-pop.-weighted avg., µg/cu. m)	49	77	74
Acute resp. infection prevalence (% of children under five)	7	5	6
Diarrhea prevalence (% of children under five)	18	14	14
Under-five mortality rate (per 1,000 live births)	71	98	82
National accounting aggregates—savings, depletion and degradation			
Gross savings (% of GNI)	12.8	26.3	24.6
Consumption of fixed capital (% of GNI)	13.5	13.0	11.8
Education expenditure (% of GNI)	4.9	3.4	3.2
Energy depletion (% of GNI)	0.0	10.3	1.4
Mineral depletion (% of GNI)	0.0	1.8	1.9
Net forest depletion (% of GNI)	8.3	1.8	4.4
CO_2 damage (% of GNI)	0.3	0.6	0.4
Particulate emissions damage (% of GNI)	0.4	1.2	1.0
Adjusted net savings (% of GNI)	-2.7	0.9	7.0

Malaysia

	Country data	East Asia & Pacific group	Upper middle-income group
Population (millions) **29.2**	Land area (1,000 sq. km)	**329**	GDP ($ billions) **305.0**

	Country data	East Asia & Pacific group	Upper middle-income group
GNI per capita, *World Bank Atlas* method ($)	9,820	4,884	6,969
Adjusted net national income per capita ($)	8,034	4,305	5,845
Change in wealth per capita (2010 $)	879	1,172	1,039
Urban population (% of total)	73.4	49.6	60.7
Agriculture			
Agricultural land (% land area)	24	48	44
Agricultural irrigated land (% of total agricultural land)	..	..	..
Agricultural productivity, value added per worker (2005 $)	9,291	794	1,131
Cereal yield (kg per hectare)	4,017	5,145	4,255
Forests and biodiversity			
Forest area (% land area)	62.0	29.7	29.1
Deforestation (avg. annual %, 2000–2010)	0.5	-0.4	0.0
Terrestrial protected areas (% of total land area)	18.4	15.1	16.1
Threatened species, mammals	71		
Threatened species, birds	45		
Threatened species, fish	71		
Threatened species, higher plants	705		
Oceans			
Total fisheries production (thousand metric tons)	2,097	108,399	90,024
Capture fisheries growth (avg. annual %, 1990–2012)	2.0	3.4	1.5
Aquaculture growth (avg. annual %, 1990–2012)	11.8	9.1	9.1
Marine protected areas (% of territorial waters)	2.0	1.4	7.3
Coral reef area (sq. km)	3,600	137,690	52,070
Mangroves area (sq. km)	7,097	56,537	50,160
Energy and emissions			
Energy use per capita (kg oil equivalent)	2,639	1,671	1,893
Energy from biomass products and waste (% of total)	4.6	10.1	8.5
Electric power consumption per capita (kWh)	4,246	2,582	2,932
Electricity generated using fossil fuel (% of total)	93.1	80.9	74.7
Electricity generated by hydropower (% of total)	5.9	14.5	20.0
CO_2 emissions per capita (metric tons)	7.7	4.9	5.4
Water and sanitation			
Internal freshwater resources per capita (cu. m)	20,168	4,438	6,791
Total freshwater withdrawal (% of internal resources)	2.3	10.9	7.4
Agriculture (% of total freshwater withdrawal)	34	73	69
Access to improved water source (% of total population)	100	91	93
Rural (% of rural population)	99	85	85
Urban (% of urban population)	100	97	98
Access to improved sanitation facilities (% of total population)	96	67	74
Rural (% of rural population)	95	58	62
Urban (% of urban population)	96	76	82
Environment and health			
Particulate matter (urban-pop.-weighted avg., µg/cu. m)	47	75	65
Acute resp. infection prevalence (% of children under five)	..	..	..
Diarrhea prevalence (% of children under five)	..	..	..
Under-five mortality rate (per 1,000 live births)	9	21	20
National accounting aggregates—savings, depletion and degradation			
Gross savings (% of GNI)	33.1	47.6	36.4
Consumption of fixed capital (% of GNI)	13.2	12.0	12.5
Education expenditure (% of GNI)	4.4	2.1	3.2
Energy depletion (% of GNI)	6.5	2.7	4.1
Mineral depletion (% of GNI)	0.2	1.4	1.2
Net forest depletion (% of GNI)	0.0	0.1	0.2
CO_2 damage (% of GNI)	0.8	1.0	0.8
Particulate emissions damage (% of GNI)	0.9	1.6	1.3
Adjusted net savings (% of GNI)	15.9	30.9	19.5

Maldives

	Population (thousands) **338**	Land area (sq. km)	**300**	GDP ($ billions)	**2.2**

	Country data	South Asia group	Upper middle-income group
GNI per capita, *World Bank Atlas* method ($)	5,750	1,437	6,969
Adjusted net national income per capita ($)	4,698	1,168	5,845
Change in wealth per capita (2010 $)	86	158	1,039
Urban population (% of total)	42.2	31.4	60.7
Agriculture			
Agricultural land (% land area)	23	55	44
Agricultural irrigated land (% of total agricultural land)	..	..	..
Agricultural productivity, value added per worker (2005 $)	3,215	669	1,131
Cereal yield (kg per hectare)	2,609	2,925	4,255
Forests and biodiversity			
Forest area (% land area)	3.0	17.1	29.1
Deforestation (avg. annual %, 2000–2010)	0.0	-0.3	0.0
Terrestrial protected areas (% of total land area)	..	6.2	16.1
Threatened species, mammals	2		
Threatened species, birds	0		
Threatened species, fish	18		
Threatened species, higher plants	0		
Oceans			
Total fisheries production (thousand metric tons)	120	13,613	90,024
Capture fisheries growth (avg. annual %, 1990–2012)	1.8	2.6	1.5
Aquaculture growth (avg. annual %, 1990–2012)	..	7.6	9.1
Marine protected areas (% of territorial waters)	..	10.7	7.3
Coral reef area (sq. km)	8,920	15,440	52,070
Mangroves area (sq. km)	..	10,343	50,160
Energy and emissions			
Energy use per capita (kg oil equivalent)	970	555	1,893
Energy from biomass products and waste (% of total)	..	26.7	8.5
Electric power consumption per capita (kWh)	..	605	2,932
Electricity generated using fossil fuel (% of total)	..	77.9	74.7
Electricity generated by hydropower (% of total)	..	13.8	20.0
CO_2 emissions per capita (metric tons)	3.3	1.4	5.4
Water and sanitation			
Internal freshwater resources per capita (cu. m)	90	1,217	6,791
Total freshwater withdrawal (% of internal resources)	19.7	51.6	7.4
Agriculture (% of total freshwater withdrawal)	0	91	69
Access to improved water source (% of total population)	99	91	93
Rural (% of rural population)	98	89	85
Urban (% of urban population)	100	95	98
Access to improved sanitation facilities (% of total population)	99	40	74
Rural (% of rural population)	100	30	62
Urban (% of urban population)	97	61	82
Environment and health			
Particulate matter (urban-pop.-weighted avg., µg/cu. m)	21	110	65
Acute resp. infection prevalence (% of children under five)	1	..	..
Diarrhea prevalence (% of children under five)	4	..	..
Under-five mortality rate (per 1,000 live births)	11	60	20
National accounting aggregates—savings, depletion and degradation			
Gross savings (% of GNI)	..	29.3	36.4
Consumption of fixed capital (% of GNI)	15.5	12.7	12.5
Education expenditure (% of GNI)	5.0	2.8	3.2
Energy depletion (% of GNI)	0.0	1.8	4.1
Mineral depletion (% of GNI)	0.0	0.8	1.2
Net forest depletion (% of GNI)	0.1	1.1	0.2
CO_2 damage (% of GNI)	0.7	1.1	0.8
Particulate emissions damage (% of GNI)	0.1	1.5	1.3
Adjusted net savings (% of GNI)	..	13.1	19.5

Mali

| | Population (millions) | **14.9** | Land area (1,000 sq. km) | **1,220** | GDP ($ billions) | **10.4** |

	Country data	Sub-Saharan Africa group	Low-Income group
GNI per capita, *World Bank Atlas* method ($)	660	1,547	594
Adjusted net national income per capita ($)	501	1,005	495
Change in wealth per capita (2010 $)	-240	-273	-39
Urban population (% of total)	35.6	36.8	28.2

Agriculture

Agricultural land (% land area)	34	44	39
Agricultural irrigated land (% of total agricultural land)	..	..	..
Agricultural productivity, value added per worker (2005 $)	842	765	367
Cereal yield (kg per hectare)	1,667	1,417	1,982

Forests and biodiversity

Forest area (% land area)	10.2	27.4	27.4
Deforestation (avg. annual %, 2000–2010)	0.6	0.5	0.6
Terrestrial protected areas (% of total land area)	6.0	16.4	13.7
Threatened species, mammals	12		
Threatened species, birds	13		
Threatened species, fish	2		
Threatened species, higher plants	7		

Oceans

Total fisheries production (thousand metric tons)	72.2	6,906	11,789
Capture fisheries growth (avg. annual %, 1990–2012)	0.0	2.1	3.8
Aquaculture growth (avg. annual %, 1990–2012)	21.8	15.9	5.1
Marine protected areas (% of territorial waters)	0.63	11.7	13.1
Coral reef area (sq. km)	..	17,980	15,120
Mangroves area (sq. km)	..	27,808	25,817

Energy and emissions

Energy use per capita (kg oil equivalent)	..	681	360
Energy from biomass products and waste (% of total)	..	57.6	66.0
Electric power consumption per capita (kWh)	..	535	233
Electricity generated using fossil fuel (% of total)	..	65.1	30.9
Electricity generated by hydropower (% of total)	..	20.0	45.5
CO_2 emissions per capita (metric tons)	0.0	0.8	0.3

Water and sanitation

Internal freshwater resources per capita (cu. m)	4,162	4,391	5,121
Total freshwater withdrawal (% of internal resources)	10.9	3.2	4.4
Agriculture (% of total freshwater withdrawal)	90	84	90
Access to improved water source (% of total population)	67	64	69
Rural (% of rural population)	54	53	61
Urban (% of urban population)	91	85	88
Access to improved sanitation facilities (% of total population)	22	30	37
Rural (% of rural population)	15	23	33
Urban (% of urban population)	35	41	46

Environment and health

Particulate matter (urban-pop.-weighted avg., µg/cu. m)	55	77	74
Acute resp. infection prevalence (% of children under five)	..	5	6
Diarrhea prevalence (% of children under five)	..	14	14
Under-five mortality rate (per 1,000 live births)	128	98	82

National accounting aggregates—savings, depletion and degradation

Gross savings (% of GNI)	8.9	26.3	24.6
Consumption of fixed capital (% of GNI)	14.2	13.0	11.8
Education expenditure (% of GNI)	4.2	3.4	3.2
Energy depletion (% of GNI)	0.0	10.3	1.4
Mineral depletion (% of GNI)	10.0	1.8	1.9
Net forest depletion (% of GNI)	0.0	1.8	4.4
CO_2 damage (% of GNI)	0.1	0.6	0.4
Particulate emissions damage (% of GNI)	1.3	1.2	1.0
Adjusted net savings (% of GNI)	–10.8	0.9	7.0

Malta

Population (thousands) **419** Land area (sq. km) **320** GDP ($ billions) **8.7**

	Country data	High-income group
GNI per capita, World Bank Atlas method ($)	19,730	38,444
Adjusted net national income per capita ($)	16,826	32,262
Change in wealth per capita (2010 $)	241	2,210
Urban population (% of total)	95.0	80.2

Agriculture

Agricultural land (% land area)	32	29
Agricultural irrigated land (% of total agricultural land)	34.0	..
Agricultural productivity, value added per worker (2005 $)	56,234	25,238
Cereal yield (kg per hectare)	5,507	4,374

Forests and biodiversity

Forest area (% land area)	0.9	35.0
Deforestation (avg. annual %, 2000–2010)	0.0	0.0
Terrestrial protected areas (% of total land area)	21.5	13.9
Threatened species, mammals	3	
Threatened species, birds	3	
Threatened species, fish	17	
Threatened species, higher plants	4	

Oceans

Total fisheries production (thousand metric tons)	6.3	37,661
Capture fisheries growth (avg. annual %, 1990–2012)	4.8	-2.0
Aquaculture growth (avg. annual %, 1990–2012)	38.8	2.5
Marine protected areas (% of territorial waters)	0.70	14.4
Coral reef area (sq. km)	..	82,210
Mangroves area (sq. km)	..	15,504

Energy and emissions

Energy use per capita (kg oil equivalent)	2,060	4,872
Energy from biomass products and waste (% of total)	5.3	4.3
Electric power consumption per capita (kWh)	4,689	8,896
Electricity generated using fossil fuel (% of total)	99.4	61.8
Electricity generated by hydropower (% of total)	0.0	12.2
CO_2 emissions per capita (metric tons)	6.2	11.6

Water and sanitation

Internal freshwater resources per capita (cu. m)	121	11,335
Total freshwater withdrawal (% of internal resources)	106.7	7.0
Agriculture (% of total freshwater withdrawal)	35	40
Access to improved water source (% of total population)	100	99
Rural (% of rural population)	100	98
Urban (% of urban population)	100	100
Access to improved sanitation facilities (% of total population)	100	96
Rural (% of rural population)	100	93
Urban (% of urban population)	100	97

Environment and health

Particulate matter (urban-pop.-weighted avg., µg/cu. m)	41	27
Acute resp. infection prevalence (% of children under five)	..	..
Diarrhea prevalence (% of children under five)	..	..
Under-five mortality rate (per 1,000 live births)	7	6

National accounting aggregates—savings, depletion and degradation

Gross savings (% of GNI)	12.4	20.1
Consumption of fixed capital (% of GNI)	13.0	14.2
Education expenditure (% of GNI)	7.0	4.7
Energy depletion (% of GNI)	0.0	1.6
Mineral depletion (% of GNI)	0.0	0.3
Net forest depletion (% of GNI)	0.0	0.0
CO_2 damage (% of GNI)	0.3	0.3
Particulate emissions damage (% of GNI)	1.1	0.3
Adjusted net savings (% of GNI)	5.2	8.1

Marshall Islands

Population (thousands) **53** Land area (sq. km) **180** GDP ($ millions) **182.4**

	Country data	East Asia & Pacific group	Upper middle-income group
GNI per capita, *World Bank Atlas* method ($)	4,040	4,884	6,969
Adjusted net national income per capita ($)	..	4,305	5,845
Change in wealth per capita (2010 $)	..	1,172	1,039
Urban population (% of total)	72.1	49.6	60.7
Agriculture			
Agricultural land (% land area)	72	48	44
Agricultural irrigated land (% of total agricultural land)	..	..	..
Agricultural productivity, value added per worker (2005 $)	..	794	1,131
Cereal yield (kg per hectare)	..	5,145	4,255
Forests and biodiversity			
Forest area (% land area)	70.2	29.7	29.1
Deforestation (avg. annual %, 2000–2010)	0.0	-0.4	0.0
Terrestrial protected areas (% of total land area)	3.0	15.1	16.1
Threatened species, mammals	2		
Threatened species, birds	4		
Threatened species, fish	12		
Threatened species, higher plants	0		
Oceans			
Total fisheries production (thousand metric tons)	75.4	108,399	90,024
Capture fisheries growth (avg. annual %, 1990–2012)	27.2	3.4	1.5
Aquaculture growth (avg. annual %, 1990–2012)	..	9.1	9.1
Marine protected areas (% of territorial waters)	0.76	1.4	7.3
Coral reef area (sq. km)	6,110	137,690	52,070
Mangroves area (sq. km)	..	56,537	50,160
Energy and emissions			
Energy use per capita (kg oil equivalent)	614	1,671	1,893
Energy from biomass products and waste (% of total)	..	10.1	8.5
Electric power consumption per capita (kWh)	..	2,582	2,932
Electricity generated using fossil fuel (% of total)	..	80.9	74.7
Electricity generated by hydropower (% of total)	..	14.5	20.0
CO_2 emissions per capita (metric tons)	2.0	4.9	5.4
Water and sanitation			
Internal freshwater resources per capita (cu. m)	..	4,438	6,791
Total freshwater withdrawal (% of internal resources)	..	10.9	7.4
Agriculture (% of total freshwater withdrawal)	..	73	69
Access to improved water source (% of total population)	95	91	93
Rural (% of rural population)	98	85	85
Urban (% of urban population)	93	97	98
Access to improved sanitation facilities (% of total population)	76	67	74
Rural (% of rural population)	56	58	62
Urban (% of urban population)	84	76	82
Environment and health			
Particulate matter (urban-pop.-weighted avg., μg/cu. m)	..	75	65
Acute resp. infection prevalence (% of children under five)	..	..	..
Diarrhea prevalence (% of children under five)	..	..	..
Under-five mortality rate (per 1,000 live births)	38	21	20
National accounting aggregates—savings, depletion and degradation			
Gross savings (% of GNI)	..	47.6	36.4
Consumption of fixed capital (% of GNI)	9.7	12.0	12.5
Education expenditure (% of GNI)	6.5	2.1	3.2
Energy depletion (% of GNI)	0.0	2.7	4.1
Mineral depletion (% of GNI)	0.0	1.4	1.2
Net forest depletion (% of GNI)	0.0	0.1	0.2
CO_2 damage (% of GNI)	0.5	1.0	0.8
Particulate emissions damage (% of GNI)	..	1.6	1.3
Adjusted net savings (% of GNI)	..	30.9	19.5

Mauritania

	Country data	Sub-Saharan Africa group	Lower middle-income group
Population (millions) **3.8** Land area (1,000 sq. km) **1,031** GDP ($ billions) **4.2**			

	Country data	Sub-Saharan Africa group	Lower middle-income group
GNI per capita, *World Bank Atlas* method ($)	1,110	1,547	1,965
Adjusted net national income per capita ($)	559	1,005	1,574
Change in wealth per capita (2010 $)	..	-273	117
Urban population (% of total)	41.8	36.8	38.9
Agriculture			
Agricultural land (% of land area)	39	44	46
Agricultural irrigated land (% of total agricultural land)	..	..	..
Agricultural productivity, value added per worker (2005 $)	1,109	765	938
Cereal yield (kg per hectare)	1,727	1,417	3,029
Forests and biodiversity			
Forest area (% land area)	0.2	27.4	26.9
Deforestation (avg. annual %, 2000–2010)	2.7	0.5	0.3
Terrestrial protected areas (% of total land area)	0.6	16.4	11.9
Threatened species, mammals	16		
Threatened species, birds	13		
Threatened species, fish	31		
Threatened species, higher plants	0		
Oceans			
Total fisheries production (thousand metric tons)	438	6,906	43,067
Capture fisheries growth (avg. annual %, 1990–2012)	9.0	2.1	2.6
Aquaculture growth (avg. annual %, 1990–2012)	..	15.9	9.9
Marine protected areas (% of territorial waters)	0.30	11.7	14.7
Coral reef area (sq. km)	..	17,980	124,480
Mangroves area (sq. km)	1.4	27,808	58,917
Energy and emissions			
Energy use per capita (kg oil equivalent)	..	681	687
Energy from biomass products and waste (% of total)	..	57.6	26.8
Electric power consumption per capita (kWh)	..	535	734
Electricity generated using fossil fuel (% of total)	..	65.1	72.3
Electricity generated by hydropower (% of total)	..	20.0	16.9
CO_2 emissions per capita (metric tons)	0.6	0.8	1.6
Water and sanitation			
Internal freshwater resources per capita (cu. m)	108	4,391	3,144
Total freshwater withdrawal (% of internal resources)	400.3	3.2	19.6
Agriculture (% of total freshwater withdrawal)	94	84	88
Access to improved water source (% of total population)	50	64	88
Rural (% of rural population)	48	53	85
Urban (% of urban population)	52	85	94
Access to improved sanitation facilities (% of total population)	27	30	48
Rural (% of rural population)	9	23	36
Urban (% of urban population)	51	41	66
Environment and health			
Particulate matter (urban-pop.-weighted avg., µg/cu. m)	46	77	90
Acute resp. infection prevalence (% of children under five)	..	5	..
Diarrhea prevalence (% of children under five)	..	14	..
Under-five mortality rate (per 1,000 live births)	84	98	61
National accounting aggregates—savings, depletion and degradation			
Gross savings (% of GNI)	..	26.3	28.6
Consumption of fixed capital (% of GNI)	14.2	13.0	11.1
Education expenditure (% of GNI)	3.6	3.4	3.1
Energy depletion (% of GNI)	0.0	10.3	4.4
Mineral depletion (% of GNI)	31.6	1.8	1.1
Net forest depletion (% of GNI)	1.9	1.8	0.8
CO_2 damage (% of GNI)	0.7	0.6	0.9
Particulate emissions damage (% of GNI)	0.5	1.2	1.4
Adjusted net savings (% of GNI)	..	0.9	12.0

Mauritius

Population (millions)	**1.3**	Land area (1,000 sq. km)	**2.0**	GDP ($ billions)	**10.5**

	Country data	Sub-Saharan Africa group	Upper middle-income group
GNI per capita, *World Bank Atlas* method ($)	8,570	1,547	6,969
Adjusted net national income per capita ($)	7,116	1,005	5,845
Change in wealth per capita (2010 $)	–422	–273	1,039
Urban population (% of total)	41.8	36.8	60.7
Agriculture			
Agricultural land (% land area)	44	44	44
Agricultural irrigated land (% of total agricultural land)	22.5	..	..
Agricultural productivity, value added per worker (2005 $)	8,155	765	1,131
Cereal yield (kg per hectare)	3,390	1,417	4,255
Forests and biodiversity			
Forest area (% land area)	17.3	27.4	29.1
Deforestation (avg. annual %, 2000–2010)	1.0	0.5	0.0
Terrestrial protected areas (% of total land area)	4.5	16.4	16.1
Threatened species, mammals	7		
Threatened species, birds	11		
Threatened species, fish	15		
Threatened species, higher plants	89		
Oceans			
Total fisheries production (thousand metric tons)	6.9	6,906	90,024
Capture fisheries growth (avg. annual %, 1990–2012)	–3.5	2.1	1.5
Aquaculture growth (avg. annual %, 1990–2012)	8.9	15.9	9.1
Marine protected areas (% of territorial waters)	0.95	11.7	7.3
Coral reef area (sq. km)	870	17,980	52,070
Mangroves area (sq. km)	1.2	27,808	50,160
Energy and emissions			
Energy use per capita (kg oil equivalent)	947	681	1,893
Energy from biomass products and waste (% of total)	..	57.6	8.5
Electric power consumption per capita (kWh)	..	535	2,932
Electricity generated using fossil fuel (% of total)	..	65.1	74.7
Electricity generated by hydropower (% of total)	..	20.0	20.0
CO_2 emissions per capita (metric tons)	3.2	0.8	5.4
Water and sanitation			
Internal freshwater resources per capita (cu. m)	2,139	4,391	6,791
Total freshwater withdrawal (% of internal resources)	26.4	3.2	7.4
Agriculture (% of total freshwater withdrawal)	68	84	69
Access to improved water source (% of total population)	100	64	93
Rural (% of rural population)	100	53	85
Urban (% of urban population)	100	85	98
Access to improved sanitation facilities (% of total population)	91	30	74
Rural (% of rural population)	90	23	62
Urban (% of urban population)	92	41	82
Environment and health			
Particulate matter (urban-pop.-weighted avg., µg/cu. m)	11	77	65
Acute resp. infection prevalence (% of children under five)	..	5	..
Diarrhea prevalence (% of children under five)	..	14	..
Under-five mortality rate (per 1,000 live births)	15	98	20
National accounting aggregates—savings, depletion and degradation			
Gross savings (% of GNI)	14.9	26.3	36.4
Consumption of fixed capital (% of GNI)	13.3	13.0	12.5
Education expenditure (% of GNI)	3.2	3.4	3.2
Energy depletion (% of GNI)	0.0	10.3	4.1
Mineral depletion (% of GNI)	0.0	1.8	1.2
Net forest depletion (% of GNI)	0.0	1.8	0.2
CO_2 damage (% of GNI)	0.4	0.6	0.8
Particulate emissions damage (% of GNI)	0.0	1.2	1.3
Adjusted net savings (% of GNI)	4.5	0.9	19.5

Mexico

Population (millions) **120.8** Land area (1,000 sq. km) **1,944** GDP ($ billions) **1,178.1**

	Country data	Latin America & Caribbean group	Upper middle-income group
GNI per capita, *World Bank Atlas* method ($)	9,640	9,070	6,969
Adjusted net national income per capita ($)	7,642	7,325	5,845
Change in wealth per capita (2010 $)	532	180	1,039
Urban population (% of total)	78.4	79.0	60.7
Agriculture			
Agricultural land (% land area)	53	37	44
Agricultural irrigated land (% of total agricultural land)	6.3	..	..
Agricultural productivity, value added per worker (2005 $)	4,103	4,135	1,131
Cereal yield (kg per hectare)	3,392	4,082	4,255
Forests and biodiversity			
Forest area (% land area)	33.3	48.1	29.1
Deforestation (avg. annual %, 2000–2010)	0.3	0.5	0.0
Terrestrial protected areas (% of total land area)	12.9	21.4	16.1
Threatened species, mammals	101		
Threatened species, birds	61		
Threatened species, fish	154		
Threatened species, higher plants	361		
Oceans			
Total fisheries production (thousand metric tons)	1,725	10,964	90,024
Capture fisheries growth (avg. annual %, 1990–2012)	0.5	-0.6	1.5
Aquaculture growth (avg. annual %, 1990–2012)	8.8	10.8	9.1
Marine protected areas (% of territorial waters)	0.06	9.0	7.3
Coral reef area (sq. km)	1,780	14,860	52,070
Mangroves area (sq. km)	6,557	39,988	50,160
Energy and emissions			
Energy use per capita (kg oil equivalent)	1,560	1,292	1,893
Energy from biomass products and waste (% of total)	4.4	16.0	8.5
Electric power consumption per capita (kWh)	2,092	1,985	2,932
Electricity generated using fossil fuel (% of total)	80.7	37.3	74.7
Electricity generated by hydropower (% of total)	12.3	55.1	20.0
CO_2 emissions per capita (metric tons)	3.8	2.7	5.4
Water and sanitation			
Internal freshwater resources per capita (cu. m)	3,427	21,735	6,791
Total freshwater withdrawal (% of internal resources)	19.5	2.0	7.4
Agriculture (% of total freshwater withdrawal)	77	68	69
Access to improved water source (% of total population)	95	94	93
Rural (% of rural population)	91	82	85
Urban (% of urban population)	96	97	98
Access to improved sanitation facilities (% of total population)	85	81	74
Rural (% of rural population)	79	62	62
Urban (% of urban population)	87	86	82
Environment and health			
Particulate matter (urban-pop.-weighted avg., µg/cu. m)	46	43	65
Acute resp. infection prevalence (% of children under five)	..	..	..
Diarrhea prevalence (% of children under five)	..	..	..
Under-five mortality rate (per 1,000 live births)	16	19	20
National accounting aggregates—savings, depletion and degradation			
Gross savings (% of GNI)	21.9	19.0	36.4
Consumption of fixed capital (% of GNI)	13.5	12.2	12.5
Education expenditure (% of GNI)	5.1	5.1	3.2
Energy depletion (% of GNI)	6.0	4.7	4.1
Mineral depletion (% of GNI)	0.7	1.2	1.2
Net forest depletion (% of GNI)	0.0	0.4	0.2
CO_2 damage (% of GNI)	0.4	0.3	0.8
Particulate emissions damage (% of GNI)	0.6	0.8	1.3
Adjusted net savings (% of GNI)	5.7	4.5	19.5

Micronesia, Fed. Sts.

Population (thousands) **103** Land area (sq. km) **700** GDP ($ millions) **326.2**

	Country data	East Asia & Pacific group	Lower middle-income group
GNI per capita, *World Bank Atlas* method ($)	3,230	4,884	1,965
Adjusted net national income per capita ($)	2,959	4,305	1,574
Change in wealth per capita (2010 $)	..	1,172	117
Urban population (% of total)	22.7	49.6	38.9

Agriculture

Agricultural land (% land area)	31	48	46
Agricultural irrigated land (% of total agricultural land)	..	..	..
Agricultural productivity, value added per worker (2005 $)	5,083	794	938
Cereal yield (kg per hectare)	1,667	5,145	3,029

Forests and biodiversity

Forest area (% land area)	91.7	29.7	26.9
Deforestation (avg. annual %, 2000–2010)	0.0	-0.4	0.3
Terrestrial protected areas (% of total land area)	4.0	15.1	11.9
Threatened species, mammals	7		
Threatened species, birds	10		
Threatened species, fish	20		
Threatened species, higher plants	5		

Oceans

Total fisheries production (thousand metric tons)	46.0	108,399	43,067
Capture fisheries growth (avg. annual %, 1990–2012)	14.4	3.4	2.6
Aquaculture growth (avg. annual %, 1990–2012)	..	9.1	9.9
Marine protected areas (% of territorial waters)	100.0	1.4	14.7
Coral reef area (sq. km)	4,340	137,690	124,480
Mangroves area (sq. km)	87.0	56,537	58,917

Energy and emissions

Energy use per capita (kg oil equivalent)	..	1,671	687
Energy from biomass products and waste (% of total)	..	10.1	26.8
Electric power consumption per capita (kWh)	..	2,582	734
Electricity generated using fossil fuel (% of total)	..	80.9	72.3
Electricity generated by hydropower (% of total)	..	14.5	16.9
CO_2 emissions per capita (metric tons)	1.0	4.9	1.6

Water and sanitation

Internal freshwater resources per capita (cu. m)	..	4,438	3,144
Total freshwater withdrawal (% of internal resources)	..	10.9	19.6
Agriculture (% of total freshwater withdrawal)	..	73	88
Access to improved water source (% of total population)	89	91	88
Rural (% of rural population)	87	85	85
Urban (% of urban population)	95	97	94
Access to improved sanitation facilities (% of total population)	57	67	48
Rural (% of rural population)	49	58	36
Urban (% of urban population)	85	76	66

Environment and health

Particulate matter (urban-pop.-weighted avg., µg/cu. m)	..	75	90
Acute resp. infection prevalence (% of children under five)	..	..	..
Diarrhea prevalence (% of children under five)	..	..	..
Under-five mortality rate (per 1,000 live births)	39	21	61

National accounting aggregates—savings, depletion and degradation

Gross savings (% of GNI)	..	47.6	28.6
Consumption of fixed capital (% of GNI)	10.8	12.0	11.1
Education expenditure (% of GNI)	..	2.1	3.1
Energy depletion (% of GNI)	0.0	2.7	4.4
Mineral depletion (% of GNI)	0.0	1.4	1.1
Net forest depletion (% of GNI)	0.1	0.1	0.8
CO_2 damage (% of GNI)	0.3	1.0	0.9
Particulate emissions damage (% of GNI)	..	1.6	1.4
Adjusted net savings (% of GNI)	..	30.9	12.0

Moldova

	Country data	Europe & Central Asia group	Lower middle-income group
Population (millions) **3.6** Land area (1,000 sq. km)	**33**	GDP ($ billions)	**7.3**

	Country data	Europe & Central Asia group	Lower middle-income group
GNI per capita, *World Bank Atlas* method ($)	2,070	6,658	1,965
Adjusted net national income per capita ($)	1,954	5,541	1,574
Change in wealth per capita (2010 $)	204	263	117
Urban population (% of total)	48.4	60.2	38.9
Agriculture			
Agricultural land (% land area)	75	66	46
Agricultural irrigated land (% of total agricultural land)	9.2	..	..
Agricultural productivity, value added per worker (2005 $)	1,884	4,866	938
Cereal yield (kg per hectare)	1,359	2,519	3,029
Forests and biodiversity			
Forest area (% land area)	11.9	10.5	26.9
Deforestation (avg. annual %, 2000–2010)	-1.8	-0.5	0.3
Terrestrial protected areas (% of total land area)	3.8	5.1	11.9
Threatened species, mammals	4		
Threatened species, birds	8		
Threatened species, fish	8		
Threatened species, higher plants	2		
Oceans			
Total fisheries production (thousand metric tons)	9.6	1,022	43,067
Capture fisheries growth (avg. annual %, 1990–2012)	-16.0	-4.0	2.6
Aquaculture growth (avg. annual %, 1990–2012)	1.3	1.8	9.9
Marine protected areas (% of territorial waters)	0.84	10.4	14.7
Coral reef area (sq. km)	..	..	124,480
Mangroves area (sq. km)	..	..	58,917
Energy and emissions			
Energy use per capita (kg oil equivalent)	936	2,078	687
Energy from biomass products and waste (% of total)	2.5	2.9	26.8
Electric power consumption per capita (kWh)	1,470	2,951	734
Electricity generated using fossil fuel (% of total)	93.9	65.8	72.3
Electricity generated by hydropower (% of total)	6.1	17.9	16.9
CO_2 emissions per capita (metric tons)	1.4	5.3	1.6
Water and sanitation			
Internal freshwater resources per capita (cu. m)	281	2,744	3,144
Total freshwater withdrawal (% of internal resources)	191.5	34.8	19.6
Agriculture (% of total freshwater withdrawal)	40	70	88
Access to improved water source (% of total population)	97	95	88
Rural (% of rural population)	94	89	85
Urban (% of urban population)	99	99	94
Access to improved sanitation facilities (% of total population)	87	94	48
Rural (% of rural population)	84	90	36
Urban (% of urban population)	89	97	66
Environment and health			
Particulate matter (urban-pop.-weighted avg., µg/cu. m)	44	48	90
Acute resp. infection prevalence (% of children under five)	..	..	..
Diarrhea prevalence (% of children under five)	..	..	..
Under-five mortality rate (per 1,000 live births)	18	22	61
National accounting aggregates—savings, depletion and degradation			
Gross savings (% of GNI)	11.9	18.9	28.6
Consumption of fixed capital (% of GNI)	10.6	12.4	11.1
Education expenditure (% of GNI)	7.3	3.8	3.1
Energy depletion (% of GNI)	0.1	4.4	4.4
Mineral depletion (% of GNI)	0.0	0.6	1.1
Net forest depletion (% of GNI)	0.4	0.0	0.8
CO_2 damage (% of GNI)	0.6	0.8	0.9
Particulate emissions damage (% of GNI)	1.3	1.8	1.4
Adjusted net savings (% of GNI)	6.2	2.8	12.0

Monaco

Population (thousands)	**38**	Land area (sq. km)	**2.0**	GDP ($ billions)	**6.1**

	Country data	High-Income group
GNI per capita, *World Bank Atlas* method ($)	*186,950*	38,444
Adjusted net national income per capita ($)	..	32,262
Change in wealth per capita (2010 $)	..	2,210
Urban population (% of total)	100.0	80.2
Agriculture		
Agricultural land (% land area)	..	29
Agricultural irrigated land (% of total agricultural land)	..	..
Agricultural productivity, value added per worker (2005 $)	..	25,238
Cereal yield (kg per hectare)	..	4,374
Forests and biodiversity		
Forest area (% land area)	*0.0*	35.0
Deforestation (avg. annual %, 2000–2010)	0.0	0.0
Terrestrial protected areas (% of total land area)	35.9	13.9
Threatened species, mammals	2	
Threatened species, birds	0	
Threatened species, fish	11	
Threatened species, higher plants	0	
Oceans		
Total fisheries production (thousand metric tons)	0.00	37,661
Capture fisheries growth (avg. annual %, 1990–2012)	-3.1	-2.0
Aquaculture growth (avg. annual %, 1990–2012)	..	2.5
Marine protected areas (% of territorial waters)	*100.0*	*14.4*
Coral reef area (sq. km)	..	82,210
Mangroves area (sq. km)	..	15,504
Energy and emissions		
Energy use per capita (kg oil equivalent)	..	4,872
Energy from biomass products and waste (% of total)	..	4.3
Electric power consumption per capita (kWh)	..	8,896
Electricity generated using fossil fuel (% of total)	..	61.8
Electricity generated by hydropower (% of total)	..	12.2
CO_2 emissions per capita (metric tons)	..	11.6
Water and sanitation		
Internal freshwater resources per capita (cu. m)	..	11,335
Total freshwater withdrawal (% of internal resources)	..	7.0
Agriculture (% of total freshwater withdrawal)	0	40
Access to improved water source (% of total population)	100	99
Rural (% of rural population)	..	98
Urban (% of urban population)	100	100
Access to improved sanitation facilities (% of total population)	100	96
Rural (% of rural population)	..	93
Urban (% of urban population)	100	97
Environment and health		
Particulate matter (urban-pop.-weighted avg., µg/cu. m)	18	27
Acute resp. infection prevalence (% of children under five)	..	..
Diarrhea prevalence (% of children under five)	..	..
Under-five mortality rate (per 1,000 live births)	4	6
National accounting aggregates—savings, depletion and degradation		
Gross savings (% of GNI)	..	20.1
Consumption of fixed capital (% of GNI)	11.7	14.2
Education expenditure (% of GNI)	1.1	4.7
Energy depletion (% of GNI)	0.0	1.6
Mineral depletion (% of GNI)	0.0	0.3
Net forest depletion (% of GNI)	..	0.0
CO_2 damage (% of GNI)	..	0.3
Particulate emissions damage (% of GNI)	..	0.3
Adjusted net savings (% of GNI)	..	8.1

Mongolia

	Population (millions)	**2.8**	Land area (1,000 sq. km)	**1,554**	GDP ($ billions)	**10.3**

	Country data	East Asia & Pacific group	Lower middle-income group
GNI per capita, *World Bank Atlas* method ($)	3,160	4,884	1,965
Adjusted net national income per capita ($)	2,591	4,305	1,574
Change in wealth per capita (2010 $)	–348	1,172	117
Urban population (% of total)	69.3	49.6	38.9
Agriculture			
Agricultural land (% land area)	73	48	46
Agricultural irrigated land (% of total agricultural land)	..	..	..
Agricultural productivity, value added per worker (2005 $)	3,078	794	938
Cereal yield (kg per hectare)	1,564	5,145	3,029
Forests and biodiversity			
Forest area (% land area)	7.0	29.7	26.9
Deforestation (avg. annual %, 2000–2010)	0.7	–0.4	0.3
Terrestrial protected areas (% of total land area)	13.8	15.1	11.9
Threatened species, mammals	11		
Threatened species, birds	20		
Threatened species, fish	2		
Threatened species, higher plants	0		
Oceans			
Total fisheries production (thousand metric tons)	0.06	108,399	43,067
Capture fisheries growth (avg. annual %, 1990–2012)	–3.2	3.4	2.6
Aquaculture growth (avg. annual %, 1990–2012)	..	9.1	9.9
Marine protected areas (% of territorial waters)	0.85	1.4	14.7
Coral reef area (sq. km)	..	137,690	124,480
Mangroves area (sq. km)	..	56,537	58,917
Energy and emissions			
Energy use per capita (kg oil equivalent)	1,310	1,671	687
Energy from biomass products and waste (% of total)	4.1	10.1	26.8
Electric power consumption per capita (kWh)	1,577	2,582	734
Electricity generated using fossil fuel (% of total)	100.0	80.9	72.3
Electricity generated by hydropower (% of total)	0.0	14.5	16.9
CO_2 emissions per capita (metric tons)	4.2	4.9	1.6
Water and sanitation			
Internal freshwater resources per capita (cu. m)	12,635	4,438	3,144
Total freshwater withdrawal (% of internal resources)	1.2	10.9	19.6
Agriculture (% of total freshwater withdrawal)	53	73	88
Access to improved water source (% of total population)	85	91	88
Rural (% of rural population)	61	85	85
Urban (% of urban population)	95	97	94
Access to improved sanitation facilities (% of total population)	56	67	48
Rural (% of rural population)	35	58	36
Urban (% of urban population)	65	76	66
Environment and health			
Particulate matter (urban-pop.-weighted avg., µg/cu. m)	284	75	90
Acute resp. infection prevalence (% of children under five)	..	..	..
Diarrhea prevalence (% of children under five)	..	..	..
Under-five mortality rate (per 1,000 live births)	28	21	61
National accounting aggregates—savings, depletion and degradation			
Gross savings (% of GNI)	35.6	47.6	28.6
Consumption of fixed capital (% of GNI)	5.1	12.0	11.1
Education expenditure (% of GNI)	5.0	2.1	3.1
Energy depletion (% of GNI)	11.2	2.7	4.4
Mineral depletion (% of GNI)	8.1	1.4	1.1
Net forest depletion (% of GNI)	0.1	0.1	0.8
CO_2 damage (% of GNI)	1.6	1.0	0.9
Particulate emissions damage (% of GNI)	3.4	1.6	1.4
Adjusted net savings (% of GNI)	11.3	30.9	12.0

Montenegro

Population (thousands) **621** Land area (1,000 sq. km) **13** GDP ($ billions) **4.4**

	Country data	Europe & Central Asia group	Upper middle-income group
GNI per capita, *World Bank Atlas* method ($)	7,220	6,658	6,969
Adjusted net national income per capita ($)	..	5,541	5,845
Change in wealth per capita (2010 $)	..	263	1,039
Urban population (% of total)	63.5	60.2	60.7

Agriculture
Agricultural land (% land area)	38	66	44
Agricultural irrigated land (% of total agricultural land)	..	..	..
Agricultural productivity, value added per worker (2005 $)	7,165	4,866	1,131
Cereal yield (kg per hectare)	2,864	2,519	4,255

Forests and biodiversity
Forest area (% land area)	40.4	10.5	29.1
Deforestation (avg. annual %, 2000–2010)	0.0	-0.5	0.0
Terrestrial protected areas (% of total land area)	14.8	5.1	16.1
Threatened species, mammals	6		
Threatened species, birds	12		
Threatened species, fish	26		
Threatened species, higher plants	2		

Oceans
Total fisheries production (thousand metric tons)	2.2	1,022	90,024
Capture fisheries growth (avg. annual %, 1990–2012)	..	-4.0	1.5
Aquaculture growth (avg. annual %, 1990–2012)	..	1.8	9.1
Marine protected areas (% of territorial waters)	0.01	10.4	7.3
Coral reef area (sq. km)	..	..	52,070
Mangroves area (sq. km)	..	..	50,160

Energy and emissions
Energy use per capita (kg oil equivalent)	1,900	2,078	1,893
Energy from biomass products and waste (% of total)	19.6	2.9	8.5
Electric power consumption per capita (kWh)	5,747	2,951	2,932
Electricity generated using fossil fuel (% of total)	54.7	65.8	74.7
Electricity generated by hydropower (% of total)	45.3	17.9	20.0
CO_2 emissions per capita (metric tons)	4.2	5.3	5.4

Water and sanitation
Internal freshwater resources per capita (cu. m)	..	2,744	6,791
Total freshwater withdrawal (% of internal resources)	..	34.8	7.4
Agriculture (% of total freshwater withdrawal)	1	70	69
Access to improved water source (% of total population)	98	95	93
Rural (% of rural population)	95	89	85
Urban (% of urban population)	100	99	98
Access to improved sanitation facilities (% of total population)	90	94	74
Rural (% of rural population)	87	90	62
Urban (% of urban population)	92	97	82

Environment and health
Particulate matter (urban-pop.-weighted avg., µg/cu. m)	30	48	65
Acute resp. infection prevalence (% of children under five)	..	..	..
Diarrhea prevalence (% of children under five)	..	..	..
Under-five mortality rate (per 1,000 live births)	6	22	20

National accounting aggregates—savings, depletion and degradation
Gross savings (% of GNI)	-0.2	18.9	36.4
Consumption of fixed capital (% of GNI)	11.1	12.4	12.5
Education expenditure (% of GNI)	..	3.8	3.2
Energy depletion (% of GNI)	0.1	4.4	4.1
Mineral depletion (% of GNI)	0.0	0.6	1.2
Net forest depletion (% of GNI)	..	0.0	0.2
CO_2 damage (% of GNI)	0.5	0.8	0.8
Particulate emissions damage (% of GNI)	..	1.8	1.3
Adjusted net savings (% of GNI)	..	2.8	19.5

Morocco

	Country data	Middle East & N. Africa group	Lower middle-income group
GNI per capita, *World Bank Atlas* method ($)	2,960	*3,451*	1,965
Adjusted net national income per capita ($)	2,411	*2,602*	1,574
Change in wealth per capita (2010 $)	465	101	117
Urban population (% of total)	57.4	59.5	38.9

Agriculture

Agricultural land (% land area)	67	23	46
Agricultural irrigated land (% of total agricultural land)	4.6	..	..
Agricultural productivity, value added per worker (2005 $)	3,737	*2,642*	938
Cereal yield (kg per hectare)	1,017	2,350	3,029

Forests and biodiversity

Forest area (% land area)	11.5	2.4	26.9
Deforestation (avg. annual %, 2000–2010)	-0.2	-0.1	0.3
Terrestrial protected areas (% of total land area)	21.5	6.1	11.9
Threatened species, mammals	17		
Threatened species, birds	11		
Threatened species, fish	44		
Threatened species, higher plants	34		

Oceans

Total fisheries production (thousand metric tons)	1,178	3,976	43,067
Capture fisheries growth (avg. annual %, 1990–2012)	3.3	3.0	2.6
Aquaculture growth (avg. annual.%, 1990–2012)	5.9	12.8	9.9
Marine protected areas (% of territorial waters)	2.4	9.1	14.7
Coral reef area (sq. km)	..	5,700	124,480
Mangroves area (sq. km)	..	217	58,917

Energy and emissions

Energy use per capita (kg oil equivalent)	539	1,376	687
Energy from biomass products and waste (% of total)	2.8	0.9	26.8
Electric power consumption per capita (kWh)	826	1,696	734
Electricity generated using fossil fuel (% of total)	89.7	91.7	72.3
Electricity generated by hydropower (% of total)	7.5	5.5	16.9
CO_2 emissions per capita (metric tons)	1.6	3.9	1.6

Water and sanitation

Internal freshwater resources per capita (cu. m)	905	679	3,144
Total freshwater withdrawal (% of internal resources)	43.5	122.1	19.6
Agriculture (% of total freshwater withdrawal)	87	86	88
Access to improved water source (% of total population)	84	90	88
Rural (% of rural population)	64	83	85
Urban (% of urban population)	98	95	94
Access to improved sanitation facilities (% of total population)	75	88	48
Rural (% of rural population)	63	80	36
Urban (% of urban population)	85	94	66

Environment and health

Particulate matter (urban-pop.-weighted avg., µg/cu. m)	66	79	90
Acute resp. infection prevalence (% of children under five)	..	..	..
Diarrhea prevalence (% of children under five)	..	..	..
Under-five mortality rate (per 1,000 live births)	31	26	61

National accounting aggregates—savings, depletion and degradation

Gross savings (% of GNI)	26.6	25.9	28.6
Consumption of fixed capital (% of GNI)	12.9	9.9	11.1
Education expenditure (% of GNI)	5.2	4.5	3.1
Energy depletion (% of GNI)	0.0	12.9	4.4
Mineral depletion (% of GNI)	2.8	0.5	1.1
Net forest depletion (% of GNI)	0.0	0.2	0.8
CO_2 damage (% of GNI)	0.6	0.7	0.9
Particulate emissions damage (% of GNI)	0.7	0.9	1.4
Adjusted net savings (% of GNI)	14.7	5.3	12.0

Population (millions) **32.5** Land area (1,000 sq. km) **446** GDP ($ billions) **96.0**

Mozambique

| | Population (millions) | **25.2** | Land area (1,000 sq. km) | **786** | GDP ($ billions) | **14.2** |

	Country data	Sub-Saharan Africa group	Low-income group
GNI per capita, *World Bank Atlas* method ($)	510	1,547	594
Adjusted net national income per capita ($)	476	1,005	495
Change in wealth per capita (2010 $)	-91	-273	-39
Urban population (% of total)	31.5	36.8	28.2
Agriculture			
Agricultural land (% land area)	63	44	39
Agricultural irrigated land (% of total agricultural land)	..	..	..
Agricultural productivity, value added per worker (2005 $)	301	765	367
Cereal yield (kg per hectare)	694	1,417	1,982
Forests and biodiversity			
Forest area (% land area)	49.4	27.4	27.4
Deforestation (avg. annual %, 2000–2010)	0.5	0.5	0.6
Terrestrial protected areas (% of total land area)	17.6	16.4	13.7
Threatened species, mammals	12		
Threatened species, birds	26		
Threatened species, fish	54		
Threatened species, higher plants	53		
Oceans			
Total fisheries production (thousand metric tons)	213	6,906	11,789
Capture fisheries growth (avg. annual %, 1990–2012)	8.4	2.1	3.8
Aquaculture growth (avg. annual %, 1990–2012)	18.3	15.9	5.1
Marine protected areas (% of territorial waters)	0.22	11.7	13.1
Coral reef area (sq. km)	1,860	17,980	15,120
Mangroves area (sq. km)	2,909	27,808	25,817
Energy and emissions			
Energy use per capita (kg oil equivalent)	415	681	360
Energy from biomass products and waste (% of total)	79.2	57.6	66.0
Electric power consumption per capita (kWh)	447	535	233
Electricity generated using fossil fuel (% of total)	0.1	65.1	30.9
Electricity generated by hydropower (% of total)	99.9	20.0	45.5
CO_2 emissions per capita (metric tons)	0.1	0.8	0.3
Water and sanitation			
Internal freshwater resources per capita (cu. m)	4,080	4,391	5,121
Total freshwater withdrawal (% of internal resources)	0.7	3.2	4.4
Agriculture (% of total freshwater withdrawal)	74	84	90
Access to improved water source (% of total population)	49	64	69
Rural (% of rural population)	35	53	61
Urban (% of urban population)	80	85	88
Access to improved sanitation facilities (% of total population)	21	30	37
Rural (% of rural population)	11	23	33
Urban (% of urban population)	44	41	46
Environment and health			
Particulate matter (urban-pop.-weighted avg., µg/cu. m)	34	77	74
Acute resp. infection prevalence (% of children under five)	2	5	6
Diarrhea prevalence (% of children under five)	11	14	14
Under-five mortality rate (per 1,000 live births)	90	98	82
National accounting aggregates—savings, depletion and degradation			
Gross savings (% of GNI)	12.4	26.3	24.6
Consumption of fixed capital (% of GNI)	12.2	13.0	11.8
Education expenditure (% of GNI)	4.0	3.4	3.2
Energy depletion (% of GNI)	3.2	10.3	1.4
Mineral depletion (% of GNI)	0.1	1.8	1.9
Net forest depletion (% of GNI)	0.0	1.8	4.4
CO_2 damage (% of GNI)	0.2	0.6	0.4
Particulate emissions damage (% of GNI)	0.3	1.2	1.0
Adjusted net savings (% of GNI)	0.4	0.9	7.0

Myanmar

	Country data	East Asia & Pacific group	Low-Income group
Population (millions) **52.8** Land area (1,000 sq. km) **653** GDP ($ millions) ..			
GNI per capita, *World Bank Atlas* method ($)	..	4,884	594
Adjusted net national income per capita ($)	..	4,305	495
Change in wealth per capita (2010 $)	..	1,172	–39
Urban population (% of total)	33.2	49.6	28.2

Agriculture

Agricultural land (% land area)	19	48	39
Agricultural irrigated land (% of total agricultural land)	24.8	..	..
Agricultural productivity, value added per worker (2005 $)	..	794	367
Cereal yield (kg per hectare)	3,864	5,145	1,982

Forests and biodiversity

Forest area (% land area)	48.2	29.7	27.4
Deforestation (avg. annual %, 2000–2010)	0.9	–0.4	0.6
Terrestrial protected areas (% of total land area)	7.3	15.1	13.7
Threatened species, mammals	46		
Threatened species, birds	44		
Threatened species, fish	40		
Threatened species, higher plants	46		

Oceans

Total fisheries production (thousand metric tons)	4,465	108,399	11,789
Capture fisheries growth (avg. annual %, 1990–2012)	7.4	3.4	3.8
Aquaculture growth (avg. annual %, 1990–2012)	24.5	9.1	5.1
Marine protected areas (% of territorial waters)	28.0	1.4	13.1
Coral reef area (sq. km)	1,870	137,690	15,120
Mangroves (sq. km)	5,029	56,537	25,817

Energy and emissions

Energy use per capita (kg oil equivalent)	268	1,671	360
Energy from biomass products and waste (% of total)	75.5	10.1	66.0
Electric power consumption per capita (kWh)	110	2,582	233
Electricity generated using fossil fuel (% of total)	29.7	80.9	30.9
Electricity generated by hydropower (% of total)	70.3	14.5	45.5
CO_2 emissions per capita (metric tons)	0.2	4.9	0.3

Water and sanitation

Internal freshwater resources per capita (cu. m)	19,159	4,438	5,121
Total freshwater withdrawal (% of internal resources)	3.3	10.9	4.4
Agriculture (% of total freshwater withdrawal)	89	73	90
Access to improved water source (% of total population)	86	91	69
Rural (% of rural population)	81	85	61
Urban (% of urban population)	95	97	88
Access to improved sanitation facilities (% of total population)	77	67	37
Rural (% of rural population)	74	58	33
Urban (% of urban population)	84	76	46

Environment and health

Particulate matter (urban-pop.-weighted avg., µg/cu. m)	67	75	74
Acute resp. infection prevalence (% of children under five)	..	..	6
Diarrhea prevalence (% of children under five)	..	..	14
Under-five mortality rate (per 1,000 live births)	52	21	82

National accounting aggregates—savings, depletion and degradation

Gross savings (% of GNI)	..	47.6	24.6
Consumption of fixed capital (% of GNI)	..	12.0	11.8
Education expenditure (% of GNI)	0.7	2.1	3.2
Energy depletion (% of GNI)	..	2.7	1.4
Mineral depletion (% of GNI)	..	1.4	1.9
Net forest depletion (% of GNI)	..	0.1	4.4
CO_2 damage (% of GNI)	..	1.0	0.4
Particulate emissions damage (% of GNI)	1.1	1.6	1.0
Adjusted net savings (% of GNI)	..	30.9	7.0

Namibia

Population (millions)	**2.3** Land area (1,000 sq. km)	**823** GDP ($ billions)	**13.1**

	Country data	Sub-Saharan Africa group	Upper middle-income group
GNI per capita, *World Bank Atlas* method ($)	5,610	1,547	6,969
Adjusted net national income per capita ($)	4,812	1,005	5,845
Change in wealth per capita (2010 $)	378	-273	1,039
Urban population (% of total)	39.0	36.8	60.7
Agriculture			
Agricultural land (% land area)	47	44	44
Agricultural irrigated land (% of total agricultural land)	..	..	..
Agricultural productivity, value added per worker (2005 $)	2,765	765	1,131
Cereal yield (kg per hectare)	460	1,417	4,255
Forests and biodiversity			
Forest area (% land area)	8.8	27.4	29.1
Deforestation (avg. annual %, 2000–2010)	1.0	0.5	0.0
Terrestrial protected areas (% of total land area)	43.2	16.4	16.1
Threatened species, mammals	12		
Threatened species, birds	26		
Threatened species, fish	27		
Threatened species, higher plants	27		
Oceans			
Total fisheries production (thousand metric tons)	469	6,906	90,024
Capture fisheries growth (avg. annual %, 1990–2012)	2.6	2.1	1.5
Aquaculture growth (avg. annual %, 1990–2012)	16.4	15.9	9.1
Marine protected areas (% of territorial waters)	8.2	11.7	7.3
Coral reef area (sq. km)	..	17,980	52,070
Mangroves area (sq. km)	..	27,808	50,160
Energy and emissions			
Energy use per capita (kg oil equivalent)	717	681	1,893
Energy from biomass products and waste (% of total)	13.3	57.6	8.5
Electric power consumption per capita (kWh)	1,549	535	2,932
Electricity generated using fossil fuel (% of total)	1.8	65.1	74.7
Electricity generated by hydropower (% of total)	98.2	20.0	20.0
CO_2 emissions per capita (metric tons)	1.5	0.8	5.4
Water and sanitation			
Internal freshwater resources per capita (cu. m)	2,778	4,391	6,791
Total freshwater withdrawal (% of internal resources)	4.9	3.2	7.4
Agriculture (% of total freshwater withdrawal)	71	84	69
Access to improved water source (% of total population)	92	64	93
Rural (% of rural population)	87	53	85
Urban (% of urban population)	98	85	98
Access to improved sanitation facilities (% of total population)	32	30	74
Rural (% of rural population)	17	23	62
Urban (% of urban population)	56	41	82
Environment and health			
Particulate matter (urban-pop.-weighted avg., µg/cu. m)	55	77	65
Acute resp. infection prevalence (% of children under five)	4	5	..
Diarrhea prevalence (% of children under five)	12	14	..
Under-five mortality rate (per 1,000 live births)	39	98	20
National accounting aggregates—savings, depletion and degradation			
Gross savings (% of GNI)	18.8	26.3	36.4
Consumption of fixed capital (% of GNI)	13.1	13.0	12.5
Education expenditure (% of GNI)	8.4	3.4	3.2
Energy depletion (% of GNI)	0.0	10.3	4.1
Mineral depletion (% of GNI)	1.4	1.8	1.2
Net forest depletion (% of GNI)	0.0	1.8	0.2
CO_2 damage (% of GNI)	0.3	0.6	0.8
Particulate emissions damage (% of GNI)	0.1	1.2	1.3
Adjusted net savings (% of GNI)	12.0	0.9	19.5

Nepal

Population (millions)	**27.5**	Land area (1,000 sq. km)	**143** GDP ($ billions)	**19.0**

	Country data	South Asia group	Low-Income group
GNI per capita, *World Bank Atlas* method ($)	700	1,437	594
Adjusted net national income per capita ($)	604	1,168	495
Change in wealth per capita (2010 $)	91	158	-39
Urban population (% of total)	17.3	31.4	28.2
Agriculture			
Agricultural land (% of land area)	30	55	39
Agricultural irrigated land (% of total agricultural land)	27.4	..	..
Agricultural productivity, value added per worker (2005 $)	270	669	367
Cereal yield (kg per hectare)	2,719	2,925	1,982
Forests and biodiversity			
Forest area (% land area)	25.4	17.1	27.4
Deforestation (avg. annual %, 2000–2010)	0.7	-0.3	0.6
Terrestrial protected areas (% of total land area)	16.4	6.2	13.7
Threatened species, mammals	31		
Threatened species, birds	33		
Threatened species, fish	7		
Threatened species, higher plants	9		
Oceans			
Total fisheries production (thousand metric tons)	56.0	13,613	11,789
Capture fisheries growth (avg. annual %, 1990–2012)	6.6	2.6	3.8
Aquaculture growth (avg. annual %, 1990–2012)	6.2	7.6	5.1
Marine protected areas (% of territorial waters)	61.8	10.7	13.1
Coral reef area (sq. km)	..	15,440	15,120
Mangroves area (sq. km)	..	10,343	25,817
Energy and emissions			
Energy use per capita (kg oil equivalent)	383	555	360
Energy from biomass products and waste (% of total)	84.1	26.7	66.0
Electric power consumption per capita (kWh)	106	605	233
Electricity generated using fossil fuel (% of total)	0.1	77.9	30.9
Electricity generated by hydropower (% of total)	99.9	13.8	45.5
CO_2 emissions per capita (metric tons)	0.1	1.4	0.3
Water and sanitation			
Internal freshwater resources per capita (cu. m)	7,298	1,217	5,121
Total freshwater withdrawal (% of internal resources)	4.9	51.6	4.4
Agriculture (% of total freshwater withdrawal)	98	91	90
Access to improved water source (% of total population)	88	91	69
Rural (% of rural population)	88	89	61
Urban (% of urban population)	90	95	88
Access to improved sanitation facilities (% of total population)	37	40	37
Rural (% of rural population)	34	30	33
Urban (% of urban population)	51	61	46
Environment and health			
Particulate matter (urban-pop.-weighted avg., µg/cu. m)	110	110	74
Acute resp. infection prevalence (% of children under five)	5	..	6
Diarrhea prevalence (% of children under five)	14	..	14
Under-five mortality rate (per 1,000 live births)	42	60	82
National accounting aggregates—savings, depletion and degradation			
Gross savings (% of GNI)	40.4	29.3	24.6
Consumption of fixed capital (% of GNI)	9.1	12.7	11.8
Education expenditure (% of GNI)	4.2	2.8	3.2
Energy depletion (% of GNI)	0.0	1.8	1.4
Mineral depletion (% of GNI)	0.0	0.8	1.9
Net forest depletion (% of GNI)	4.3	1.1	4.4
CO_2 damage (% of GNI)	0.2	1.1	0.4
Particulate emissions damage (% of GNI)	1.0	1.5	1.0
Adjusted net savings (% of GNI)	30.0	13.1	7.0

Netherlands

Population (millions)	**16.8**	Land area (1,000 sq. km)	**34**	GDP ($ billions)	**770.1**

	Country data	High-income group
GNI per capita, *World Bank Atlas* method ($)	48,110	38,444
Adjusted net national income per capita ($)	40,343	32,262
Change in wealth per capita (2010 $)	4,891	2,210
Urban population (% of total)	83.5	80.2
Agriculture		
Agricultural land (% land area)	56	29
Agricultural irrigated land (% of total agricultural land)	10.6	..
Agricultural productivity, value added per worker (2005 $)	60,398	25,238
Cereal yield (kg per hectare)	8,545	4,374
Forests and biodiversity		
Forest area (% land area)	10.8	35.0
Deforestation (avg. annual %, 2000–2010)	-0.1	0.0
Terrestrial protected areas (% of total land area)	19.5	13.9
Threatened species, mammals	3	
Threatened species, birds	4	
Threatened species, fish	13	
Threatened species, higher plants	0	
Oceans		
Total fisheries production (thousand metric tons)	393	37,661
Capture fisheries growth (avg. annual %, 1990–2012)	-0.7	-2.0
Aquaculture growth (avg. annual %, 1990–2012)	-3.5	2.5
Marine protected areas (% of territorial waters)	0.54	14.4
Coral reef area (sq. km)	..	82,210
Mangroves area (sq. km)	..	15,504
Energy and emissions		
Energy use per capita (kg oil equivalent)	4,638	4,872
Energy from biomass products and waste (% of total)	4.6	4.3
Electric power consumption per capita (kWh)	7,036	8,896
Electricity generated using fossil fuel (% of total)	83.8	61.8
Electricity generated by hydropower (% of total)	0.1	12.2
CO_2 emissions per capita (metric tons)	11.0	11.6
Water and sanitation		
Internal freshwater resources per capita (cu. m)	659	11,335
Total freshwater withdrawal (% of internal resources)	96.5	7.0
Agriculture (% of total freshwater withdrawal)	1	40
Access to improved water source (% of total population)	100	99
Rural (% of rural population)	100	98
Urban (% of urban population)	100	100
Access to improved sanitation facilities (% of total population)	100	96
Rural (% of rural population)	100	93
Urban (% of urban population)	100	97
Environment and health		
Particulate matter (urban-pop.-weighted avg., µg/cu. m)	25	27
Acute resp. infection prevalence (% of children under five)	..	..
Diarrhea prevalence (% of children under five)	..	..
Under-five mortality rate (per 1,000 live births)	4	6
National accounting aggregates—savings, depletion and degradation		
Gross savings (% of GNI)	24.5	20.1
Consumption of fixed capital (% of GNI)	12.4	14.2
Education expenditure (% of GNI)	6.1	4.7
Energy depletion (% of GNI)	0.7	1.6
Mineral depletion (% of GNI)	0.0	0.3
Net forest depletion (% of GNI)	0.0	0.0
CO_2 damage (% of GNI)	0.2	0.3
Particulate emissions damage (% of GNI)	0.4	0.3
Adjusted net savings (% of GNI)	16.9	8.1

New Caledonia

Population (thousands) **258** Land area (1,000 sq. km) **18** GDP ($ millions) ..

	Country data	High-income group
GNI per capita, *World Bank Atlas* method ($)	..	38,444
Adjusted net national income per capita ($)	..	32,262
Change in wealth per capita (2010 $)	..	2,210
Urban population (% of total)	61.6	80.2

Agriculture
Agricultural land (% land area)	14	29
Agricultural irrigated land (% of total agricultural land)	..	..
Agricultural productivity, value added per worker (2005 $)	..	25,238
Cereal yield (kg per hectare)	3,133	4,374

Forests and biodiversity
Forest area (% land area)	45.9	35.0
Deforestation (avg. annual %, 2000-2010)	0.0	0.0
Terrestrial protected areas (% of total land area)	61.3	13.9
Threatened species, mammals	9	
Threatened species, birds	15	
Threatened species, fish	30	
Threatened species, higher plants	258	

Oceans
Total fisheries production (thousand metric tons)	5.4	37,661
Capture fisheries growth (avg. annual %, 1990-2012)	-1.2	-2.0
Aquaculture growth (avg. annual %, 1990-2012)	4.5	2.5
Marine protected areas (% of territorial waters)	12.4	14.4
Coral reef area (sq. km)	5,980	82,210
Mangroves area (sq. km)	227	15,504

Energy and emissions
Energy use per capita (kg oil equivalent)	..	4,872
Energy from biomass products and waste (% of total)	..	4.3
Electric power consumption per capita (kWh)	..	8,896
Electricity generated using fossil fuel (% of total)	..	61.8
Electricity generated by hydropower (% of total)	..	12.2
CO_2 emissions per capita (metric tons)	15.7	11.6

Water and sanitation
Internal freshwater resources per capita (cu. m)	..	11,335
Total freshwater withdrawal (% of internal resources)	..	7.0
Agriculture (% of total freshwater withdrawal)	..	40
Access to improved water source (% of total population)	98	99
Rural (% of rural population)	98	98
Urban (% of urban population)	98	100
Access to improved sanitation facilities (% of total population)	100	96
Rural (% of rural population)	100	93
Urban (% of urban population)	100	97

Environment and health
Particulate matter (urban-pop.-weighted avg., µg/cu. m)	29	27
Acute resp. infection prevalence (% of children under five)	..	..
Diarrhea prevalence (% of children under five)	..	..
Under-five mortality rate (per 1,000 live births)	..	6

National accounting aggregates—savings, depletion and degradation
Gross savings (% of GNI)	..	20.1
Consumption of fixed capital (% of GNI)	..	14.2
Education expenditure (% of GNI)	..	4.7
Energy depletion (% of GNI)	..	1.6
Mineral depletion (% of GNI)	..	0.3
Net forest depletion (% of GNI)	..	0.0
CO_2 damage (% of GNI)	..	0.3
Particulate emissions damage (% of GNI)	..	0.3
Adjusted net savings (% of GNI)	..	8.1

New Zealand

Population (millions)	**4.4**	Land area (1,000 sq. km)	**263**	GDP ($ billions)	**171.3**

	Country data	High-income group
GNI per capita, *World Bank Atlas* method ($)	36,900	38,444
Adjusted net national income per capita ($)	33,037	32,262
Change in wealth per capita (2010 $)	1,459	2,210
Urban population (% of total)	86.3	80.2
Agriculture		
Agricultural land (% land area)	43	29
Agricultural irrigated land (% of total agricultural land)	..	..
Agricultural productivity, value added per worker (2005 $)	..	25,238
Cereal yield (kg per hectare)	8,012	4,374
Forests and biodiversity		
Forest area (% land area)	31.4	35.0
Deforestation (avg. annual %, 2000–2010)	0.0	0.0
Terrestrial protected areas (% of total land area)	27.3	13.9
Threatened species, mammals	9	
Threatened species, birds	70	
Threatened species, fish	23	
Threatened species, higher plants	21	
Oceans		
Total fisheries production (thousand metric tons)	542	37,661
Capture fisheries growth (avg. annual %, 1990–2012)	1.0	-2.0
Aquaculture growth (avg. annual %, 1990–2012)	5.9	2.5
Marine protected areas (% of territorial waters)	37.7	14.4
Coral reef area (sq. km)	..	82,210
Mangroves area (sq. km)	261	15,504
Energy and emissions		
Energy use per capita (kg oil equivalent)	4,124	4,872
Energy from biomass products and waste (% of total)	6.6	4.3
Electric power consumption per capita (kWh)	9,399	8,896
Electricity generated using fossil fuel (% of total)	24.0	61.8
Electricity generated by hydropower (% of total)	56.4	12.2
CO_2 emissions per capita (metric tons)	7.2	11.6
Water and sanitation		
Internal freshwater resources per capita (cu. m)	74,230	11,335
Total freshwater withdrawal (% of internal resources)	1.5	7.0
Agriculture (% of total freshwater withdrawal)	74	40
Access to improved water source (% of total population)	100	99
Rural (% of rural population)	100	98
Urban (% of urban population)	100	100
Access to improved sanitation facilities (% of total population)	..	96
Rural (% of rural population)	..	93
Urban (% of urban population)	..	97
Environment and health		
Particulate matter (urban-pop.-weighted avg., µg/cu. m)	16	27
Acute resp. infection prevalence (% of children under five)	..	..
Diarrhea prevalence (% of children under five)	..	..
Under-five mortality rate (per 1,000 live births)	6	6
National accounting aggregates—savings, depletion and degradation		
Gross savings (% of GNI)	15.4	20.1
Consumption of fixed capital (% of GNI)	12.8	14.2
Education expenditure (% of GNI)	7.3	4.7
Energy depletion (% of GNI)	0.5	1.6
Mineral depletion (% of GNI)	0.4	0.3
Net forest depletion (% of GNI)	0.0	0.0
CO_2 damage (% of GNI)	0.2	0.3
Particulate emissions damage (% of GNI)	0.1	0.3
Adjusted net savings (% of GNI)	8.0	8.1

Nicaragua

	Country data	Latin America & Caribbean group	Lower middle-income group
Population (millions) **6.0** Land area (1,000 sq. km) **120** GDP ($ billions) **10.5**			

	Country data	Latin America & Caribbean group	Lower middle-income group
GNI per capita, *World Bank Atlas* method ($)	1,650	9,070	1,965
Adjusted net national income per capita ($)	1,409	7,325	1,574
Change in wealth per capita (2010 $)	-58	180	117
Urban population (% of total)	57.9	79.0	38.9
Agriculture			
Agricultural land (% land area)	43	37	46
Agricultural irrigated land (% of total agricultural land)	..	..	..
Agricultural productivity, value added per worker (2005 $)	3,832	4,135	938
Cereal yield (kg per hectare)	2,093	4,082	3,029
Forests and biodiversity			
Forest area (% land area)	25.3	48.1	26.9
Deforestation (avg. annual %, 2000–2010)	2.0	0.5	0.3
Terrestrial protected areas (% of total land area)	30.8	21.4	11.9
Threatened species, mammals	7		
Threatened species, birds	14		
Threatened species, fish	31		
Threatened species, higher plants	43		
Oceans			
Total fisheries production (thousand metric tons)	58.2	10,964	43,067
Capture fisheries growth (avg. annual %, 1990–2012)	11.5	-0.6	2.6
Aquaculture growth (avg. annual %, 1990–2012)	30.1	10.8	9.9
Marine protected areas (% of territorial waters)	37.2	9.0	14.7
Coral reef area (sq. km)	710	14,860	124,480
Mangroves area (sq. km)	671	39,988	58,917
Energy and emissions			
Energy use per capita (kg oil equivalent)	515	1,292	687
Energy from biomass products and waste (% of total)	40.8	16.0	26.8
Electric power consumption per capita (kWh)	522	1,985	734
Electricity generated using fossil fuel (% of total)	66.0	37.3	72.3
Electricity generated by hydropower (% of total)	11.6	55.1	16.9
CO_2 emissions per capita (metric tons)	0.8	2.7	1.6
Water and sanitation			
Internal freshwater resources per capita (cu. m)	32,125	21,735	3,144
Total freshwater withdrawal (% of internal resources)	0.7	2.0	19.6
Agriculture (% of total freshwater withdrawal)	84	68	88
Access to improved water source (% of total population)	85	94	88
Rural (% of rural population)	68	82	85
Urban (% of urban population)	98	97	94
Access to improved sanitation facilities (% of total population)	52	81	48
Rural (% of rural population)	37	62	36
Urban (% of urban population)	63	86	66
Environment and health			
Particulate matter (urban-pop.-weighted avg., µg/cu. m)	49	43	90
Acute resp. infection prevalence (% of children under five)	..	..	..
Diarrhea prevalence (% of children under five)	..	..	..
Under-five mortality rate (per 1,000 live births)	24	19	61
National accounting aggregates—savings, depletion and degradation			
Gross savings (% of GNI)	17.8	19.0	28.6
Consumption of fixed capital (% of GNI)	13.0	12.2	11.1
Education expenditure (% of GNI)	4.2	5.1	3.1
Energy depletion (% of GNI)	0.0	4.7	4.4
Mineral depletion (% of GNI)	1.2	1.2	1.1
Net forest depletion (% of GNI)	3.2	0.4	0.8
CO_2 damage (% of GNI)	0.5	0.3	0.9
Particulate emissions damage (% of GNI)	0.4	0.8	1.4
Adjusted net savings (% of GNI)	3.7	4.5	12.0

Niger

| Population (millions) | **17.2** | Land area (1,000 sq. km) | **1,267** | GDP ($ billions) | **6.8** |

	Country data	Sub-Saharan Africa group	Low-Income group
GNI per capita, *World Bank Atlas* method ($)	390	1,547	594
Adjusted net national income per capita ($)	342	1,005	495
Change in wealth per capita (2010 $)	−77	−273	−39
Urban population (% of total)	18.1	36.8	28.2
Agriculture			
Agricultural land (% land area)	35	44	39
Agricultural irrigated land (% of total agricultural land)	0.2	..	..
Agricultural productivity, value added per worker (2005 $)	..	765	367
Cereal yield (kg per hectare)	470	1,417	1,982
Forests and biodiversity			
Forest area (% land area)	0.9	27.4	27.4
Deforestation (avg. annual %, 2000–2010)	1.0	0.5	0.6
Terrestrial protected areas (% of total land area)	16.7	16.4	13.7
Threatened species, mammals	12		
Threatened species, birds	9		
Threatened species, fish	4		
Threatened species, higher plants	3		
Oceans			
Total fisheries production (thousand metric tons)	46.6	6,906	11,789
Capture fisheries growth (avg. annual %, 1990–2012)	12.8	2.1	3.8
Aquaculture growth (avg. annual %, 1990–2012)	4.8	15.9	5.1
Marine protected areas (% of territorial waters)	0.21	11.7	13.1
Coral reef area (sq. km)	..	17,980	15,120
Mangroves area (sq. km)	..	27,808	25,817
Energy and emissions			
Energy use per capita (kg oil equivalent)	..	681	360
Energy from biomass products and waste (% of total)	..	57.6	66.0
Electric power consumption per capita (kWh)	..	535	233
Electricity generated using fossil fuel (% of total)	..	65.1	30.9
Electricity generated by hydropower (% of total)	..	20.0	45.5
CO_2 emissions per capita (metric tons)	0.1	0.8	0.3
Water and sanitation			
Internal freshwater resources per capita (cu. m)	212	4,391	5,121
Total freshwater withdrawal (% of internal resources)	67.5	3.2	4.4
Agriculture (% of total freshwater withdrawal)	88	84	90
Access to improved water source (% of total population)	52	64	69
Rural (% of rural population)	42	53	61
Urban (% of urban population)	99	85	88
Access to improved sanitation facilities (% of total population)	9	30	37
Rural (% of rural population)	4	23	33
Urban (% of urban population)	33	41	46
Environment and health			
Particulate matter (urban-pop.-weighted avg., µg/cu. m)	50	77	74
Acute resp. infection prevalence (% of children under five)	4	5	6
Diarrhea prevalence (% of children under five)	14	14	14
Under-five mortality rate (per 1,000 live births)	114	98	82
National accounting aggregates—savings, depletion and degradation			
Gross savings (% of GNI)	*20.3*	26.3	24.6
Consumption of fixed capital (% of GNI)	3.5	13.0	11.8
Education expenditure (% of GNI)	4.0	3.4	3.2
Energy depletion (% of GNI)	0.0	10.3	1.4
Mineral depletion (% of GNI)	0.4	1.8	1.9
Net forest depletion (% of GNI)	8.1	1.8	4.4
CO_2 damage (% of GNI)	0.3	0.6	0.4
Particulate emissions damage (% of GNI)	1.0	1.2	1.0
Adjusted net savings (% of GNI)	*10.0*	0.9	7.0

Nigeria

	Country data	Sub-Saharan Africa group	Lower middle-income group
Population (millions) **168.8** Land area (1,000 sq. km)	**911**	GDP ($ billions)	**459.6**

	Country data	Sub-Saharan Africa group	Lower middle-income group
GNI per capita, *World Bank Atlas* method ($)	2,490	1,547	1,965
Adjusted net national income per capita ($)	938	1,005	1,574
Change in wealth per capita (2010 $)	-381	-273	117
Urban population (% of total)	50.2	36.8	38.9
Agriculture			
Agricultural land (% land area)	84	44	46
Agricultural irrigated land (% of total agricultural land)	..	..	..
Agricultural productivity, value added per worker (2005 $)	4,310	765	938
Cereal yield (kg per hectare)	1,363	1,417	3,029
Forests and biodiversity			
Forest area (% land area)	9.5	27.4	26.9
Deforestation (avg. annual %, 2000-2010)	3.7	0.5	0.3
Terrestrial protected areas (% of total land area)	14.1	16.4	11.9
Threatened species, mammals	26		
Threatened species, birds	18		
Threatened species, fish	60		
Threatened species, higher plants	169		
Oceans			
Total fisheries production (thousand metric tons)	923	6,906	43,067
Capture fisheries growth (avg. annual %, 1990-2012)	3.6	2.1	2.6
Aquaculture growth (avg. annual %, 1990-2012)	17.5	15.9	9.9
Marine protected areas (% of territorial waters)	1.2	11.7	14.7
Coral reef area (sq. km)	..	17,980	124,480
Mangroves area (sq. km)	7,356	27,808	58,917
Energy and emissions			
Energy use per capita (kg oil equivalent)	721	681	687
Energy from biomass products and waste (% of total)	82.2	57.6	26.8
Electric power consumption per capita (kWh)	149	535	734
Electricity generated using fossil fuel (% of total)	79.1	65.1	72.3
Electricity generated by hydropower (% of total)	20.9	20.0	16.9
CO_2 emissions per capita (metric tons)	0.5	0.8	1.6
Water and sanitation			
Internal freshwater resources per capita (cu. m)	1,346	4,391	3,144
Total freshwater withdrawal (% of internal resources)	4.7	3.2	19.6
Agriculture (% of total freshwater withdrawal)	53	84	88
Access to improved water source (% of total population)	64	64	88
Rural (% of rural population)	49	53	85
Urban (% of urban population)	79	85	94
Access to improved sanitation facilities (% of total population)	28	30	48
Rural (% of rural population)	25	23	36
Urban (% of urban population)	31	41	66
Environment and health			
Particulate matter (urban-pop.-weighted avg., µg/cu. m)	149	77	90
Acute resp. infection prevalence (% of children under five)	3	5	..
Diarrhea prevalence (% of children under five)	10	14	..
Under-five mortality rate (per 1,000 live births)	124	98	61
National accounting aggregates—savings, depletion and degradation			
Gross savings (% of GNI)	44.4	26.3	28.6
Consumption of fixed capital (% of GNI)	13.2	13.0	11.1
Education expenditure (% of GNI)	0.9	3.4	3.1
Energy depletion (% of GNI)	19.6	10.3	4.4
Mineral depletion (% of GNI)	0.0	1.8	1.1
Net forest depletion (% of GNI)	1.4	1.8	0.8
CO_2 damage (% of GNI)	0.3	0.6	0.9
Particulate emissions damage (% of GNI)	2.7	1.2	1.4
Adjusted net savings (% of GNI)	8.2	0.9	12.0

Northern Mariana Islands

Population (thousands) **53** Land area (sq. km)	**460** GDP ($ millions)	..

	Country data	High-income group
GNI per capita, *World Bank Atlas* method ($)	..	38,444
Adjusted net national income per capita ($)	..	32,262
Change in wealth per capita (2010 $)	..	2,210
Urban population (% of total)	91.6	80.2
Agriculture		
Agricultural land (% land area)	7	29
Agricultural irrigated land (% of total agricultural land)	..	
Agricultural productivity, value added per worker (2005 $)	..	25,238
Cereal yield (kg per hectare)	..	4,374
Forests and biodiversity		
Forest area (% land area)	65.5	35.0
Deforestation (avg. annual %, 2000–2010)	0.5	0.0
Terrestrial protected areas (% of total land area)	3.1	13.9
Threatened species, mammals	4	
Threatened species, birds	15	
Threatened species, fish	12	
Threatened species, higher plants	5	
Oceans		
Total fisheries production (thousand metric tons)	0.25	37,661
Capture fisheries growth (avg. annual %, 1990–2012)	1.1	-2.0
Aquaculture growth (avg. annual %, 1990–2012)	..	2.5
Marine protected areas (% of territorial waters)	2.8	14.4
Coral reef area (sq. km)	<50	82,210
Mangroves area (sq. km)	0.07	15,504
Energy and emissions		
Energy use per capita (kg oil equivalent)	..	4,872
Energy from biomass products and waste (% of total)	..	4.3
Electric power consumption per capita (kWh)	..	8,896
Electricity generated using fossil fuel (% of total)	..	61.8
Electricity generated by hydropower (% of total)	..	12.2
CO_2 emissions per capita (metric tons)	..	11.6
Water and sanitation		
Internal freshwater resources per capita (cu. m)	..	11,335
Total freshwater withdrawal (% of internal resources)	..	7.0
Agriculture (% of total freshwater withdrawal)	..	40
Access to improved water source (% of total population)	98	99
Rural (% of rural population)	98	98
Urban (% of urban population)	98	100
Access to improved sanitation facilities (% of total population)	80	96
Rural (% of rural population)	80	93
Urban (% of urban population)	80	97
Environment and health		
Particulate matter (urban-pop.-weighted avg., µg/cu. m)	..	27
Acute resp. infection prevalence (% of children under five)	..	..
Diarrhea prevalence (% of children under five)	..	..
Under-five mortality rate (per 1,000 live births)	..	6
National accounting aggregates—savings, depletion and degradation		
Gross savings (% of GNI)	..	20.1
Consumption of fixed capital (% of GNI)	..	14.2
Education expenditure (% of GNI)	..	4.7
Energy depletion (% of GNI)	..	1.6
Mineral depletion (% of GNI)	..	0.3
Net forest depletion (% of GNI)	..	0.0
CO_2 damage (% of GNI)	..	0.3
Particulate emissions damage (% of GNI)	..	0.3
Adjusted net savings (% of GNI)		

Norway

	Country data	High-Income group
GNI per capita, *World Bank Atlas* method ($)	98,780	38,444
Adjusted net national income per capita ($)	78,775	32,262
Change in wealth per capita (2010 $)	8,078	2,210
Urban population (% of total)	79.6	80.2

Agriculture

Agricultural land (% land area)	3	29
Agricultural irrigated land (% of total agricultural land)	4.3	..
Agricultural productivity, value added per worker (2005 $)	65,249	25,238
Cereal yield (kg per hectare)	3,467	4,374

Forests and biodiversity

Forest area (% land area)	33.3	35.0
Deforestation (avg. annual %, 2000–2010)	-0.8	0.0
Terrestrial protected areas (% of total land area)	16.3	13.9
Threatened species, mammals	7	
Threatened species, birds	4	
Threatened species, fish	19	
Threatened species, higher plants	3	

Oceans

Total fisheries production (thousand metric tons)	3,612	37,661
Capture fisheries growth (avg. annual %, 1990–2012)	1.1	-2.0
Aquaculture growth (avg. annual %, 1990–2012)	10.4	2.5
Marine protected areas (% of territorial waters)	1.3	14.4
Coral reef area (sq. km)	..	82,210
Mangroves area (sq. km)	..	15,504

Energy and emissions

Energy use per capita (kg oil equivalent)	5,681	4,872
Energy from biomass products and waste (% of total)	6.4	4.3
Electric power consumption per capita (kWh)	23,174	8,896
Electricity generated using fossil fuel (% of total)	3.3	61.8
Electricity generated by hydropower (% of total)	95.2	12.2
CO_2 emissions per capita (metric tons)	11.7	11.6

Water and sanitation

Internal freshwater resources per capita (cu. m)	77,124	11,335
Total freshwater withdrawal (% of internal resources)	0.8	7.0
Agriculture (% of total freshwater withdrawal)	29	40
Access to improved water source (% of total population)	100	99
Rural (% of rural population)	100	98
Urban (% of urban population)	100	100
Access to improved sanitation facilities (% of total population)	100	96
Rural (% of rural population)	100	93
Urban (% of urban population)	100	97

Environment and health

Particulate matter (urban-pop.-weighted avg., µg/cu. m)	24	27
Acute resp. infection prevalence (% of children under five)	..	..
Diarrhea prevalence (% of children under five)	..	..
Under-five mortality rate (per 1,000 live births)	3	6

National accounting aggregates—savings, depletion and degradation

Gross savings (% of GNI)	38.3	20.1
Consumption of fixed capital (% of GNI)	13.4	14.2
Education expenditure (% of GNI)	6.2	4.7
Energy depletion (% of GNI)	9.1	1.6
Mineral depletion (% of GNI)	0.0	0.3
Net forest depletion (% of GNI)	0.0	0.0
CO_2 damage (% of GNI)	0.1	0.3
Particulate emissions damage (% of GNI)	0.2	0.3
Adjusted net savings (% of GNI)	21.7	8.1

Oman

	Population (millions)	**3.3** Land area (1,000 sq. km)	**310** GDP ($ billions)	**78.1**

	Country data	High-income group
GNI per capita, *World Bank Atlas* method ($)	19,450	38,444
Adjusted net national income per capita ($)	11,665	32,262
Change in wealth per capita (2010 $)	–3,022	2,210
Urban population (% of total)	73.7	80.2
Agriculture		
Agricultural land (% land area)	6	29
Agricultural irrigated land (% of total agricultural land)	4.2	..
Agricultural productivity, value added per worker (2005 $)	..	25,238
Cereal yield (kg per hectare)	10,894	4,374
Forests and biodiversity		
Forest area (% land area)	0.0	35.0
Deforestation (avg. annual %, 2000–2010)	0.0	0.0
Terrestrial protected areas (% of total land area)	10.7	13.9
Threatened species, mammals	10	
Threatened species, birds	10	
Threatened species, fish	25	
Threatened species, higher plants	6	
Oceans		
Total fisheries production (thousand metric tons)	192	37,661
Capture fisheries growth (avg. annual %, 1990–2012)	2.2	-2.0
Aquaculture growth (avg. annual %, 1990–2012)	..	2.5
Marine protected areas (% of territorial waters)	5.9	14.4
Coral reef area (sq. km)	530	82,210
Mangroves area (sq. km)	10.9	15,504
Energy and emissions		
Energy use per capita (kg oil equivalent)	8,356	4,872
Energy from biomass products and waste (% of total)	0.0	4.3
Electric power consumption per capita (kWh)	6,292	8,896
Electricity generated using fossil fuel (% of total)	100.0	61.8
Electricity generated by hydropower (% of total)	0.0	12.2
CO_2 emissions per capita (metric tons)	20.4	11.6
Water and sanitation		
Internal freshwater resources per capita (cu. m)	463	11,335
Total freshwater withdrawal (% of internal resources)	94.4	7.0
Agriculture (% of total freshwater withdrawal)	88	40
Access to improved water source (% of total population)	93	99
Rural (% of rural population)	86	98
Urban (% of urban population)	95	100
Access to improved sanitation facilities (% of total population)	97	96
Rural (% of rural population)	95	93
Urban (% of urban population)	97	97
Environment and health		
Particulate matter (urban-pop.-weighted avg., µg/cu. m)	32	27
Acute resp. infection prevalence (% of children under five)	..	..
Diarrhea prevalence (% of children under five)	..	..
Under-five mortality rate (per 1,000 live births)	12	6
National accounting aggregates—savings, depletion and degradation		
Gross savings (% of GNI)	39.6	20.1
Consumption of fixed capital (% of GNI)	12.5	14.2
Education expenditure (% of GNI)	4.2	4.7
Energy depletion (% of GNI)	34.6	1.6
Mineral depletion (% of GNI)	0.0	0.3
Net forest depletion (% of GNI)	0.0	0.0
CO_2 damage (% of GNI)	0.8	0.3
Particulate emissions damage (% of GNI)	0.3	0.3
Adjusted net savings (% of GNI)	–6.9	8.1

Pakistan

Population (millions)	**179.2**	Land area (1,000 sq. km)	**771** GDP ($ billions) **225.1**

	Country data	South Asia group	Lower middle-income group
GNI per capita, *World Bank Atlas* method ($)	1,260	1,437	1,965
Adjusted net national income per capita ($)	1,121	1,168	1,574
Change in wealth per capita (2010 $)	-106	158	117
Urban population (% of total)	36.5	31.4	38.9
Agriculture			
Agricultural land (% land area)	34	55	46
Agricultural irrigated land (% of total agricultural land)	70.2	..	..
Agricultural productivity, value added per worker (2005 $)	1,063	669	938
Cereal yield (kg per hectare)	2,834	2,925	3,029
Forests and biodiversity			
Forest area (% land area)	2.1	17.1	26.9
Deforestation (avg. annual %, 2000–2010)	2.2	-0.3	0.3
Terrestrial protected areas (% of total land area)	10.7	6.2	11.9
Threatened species, mammals	24		
Threatened species, birds	29		
Threatened species, fish	34		
Threatened species, higher plants	4		
Oceans			
Total fisheries production (thousand metric tons)	612	13,613	43,067
Capture fisheries growth (avg. annual %, 1990–2012)	0.0	2.6	2.6
Aquaculture growth (avg. annual %, 1990–2012)	12.8	7.6	9.9
Marine protected areas (% of territorial waters)	30.3	10.7	14.7
Coral reef area (sq. km)	..	15,440	124,480
Mangroves area (sq. km)	977	10,343	58,917
Energy and emissions			
Energy use per capita (kg oil equivalent)	482	555	687
Energy from biomass products and waste (% of total)	34.6	26.7	26.8
Electric power consumption per capita (kWh)	449	605	734
Electricity generated using fossil fuel (% of total)	64.5	77.9	72.3
Electricity generated by hydropower (% of total)	29.9	13.8	16.9
CO_2 emissions per capita (metric tons)	0.9	1.4	1.6
Water and sanitation			
Internal freshwater resources per capita (cu. m)	312	1,217	3,144
Total freshwater withdrawal (% of internal resources)	333.6	51.6	19.6
Agriculture (% of total freshwater withdrawal)	94	91	88
Access to improved water source (% of total population)	91	91	88
Rural (% of rural population)	89	89	85
Urban (% of urban population)	96	95	94
Access to improved sanitation facilities (% of total population)	48	40	48
Rural (% of rural population)	34	30	36
Urban (% of urban population)	72	61	66
Environment and health			
Particulate matter (urban-pop.-weighted avg., µg/cu. m)	171	110	90
Acute resp. infection prevalence (% of children under five)	14	..	..
Diarrhea prevalence (% of children under five)	22	..	..
Under-five mortality rate (per 1,000 live births)	86	60	61
National accounting aggregates—savings, depletion and degradation			
Gross savings (% of GNI)	19.3	29.3	28.6
Consumption of fixed capital (% of GNI)	12.5	12.7	11.1
Education expenditure (% of GNI)	1.5	2.8	3.1
Energy depletion (% of GNI)	1.8	1.8	4.4
Mineral depletion (% of GNI)	0.0	0.8	1.1
Net forest depletion (% of GNI)	0.9	1.1	0.8
CO_2 damage (% of GNI)	0.7	1.1	0.9
Particulate emissions damage (% of GNI)	1.2	1.5	1.4
Adjusted net savings (% of GNI)	3.7	13.1	12.0

Palau

| Population (thousands) | 21 | Land area (sq. km) | **460** | GDP ($ millions) | **228.4** |

	Country data	East Asia & Pacific group	Upper middle-income group
GNI per capita, *World Bank Atlas* method ($)	9,860	4,884	6,969
Adjusted net national income per capita ($)	..	4,305	5,845
Change in wealth per capita (2010 $)		1,172	1,039
Urban population (% of total)	84.9	49.6	60.7
Agriculture			
Agricultural land (% land area)	11	48	44
Agricultural irrigated land (% of total agricultural land)	..	..	..
Agricultural productivity, value added per worker (2005 $)	3,989	794	1,131
Cereal yield (kg per hectare)	..	5,145	4,255
Forests and biodiversity			
Forest area (% land area)	87.6	29.7	29.1
Deforestation (avg. annual %, 2000–2010)	-0.2	-0.4	0.0
Terrestrial protected areas (% of total land area)	15.9	15.1	16.1
Threatened species, mammals	4		
Threatened species, birds	4		
Threatened species, fish	15		
Threatened species, higher plants	4		
Oceans			
Total fisheries production (thousand metric tons)	0.94	108,399	90,024
Capture fisheries growth (avg. annual %, 1990–2012)	-0.8	3.4	1.5
Aquaculture growth (avg. annual %, 1990–2012)	14.0	9.1	9.1
Marine protected areas (% of territorial waters)	7.4	1.4	7.3
Coral reef area (sq. km)	1,150	137,690	52,070
Mangroves area (sq. km)	48.5	56,537	50,160
Energy and emissions			
Energy use per capita (kg oil equivalent)	..	1,671	1,893
Energy from biomass products and waste (% of total)	..	10.1	8.5
Electric power consumption per capita (kWh)	..	2,582	2,932
Electricity generated using fossil fuel (% of total)	..	80.9	74.7
Electricity generated by hydropower (% of total)	..	14.5	20.0
CO_2 emissions per capita (metric tons)	10.6	4.9	5.4
Water and sanitation			
Internal freshwater resources per capita (cu. m)	..	4,438	6,791
Total freshwater withdrawal (% of internal resources)	..	10.9	7.4
Agriculture (% of total freshwater withdrawal)	..	73	69
Access to improved water source (% of total population)	95	91	93
Rural (% of rural population)	86	85	85
Urban (% of urban population)	97	97	98
Access to improved sanitation facilities (% of total population)	100	67	74
Rural (% of rural population)	100	58	62
Urban (% of urban population)	100	76	82
Environment and health			
Particulate matter (urban-pop.-weighted avg., µg/cu. m)	..	75	65
Acute resp. infection prevalence (% of children under five)	..	..	..
Diarrhea prevalence (% of children under five)	..	..	..
Under-five mortality rate (per 1,000 live births)	21	21	20
National accounting aggregates—savings, depletion and degradation			
Gross savings (% of GNI)	..	47.6	36.4
Consumption of fixed capital (% of GNI)	13.4	12.0	12.5
Education expenditure (% of GNI)	..	2.1	3.2
Energy depletion (% of GNI)	0.0	2.7	4.1
Mineral depletion (% of GNI)	0.0	1.4	1.2
Net forest depletion (% of GNI)	..	0.1	0.2
CO_2 damage (% of GNI)	1.4	1.0	0.8
Particulate emissions damage (% of GNI)	..	1.6	1.3
Adjusted net savings (% of GNI)	..	30.9	19.5

Panama

	Country data	Latin America & Caribbean group	Upper middle-income group
Population (millions) **3.8** Land area (1,000 sq. km) **74** GDP ($ billions) **36.3**			

	Country data	Latin America & Caribbean group	Upper middle-income group
GNI per capita, *World Bank Atlas* method ($)	8,510	9,070	6,969
Adjusted net national income per capita ($)	8,203	7,325	5,845
Change in wealth per capita (2010 $)	1,738	180	1,039
Urban population (% of total)	75.8	79.0	60.7
Agriculture			
Agricultural land (% land area)	30	37	44
Agricultural irrigated land (% of total agricultural land)	..	..	..
Agricultural productivity, value added per worker (2005 $)	3,844	4,135	1,131
Cereal yield (kg per hectare)	2,214	4,082	4,255
Forests and biodiversity			
Forest area (% land area)	43.6	48.1	29.1
Deforestation (avg. annual %, 2000-2010)	0.4	0.5	0.0
Terrestrial protected areas (% of total land area)	20.6	21.4	16.1
Threatened species, mammals	16		
Threatened species, birds	19		
Threatened species, fish	42		
Threatened species, higher plants	202		
Oceans			
Total fisheries production (thousand metric tons)	154	10,964	90,024
Capture fisheries growth (avg. annual %, 1990-2012)	0.6	-0.6	1.5
Aquaculture growth (avg. annual %, 1990-2012)	3.6	10.8	9.1
Marine protected areas (% of territorial waters)	0.35	9.0	7.3
Coral reef area (sq. km)	720	14,860	52,070
Mangroves area (sq. km)	1,744	39,988	50,160
Energy and emissions			
Energy use per capita (kg oil equivalent)	1,085	1,292	1,893
Energy from biomass products and waste (% of total)	11.5	16.0	8.5
Electric power consumption per capita (kWh)	1,829	1,985	2,932
Electricity generated using fossil fuel (% of total)	47.5	37.3	74.7
Electricity generated by hydropower (% of total)	52.2	55.1	20.0
CO_2 emissions per capita (metric tons)	2.6	2.7	5.4
Water and sanitation			
Internal freshwater resources per capita (cu. m)	39,409	21,735	6,791
Total freshwater withdrawal (% of internal resources)	0.3	2.0	7.4
Agriculture (% of total freshwater withdrawal)	51	68	69
Access to improved water source (% of total population)	94	94	93
Rural (% of rural population)	87	82	85
Urban (% of urban population)	97	97	98
Access to improved sanitation facilities (% of total population)	73	81	74
Rural (% of rural population)	52	62	62
Urban (% of urban population)	80	86	82
Environment and health			
Particulate matter (urban-pop.-weighted avg., µg/cu. m)	49	43	65
Acute resp. infection prevalence (% of children under five)	..	..	..
Diarrhea prevalence (% of children under five)	..	..	..
Under-five mortality rate (per 1,000 live births)	19	19	20
National accounting aggregates—savings, depletion and degradation			
Gross savings (% of GNI)	28.8	19.0	36.4
Consumption of fixed capital (% of GNI)	6.7	12.2	12.5
Education expenditure (% of GNI)	2.6	5.1	3.2
Energy depletion (% of GNI)	0.0	4.7	4.1
Mineral depletion (% of GNI)	0.5	1.2	1.2
Net forest depletion (% of GNI)	0.0	0.4	0.2
CO_2 damage (% of GNI)	0.4	0.3	0.8
Particulate emissions damage (% of GNI)	0.6	0.8	1.3
Adjusted net savings (% of GNI)	23.3	4.5	19.5

Papua New Guinea

Population (millions)	**7.2**	Land area (1,000 sq. km)	**453**	GDP ($ billions)	**15.7**

	Country data	East Asia & Pacific group	Lower middle-income group
GNI per capita, *World Bank Atlas* method ($)	1,790	4,884	1,965
Adjusted net national income per capita ($)	1,592	4,305	1,574
Change in wealth per capita (2010 $)	..	1,172	117
Urban population (% of total)	12.6	49.6	38.9
Agriculture			
Agricultural land (% land area)	3	48	46
Agricultural irrigated land (% of total agricultural land)	..	..	..
Agricultural productivity, value added per worker (2005 $)	..	794	938
Cereal yield (kg per hectare)	4,486	5,145	3,029
Forests and biodiversity			
Forest area (% land area)	63.1	29.7	26.9
Deforestation (avg. annual %, 2000–2010)	0.5	-0.4	0.3
Terrestrial protected areas (% of total land area)	3.1	15.1	11.9
Threatened species, mammals	39		
Threatened species, birds	37		
Threatened species, fish	47		
Threatened species, higher plants	145		
Oceans			
Total fisheries production (thousand metric tons)	259	108,399	43,067
Capture fisheries growth (avg. annual %, 1990–2012)	10.9	3.4	2.6
Aquaculture growth (avg. annual %, 1990–2012)	28.8	9.1	9.9
Marine protected areas (% of territorial waters)	0.32	1.4	14.7
Coral reef area (sq. km)	13,840	137,690	124,480
Mangroves area (sq. km)	4,265	56,537	58,917
Energy and emissions			
Energy use per capita (kg oil equivalent)	..	1,671	687
Energy from biomass products and waste (% of total)	..	10.1	26.8
Electric power consumption per capita (kWh)	..	2,582	734
Electricity generated using fossil fuel (% of total)	..	80.9	72.3
Electricity generated by hydropower (% of total)	..	14.5	16.9
CO_2 emissions per capita (metric tons)	0.5	4.9	1.6
Water and sanitation			
Internal freshwater resources per capita (cu. m)	114,217	4,438	3,144
Total freshwater withdrawal (% of internal resources)	0.0	10.9	19.6
Agriculture (% of total freshwater withdrawal)	0	73	88
Access to improved water source (% of total population)	40	91	88
Rural (% of rural population)	33	85	85
Urban (% of urban population)	88	97	94
Access to improved sanitation facilities (% of total population)	19	67	48
Rural (% of rural population)	13	58	36
Urban (% of urban population)	56	76	66
Environment and health			
Particulate matter (urban-pop.-weighted avg., µg/cu. m)	32	75	90
Acute resp. infection prevalence (% of children under five)	..	..	..
Diarrhea prevalence (% of children under five)	..	..	..
Under-five mortality rate (per 1,000 live births)	63	21	61
National accounting aggregates—savings, depletion and degradation			
Gross savings (% of GNI)	..	47.6	28.6
Consumption of fixed capital (% of GNI)	6.1	12.0	11.1
Education expenditure (% of GNI)	..	2.1	3.1
Energy depletion (% of GNI)	0.0	2.7	4.4
Mineral depletion (% of GNI)	17.0	1.4	1.1
Net forest depletion (% of GNI)	1.0	0.1	0.8
CO_2 damage (% of GNI)	0.2	1.0	0.9
Particulate emissions damage (% of GNI)	0.1	1.6	1.4
Adjusted net savings (% of GNI)	..	30.9	12.0

Paraguay

	Country data	Latin America & Caribbean group	Lower middle-income group
Population (millions) **6.7** Land area (1,000 sq. km) **397** GDP ($ billions) **25.5**			

	Country data	Latin America & Caribbean group	Lower middle-income group
GNI per capita, *World Bank Atlas* method ($)	3,400	9,070	1,965
Adjusted net national income per capita ($)	3,243	7,325	1,574
Change in wealth per capita (2010 $)	-96	180	117
Urban population (% of total)	62.4	79.0	38.9
Agriculture			
Agricultural land (% land area)	53	37	46
Agricultural irrigated land (% of total agricultural land)	..	..	..
Agricultural productivity, value added per worker (2005 $)	2,209	4,135	938
Cereal yield (kg per hectare)	3,439	4,082	3,029
Forests and biodiversity			
Forest area (% land area)	43.8	48.1	26.9
Deforestation (avg. annual %, 2000–2010)	1.0	0.5	0.3
Terrestrial protected areas (% of total land area)	6.4	21.4	11.9
Threatened species, mammals	9		
Threatened species, birds	28		
Threatened species, fish	0		
Threatened species, higher plants	19		
Oceans			
Total fisheries production (thousand metric tons)	22.4	10,964	43,067
Capture fisheries growth (avg. annual %, 1990–2012)	1.4	-0.6	2.6
Aquaculture growth (avg. annual %, 1990–2012)	22.6	10.8	9.9
Marine protected areas (% of territorial waters)	3.9	9.0	14.7
Coral reef area (sq. km)	..	14,860	124,480
Mangroves area (sq. km)	..	39,988	58,917
Energy and emissions			
Energy use per capita (kg oil equivalent)	739	1,292	687
Energy from biomass products and waste (% of total)	45.8	16.0	26.8
Electric power consumption per capita (kWh)	1,228	1,985	734
Electricity generated using fossil fuel (% of total)	0.0	37.3	72.3
Electricity generated by hydropower (% of total)	100.0	55.1	16.9
CO_2 emissions per capita (metric tons)	0.8	2.7	1.6
Water and sanitation			
Internal freshwater resources per capita (cu. m)	14,301	21,735	3,144
Total freshwater withdrawal (% of internal resources)	0.5	2.0	19.6
Agriculture (% of total freshwater withdrawal)	71	68	88
Access to improved water source (% of total population)	94	94	88
Rural (% of rural population)	83	82	85
Urban (% of urban population)	100	97	94
Access to improved sanitation facilities (% of total population)	80	81	48
Rural (% of rural population)	53	62	36
Urban (% of urban population)	96	86	66
Environment and health			
Particulate matter (urban-pop.-weighted avg., µg/cu. m)	32	43	90
Acute resp. infection prevalence (% of children under five)	..	..	..
Diarrhea prevalence (% of children under five)	..	..	..
Under-five mortality rate (per 1,000 live births)	22	19	61
National accounting aggregates—savings, depletion and degradation			
Gross savings (% of GNI)	13.0	19.0	28.6
Consumption of fixed capital (% of GNI)	5.9	12.2	11.1
Education expenditure (% of GNI)	3.8	5.1	3.1
Energy depletion (% of GNI)	0.0	4.7	4.4
Mineral depletion (% of GNI)	0.0	1.2	1.1
Net forest depletion (% of GNI)	4.3	0.4	0.8
CO_2 damage (% of GNI)	0.2	0.3	0.9
Particulate emissions damage (% of GNI)	0.3	0.8	1.4
Adjusted net savings (% of GNI)	6.1	4.5	12.0

Peru

| Population (millions) | **30.0** | Land area (1,000 sq. km) | **1,280** | GDP ($ billions) | **203.8** |

	Country data	Latin America & Caribbean group	Upper middle-income group
GNI per capita, *World Bank Atlas* method ($)	6,060	9,070	6,969
Adjusted net national income per capita ($)	5,042	7,325	5,845
Change in wealth per capita (2010 $)	68	180	1,039
Urban population (% of total)	77.6	79.0	60.7
Agriculture			
Agricultural land (% of land area)	17	37	44
Agricultural irrigated land (% of total agricultural land)	..	..	..
Agricultural productivity, value added per worker (2005 $)	1,957	4,135	1,131
Cereal yield (kg per hectare)	4,136	4,082	4,255
Forests and biodiversity			
Forest area (% land area)	53.0	48.1	29.1
Deforestation (avg. annual %, 2000–2010)	0.2	0.5	0.0
Terrestrial protected areas (% of total land area)	19.1	21.4	16.1
Threatened species, mammals	55		
Threatened species, birds	124		
Threatened species, fish	21		
Threatened species, higher plants	318		
Oceans			
Total fisheries production (thousand metric tons)	4,917	10,964	90,024
Capture fisheries growth (avg. annual %, 1990–2012)	-1.6	-0.6	1.5
Aquaculture growth (avg. annual %, 1990–2012)	12.7	10.8	9.1
Marine protected areas (% of territorial waters)	2.5	9.0	7.3
Coral reef area (sq. km)	..	14,860	52,070
Mangroves area (sq. km)	53.1	39,988	50,160
Energy and emissions			
Energy use per capita (kg oil equivalent)	695	1,292	1,893
Energy from biomass products and waste (% of total)	15.0	16.0	8.5
Electric power consumption per capita (kWh)	1,248	1,985	2,932
Electricity generated using fossil fuel (% of total)	43.1	37.3	74.7
Electricity generated by hydropower (% of total)	55.0	55.1	20.0
CO_2 emissions per capita (metric tons)	2.0	2.7	5.4
Water and sanitation			
Internal freshwater resources per capita (cu. m)	54,567	21,735	6,791
Total freshwater withdrawal (% of internal resources)	1.2	2.0	7.4
Agriculture (% of total freshwater withdrawal)	85	68	69
Access to improved water source (% of total population)	87	94	93
Rural (% of rural population)	72	82	85
Urban (% of urban population)	91	97	98
Access to improved sanitation facilities (% of total population)	73	81	74
Rural (% of rural population)	45	62	62
Urban (% of urban population)	81	86	82
Environment and health			
Particulate matter (urban-pop.-weighted avg., µg/cu. m)	63	43	65
Acute resp. infection prevalence (% of children under five)	7	..	..
Diarrhea prevalence (% of children under five)	12	..	..
Under-five mortality rate (per 1,000 live births)	18	19	20
National accounting aggregates—savings, depletion and degradation			
Gross savings (% of GNI)	27.1	19.0	36.4
Consumption of fixed capital (% of GNI)	12.9	12.2	12.5
Education expenditure (% of GNI)	2.2	5.1	3.2
Energy depletion (% of GNI)	1.7	4.7	4.1
Mineral depletion (% of GNI)	6.3	1.2	1.2
Net forest depletion (% of GNI)	0.0	0.4	0.2
CO_2 damage (% of GNI)	0.4	0.3	0.8
Particulate emissions damage (% of GNI)	0.8	0.8	1.3
Adjusted net savings (% of GNI)	7.3	4.5	19.5

Philippines

	Country data	East Asia & Pacific group	Lower middle-income group

Population (millions) **96.7** Land area (1,000 sq. km) **298** GDP ($ billions) **250.2**

	Country data	East Asia & Pacific group	Lower middle-income group
GNI per capita, *World Bank Atlas* method ($)	2,500	4,884	1,965
Adjusted net national income per capita ($)	2,204	4,305	1,574
Change in wealth per capita (2010 $)	106	1,172	117
Urban population (% of total)	49.1	49.6	38.9
Agriculture			
Agricultural land (% of land area)	41	48	46
Agricultural irrigated land (% of total agricultural land)	9.4	..	..
Agricultural productivity, value added per worker (2005 $)	1,129	794	938
Cereal yield (kg per hectare)	3,493	5,145	3,029
Forests and biodiversity			
Forest area (% land area)	25.9	29.7	26.9
Deforestation (avg. annual %, 2000–2010)	-0.7	-0.4	0.3
Terrestrial protected areas (% of total land area)	10.9	15.1	11.9
Threatened species, mammals	38		
Threatened species, birds	74		
Threatened species, fish	72		
Threatened species, higher plants	229		
Oceans			
Total fisheries production (thousand metric tons)	4,869	108,399	43,067
Capture fisheries growth (avg. annual %, 1990–2012)	1.1	3.4	2.6
Aquaculture growth (avg. annual %, 1990–2012)	6.2	9.1	9.9
Marine protected areas (% of territorial waters)	52.8	1.4	14.7
Coral reef area (sq. km)	25,060	137,690	124,480
Mangroves area (sq. km)	2,565	56,537	58,917
Energy and emissions			
Energy use per capita (kg oil equivalent)	426	1,671	687
Energy from biomass products and waste (% of total)	17.1	10.1	26.8
Electric power consumption per capita (kWh)	647	2,582	734
Electricity generated using fossil fuel (% of total)	71.3	80.9	72.3
Electricity generated by hydropower (% of total)	14.0	14.5	16.9
CO_2 emissions per capita (metric tons)	0.9	4.9	1.6
Water and sanitation			
Internal freshwater resources per capita (cu. m)	5,039	4,438	3,144
Total freshwater withdrawal (% of internal resources)	17.0	10.9	19.6
Agriculture (% of total freshwater withdrawal)	82	73	88
Access to improved water source (% of total population)	92	91	88
Rural (% of rural population)	91	85	85
Urban (% of urban population)	92	97	94
Access to improved sanitation facilities (% of total population)	74	67	48
Rural (% of rural population)	69	58	36
Urban (% of urban population)	79	76	66
Environment and health			
Particulate matter (urban-pop.-weighted avg., µg/cu. m)	45	75	90
Acute resp. infection prevalence (% of children under five)	5	..	..
Diarrhea prevalence (% of children under five)	9	..	..
Under-five mortality rate (per 1,000 live births)	30	21	61
National accounting aggregates—savings, depletion and degradation			
Gross savings (% of GNI)	23.7	47.6	28.6
Consumption of fixed capital (% of GNI)	13.0	12.0	11.1
Education expenditure (% of GNI)	2.4	2.1	3.1
Energy depletion (% of GNI)	0.3	2.7	4.4
Mineral depletion (% of GNI)	2.0	1.4	1.1
Net forest depletion (% of GNI)	0.2	0.1	0.8
CO_2 damage (% of GNI)	0.4	1.0	0.9
Particulate emissions damage (% of GNI)	0.7	1.6	1.4
Adjusted net savings (% of GNI)	9.4	30.9	12.0

Poland

	Country data	High-income group
Population (millions) **38.5** Land area (1,000 sq. km) **304** GDP ($ billions) **489.8**		

	Country data	High-income group
GNI per capita, *World Bank Atlas* method ($)	12,660	38,444
Adjusted net national income per capita ($)	10,401	32,262
Change in wealth per capita (2010 $)	1,146	2,210
Urban population (% of total)	60.8	80.2
Agriculture		
Agricultural land (% land area)	49	29
Agricultural irrigated land (% of total agricultural land)	0.4	..
Agricultural productivity, value added per worker (2005 $)	4,111	25,238
Cereal yield (kg per hectare)	3,585	4,374
Forests and biodiversity		
Forest area (% land area)	30.8	35.0
Deforestation (avg. annual %, 2000–2010)	–0.3	0.0
Terrestrial protected areas (% of total land area)	34.2	13.9
Threatened species, mammals	5	
Threatened species, birds	8	
Threatened species, fish	7	
Threatened species, higher plants	11	
Oceans		
Total fisheries production (thousand metric tons)	231	37,661
Capture fisheries growth (avg. annual %, 1990–2012)	–3.6	–2.0
Aquaculture growth (avg. annual %, 1990–2012)	0.9	2.5
Marine protected areas (% of territorial waters)	4.1	14.4
Coral reef area (sq. km)	..	82,210
Mangroves area (sq. km)	..	15,504
Energy and emissions		
Energy use per capita (kg oil equivalent)	2,629	4,872
Energy from biomass products and waste (% of total)	8.1	4.3
Electric power consumption per capita (kWh)	3,832	8,896
Electricity generated using fossil fuel (% of total)	91.8	61.8
Electricity generated by hydropower (% of total)	1.4	12.2
CO_2 emissions per capita (metric tons)	8.3	11.6
Water and sanitation		
Internal freshwater resources per capita (cu. m)	1,391	11,335
Total freshwater withdrawal (% of internal resources)	22.3	7.0
Agriculture (% of total freshwater withdrawal)	10	40
Access to improved water source (% of total population)	..	99
Rural (% of rural population)	..	98
Urban (% of urban population)	100	100
Access to improved sanitation facilities (% of total population)	..	96
Rural (% of rural population)	..	93
Urban (% of urban population)	96	97
Environment and health		
Particulate matter (urban-pop.-weighted avg., µg/cu. m)	34	27
Acute resp. infection prevalence (% of children under five)	..	..
Diarrhea prevalence (% of children under five)	..	..
Under-five mortality rate (per 1,000 live births)	5	6
National accounting aggregates—savings, depletion and degradation		
Gross savings (% of GNI)	18.4	20.1
Consumption of fixed capital (% of GNI)	13.0	14.2
Education expenditure (% of GNI)	5.1	4.7
Energy depletion (% of GNI)	0.6	1.6
Mineral depletion (% of GNI)	0.4	0.3
Net forest depletion (% of GNI)	0.3	0.0
CO_2 damage (% of GNI)	0.7	0.3
Particulate emissions damage (% of GNI)	0.6	0.3
Adjusted net savings (% of GNI)	7.9	8.1

Portugal

| | Population (millions) | **10.5** | Land area (1,000 sq. km) | **91** | GDP ($ billions) | **212.1** |

	Country data	High-income group
GNI per capita, *World Bank Atlas* method ($)	20,690	38,444
Adjusted net national income per capita ($)	17,233	32,262
Change in wealth per capita (2010 $)	–507	2,210
Urban population (% of total)	61.6	80.2

Agriculture
Agricultural land (% land area)	40	29
Agricultural irrigated land (% of total agricultural land)	12.7	..
Agricultural productivity, value added per worker (2005 $)	8,906	25,238
Cereal yield (kg per hectare)	4,303	4,374

Forests and biodiversity
Forest area (% land area)	37.8	35.0
Deforestation (avg. annual %, 2000–2010)	–0.1	0.0
Terrestrial protected areas (% of total land area)	22.3	13.9
Threatened species, mammals	11	
Threatened species, birds	9	
Threatened species, fish	55	
Threatened species, higher plants	81	

Oceans
Total fisheries production (thousand metric tons)	209	37,661
Capture fisheries growth (avg. annual %, 1990–2012)	–2.3	–2.0
Aquaculture growth (avg. annual %, 1990–2012)	3.4	2.5
Marine protected areas (% of territorial waters)	1.7	14.4
Coral reef area (sq. km)	..	82,210
Mangroves area (sq. km)	..	15,504

Energy and emissions
Energy use per capita (kg oil equivalent)	2,187	4,872
Energy from biomass products and waste (% of total)	13.9	4.3
Electric power consumption per capita (kWh)	4,848	8,896
Electricity generated using fossil fuel (% of total)	52.9	61.8
Electricity generated by hydropower (% of total)	22.2	12.2
CO_2 emissions per capita (metric tons)	5.0	11.6

Water and sanitation
Internal freshwater resources per capita (cu. m)	3,599	11,335
Total freshwater withdrawal (% of internal resources)	22.3	7.0
Agriculture (% of total freshwater withdrawal)	73	40
Access to improved water source (% of total population)	100	99
Rural (% of rural population)	100	98
Urban (% of urban population)	100	100
Access to improved sanitation facilities (% of total population)	100	96
Rural (% of rural population)	100	93
Urban (% of urban population)	100	97

Environment and health
Particulate matter (urban-pop.-weighted avg., µg/cu. m)	28	27
Acute resp. infection prevalence (% of children under five)	..	..
Diarrhea prevalence (% of children under five)	..	..
Under-five mortality rate (per 1,000 live births)	4	6

National accounting aggregates—savings, depletion and degradation
Gross savings (% of GNI)	16.3	20.1
Consumption of fixed capital (% of GNI)	12.4	14.2
Education expenditure (% of GNI)	5.7	4.7
Energy depletion (% of GNI)	0.0	1.6
Mineral depletion (% of GNI)	0.1	0.3
Net forest depletion (% of GNI)	0.0	0.0
CO_2 damage (% of GNI)	0.2	0.3
Particulate emissions damage (% of GNI)	0.5	0.3
Adjusted net savings (% of GNI)		

Puerto Rico

| Population (millions) | **3.7** | Land area (1,000 sq. km) | **8.9** | GDP ($ billions) | **101.5** |

	Country data	High-income group
GNI per capita, *World Bank Atlas* method ($)	18,000	38,444
Adjusted net national income per capita ($)	..	32,262
Change in wealth per capita (2010 $)	..	2,210
Urban population (% of total)	99.0	80.2
Agriculture		
Agricultural land (% land area)	21	29
Agricultural irrigated land (% of total agricultural land)	8.6	..
Agricultural productivity, value added per worker (2005 $)	..	25,238
Cereal yield (kg per hectare)	1,952	4,374
Forests and biodiversity		
Forest area (% land area)	63.2	35.0
Deforestation (avg. annual %, 2000–2010)	-1.8	0.0
Terrestrial protected areas (% of total land area)	10.3	13.9
Threatened species, mammals	3	
Threatened species, birds	8	
Threatened species, fish	21	
Threatened species, higher plants	54	
Oceans		
Total fisheries production (thousand metric tons)	1.3	37,661
Capture fisheries growth (avg. annual %, 1990–2012)	-1.9	-2.0
Aquaculture growth (avg. annual %, 1990–2012)	-7.6	2.5
Marine protected areas (% of territorial waters)	1.6	14.4
Coral reef area (sq. km)	480	82,210
Mangroves area (sq. km)	73.9	15,504
Energy and emissions		
Energy use per capita (kg oil equivalent)	..	4,872
Energy from biomass products and waste (% of total)	..	4.3
Electric power consumption per capita (kWh)	..	8,896
Electricity generated using fossil fuel (% of total)	..	61.8
Electricity generated by hydropower (% of total)	..	12.2
CO_2 emissions per capita (metric tons)	..	11.6
Water and sanitation		
Internal freshwater resources per capita (cu. m)	1,922	11,335
Total freshwater withdrawal (% of internal resources)	14.0	7.0
Agriculture (% of total freshwater withdrawal)	7	40
Access to improved water source (% of total population)	..	99
Rural (% of rural population)	..	98
Urban (% of urban population)	..	100
Access to improved sanitation facilities (% of total population)	99	96
Rural (% of rural population)	99	93
Urban (% of urban population)	99	97
Environment and health		
Particulate matter (urban-pop.-weighted avg., μg/cu. m)	15	27
Acute resp. infection prevalence (% of children under five)	..	..
Diarrhea prevalence (% of children under five)	..	..
Under-five mortality rate (per 1,000 live births)	..	6
National accounting aggregates—savings, depletion and degradation		
Gross savings (% of GNI)	..	20.1
Consumption of fixed capital (% of GNI)	8.6	14.2
Education expenditure (% of GNI)	..	4.7
Energy depletion (% of GNI)	0.0	1.6
Mineral depletion (% of GNI)	0.0	0.3
Net forest depletion (% of GNI)	..	0.0
CO_2 damage (% of GNI)	..	0.3
Particulate emissions damage (% of GNI)	..	0.3
Adjusted net savings (% of GNI)	..	8.1

Qatar

| Population (millions) | **2.1** | Land area (1,000 sq. km) | **12** | GDP ($ billions) | **192.4** |

	Country data	High-income group
GNI per capita, *World Bank Atlas* method ($)	74,600	38,444
Adjusted net national income per capita ($)	65,820	32,262
Change in wealth per capita (2010 $)	..	2,210
Urban population (% of total)	98.9	80.2
Agriculture		
Agricultural land (% land area)	6	29
Agricultural irrigated land (% of total agricultural land)	..	..
Agricultural productivity, value added per worker (2005 $)	..	25,238
Cereal yield (kg per hectare)	6,485	4,374
Forests and biodiversity		
Forest area (% land area)	0.0	35.0
Deforestation (avg. annual %, 2000–2010)	0.0	0.0
Terrestrial protected areas (% of total land area)	3.2	13.9
Threatened species, mammals	3	
Threatened species, birds	4	
Threatened species, fish	12	
Threatened species, higher plants	0	
Oceans		
Total fisheries production (thousand metric tons)	11.3	37,661
Capture fisheries growth (avg. annual %, 1990–2012)	3.1	-2.0
Aquaculture growth (avg. annual %, 1990–2012)	..	2.5
Marine protected areas (% of territorial waters)	0.25	14.4
Coral reef area (sq. km)	700	82,210
Mangroves area (sq. km)	12.3	15,504
Energy and emissions		
Energy use per capita (kg oil equivalent)	17,419	4,872
Energy from biomass products and waste (% of total)	0.0	4.3
Electric power consumption per capita (kWh)	15,755	8,896
Electricity generated using fossil fuel (% of total)	100.0	61.8
Electricity generated by hydropower (% of total)	0.0	12.2
CO_2 emissions per capita (metric tons)	40.3	11.6
Water and sanitation		
Internal freshwater resources per capita (cu. m)	29	11,335
Total freshwater withdrawal (% of internal resources)	792.9	7.0
Agriculture (% of total freshwater withdrawal)	59	40
Access to improved water source (% of total population)	100	99
Rural (% of rural population)	100	98
Urban (% of urban population)	100	100
Access to improved sanitation facilities (% of total population)	100	96
Rural (% of rural population)	100	93
Urban (% of urban population)	100	97
Environment and health		
Particulate matter (urban-pop.-weighted avg., µg/cu. m)	28	27
Acute resp. infection prevalence (% of children under five)	..	..
Diarrhea prevalence (% of children under five)	..	..
Under-five mortality rate (per 1,000 live births)	7	6
National accounting aggregates—savings, depletion and degradation		
Gross savings (% of GNI)	68.7	20.1
Consumption of fixed capital (% of GNI)	5.2	14.2
Education expenditure (% of GNI)	1.8	4.7
Energy depletion (% of GNI)	18.6	1.6
Mineral depletion (% of GNI)	0.0	0.3
Net forest depletion (% of GNI)	0.0	0.0
CO_2 damage (% of GNI)	0.4	0.3
Particulate emissions damage (% of GNI)	0.2	0.3
Adjusted net savings (% of GNI)	46.1	8.1

Romania

Population (millions)	**20.1**	Land area (1,000 sq. km)	**230**	GDP ($ billions)	**169.4**

	Country data	Europe & Central Asia group	Upper middle-income group
GNI per capita, *World Bank Atlas* method ($)	8,560	6,658	6,969
Adjusted net national income per capita ($)	6,753	5,541	5,845
Change in wealth per capita (2010 $)	691	263	1,039
Urban population (% of total)	52.8	60.2	60.7
Agriculture			
Agricultural land (% land area)	61	66	44
Agricultural irrigated land (% of total agricultural land)	0.7	..	..
Agricultural productivity, value added per worker (2005 $)	9,117	4,866	1,131
Cereal yield (kg per hectare)	2,364	2,519	4,255
Forests and biodiversity			
Forest area (% land area)	28.7	10.5	29.1
Deforestation (avg. annual %, 2000–2010)	-0.3	-0.5	0.0
Terrestrial protected areas (% of total land area)	18.7	5.1	16.1
Threatened species, mammals	7		
Threatened species, birds	14		
Threatened species, fish	19		
Threatened species, higher plants	5		
Oceans			
Total fisheries production (thousand metric tons)	13.5	1,022	90,024
Capture fisheries growth (avg. annual %, 1990–2012)	-13.8	-4.0	1.5
Aquaculture growth (avg. annual %, 1990–2012)	-5.5	1.8	9.1
Marine protected areas (% of territorial waters)	11.6	10.4	7.3
Coral reef area (sq. km)	..	..	52,070
Mangroves area (sq. km)	..	..	50,160
Energy and emissions			
Energy use per capita (kg oil equivalent)	1,778	2,078	1,893
Energy from biomass products and waste (% of total)	10.3	2.9	8.5
Electric power consumption per capita (kWh)	2,639	2,951	2,932
Electricity generated using fossil fuel (% of total)	54.7	65.8	74.7
Electricity generated by hydropower (% of total)	23.8	17.9	20.0
CO_2 emissions per capita (metric tons)	3.9	5.3	5.4
Water and sanitation			
Internal freshwater resources per capita (cu. m)	2,100	2,744	6,791
Total freshwater withdrawal (% of internal resources)	16.3	34.8	7.4
Agriculture (% of total freshwater withdrawal)	17	70	69
Access to improved water source (% of total population)	..	95	93
Rural (% of rural population)	..	89	85
Urban (% of urban population)	99	99	98
Access to improved sanitation facilities (% of total population)	..	94	74
Rural (% of rural population)	..	90	62
Urban (% of urban population)	..	97	82
Environment and health			
Particulate matter (urban-pop.-weighted avg., µg/cu. m)	35	48	65
Acute resp. infection prevalence (% of children under five)	..	..	..
Diarrhea prevalence (% of children under five)	..	..	..
Under-five mortality rate (per 1,000 live births)	12	22	20
National accounting aggregates—savings, depletion and degradation			
Gross savings (% of GNI)	22.7	18.9	36.4
Consumption of fixed capital (% of GNI)	16.5	12.4	12.5
Education expenditure (% of GNI)	3.7	3.8	3.2
Energy depletion (% of GNI)	1.5	4.4	4.1
Mineral depletion (% of GNI)	0.0	0.6	1.2
Net forest depletion (% of GNI)	0.0	0.0	0.2
CO_2 damage (% of GNI)	0.4	0.8	0.8
Particulate emissions damage (% of GNI)	0.9	1.8	1.3
Adjusted net savings (% of GNI)	7.0	2.8	19.5

Russian Federation

Population (millions) **143.5**   Land area (1,000 sq. km) **16,377**   GDP ($ billions) **2,014.8**

	Country data	High-income group
GNI per capita, *World Bank Atlas* method ($)	12,700	38,444
Adjusted net national income per capita ($)	11,263	32,262
Change in wealth per capita (2010 $)	1,009	2,210
Urban population (% of total)	74.0	80.2

Agriculture

Agricultural land (% land area)	13	29
Agricultural irrigated land (% of total agricultural land)	2.0	..
Agricultural productivity, value added per worker (2005 $)	5,969	25,238
Cereal yield (kg per hectare)	1,859	4,374

Forests and biodiversity

Forest area (% land area)	49.4	35.0
Deforestation (avg. annual %, 2000–2010)	0.0	0.0
Terrestrial protected areas (% of total land area)	11.3	13.9
Threatened species, mammals	31	
Threatened species, birds	83	
Threatened species, fish	36	
Threatened species, higher plants	12	

Oceans

Total fisheries production (thousand metric tons)	4,484	37,661
Capture fisheries growth (avg. annual %, 1990–2012)	-2.4	-2.0
Aquaculture growth (avg. annual %, 1990–2012)	-2.6	2.5
Marine protected areas (% of territorial waters)	10.8	14.4
Coral reef area (sq. km)	..	82,210
Mangroves area (sq. km)	..	15,504

Energy and emissions

Energy use per capita (kg oil equivalent)	5,113	4,872
Energy from biomass products and waste (% of total)	1.0	4.3
Electric power consumption per capita (kWh)	6,486	8,896
Electricity generated using fossil fuel (% of total)	67.4	61.8
Electricity generated by hydropower (% of total)	15.7	12.2
CO_2 emissions per capita (metric tons)	12.2	11.6

Water and sanitation

Internal freshwater resources per capita (cu. m)	30,169	11,335
Total freshwater withdrawal (% of internal resources)	1.5	7.0
Agriculture (% of total freshwater withdrawal)	20	40
Access to improved water source (% of total population)	97	99
Rural (% of rural population)	92	98
Urban (% of urban population)	99	100
Access to improved sanitation facilities (% of total population)	70	96
Rural (% of rural population)	59	93
Urban (% of urban population)	74	97

Environment and health

Particulate matter (urban-pop.-weighted avg., µg/cu. m)	27	27
Acute resp. infection prevalence (% of children under five)	..	..
Diarrhea prevalence (% of children under five)	..	..
Under-five mortality rate (per 1,000 live births)	10	6

National accounting aggregates—savings, depletion and degradation

Gross savings (% of GNI)	30.7	20.1
Consumption of fixed capital (% of GNI)	4.7	14.2
Education expenditure (% of GNI)	3.5	4.7
Energy depletion (% of GNI)	11.4	1.6
Mineral depletion (% of GNI)	0.9	0.3
Net forest depletion (% of GNI)	0.0	0.0
CO_2 damage (% of GNI)	0.9	0.3
Particulate emissions damage (% of GNI)	1.2	0.3
Adjusted net savings (% of GNI)	15.0	8.1

Rwanda

Population (millions)	**11.5**	Land area (1,000 sq. km)	**25**	GDP ($ billions)	**7.1**

	Country data	Sub-Saharan Africa group	Low-Income group
GNI per capita, *World Bank Atlas* method ($)	600	1,547	594
Adjusted net national income per capita ($)	497	1,005	495
Change in wealth per capita (2010 $)	-136	-273	-39
Urban population (% of total)	19.4	36.8	28.2
Agriculture			
Agricultural land (% land area)	78	44	39
Agricultural irrigated land (% of total agricultural land)	..	..	
Agricultural productivity, value added per worker (2005 $)	294	765	367
Cereal yield (kg per hectare)	2,169	1,417	1,982
Forests and biodiversity			
Forest area (% land area)	18.0	27.4	27.4
Deforestation (avg. annual %, 2000–2010)	-2.4	0.5	0.6
Terrestrial protected areas (% of total land area)	10.5	16.4	13.7
Threatened species, mammals	20		
Threatened species, birds	14		
Threatened species, fish	9		
Threatened species, higher plants	6		
Oceans			
Total fisheries production (thousand metric tons)	20.0	6,906	11,789
Capture fisheries growth (avg. annual %, 1990–2012)	10.1	2.1	3.8
Aquaculture growth (avg. annual %, 1990–2012)	5.3	15.9	5.1
Marine protected areas (% of territorial waters)	31.2	11.7	13.1
Coral reef area (sq. km)	..	17,980	15,120
Mangroves area (sq. km)	..	27,808	25,817
Energy and emissions			
Energy use per capita (kg oil equivalent)	..	681	360
Energy from biomass products and waste (% of total)	..	57.6	66.0
Electric power consumption per capita (kWh)	..	535	233
Electricity generated using fossil fuel (% of total)	..	65.1	30.9
Electricity generated by hydropower (% of total)	..	20.0	45.5
CO_2 emissions per capita (metric tons)	0.1	0.8	0.3
Water and sanitation			
Internal freshwater resources per capita (cu. m)	852	4,391	5,121
Total freshwater withdrawal (% of internal resources)	1.6	3.2	4.4
Agriculture (% of total freshwater withdrawal)	68	84	90
Access to improved water source (% of total population)	71	64	69
Rural (% of rural population)	68	53	61
Urban (% of urban population)	81	85	88
Access to improved sanitation facilities (% of total population)	64	30	37
Rural (% of rural population)	64	23	33
Urban (% of urban population)	61	41	46
Environment and health			
Particulate matter (urban-pop.-weighted avg., µg/cu. m)	30	77	74
Acute resp. infection prevalence (% of children under five)	4	5	6
Diarrhea prevalence (% of children under five)	13	14	14
Under-five mortality rate (per 1,000 live births)	55	98	82
National accounting aggregates—savings, depletion and degradation			
Gross savings (% of GNI)	11.7	26.3	24.6
Consumption of fixed capital (% of GNI)	13.9	13.0	11.8
Education expenditure (% of GNI)	4.1	3.4	3.2
Energy depletion (% of GNI)	0.0	10.3	1.4
Mineral depletion (% of GNI)	0.2	1.8	1.9
Net forest depletion (% of GNI)	4.9	1.8	4.4
CO_2 damage (% of GNI)	0.1	0.6	0.4
Particulate emissions damage (% of GNI)	0.3	1.2	1.0
Adjusted net savings (% of GNI)	-3.7	0.9	7.0

Samoa

Population (thousands) **189**	Land area (1,000 sq. km)	**2.8**	GDP ($ millions)	**683.7**

	Country data	East Asia & Pacific group	Lower middle-income group
GNI per capita, *World Bank Atlas* method ($)	3,260	4,884	1,965
Adjusted net national income per capita ($)	2,970	4,305	1,574
Change in wealth per capita (2010 $)	..	1,172	117
Urban population (% of total)	19.7	49.6	38.9
Agriculture			
Agricultural land (% land area)	12	48	46
Agricultural irrigated land (% of total agricultural land)	..	..	..
Agricultural productivity, value added per worker (2005 $)	2,461	794	938
Cereal yield (kg per hectare)	..	5,145	3,029
Forests and biodiversity			
Forest area (% land area)	60.4	29.7	26.9
Deforestation (avg. annual %, 2000–2010)	0.0	-0.4	0.3
Terrestrial protected areas (% of total land area)	6.7	15.1	11.9
Threatened species, mammals	2		
Threatened species, birds	6		
Threatened species, fish	13		
Threatened species, higher plants	2		
Oceans			
Total fisheries production (thousand metric tons)	12.1	108,399	43,067
Capture fisheries growth (avg. annual %, 1990–2012)	9.9	3.4	2.6
Aquaculture growth (avg. annual %, 1990–2012)	..	9.1	9.9
Marine protected areas (% of territorial waters)	0.55	1.4	14.7
Coral reef area (sq. km)	490	137,690	124,480
Mangroves area (sq. km)	3.7	56,537	58,917
Energy and emissions			
Energy use per capita (kg oil equivalent)	318	1,671	687
Energy from biomass products and waste (% of total)	..	10.1	26.8
Electric power consumption per capita (kWh)	..	2,582	734
Electricity generated using fossil fuel (% of total)	..	80.9	72.3
Electricity generated by hydropower (% of total)	..	14.5	16.9
CO_2 emissions per capita (metric tons)	0.9	4.9	1.6
Water and sanitation			
Internal freshwater resources per capita (cu. m)	..	4,438	3,144
Total freshwater withdrawal (% of internal resources)	..	10.9	19.6
Agriculture (% of total freshwater withdrawal)	..	73	88
Access to improved water source (% of total population)	99	91	88
Rural (% of rural population)	99	85	85
Urban (% of urban population)	97	97	94
Access to improved sanitation facilities (% of total population)	92	67	48
Rural (% of rural population)	91	58	36
Urban (% of urban population)	93	76	66
Environment and health			
Particulate matter (urban-pop.-weighted avg., µg/cu. m)	..	75	90
Acute resp. infection prevalence (% of children under five)	..	..	..
Diarrhea prevalence (% of children under five)	..	..	..
Under-five mortality rate (per 1,000 live births)	18	21	61
National accounting aggregates—savings, depletion and degradation			
Gross savings (% of GNI)	..	47.6	28.6
Consumption of fixed capital (% of GNI)	12.4	12.0	11.1
Education expenditure (% of GNI)	4.8	2.1	3.1
Energy depletion (% of GNI)	0.0	2.7	4.4
Mineral depletion (% of GNI)	0.0	1.4	1.1
Net forest depletion (% of GNI)	0.9	0.1	0.8
CO_2 damage (% of GNI)	0.3	1.0	0.9
Particulate emissions damage (% of GNI)	..	1.6	1.4
Adjusted net savings (% of GNI)	..	30.9	12.0

San Marino

Population (thousands)	**31**	Land area (sq. km)	**60**	GDP ($ billions)	*1.9*

	Country data	High-income group
GNI per capita, *World Bank Atlas* method ($)	*51,470*	38,444
Adjusted net national income per capita ($)	..	32,262
Change in wealth per capita (2010 $)	..	2,210
Urban population (% of total)	94.1	80.2
Agriculture		
Agricultural land (% land area)	17	29
Agricultural irrigated land (% of total agricultural land)	..	..
Agricultural productivity, value added per worker (2005 $)	..	25,238
Cereal yield (kg per hectare)	..	4,374
Forests and biodiversity		
Forest area (% land area)	0.0	35.0
Deforestation (avg. annual %, 2000–2010)	0.0	0.0
Terrestrial protected areas (% of total land area)	..	13.9
Threatened species, mammals	*0*	
Threatened species, birds	*0*	
Threatened species, fish	*0*	
Threatened species, higher plants	*0*	
Oceans		
Total fisheries production (thousand metric tons)	..	37,661
Capture fisheries growth (avg. annual %, 1990–2012)	..	-2.0
Aquaculture growth (avg. annual %, 1990–2012)	..	2.5
Marine protected areas (% of territorial waters)	0.0	*14.4*
Coral reef area (sq. km)	..	82,210
Mangroves area (sq. km)	..	15,504
Energy and emissions		
Energy use per capita (kg oil equivalent)	..	4,872
Energy from biomass products and waste (% of total)	..	4.3
Electric power consumption per capita (kWh)	..	8,896
Electricity generated using fossil fuel (% of total)	..	61.8
Electricity generated by hydropower (% of total)	..	12.2
CO_2 emissions per capita (metric tons)	..	11.6
Water and sanitation		
Internal freshwater resources per capita (cu. m)	..	11,335
Total freshwater withdrawal (% of internal resources)	..	7.0
Agriculture (% of total freshwater withdrawal)	..	40
Access to improved water source (% of total population)	..	99
Rural (% of rural population)	..	98
Urban (% of urban population)	..	100
Access to improved sanitation facilities (% of total population)	..	96
Rural (% of rural population)	..	93
Urban (% of urban population)	..	97
Environment and health		
Particulate matter (urban-pop.-weighted avg., µg/cu. m)	20	27
Acute resp. infection prevalence (% of children under five)	..	..
Diarrhea prevalence (% of children under five)	..	..
Under-five mortality rate (per 1,000 live births)	3	6
National accounting aggregates—savings, depletion and degradation		
Gross savings (% of GNI)	..	20.1
Consumption of fixed capital (% of GNI)	*12.7*	14.2
Education expenditure (% of GNI)	3.6	4.7
Energy depletion (% of GNI)	0.0	1.6
Mineral depletion (% of GNI)	*0.0*	0.3
Net forest depletion (% of GNI)	..	0.0
CO_2 damage (% of GNI)	..	0.3
Particulate emissions damage (% of GNI)	..	0.3
Adjusted net savings (% of GNI)	..	8.1

São Tomé and Príncipe

Population (thousands) **188** Land area (sq. km) **960** GDP ($ millions) **263.4**

	Country data	Sub-Saharan Africa group	Lower middle-income group
GNI per capita, *World Bank Atlas* method ($)	1,310	1,547	1,965
Adjusted net national income per capita ($)	1,147	1,005	1,574
Change in wealth per capita (2010 $)	..	-273	117
Urban population (% of total)	63.3	36.8	38.9

Agriculture

Agricultural land (% land area)	51	44	46
Agricultural irrigated land (% of total agricultural land)	..	..	..
Agricultural productivity, value added per worker (2005 $)	..	765	938
Cereal yield (kg per hectare)	3,077	1,417	3,029

Forests and biodiversity

Forest area (% land area)	28.1	27.4	26.9
Deforestation (avg. annual %, 2000–2010)	0.0	0.5	0.3
Terrestrial protected areas (% of total land area)	..	16.4	11.9
Threatened species, mammals	5		
Threatened species, birds	13		
Threatened species, fish	13		
Threatened species, higher plants	37		

Oceans

Total fisheries production (thousand metric tons)	5.3	6,906	43,067
Capture fisheries growth (avg. annual %, 1990–2012)	1.4	2.1	2.6
Aquaculture growth (avg. annual %, 1990–2012)	..	15.9	9.9
Marine protected areas (% of territorial waters)	3.4	11.7	14.7
Coral reef area (sq. km)	..	17,980	124,480
Mangroves area (sq. km)	1.4	27,808	58,917

Energy and emissions

Energy use per capita (kg oil equivalent)	*269*	681	687
Energy from biomass products and waste (% of total)	..	57.6	26.8
Electric power consumption per capita (kWh)	..	535	734
Electricity generated using fossil fuel (% of total)	..	65.1	72.3
Electricity generated by hydropower (% of total)	..	20.0	16.9
CO_2 emissions per capita (metric tons)	0.6	0.8	1.6

Water and sanitation

Internal freshwater resources per capita (cu. m)	11,901	4,391	3,144
Total freshwater withdrawal (% of internal resources)	0.3	3.2	19.6
Agriculture (% of total freshwater withdrawal)	..	84	88
Access to improved water source (% of total population)	97	64	88
Rural (% of rural population)	94	53	85
Urban (% of urban population)	99	85	94
Access to improved sanitation facilities (% of total population)	34	30	48
Rural (% of rural population)	23	23	36
Urban (% of urban population)	41	41	66

Environment and health

Particulate matter (urban-pop.-weighted avg., µg/cu. m)	14	77	90
Acute resp. infection prevalence (% of children under five)	9	5	..
Diarrhea prevalence (% of children under five)	16	14	..
Under-five mortality rate (per 1,000 live births)	53	98	61

National accounting aggregates—savings, depletion and degradation

Gross savings (% of GNI)	..	26.3	28.6
Consumption of fixed capital (% of GNI)	15.3	13.0	11.1
Education expenditure (% of GNI)	7.7	3.4	3.1
Energy depletion (% of GNI)	0.0	10.3	4.4
Mineral depletion (% of GNI)	0.0	1.8	1.1
Net forest depletion (% of GNI)	2.1	1.8	0.8
CO_2 damage (% of GNI)	0.4	0.6	0.9
Particulate emissions damage (% of GNI)	0.0	1.2	1.4
Adjusted net savings (% of GNI)	..	0.9	12.0

Saudi Arabia

Population (millions)	**28.3**	Land area (1,000 sq. km)	**2,150**	GDP ($ billions)	**711.0**

	Country data	High-income group
GNI per capita, *World Bank Atlas* method ($)	24,310	38,444
Adjusted net national income per capita ($)	14,390	32,262
Change in wealth per capita (2010 $)	–1,718	2,210
Urban population (% of total)	82.5	80.2
Agriculture		
Agricultural land (% land area)	81	29
Agricultural irrigated land (% of total agricultural land)	..	..
Agricultural productivity, value added per worker (2005 $)	24,309	25,238
Cereal yield (kg per hectare)	5,166	4,374
Forests and biodiversity		
Forest area (% land area)	0.5	35.0
Deforestation (avg. annual %, 2000–2010)	0.0	0.0
Terrestrial protected areas (% of total land area)	31.3	13.9
Threatened species, mammals	10	
Threatened species, birds	15	
Threatened species, fish	24	
Threatened species, higher plants	3	
Oceans		
Total fisheries production (thousand metric tons)	91.0	37,661
Capture fisheries growth (avg. annual %, 1990–2012)	2.2	–2.0
Aquaculture growth (avg. annual %, 1990–2012)	12.4	2.5
Marine protected areas (% of territorial waters)	14.4	14.4
Coral reef area (sq. km)	6,660	82,210
Mangroves area (sq. km)	204	15,504
Energy and emissions		
Energy use per capita (kg oil equivalent)	6,738	4,872
Energy from biomass products and waste (% of total)	0.0	4.3
Electric power consumption per capita (kWh)	8,161	8,896
Electricity generated using fossil fuel (% of total)	69.8	61.8
Electricity generated by hydropower (% of total)	0.0	12.2
CO_2 emissions per capita (metric tons)	17.0	11.6
Water and sanitation		
Internal freshwater resources per capita (cu. m)	86	11,335
Total freshwater withdrawal (% of internal resources)	986.3	7.0
Agriculture (% of total freshwater withdrawal)	88	40
Access to improved water source (% of total population)	97	99
Rural (% of rural population)	97	98
Urban (% of urban population)	97	100
Access to improved sanitation facilities (% of total population)	100	96
Rural (% of rural population)	100	93
Urban (% of urban population)	100	97
Environment and health		
Particulate matter (urban-pop.-weighted avg., µg/cu. m)	108	27
Acute resp. infection prevalence (% of children under five)	..	..
Diarrhea prevalence (% of children under five)	..	..
Under-five mortality rate (per 1,000 live births)	9	6
National accounting aggregates—savings, depletion and degradation		
Gross savings (% of GNI)	49.7	20.1
Consumption of fixed capital (% of GNI)	13.0	14.2
Education expenditure (% of GNI)	7.2	4.7
Energy depletion (% of GNI)	30.6	1.6
Mineral depletion (% of GNI)	0.0	0.3
Net forest depletion (% of GNI)	0.0	0.0
CO_2 damage (% of GNI)	0.7	0.3
Particulate emissions damage (% of GNI)	2.0	0.3
Adjusted net savings (% of GNI)	10.0	8.1

Senegal

	Country data	Sub-Saharan Africa group	Lower middle-income group
Population (millions) **13.7** Land area (1,000 sq. km) **193** GDP ($ billions) **14.0**			

	Country data	Sub-Saharan Africa group	Lower middle-income group
GNI per capita, *World Bank Atlas* method ($)	1,030	1,547	1,965
Adjusted net national income per capita ($)	915	1,005	1,574
Change in wealth per capita (2010 $)	–4	–273	117
Urban population (% of total)	42.9	36.8	38.9
Agriculture			
Agricultural land (% land area)	49	44	46
Agricultural irrigated land (% of total agricultural land)	0.7	..	..
Agricultural productivity, value added per worker (2005 $)	363	765	938
Cereal yield (kg per hectare)	1,310	1,417	3,029
Forests and biodiversity			
Forest area (% land area)	43.8	27.4	26.9
Deforestation (avg. annual %, 2000–2010)	0.5	0.5	0.3
Terrestrial protected areas (% of total land area)	24.8	16.4	11.9
Threatened species, mammals	16		
Threatened species, birds	13		
Threatened species, fish	46		
Threatened species, higher plants	10		
Oceans			
Total fisheries production (thousand metric tons)	462	6,906	43,067
Capture fisheries growth (avg. annual %, 1990–2012)	1.8	2.1	2.6
Aquaculture growth (avg. annual %, 1990–2012)	20.2	15.9	9.9
Marine protected areas (% of territorial waters)	12.4	11.7	14.7
Coral reef area (sq. km)	..	17,980	124,480
Mangroves area (sq. km)	1,279	27,808	58,917
Energy and emissions			
Energy use per capita (kg oil equivalent)	264	681	687
Energy from biomass products and waste (% of total)	45.8	57.6	26.8
Electric power consumption per capita (kWh)	187	535	734
Electricity generated using fossil fuel (% of total)	88.0	65.1	72.3
Electricity generated by hydropower (% of total)	8.5	20.0	16.9
CO_2 emissions per capita (metric tons)	0.5	0.8	1.6
Water and sanitation			
Internal freshwater resources per capita (cu. m)	1,935	4,391	3,144
Total freshwater withdrawal (% of internal resources)	8.6	3.2	19.6
Agriculture (% of total freshwater withdrawal)	93	84	88
Access to improved water source (% of total population)	74	64	88
Rural (% of rural population)	60	53	85
Urban (% of urban population)	92	85	94
Access to improved sanitation facilities (% of total population)	52	30	48
Rural (% of rural population)	40	23	36
Urban (% of urban population)	67	41	66
Environment and health			
Particulate matter (urban-pop.-weighted avg., µg/cu. m)	147	77	90
Acute resp. infection prevalence (% of children under five)	5	5	..
Diarrhea prevalence (% of children under five)	21	14	..
Under-five mortality rate (per 1,000 live births)	60	98	61
National accounting aggregates—savings, depletion and degradation			
Gross savings (% of GNI)	22.1	26.3	28.6
Consumption of fixed capital (% of GNI)	7.4	13.0	11.1
Education expenditure (% of GNI)	5.2	3.4	3.1
Energy depletion (% of GNI)	0.0	10.3	4.4
Mineral depletion (% of GNI)	2.0	1.8	1.1
Net forest depletion (% of GNI)	0.0	1.8	0.8
CO_2 damage (% of GNI)	0.6	0.6	0.9
Particulate emissions damage (% of GNI)	1.9	1.2	1.4
Adjusted net savings (% of GNI)	15.9	0.9	12.0

Serbia

	Country data	Europe & Central Asia group	Upper middle-income group
Population (millions) **7.2** Land area (1,000 sq. km)		**87** GDP ($ billions)	**37.5**

	Country data	Europe & Central Asia group	Upper middle-income group
GNI per capita, *World Bank Atlas* method ($)	5,280	6,658	6,969
Adjusted net national income per capita ($)	..	5,541	5,845
Change in wealth per capita (2010 $)	..	263	1,039
Urban population (% of total)	56.7	60.2	60.7
Agriculture			
Agricultural land (% land area)	58	66	44
Agricultural irrigated land (% of total agricultural land)	0.7	..	..
Agricultural productivity, value added per worker (2005 $)	*3,904*	4,866	1,131
Cereal yield (kg per hectare)	3,118	2,519	4,255
Forests and biodiversity			
Forest area (% land area)	31.6	10.5	29.1
Deforestation (avg. annual %, 2000–2010)	-1.0	-0.5	0.0
Terrestrial protected areas (% of total land area)	6.3	5.1	16.1
Threatened species, mammals	6		
Threatened species, birds	11		
Threatened species, fish	11		
Threatened species, higher plants	4		
Oceans			
Total fisheries production (thousand metric tons)	12.5	1,022	90,024
Capture fisheries growth (avg. annual %, 1990–2012)	..	-4.0	1.5
Aquaculture growth (avg. annual %, 1990–2012)	..	1.8	9.1
Marine protected areas (% of territorial waters)	0.85	10.4	7.3
Coral reef area (sq. km)	..	..	52,070
Mangroves area (sq. km)	..	..	50,160
Energy and emissions			
Energy use per capita (kg oil equivalent)	2,230	2,078	1,893
Energy from biomass products and waste (% of total)	6.4	2.9	8.5
Electric power consumption per capita (kWh)	4,474	2,951	2,932
Electricity generated using fossil fuel (% of total)	77.2	65.8	74.7
Electricity generated by hydropower (% of total)	22.8	17.9	20.0
CO_2 emissions per capita (metric tons)	6.3	5.3	5.4
Water and sanitation			
Internal freshwater resources per capita (cu. m)	1,158	2,744	6,791
Total freshwater withdrawal (% of internal resources)	49.0	34.8	7.4
Agriculture (% of total freshwater withdrawal)	2	70	69
Access to improved water source (% of total population)	99	95	93
Rural (% of rural population)	99	89	85
Urban (% of urban population)	99	99	98
Access to improved sanitation facilities (% of total population)	97	94	74
Rural (% of rural population)	96	90	62
Urban (% of urban population)	99	97	82
Environment and health			
Particulate matter (urban-pop.-weighted avg., µg/cu. m)	43	48	65
Acute resp. infection prevalence (% of children under five)	..	..	..
Diarrhea prevalence (% of children under five)	..	..	..
Under-five mortality rate (per 1,000 live births)	7	22	20
National accounting aggregates—savings, depletion and degradation			
Gross savings (% of GNI)	*18.4*	18.9	36.4
Consumption of fixed capital (% of GNI)	13.6	12.4	12.5
Education expenditure (% of GNI)	4.8	3.8	3.2
Energy depletion (% of GNI)	1.6	4.4	4.1
Mineral depletion (% of GNI)	0.3	0.6	1.2
Net forest depletion (% of GNI)	..	0.0	0.2
CO_2 damage (% of GNI)	1.1	0.8	0.8
Particulate emissions damage (% of GNI)	..	1.8	1.3
Adjusted net savings (% of GNI)	..	2.8	19.5

Seychelles

	Country data	Sub-Saharan Africa group	Upper middle-income group
Population (thousands) **88** Land area (sq. km)	**460** GDP ($ billions)		**1.1**

	Country data	Sub-Saharan Africa group	Upper middle-income group
GNI per capita, World Bank Atlas method ($)	12,180	1,547	6,969
Adjusted net national income per capita ($)	10,632	1,005	5,845
Change in wealth per capita (2010 $)	..	-273	1,039
Urban population (% of total)	54.0	36.8	60.7
Agriculture			
Agricultural land (% land area)	7	44	44
Agricultural irrigated land (% of total agricultural land)	..	..	..
Agricultural productivity, value added per worker (2005 $)	777	765	1,131
Cereal yield (kg per hectare)	..	1,417	4,255
Forests and biodiversity			
Forest area (% land area)	88.5	27.4	29.1
Deforestation (avg. annual %, 2000–2010)	0.0	0.5	0.0
Terrestrial protected areas (% of total land area)	42.0	16.4	16.1
Threatened species, mammals	6		
Threatened species, birds	10		
Threatened species, fish	19		
Threatened species, higher plants	62		
Oceans			
Total fisheries production (thousand metric tons)	68.8	6,906	90,024
Capture fisheries growth (avg. annual %, 1990–2012)	12.2	2.1	1.5
Aquaculture growth (avg. annual %, 1990–2012)	..	15.9	9.1
Marine protected areas (% of territorial waters)	8.6	11.7	7.3
Coral reef area (sq. km)	1,690	17,980	52,070
Mangroves area (sq. km)	32.3	27,808	50,160
Energy and emissions			
Energy use per capita (kg oil equivalent)	2,411	681	1,893
Energy from biomass products and waste (% of total)	..	57.6	8.5
Electric power consumption per capita (kWh)	..	535	2,932
Electricity generated using fossil fuel (% of total)	..	65.1	74.7
Electricity generated by hydropower (% of total)	..	20.0	20.0
CO_2 emissions per capita (metric tons)	7.8	0.8	5.4
Water and sanitation			
Internal freshwater resources per capita (cu. m)	..	4,391	6,791
Total freshwater withdrawal (% of internal resources)	..	3.2	7.4
Agriculture (% of total freshwater withdrawal)	7	84	69
Access to improved water source (% of total population)	96	64	93
Rural (% of rural population)	96	53	85
Urban (% of urban population)	96	85	98
Access to improved sanitation facilities (% of total population)	97	30	74
Rural (% of rural population)	97	23	62
Urban (% of urban population)	97	41	82
Environment and health			
Particulate matter (urban-pop.-weighted avg., µg/cu. m)	..	77	65
Acute resp. infection prevalence (% of children under five)	..	5	..
Diarrhea prevalence (% of children under five)	..	14	..
Under-five mortality rate (per 1,000 live births)	13	98	20
National accounting aggregates—savings, depletion and degradation			
Gross savings (% of GNI)	..	26.3	36.4
Consumption of fixed capital (% of GNI)	13.5	13.0	12.5
Education expenditure (% of GNI)	3.4	3.4	3.2
Energy depletion (% of GNI)	0.0	10.3	4.1
Mineral depletion (% of GNI)	0.0	1.8	1.2
Net forest depletion (% of GNI)	0.1	1.8	0.2
CO_2 damage (% of GNI)	0.7	0.6	0.8
Particulate emissions damage (% of GNI)	..	1.2	1.3
Adjusted net savings (% of GNI)	..	0.9	19.5

Sierra Leone

Population (millions)	**6.0**	Land area (1,000 sq. km)	**72**	GDP ($ billions)	**3.8**

	Country data	Sub-Saharan Africa group	Low-income group
GNI per capita, *World Bank Atlas* method ($)	580	1,547	594
Adjusted net national income per capita ($)	494	1,005	495
Change in wealth per capita (2010 $)	-142	-273	-39
Urban population (% of total)	39.6	36.8	28.2
Agriculture			
Agricultural land (% land area)	48	44	39
Agricultural irrigated land (% of total agricultural land)	..	..	..
Agricultural productivity, value added per worker (2005 $)	875	765	367
Cereal yield (kg per hectare)	1,768	1,417	1,982
Forests and biodiversity			
Forest area (% land area)	37.8	27.4	27.4
Deforestation (avg. annual %, 2000–2010)	0.7	0.5	0.6
Terrestrial protected areas (% of total land area)	10.5	16.4	13.7
Threatened species, mammals	17		
Threatened species, birds	13		
Threatened species, fish	48		
Threatened species, higher plants	54		
Oceans			
Total fisheries production (thousand metric tons)	204	6,906	11,789
Capture fisheries growth (avg. annual %, 1990–2012)	6.0	2.1	3.8
Aquaculture growth (avg. annual %, 1990–2012)	6.5	15.9	5.1
Marine protected areas (% of territorial waters)	1.4	11.7	13.1
Coral reef area (sq. km)	..	17,980	15,120
Mangroves area (sq. km)	1,049	27,808	25,817
Energy and emissions			
Energy use per capita (kg oil equivalent)	..	681	360
Energy from biomass products and waste (% of total)	..	57.6	66.0
Electric power consumption per capita (kWh)	..	535	233
Electricity generated using fossil fuel (% of total)	..	65.1	30.9
Electricity generated by hydropower (% of total)	..	20.0	45.5
CO_2 emissions per capita (metric tons)	0.1	0.8	0.3
Water and sanitation			
Internal freshwater resources per capita (cu. m)	27,278	4,391	5,121
Total freshwater withdrawal (% of internal resources)	0.3	3.2	4.4
Agriculture (% of total freshwater withdrawal)	71	84	90
Access to improved water source (% of total population)	60	64	69
Rural (% of rural population)	42	53	61
Urban (% of urban population)	87	85	88
Access to improved sanitation facilities (% of total population)	13	30	37
Rural (% of rural population)	7	23	33
Urban (% of urban population)	22	41	46
Environment and health			
Particulate matter (urban-pop.-weighted avg., µg/cu. m)	29	77	74
Acute resp. infection prevalence (% of children under five)	7	5	6
Diarrhea prevalence (% of children under five)	13	14	14
Under-five mortality rate (per 1,000 live births)	182	98	82
National accounting aggregates—savings, depletion and degradation			
Gross savings (% of GNI)	*10.4*	26.3	24.6
Consumption of fixed capital (% of GNI)	14.5	13.0	11.8
Education expenditure (% of GNI)	2.7	3.4	3.2
Energy depletion (% of GNI)	0.0	10.3	1.4
Mineral depletion (% of GNI)	0.5	1.8	1.9
Net forest depletion (% of GNI)	7.2	1.8	4.4
CO_2 damage (% of GNI)	0.2	0.6	0.4
Particulate emissions damage (% of GNI)	0.9	1.2	1.0
Adjusted net savings (% of GNI)	-22.7	0.9	7.0

Singapore

	Country data	High-Income group
Population (millions) **5.3** Land area (sq. km)	**700** GDP ($ billions)	**276.5**

	Country data	High-Income group
GNI per capita, *World Bank Atlas* method ($)	49,710	38,444
Adjusted net national income per capita ($)	41,936	32,262
Change in wealth per capita (2010 $)	10,888	2,210
Urban population (% of total)	100.0	80.2
Agriculture		
Agricultural land (% land area)	1	29
Agricultural irrigated land (% of total agricultural land)	..	..
Agricultural productivity, value added per worker (2005 $)	35,839	25,238
Cereal yield (kg per hectare)	..	4,374
Forests and biodiversity		
Forest area (% land area)	3.3	35.0
Deforestation (avg. annual %, 2000–2010)	0.0	-0.0
Terrestrial protected areas (% of total land area)	5.4	13.9
Threatened species, mammals	11	
Threatened species, birds	15	
Threatened species, fish	25	
Threatened species, higher plants	58	
Oceans		
Total fisheries production (thousand metric tons)	5.6	37,661
Capture fisheries growth (avg. annual %, 1990–2012)	-7.7	-2.0
Aquaculture growth (avg. annual %, 1990–2012)	3.0	2.5
Marine protected areas (% of territorial waters)	1.4	14.4
Coral reef area (sq. km)	<100	82,210
Mangroves area (sq. km)	4.6	15,504
Energy and emissions		
Energy use per capita (kg oil equivalent)	6,452	4,872
Energy from biomass products and waste (% of total)	2.8	4.3
Electric power consumption per capita (kWh)	8,404	8,896
Electricity generated using fossil fuel (% of total)	96.4	61.8
Electricity generated by hydropower (% of total)	0.0	12.2
CO_2 emissions per capita (metric tons)	2.7	11.6
Water and sanitation		
Internal freshwater resources per capita (cu. m)	116	11,335
Total freshwater withdrawal (% of internal resources)	31.7	7.0
Agriculture (% of total freshwater withdrawal)	4	40
Access to improved water source (% of total population)	100	99
Rural (% of rural population)	..	98
Urban (% of urban population)	100	100
Access to improved sanitation facilities (% of total population)	100	96
Rural (% of rural population)	..	93
Urban (% of urban population)	100	97
Environment and health		
Particulate matter (urban-pop.-weighted avg., µg/cu. m)	25	27
Acute resp. infection prevalence (% of children under five)	..	..
Diarrhea prevalence (% of children under five)	..	..
Under-five mortality rate (per 1,000 live births)	3	6
National accounting aggregates—savings, depletion and degradation		
Gross savings (% of GNI)	46.1	20.1
Consumption of fixed capital (% of GNI)	18.0	14.2
Education expenditure (% of GNI)	2.9	4.7
Energy depletion (% of GNI)	0.0	1.6
Mineral depletion (% of GNI)	0.0	0.3
Net forest depletion (% of GNI)	0.0	0.0
CO_2 damage (% of GNI)	0.1	0.3
Particulate emissions damage (% of GNI)	0.4	0.3
Adjusted net savings (% of GNI)	30.7	8.1

Sint Maarten (Dutch part)

Population (thousands) **39** Land area (sq. km) **34** GDP ($ millions) ..

	Country data	High-income group
GNI per capita, *World Bank Atlas* method ($)	..	38,444
Adjusted net national income per capita ($)	..	32,262
Change in wealth per capita (2010 $)	..	2,210
Urban population (% of total)	..	80.2
Agriculture		
Agricultural land (% land area)	..	29
Agricultural irrigated land (% of total agricultural land)	..	..
Agricultural productivity, value added per worker (2005 $)	..	25,238
Cereal yield (kg per hectare)	..	4,374
Forests and biodiversity		
Forest area (% land area)	..	35.0
Deforestation (avg. annual %, 2000–2010)	..	-0.0
Terrestrial protected areas (% of total land area)	..	13.9
Threatened species, mammals	0	
Threatened species, birds	1	
Threatened species, fish	1	
Threatened species, higher plants	0	
Oceans		
Total fisheries production (thousand metric tons)	0.18	37,661
Capture fisheries growth (avg. annual %, 1990–2012)	..	-2.0
Aquaculture growth (avg. annual %, 1990–2012)	..	2.5
Marine protected areas (% of territorial waters)	..	14.4
Coral reef area (sq. km)	..	82,210
Mangroves area (sq. km)	..	15,504
Energy and emissions		
Energy use per capita (kg oil equivalent)	..	4,872
Energy from biomass products and waste (% of total)	..	4.3
Electric power consumption per capita (kWh)	..	8,896
Electricity generated using fossil fuel (% of total)	..	61.8
Electricity generated by hydropower (% of total)	..	12.2
CO_2 emissions per capita (metric tons)	..	11.6
Water and sanitation		
Internal freshwater resources per capita (cu. m)	..	11,335
Total freshwater withdrawal (% of internal resources)	..	7.0
Agriculture (% of total freshwater withdrawal)	..	40
Access to improved water source (% of total population)	..	99
Rural (% of rural population)	..	98
Urban (% of urban population)	..	100
Access to improved sanitation facilities (% of total population)	..	96
Rural (% of rural population)	..	93
Urban (% of urban population)	..	97
Environment and health		
Particulate matter (urban-pop.-weighted avg., µg/cu. m)	..	27
Acute resp. infection prevalence (% of children under five)	..	..
Diarrhea prevalence (% of children under five)	..	..
Under-five mortality rate (per 1,000 live births)	..	6
National accounting aggregates—savings, depletion and degradation		
Gross savings (% of GNI)	..	20.1
Consumption of fixed capital (% of GNI)	..	14.2
Education expenditure (% of GNI)	..	4.7
Energy depletion (% of GNI)	..	1.6
Mineral depletion (% of GNI)	..	0.3
Net forest depletion (% of GNI)	..	0.0
CO_2 damage (% of GNI)	..	0.3
Particulate emissions damage (% of GNI)	..	0.3
Adjusted net savings (% of GNI)	..	8.1

Slovak Republic

Population (millions) **5.4**	Land area (1,000 sq. km) **48**	GDP ($ billions) **91.3**

	Country data	High-income group
GNI per capita, *World Bank Atlas* method ($)	17,200	38,444
Adjusted net national income per capita ($)	13,415	32,262
Change in wealth per capita (2010 $)	–66	2,210
Urban population (% of total)	54.7	80.2

Agriculture

Agricultural land (% of land area)	40	29
Agricultural irrigated land (% of total agricultural land)	0.7	..
Agricultural productivity, value added per worker (2005 $)	*12,735*	*25,238*
Cereal yield (kg per hectare)	4,331	4,374

Forests and biodiversity

Forest area (% land area)	40.2	35.0
Deforestation (avg. annual %, 2000–2010)	–0.1	0.0
Terrestrial protected areas (% of total land area)	36.1	13.9
Threatened species, mammals	3	
Threatened species, birds	8	
Threatened species, fish	5	
Threatened species, higher plants	7	

Oceans

Total fisheries production (thousand metric tons)	3.2	37,661
Capture fisheries growth (avg. annual %, 1990–2012)	..	–2.0
Aquaculture growth (avg. annual %, 1990–2012)	..	2.5
Marine protected areas (% of territorial waters)	98.4	*14.4*
Coral reef area (sq. km)	..	82,210
Mangroves area (sq. km)	..	15,504

Energy and emissions

Energy use per capita (kg oil equivalent)	3,214	4,872
Energy from biomass products and waste (% of total)	5.5	4.3
Electric power consumption per capita (kWh)	5,348	8,896
Electricity generated using fossil fuel (% of total)	27.5	61.8
Electricity generated by hydropower (% of total)	13.4	12.2
CO_2 emissions per capita (metric tons)	6.7	11.6

Water and sanitation

Internal freshwater resources per capita (cu. m)	2,334	11,335
Total freshwater withdrawal (% of internal resources)	5.5	7.0
Agriculture (% of total freshwater withdrawal)	3	40
Access to improved water source (% of total population)	100	99
Rural (% of rural population)	100	98
Urban (% of urban population)	100	100
Access to improved sanitation facilities (% of total population)	100	96
Rural (% of rural population)	100	93
Urban (% of urban population)	100	97

Environment and health

Particulate matter (urban-pop.-weighted avg., µg/cu. m)	30	27
Acute resp. infection prevalence (% of children under five)	..	..
Diarrhea prevalence (% of children under five)	..	..
Under-five mortality rate (per 1,000 live births)	8	6

National accounting aggregates—savings, depletion and degradation

Gross savings (% of GNI)	*22.4*	20.1
Consumption of fixed capital (% of GNI)	18.4	14.2
Education expenditure (% of GNI)	3.9	4.7
Energy depletion (% of GNI)	0.0	1.6
Mineral depletion (% of GNI)	0.0	0.3
Net forest depletion (% of GNI)	0.7	0.0
CO_2 damage (% of GNI)	0.4	0.3
Particulate emissions damage (% of GNI)	0.5	0.3
Adjusted net savings (% of GNI)	*6.1*	8.1

Slovenia

Population (millions)	**2.1**	Land area (1,000 sq. km)	**20**	GDP ($ billions)	**45.4**

	Country data	High-income group
GNI per capita, *World Bank Atlas* method ($)	22,830	38,444
Adjusted net national income per capita ($)	18,198	32,262
Change in wealth per capita (2010 $)	2,075	2,210
Urban population (% of total)	49.9	80.2
Agriculture		
Agricultural land (% land area)	23	29
Agricultural irrigated land (% of total agricultural land)	0.9	..
Agricultural productivity, value added per worker (2005 $)	*112,484*	*25,238*
Cereal yield (kg per hectare)	5,751	4,374
Forests and biodiversity		
Forest area (% land area)	62.3	35.0
Deforestation (avg. annual %, 2000–2010)	–0.2	0.0
Terrestrial protected areas (% of total land area)	54.5	13.9
Threatened species, mammals	5	
Threatened species, birds	5	
Threatened species, fish	29	
Threatened species, higher plants	7	
Oceans		
Total fisheries production (thousand metric tons)	1.7	37,661
Capture fisheries growth (avg. annual %, 1990–2012)	..	-2.0
Aquaculture growth (avg. annual %, 1990–2012)	..	2.5
Marine protected areas (% of territorial waters)	0.90	*14.4*
Coral reef area (sq. km)	..	82,210
Mangroves area (sq. km)	..	15,504
Energy and emissions		
Energy use per capita (kg oil equivalent)	3,531	4,872
Energy from biomass products and waste (% of total)	8.5	4.3
Electric power consumption per capita (kWh)	6,806	8,896
Electricity generated using fossil fuel (% of total)	36.5	61.8
Electricity generated by hydropower (% of total)	22.4	12.2
CO_2 emissions per capita (metric tons)	7.5	11.6
Water and sanitation		
Internal freshwater resources per capita (cu. m)	9,095	11,335
Total freshwater withdrawal (% of internal resources)	5.0	7.0
Agriculture (% of total freshwater withdrawal)	0	40
Access to improved water source (% of total population)	100	99
Rural (% of rural population)	99	98
Urban (% of urban population)	100	100
Access to improved sanitation facilities (% of total population)	100	96
Rural (% of rural population)	100	93
Urban (% of urban population)	100	97
Environment and health		
Particulate matter (urban-pop.-weighted avg., µg/cu. m)	31	27
Acute resp. infection prevalence (% of children under five)	..	..
Diarrhea prevalence (% of children under five)	..	..
Under-five mortality rate (per 1,000 live births)	3	6
National accounting aggregates—savings, depletion and degradation		
Gross savings (% of GNI)	*21.7*	20.1
Consumption of fixed capital (% of GNI)	16.2	14.2
Education expenditure (% of GNI)	5.4	4.7
Energy depletion (% of GNI)	0.0	1.6
Mineral depletion (% of GNI)	0.0	0.3
Net forest depletion (% of GNI)	0.4	0.0
CO_2 damage (% of GNI)	0.3	0.3
Particulate emissions damage (% of GNI)	0.5	0.3
Adjusted net savings (% of GNI)	9.5	8.1

Solomon Islands

Population (thousands) **550**	Land area (1,000 sq. km)	**28**	GDP ($ billions)	**1.0**

	Country data	East Asia & Pacific group	Lower middle-income group
GNI per capita, *World Bank Atlas* method ($)	1,130	4,884	1,965
Adjusted net national income per capita ($)	565	4,305	1,574
Change in wealth per capita (2010 $)	–472	1,172	117
Urban population (% of total)	20.9	49.6	38.9
Agriculture			
Agricultural land (% land area)	3	48	46
Agricultural irrigated land (% of total agricultural land)	..	..	..
Agricultural productivity, value added per worker (2005 $)	*1,177*	794	938
Cereal yield (kg per hectare)	4,000	5,145	3,029
Forests and biodiversity			
Forest area (% land area)	78.9	29.7	26.9
Deforestation (avg. annual %, 2000–2010)	0.2	–0.4	0.3
Terrestrial protected areas (% of total land area)	2.2	15.1	11.9
Threatened species, mammals	20		
Threatened species, birds	20		
Threatened species, fish	18		
Threatened species, higher plants	17		
Oceans			
Total fisheries production (thousand metric tons)	51.8	108,399	43,067
Capture fisheries growth (avg. annual %, 1990–2012)	–0.3	3.4	2.6
Aquaculture growth (avg. annual %, 1990–2012)	43.0	9.1	9.9
Marine protected areas (% of territorial waters)	0.0	1.4	14.7
Coral reef area (sq. km)	5,750	137,690	124,480
Mangroves area (sq. km)	603	56,537	58,917
Energy and emissions			
Energy use per capita (kg oil equivalent)	*130*	1,671	687
Energy from biomass products and waste (% of total)	..	10.1	26.8
Electric power consumption per capita (kWh)	..	2,582	734
Electricity generated using fossil fuel (% of total)	..	80.9	72.3
Electricity generated by hydropower (% of total)	..	14.5	16.9
CO_2 emissions per capita (metric tons)	0.4	4.9	1.6
Water and sanitation			
Internal freshwater resources per capita (cu. m)	83,086	4,438	3,144
Total freshwater withdrawal (% of internal resources)	..	10.9	19.6
Agriculture (% of total freshwater withdrawal)	..	73	88
Access to improved water source (% of total population)	81	91	88
Rural (% of rural population)	77	85	85
Urban (% of urban population)	93	97	94
Access to improved sanitation facilities (% of total population)	29	67	48
Rural (% of rural population)	15	58	36
Urban (% of urban population)	81	76	66
Environment and health			
Particulate matter (urban-pop.-weighted avg., µg/cu. m)	25	75	90
Acute resp. infection prevalence (% of children under five)	..	..	..
Diarrhea prevalence (% of children under five)	..	..	..
Under-five mortality rate (per 1,000 live births)	31	21	61
National accounting aggregates—savings, depletion and degradation			
Gross savings (% of GNI)	..	47.6	28.6
Consumption of fixed capital (% of GNI)	17.7	12.0	11.1
Education expenditure (% of GNI)	3.8	2.1	3.1
Energy depletion (% of GNI)	0.0	2.7	4.4
Mineral depletion (% of GNI)	5.9	1.4	1.1
Net forest depletion (% of GNI)	32.0	0.1	0.8
CO_2 damage (% of GNI)	0.3	1.0	0.9
Particulate emissions damage (% of GNI)	0.1	1.6	1.4
Adjusted net savings (% of GNI)	..	30.9	12.0

Somalia

| | Population (millions) | **10.2** | Land area (1,000 sq. km) | **627** | GDP ($ millions) | .. |

	Country data	Sub-Saharan Africa group	Low-Income group
GNI per capita, *World Bank Atlas* method ($)	..	1,547	594
Adjusted net national income per capita ($)	..	1,005	495
Change in wealth per capita (2010 $)	..	-273	-39
Urban population (% of total)	38.2	36.8	28.2

Agriculture
Agricultural land (% land area)	70	44	39
Agricultural irrigated land (% of total agricultural land)	..	..	..
Agricultural productivity, value added per worker (2005 $)	..	765	367
Cereal yield (kg per hectare)	528	1,417	1,982

Forests and biodiversity
Forest area (% land area)	10.6	27.4	27.4
Deforestation (avg. annual %, 2000–2010)	1.1	0.5	0.6
Terrestrial protected areas (% of total land area)	0.6	16.4	13.7
Threatened species, mammals	15		
Threatened species, birds	14		
Threatened species, fish	26		
Threatened species, higher plants	24		

Oceans
Total fisheries production (thousand metric tons)	30.0	6,906	11,789
Capture fisheries growth (avg. annual %, 1990–2012)	1.3	2.1	3.8
Aquaculture growth (avg. annual %, 1990–2012)	..	15.9	5.1
Marine protected areas (% of territorial waters)	12.8	11.7	13.1
Coral reef area (sq. km)	710	17,980	15,120
Mangroves area (sq. km)	48.0	27,808	25,817

Energy and emissions
Energy use per capita (kg oil equivalent)	..	681	360
Energy from biomass products and waste (% of total)	..	57.6	66.0
Electric power consumption per capita (kWh)	..	535	233
Electricity generated using fossil fuel (% of total)	..	65.1	30.9
Electricity generated by hydropower (% of total)	..	20.0	45.5
CO_2 emissions per capita (metric tons)	0.1	0.8	0.3

Water and sanitation
Internal freshwater resources per capita (cu. m)	606	4,391	5,121
Total freshwater withdrawal (% of internal resources)	55.0	3.2	4.4
Agriculture (% of total freshwater withdrawal)	99	84	90
Access to improved water source (% of total population)	31	64	69
Rural (% of rural population)	9	53	61
Urban (% of urban population)	70	85	88
Access to improved sanitation facilities (% of total population)	23	30	37
Rural (% of rural population)	6	23	33
Urban (% of urban population)	52	41	46

Environment and health
Particulate matter (urban-pop.-weighted avg., µg/cu. m)	32	77	74
Acute resp. infection prevalence (% of children under five)	..	5	6
Diarrhea prevalence (% of children under five)	..	14	14
Under-five mortality rate (per 1,000 live births)	147	98	82

National accounting aggregates—savings, depletion and degradation
Gross savings (% of GNI)	..	26.3	24.6
Consumption of fixed capital (% of GNI)	..	13.0	11.8
Education expenditure (% of GNI)	..	3.4	3.2
Energy depletion (% of GNI)	..	10.3	1.4
Mineral depletion (% of GNI)	..	1.8	1.9
Net forest depletion (% of GNI)	..	1.8	4.4
CO_2 damage (% of GNI)	..	0.6	0.4
Particulate emissions damage (% of GNI)	0.9	1.2	1.0
Adjusted net savings (% of GNI)	..	0.9	7.0

South Africa

	Country data	Sub-Saharan Africa group	Upper middle-income group
Population (millions) **52.3** Land area (1,000 sq. km) **1,213** GDP ($ billions) **384.3**			

	Country data	Sub-Saharan Africa group	Upper middle-income group
GNI per capita, *World Bank Atlas* method ($)	7,460	1,547	6,969
Adjusted net national income per capita ($)	5,890	1,005	5,845
Change in wealth per capita (2010 $)	-151	-273	1,039
Urban population (% of total)	62.4	36.8	60.7
Agriculture			
Agricultural land (% land area)	79	44	44
Agricultural irrigated land (% of total agricultural land)	1.7	..	..
Agricultural productivity, value added per worker (2005 $)	5,967	765	1,131
Cereal yield (kg per hectare)	3,650	1,417	4,255
Forests and biodiversity			
Forest area (% land area)	7.6	27.4	29.1
Deforestation (avg. annual %, 2000–2010)	0.0	0.5	0.0
Terrestrial protected areas (% of total land area)	6.2	16.4	16.1
Threatened species, mammals	24		
Threatened species, birds	41		
Threatened species, fish	87		
Threatened species, higher plants	100		
Oceans			
Total fisheries production (thousand metric tons)	722	6,906	90,024
Capture fisheries growth (avg. annual %, 1990–2012)	1.2	2.1	1.5
Aquaculture growth (avg. annual %, 1990–2012)	2.3	15.9	9.1
Marine protected areas (% of territorial waters)	9.4	11.7	7.3
Coral reef area (sq. km)	..	17,980	52,070
Mangroves area (sq. km)	30.5	27,808	50,160
Energy and emissions			
Energy use per capita (kg oil equivalent)	2,741	681	1,893
Energy from biomass products and waste (% of total)	10.3	57.6	8.5
Electric power consumption per capita (kWh)	4,604	535	2,932
Electricity generated using fossil fuel (% of total)	93.8	65.1	74.7
Electricity generated by hydropower (% of total)	0.8	20.0	20.0
CO_2 emissions per capita (metric tons)	9.0	0.8	5.4
Water and sanitation			
Internal freshwater resources per capita (cu. m)	869	4,391	6,791
Total freshwater withdrawal (% of internal resources)	27.9	3.2	7.4
Agriculture (% of total freshwater withdrawal)	63	84	69
Access to improved water source (% of total population)	95	64	93
Rural (% of rural population)	88	53	85
Urban (% of urban population)	99	85	98
Access to improved sanitation facilities (% of total population)	74	30	74
Rural (% of rural population)	62	23	62
Urban (% of urban population)	82	41	82
Environment and health			
Particulate matter (urban-pop.-weighted avg., µg/cu. m)	40	77	65
Acute resp. infection prevalence (% of children under five)	..	5	..
Diarrhea prevalence (% of children under five)	..	14	..
Under-five mortality rate (per 1,000 live births)	45	98	20
National accounting aggregates—savings, depletion and degradation			
Gross savings (% of GNI)	13.5	26.3	36.4
Consumption of fixed capital (% of GNI)	13.1	13.0	12.5
Education expenditure (% of GNI)	5.5	3.4	3.2
Energy depletion (% of GNI)	2.2	10.3	4.1
Mineral depletion (% of GNI)	2.7	1.8	1.2
Net forest depletion (% of GNI)	0.0	1.8	0.2
CO_2 damage (% of GNI)	1.4	0.6	0.8
Particulate emissions damage (% of GNI)	0.4	1.2	1.3
Adjusted net savings (% of GNI)	-0.9	0.9	19.5

South Sudan

Population (millions)	**10.8**	Land area (sq. km)	..	GDP ($ billions)	**10.2**

	Country data	Sub-Saharan Africa group	Low-Income group
GNI per capita, *World Bank Atlas* method ($)	790	1,547	594
Adjusted net national income per capita ($)	..	1,005	495
Change in wealth per capita (2010 $)	..	–273	–39
Urban population (% of total)	18.3	36.8	28.2

Agriculture

Agricultural land (% land area)	..	44	39
Agricultural irrigated land (% of total agricultural land)	..	..	..
Agricultural productivity, value added per worker (2005 $)	..	765	367
Cereal yield (kg per hectare)	..	1,417	1,982

Forests and biodiversity

Forest area (% land area)	..	27.4	27.4
Deforestation (avg. annual %, 2000–2010)	..	0.5	0.6
Terrestrial protected areas (% of total land area)	..	16.4	13.7
Threatened species, mammals	0		
Threatened species, birds	14		
Threatened species, fish	0		
Threatened species, higher plants	0		

Oceans

Total fisheries production (thousand metric tons)	37.0	6,906	11,789
Capture fisheries growth (avg. annual %, 1990–2012)	..	2.1	3.8
Aquaculture growth (avg. annual %, 1990–2012)	..	15.9	5.1
Marine protected areas (% of territorial waters)	..	11.7	13.1
Coral reef area (sq. km)	..	17,980	15,120
Mangroves area (sq. km)	..	27,808	25,817

Energy and emissions

Energy use per capita (kg oil equivalent)	..	681	360
Energy from biomass products and waste (% of total)	..	57.6	66.0
Electric power consumption per capita (kWh)	..	535	233
Electricity generated using fossil fuel (% of total)	..	65.1	30.9
Electricity generated by hydropower (% of total)	..	20.0	45.5
CO_2 emissions per capita (metric tons)	..	0.8	0.3

Water and sanitation

Internal freshwater resources per capita (cu. m)	..	4,391	5,121
Total freshwater withdrawal (% of internal resources)	..	3.2	4.4
Agriculture (% of total freshwater withdrawal)	..	84	90
Access to improved water source (% of total population)	57	64	69
Rural (% of rural population)	55	53	61
Urban (% of urban population)	63	85	88
Access to improved sanitation facilities (% of total population)	9	30	37
Rural (% of rural population)	7	23	33
Urban (% of urban population)	16	41	46

Environment and health

Particulate matter (urban-pop.-weighted avg., µg/cu. m)	..	77	74
Acute resp. infection prevalence (% of children under five)	..	5	6
Diarrhea prevalence (% of children under five)	..	14	14
Under-five mortality rate (per 1,000 live births)	104	98	82

National accounting aggregates—savings, depletion and degradation

Gross savings (% of GNI)	..	26.3	24.6
Consumption of fixed capital (% of GNI)	12.6	13.0	11.8
Education expenditure (% of GNI)	..	3.4	3.2
Energy depletion (% of GNI)	0.0	10.3	1.4
Mineral depletion (% of GNI)	0.0	1.8	1.9
Net forest depletion (% of GNI)	..	1.8	4.4
CO_2 damage (% of GNI)	..	0.6	0.4
Particulate emissions damage (% of GNI)	..	1.2	1.0
Adjusted net savings (% of GNI)	..	0.9	7.0

Spain

| | Population (millions) | 46.8 | Land area (1,000 sq. km) | 499 | GDP ($ billions) | 1,322.1 |

	Country data	High-income group
GNI per capita, *World Bank Atlas* method ($)	29,340	38,444
Adjusted net national income per capita ($)	23,147	32,262
Change in wealth per capita (2010 $)	1,585	2,210
Urban population (% of total)	77.6	80.2
Agriculture		
Agricultural land (% land area)	55	29
Agricultural irrigated land (% of total agricultural land)	12.0	..
Agricultural productivity, value added per worker (2005 $)	33,681	25,238
Cereal yield (kg per hectare)	2,886	4,374
Forests and biodiversity		
Forest area (% land area)	36.8	35.0
Deforestation (avg. annual %, 2000–2010)	-0.7	0.0
Terrestrial protected areas (% of total land area)	29.0	13.9
Threatened species, mammals	16	
Threatened species, birds	12	
Threatened species, fish	70	
Threatened species, higher plants	213	
Oceans		
Total fisheries production (thousand metric tons)	1,195	37,661
Capture fisheries growth (avg. annual %, 1990–2012)	-0.9	-2.0
Aquaculture growth (avg. annual %, 1990–2012)	1.2	2.5
Marine protected areas (% of territorial waters)	1.3	14.4
Coral reef area (sq. km)	..	82,210
Mangroves area (sq. km)	..	15,504
Energy and emissions		
Energy use per capita (kg oil equivalent)	2,686	4,872
Energy from biomass products and waste (% of total)	5.7	4.3
Electric power consumption per capita (kWh)	5,530	8,896
Electricity generated using fossil fuel (% of total)	49.9	61.8
Electricity generated by hydropower (% of total)	10.6	12.2
CO_2 emissions per capita (metric tons)	5.8	11.6
Water and sanitation		
Internal freshwater resources per capita (cu. m)	2,379	11,335
Total freshwater withdrawal (% of internal resources)	29.2	7.0
Agriculture (% of total freshwater withdrawal)	61	40
Access to improved water source (% of total population)	100	99
Rural (% of rural population)	100	98
Urban (% of urban population)	100	100
Access to improved sanitation facilities (% of total population)	100	96
Rural (% of rural population)	100	93
Urban (% of urban population)	100	97
Environment and health		
Particulate matter (urban-pop.-weighted avg., μg/cu. m)	27	27
Acute resp. infection prevalence (% of children under five)	..	..
Diarrhea prevalence (% of children under five)	..	..
Under-five mortality rate (per 1,000 live births)	5	6
National accounting aggregates—savings, depletion and degradation		
Gross savings (% of GNI)	19.2	20.1
Consumption of fixed capital (% of GNI)	17.2	14.2
Education expenditure (% of GNI)	4.5	4.7
Energy depletion (% of GNI)	0.0	1.6
Mineral depletion (% of GNI)	0.0	0.3
Net forest depletion (% of GNI)	0.0	0.0
CO_2 damage (% of GNI)	0.2	0.3
Particulate emissions damage (% of GNI)	0.4	0.3
Adjusted net savings (% of GNI)	5.9	8.1

Sri Lanka

Population (millions)	**20.3**	Land area (1,000 sq. km)	**63**	GDP ($ billions)	**59.4**

	Country data	South Asia group	Lower middle-income group
GNI per capita, *World Bank Atlas* method ($)	2,920	1,437	1,965
Adjusted net national income per capita ($)	2,696	1,168	1,574
Change in wealth per capita (2010 $)	421	158	117
Urban population (% of total)	15.2	31.4	38.9
Agriculture			
Agricultural land (% land area)	42	55	46
Agricultural irrigated land (% of total agricultural land)	..	..	..
Agricultural productivity, value added per worker (2005 $)	999	669	938
Cereal yield (kg per hectare)	3,862	2,925	3,029
Forests and biodiversity			
Forest area (% land area)	29.4	17.1	26.9
Deforestation (avg. annual %, 2000–2010)	1.1	-0.3	0.3
Terrestrial protected areas (% of total land area)	22.0	6.2	11.9
Threatened species, mammals	30		
Threatened species, birds	15		
Threatened species, fish	43		
Threatened species, higher plants	286		
Oceans			
Total fisheries production (thousand metric tons)	485	13,613	43,067
Capture fisheries growth (avg. annual %, 1990–2012)	4.4	2.6	2.6
Aquaculture growth (avg. annual %, 1990–2012)	10.3	7.6	9.9
Marine protected areas (% of territorial waters)	1.1	10.7	14.7
Coral reef area (sq. km)	680	15,440	124,480
Mangroves area (sq. km)	88.8	10,343	58,917
Energy and emissions			
Energy use per capita (kg oil equivalent)	499	555	687
Energy from biomass products and waste (% of total)	47.4	26.7	26.8
Electric power consumption per capita (kWh)	490	605	734
Electricity generated using fossil fuel (% of total)	59.1	77.9	72.3
Electricity generated by hydropower (% of total)	39.7	13.8	16.9
CO_2 emissions per capita (metric tons)	0.6	1.4	1.6
Water and sanitation			
Internal freshwater resources per capita (cu. m)	2,530	1,217	3,144
Total freshwater withdrawal (% of internal resources)	24.5	51.6	19.6
Agriculture (% of total freshwater withdrawal)	87	91	88
Access to improved water source (% of total population)	94	91	88
Rural (% of rural population)	93	89	85
Urban (% of urban population)	99	95	94
Access to improved sanitation facilities (% of total population)	92	40	48
Rural (% of rural population)	94	30	36
Urban (% of urban population)	83	61	66
Environment and health			
Particulate matter (urban-pop.-weighted avg., µg/cu. m)	62	110	90
Acute resp. infection prevalence (% of children under five)	..	..	..
Diarrhea prevalence (% of children under five)	..	..	..
Under-five mortality rate (per 1,000 live births)	10	60	61
National accounting aggregates—savings, depletion and degradation			
Gross savings (% of GNI)	24.6	29.3	28.6
Consumption of fixed capital (% of GNI)	5.5	12.7	11.1
Education expenditure (% of GNI)	1.7	2.8	3.1
Energy depletion (% of GNI)	0.0	1.8	4.4
Mineral depletion (% of GNI)	0.0	0.8	1.1
Net forest depletion (% of GNI)	0.5	1.1	0.8
CO_2 damage (% of GNI)	0.2	1.1	0.9
Particulate emissions damage (% of GNI)	0.4	1.5	1.4
Adjusted net savings (% of GNI)	19.7	13.1	12.0

St. Kitts and Nevis

Population (thousands)	**54**	Land area (sq. km)	**260**	GDP ($ millions)	**767.0**

	Country data	High-income group
GNI per capita, *World Bank Atlas* method ($)	13,610	38,444
Adjusted net national income per capita ($)	..	32,262
Change in wealth per capita (2010 $)	..	2,210
Urban population (% of total)	32.1	80.2
Agriculture		
Agricultural land (% land area)	23	29
Agricultural irrigated land (% of total agricultural land)	13.3	..
Agricultural productivity, value added per worker (2005 $)	1,217	25,238
Cereal yield (kg per hectare)	..	4,374
Forests and biodiversity		
Forest area (% land area)	42.3	35.0
Deforestation (avg. annual %, 2000–2010)	0.0	0.0
Terrestrial protected areas (% of total land area)	3.6	13.9
Threatened species, mammals	2	
Threatened species, birds	1	
Threatened species, fish	20	
Threatened species, higher plants	2	
Oceans		
Total fisheries production (thousand metric tons)	21.8	37,661
Capture fisheries growth (avg. annual %, 1990–2012)	17.6	-2.0
Aquaculture growth (avg. annual %, 1990–2012)	-4.9	2.5
Marine protected areas (% of territorial waters)	0.16	14.4
Coral reef area (sq. km)	180	82,210
Mangroves area (sq. km)	0.68	15,504
Energy and emissions		
Energy use per capita (kg oil equivalent)	1,644	4,872
Energy from biomass products and waste (% of total)	..	4.3
Electric power consumption per capita (kWh)	..	8,896
Electricity generated using fossil fuel (% of total)	..	61.8
Electricity generated by hydropower (% of total)	..	12.2
CO_2 emissions per capita (metric tons)	4.8	11.6
Water and sanitation		
Internal freshwater resources per capita (cu. m)	453	11,335
Total freshwater withdrawal (% of internal resources)	..	7.0
Agriculture (% of total freshwater withdrawal)	..	40
Access to improved water source (% of total population)	98	99
Rural (% of rural population)	98	98
Urban (% of urban population)	98	100
Access to improved sanitation facilities (% of total population)	..	96
Rural (% of rural population)	..	93
Urban (% of urban population)	..	97
Environment and health		
Particulate matter (urban-pop.-weighted avg., µg/cu. m)	9	27
Acute resp. infection prevalence (% of children under five)	..	..
Diarrhea prevalence (% of children under five)	..	..
Under-five mortality rate (per 1,000 live births)	9	6
National accounting aggregates—savings, depletion and degradation		
Gross savings (% of GNI)	19.1	20.1
Consumption of fixed capital (% of GNI)	13.0	14.2
Education expenditure (% of GNI)	3.3	4.7
Energy depletion (% of GNI)	0.0	1.6
Mineral depletion (% of GNI)	0.0	0.3
Net forest depletion (% of GNI)	..	0.0
CO_2 damage (% of GNI)	0.4	0.3
Particulate emissions damage (% of GNI)	..	0.3
Adjusted net savings (% of GNI)	..	8.1

St. Lucia

Population (thousands) **181**	Land area (sq. km)	**610**	GDP ($ billions)	**1.2**

	Country data	Latin America & Caribbean group	Upper middle-income group
GNI per capita, *World Bank Atlas* method ($)	6,890	9,070	6,969
Adjusted net national income per capita ($)	5,926	7,325	5,845
Change in wealth per capita (2010 $)	446	180	1,039
Urban population (% of total)	17.0	79.0	60.7
Agriculture			
Agricultural land (% land area)	18	37	44
Agricultural irrigated land (% of total agricultural land)	..	..	..
Agricultural productivity, value added per worker (2005 $)	1,981	4,135	1,131
Cereal yield (kg per hectare)	..	4,082	4,255
Forests and biodiversity			
Forest area (% land area)	77.0	48.1	29.1
Deforestation (avg. annual %, 2000–2010)	-0.1	0.5	0.0
Terrestrial protected areas (% of total land area)	16.9	21.4	16.1
Threatened species, mammals	2		
Threatened species, birds	5		
Threatened species, fish	21		
Threatened species, higher plants	6		
Oceans			
Total fisheries production (thousand metric tons)	2.2	10,964	90,024
Capture fisheries growth (avg. annual %, 1990–2012)	3.9	-0.6	1.5
Aquaculture growth (avg. annual %, 1990–2012)	-1.6	10.8	9.1
Marine protected areas (% of territorial waters)	2.1	9.0	7.3
Coral reef area (sq. km)	160	14,860	52,070
Mangroves area (sq. km)	1.9	39,988	50,160
Energy and emissions			
Energy use per capita (kg oil equivalent)	752	1,292	1,893
Energy from biomass products and waste (% of total)	..	16.0	8.5
Electric power consumption per capita (kWh)	..	1,985	2,932
Electricity generated using fossil fuel (% of total)	..	37.3	74.7
Electricity generated by hydropower (% of total)	..	55.1	20.0
CO_2 emissions per capita (metric tons)	2.3	2.7	5.4
Water and sanitation			
Internal freshwater resources per capita (cu. m)	..	21,735	6,791
Total freshwater withdrawal (% of internal resources)	..	2.0	7.4
Agriculture (% of total freshwater withdrawal)	..	68	69
Access to improved water source (% of total population)	94	94	93
Rural (% of rural population)	93	82	85
Urban (% of urban population)	99	97	98
Access to improved sanitation facilities (% of total population)	65	81	74
Rural (% of rural population)	64	62	62
Urban (% of urban population)	70	86	82
Environment and health			
Particulate matter (urban-pop.-weighted avg., µg/cu. m)	11	43	65
Acute resp. infection prevalence (% of children under five)	..	..	..
Diarrhea prevalence (% of children under five)	..	..	..
Under-five mortality rate (per 1,000 live births)	18	19	20
National accounting aggregates—savings, depletion and degradation			
Gross savings (% of GNI)	13.1	19.0	36.4
Consumption of fixed capital (% of GNI)	12.4	12.2	12.5
Education expenditure (% of GNI)	4.2	5.1	3.2
Energy depletion (% of GNI)	0.0	4.7	4.1
Mineral depletion (% of GNI)	0.0	1.2	1.2
Net forest depletion (% of GNI)	0.0	0.4	0.2
CO_2 damage (% of GNI)	0.3	0.3	0.8
Particulate emissions damage (% of GNI)	0.0	0.8	1.3
Adjusted net savings (% of GNI)	4.5	4.5	19.5

St. Martin (French part)

Population (thousands) **31** Land area (sq. km) **54** GDP ($ millions) ..

	Country data	High-income group
GNI per capita, *World Bank Atlas* method ($)	..	38,444
Adjusted net national income per capita ($)	..	32,262
Change in wealth per capita (2010 $)	..	2,210
Urban population (% of total)	..	80.2

Agriculture

Agricultural land (% land area)	..	29
Agricultural irrigated land (% of total agricultural land)	..	..
Agricultural productivity, value added per worker (2005 $)	..	25,238
Cereal yield (kg per hectare)	..	4,374

Forests and biodiversity

Forest area (% land area)	..	35.0
Deforestation (avg. annual %, 2000-2010)	0.0	0.0
Terrestrial protected areas (% of total land area)	..	13.9
Threatened species, mammals	1	
Threatened species, birds	0	
Threatened species, fish	5	
Threatened species, higher plants	2	

Oceans

Total fisheries production (thousand metric tons)	0.20	37,661
Capture fisheries growth (avg. annual %, 1990-2012)	..	-2.0
Aquaculture growth (avg. annual %, 1990-2012)	..	2.5
Marine protected areas (% of territorial waters)	..	14.4
Coral reef area (sq. km)	..	82,210
Mangroves area (sq. km)	..	15,504

Energy and emissions

Energy use per capita (kg oil equivalent)	..	4,872
Energy from biomass products and waste (% of total)	..	4.3
Electric power consumption per capita (kWh)	..	8,896
Electricity generated using fossil fuel (% of total)	..	61.8
Electricity generated by hydropower (% of total)	..	12.2
CO_2 emissions per capita (metric tons)	..	11.6

Water and sanitation

Internal freshwater resources per capita (cu. m)	..	11,335
Total freshwater withdrawal (% of internal resources)	..	7.0
Agriculture (% of total freshwater withdrawal)	..	40
Access to improved water source (% of total population)	..	99
Rural (% of rural population)	..	98
Urban (% of urban population)	..	100
Access to improved sanitation facilities (% of total population)	..	96
Rural (% of rural population)	..	93
Urban (% of urban population)	..	97

Environment and health

Particulate matter (urban-pop.-weighted avg., µg/cu. m)	..	27
Acute resp. infection prevalence (% of children under five)	..	..
Diarrhea prevalence (% of children under five)	..	..
Under-five mortality rate (per 1,000 live births)	..	6

National accounting aggregates—savings, depletion and degradation

Gross savings (% of GNI)	..	20.1
Consumption of fixed capital (% of GNI)	..	14.2
Education expenditure (% of GNI)	..	4.7
Energy depletion (% of GNI)	..	1.6
Mineral depletion (% of GNI)	..	0.3
Net forest depletion (% of GNI)	..	0.0
CO_2 damage (% of GNI)	..	0.3
Particulate emissions damage (% of GNI)	..	0.3
Adjusted net savings (% of GNI)	..	8.1

St. Vincent and the Grenadines

| Population (thousands) **109** | Land area (sq. km) | **390** GDP ($ millions) | **712.6** |

	Country data	Latin America & Caribbean group	Upper middle-income group
GNI per capita, *World Bank Atlas* method ($)	6,400	9,070	6,969
Adjusted net national income per capita ($)	5,615	7,325	5,845
Change in wealth per capita (2010 $)	–864	180	1,039
Urban population (% of total)	49.7	79.0	60.7
Agriculture			
Agricultural land (% land area)	26	37	44
Agricultural irrigated land (% of total agricultural land)	..	..	..
Agricultural productivity, value added per worker (2005 $)	2,851	4,135	1,131
Cereal yield (kg per hectare)	25,879	4,082	4,255
Forests and biodiversity			
Forest area (% land area)	68.7	48.1	29.1
Deforestation (avg. annual %, 2000–2010)	–0.3	0.5	0.0
Terrestrial protected areas (% of total land area)	10.9	21.4	16.1
Threatened species, mammals	2		
Threatened species, birds	2		
Threatened species, fish	21		
Threatened species, higher plants	4		
Oceans			
Total fisheries production (thousand metric tons)	10.4	10,964	90,024
Capture fisheries growth (avg. annual %, 1990–2012)	0.7	–0.6	1.5
Aquaculture growth (avg. annual %, 1990–2012)	..	10.8	9.1
Marine protected areas (% of territorial waters)	1.1	9.0	7.3
Coral reef area (sq. km)	140	14,860	52,070
Mangroves area (sq. km)	0.90	39,988	50,160
Energy and emissions			
Energy use per capita (kg oil equivalent)	642	1,292	1,893
Energy from biomass products and waste (% of total)	..	16.0	8.5
Electric power consumption per capita (kWh)	..	1,985	2,932
Electricity generated using fossil fuel (% of total)	..	37.3	74.7
Electricity generated by hydropower (% of total)	..	55.1	20.0
CO_2 emissions per capita (metric tons)	1.9	2.7	5.4
Water and sanitation			
Internal freshwater resources per capita (cu. m)	..	21,735	6,791
Total freshwater withdrawal (% of internal resources)	..	2.0	7.4
Agriculture (% of total freshwater withdrawal)	..	68	69
Access to improved water source (% of total population)	95	94	93
Rural (% of rural population)	95	82	85
Urban (% of urban population)	95	97	98
Access to improved sanitation facilities (% of total population)	..	81	74
Rural (% of rural population)	..	62	62
Urban (% of urban population)	..	86	82
Environment and health			
Particulate matter (urban-pop.-weighted avg., µg/cu. m)	14	43	65
Acute resp. infection prevalence (% of children under five)	..	..	..
Diarrhea prevalence (% of children under five)	..	..	..
Under-five mortality rate (per 1,000 live births)	23	19	20
National accounting aggregates—savings, depletion and degradation			
Gross savings (% of GNI)	–6.8	19.0	36.4
Consumption of fixed capital (% of GNI)	12.3	12.2	12.5
Education expenditure (% of GNI)	4.5	5.1	3.2
Energy depletion (% of GNI)	0.0	4.7	4.1
Mineral depletion (% of GNI)	0.0	1.2	1.2
Net forest depletion (% of GNI)	0.1	0.4	0.2
CO_2 damage (% of GNI)	0.3	0.3	0.8
Particulate emissions damage (% of GNI)	0.0	0.8	1.3
Adjusted net savings (% of GNI)	–14.9	4.5	19.5

Sudan

	Country data	Sub-Saharan Africa group	Lower middle-income group
Population (millions) **37.2**[c] Land area (1,000 sq. km) **2,376** GDP ($ billions) **58.8**[c]			

	Country data	Sub-Saharan Africa group	Lower middle-income group
GNI per capita, *World Bank Atlas* method ($)	1,500[c]	1,547	1,965
Adjusted net national income per capita ($)	1,262	1,005	1,574
Change in wealth per capita (2010 $)	–343	–273	117
Urban population (% of total)	33.4[c]	36.8	38.9
Agriculture			
Agricultural land (% land area)	46	44	46
Agricultural irrigated land (% of total agricultural land)	1.4	..	..
Agricultural productivity, value added per worker (2005 $)	1,683	765	938
Cereal yield (kg per hectare)	472	1,417	3,029
Forests and biodiversity			
Forest area (% land area)	23.2	27.4	26.9
Deforestation (avg. annual %, 2000-2010)	0.1	0.5	0.3
Terrestrial protected areas (% of total land area)	6.8	16.4	11.9
Threatened species, mammals	16[c]		
Threatened species, birds	17[c]		
Threatened species, fish	21[c]		
Threatened species, higher plants	18[c]		
Oceans			
Total fisheries production (thousand metric tons)	73.0	6,906	43,067
Capture fisheries growth (avg. annual %, 1990-2012)	3.8	2.1	2.6
Aquaculture growth (avg. annual %, 1990-2012)	10.2	15.9	9.9
Marine protected areas (% of territorial waters)	22.9	11.7	14.7
Coral reef area (sq. km)	2,720	17,980	124,480
Mangroves area (sq. km)	9.8	27,808	58,917
Energy and emissions			
Energy use per capita (kg oil equivalent)	355	681	687
Energy from biomass products and waste (% of total)	67.1	57.6	26.8
Electric power consumption per capita (kWh)	143	535	734
Electricity generated using fossil fuel (% of total)	24.8	65.1	72.3
Electricity generated by hydropower (% of total)	75.2	20.0	16.9
CO_2 emissions per capita (metric tons)	0.3	0.8	1.6
Water and sanitation			
Internal freshwater resources per capita (cu. m)	641	4,391	3,144
Total freshwater withdrawal (% of internal resources)	123.8	3.2	19.6
Agriculture (% of total freshwater withdrawal)	97	84	88
Access to improved water source (% of total population)	55[c]	64	88
Rural (% of rural population)	50[c]	53	85
Urban (% of urban population)	66[c]	85	94
Access to improved sanitation facilities (% of total population)	24[c]	30	48
Rural (% of rural population)	13[c]	23	36
Urban (% of urban population)	44[c]	41	66
Environment and health			
Particulate matter (urban-pop.-weighted avg., μg/cu. m)	62	77	90
Acute resp. infection prevalence (% of children under five)	..	5	..
Diarrhea prevalence (% of children under five)	..	14	..
Under-five mortality rate (per 1,000 live births)	73[c]	98	61
National accounting aggregates—savings, depletion and degradation			
Gross savings (% of GNI)	10.3[c]	26.3	28.6
Consumption of fixed capital (% of GNI)	11.6[c]	13.0	11.1
Education expenditure (% of GNI)	0.9	3.4	3.1
Energy depletion (% of GNI)	3.4	10.3	4.4
Mineral depletion (% of GNI)	1.7	1.8	1.1
Net forest depletion (% of GNI)	0.0[c]	1.8	0.8
CO_2 damage (% of GNI)	0.2	0.6	0.9
Particulate emissions damage (% of GNI)	0.9	1.2	1.4
Adjusted net savings (% of GNI)	–6.7	0.9	12.0

Suriname

	Country data	Latin America & Caribbean group	Upper middle-income group
Population (thousands) **535**	Land area (1,000 sq. km) **156**	GDP ($ billions)	**5.0**

	Country data	Latin America & Caribbean group	Upper middle-income group
GNI per capita, *World Bank Atlas* method ($)	8,680	9,070	6,969
Adjusted net national income per capita ($)	6,402	7,325	5,845
Change in wealth per capita (2010 $)	..	180	1,039
Urban population (% of total)	70.1	79.0	60.7
Agriculture			
Agricultural land (% land area)	1	37	44
Agricultural irrigated land (% of total agricultural land)	..	..	..
Agricultural productivity, value added per worker (2005 $)	4,132	4,135	1,131
Cereal yield (kg per hectare)	4,000	4,082	4,255
Forests and biodiversity			
Forest area (% land area)	94.6	48.1	29.1
Deforestation (avg. annual %, 2000–2010)	0.0	0.5	0.0
Terrestrial protected areas (% of total land area)	14.7	21.4	16.1
Threatened species, mammals	9		
Threatened species, birds	7		
Threatened species, fish	26		
Threatened species, higher plants	26		
Oceans			
Total fisheries production (thousand metric tons)	36.7	10,964	90,024
Capture fisheries growth (avg. annual %, 1990–2012)	8.2	-0.6	1.5
Aquaculture growth (avg. annual %, 1990–2012)	..	10.8	9.1
Marine protected areas (% of territorial waters)	22.9	9.0	7.3
Coral reef area (sq. km)	..	14,860	52,070
Mangroves area (sq. km)	510	39,988	50,160
Energy and emissions			
Energy use per capita (kg oil equivalent)	1,399	1,292	1,893
Energy from biomass products and waste (% of total)	..	16.0	8.5
Electric power consumption per capita (kWh)	..	1,985	2,932
Electricity generated using fossil fuel (% of total)	..	37.3	74.7
Electricity generated by hydropower (% of total)	..	55.1	20.0
CO_2 emissions per capita (metric tons)	4.5	2.7	5.4
Water and sanitation			
Internal freshwater resources per capita (cu. m)	166,113	21,735	6,791
Total freshwater withdrawal (% of internal resources)	0.8	2.0	7.4
Agriculture (% of total freshwater withdrawal)	93	68	69
Access to improved water source (% of total population)	95	94	93
Rural (% of rural population)	88	82	85
Urban (% of urban population)	98	97	98
Access to improved sanitation facilities (% of total population)	80	81	74
Rural (% of rural population)	61	62	62
Urban (% of urban population)	88	86	82
Environment and health			
Particulate matter (urban-pop.-weighted avg., µg/cu. m)	18	43	65
Acute resp. infection prevalence (% of children under five)	..	..	..
Diarrhea prevalence (% of children under five)	..	..	..
Under-five mortality rate (per 1,000 live births)	21	19	20
National accounting aggregates—savings, depletion and degradation			
Gross savings (% of GNI)	..	19.0	36.4
Consumption of fixed capital (% of GNI)	12.8	12.2	12.5
Education expenditure (% of GNI)	..	5.1	3.2
Energy depletion (% of GNI)	0.0	4.7	4.1
Mineral depletion (% of GNI)	16.2	1.2	1.2
Net forest depletion (% of GNI)	0.0	0.4	0.2
CO_2 damage (% of GNI)	0.5	0.3	0.8
Particulate emissions damage (% of GNI)	0.1	0.8	1.3
Adjusted net savings (% of GNI)	..	4.5	19.5

Swaziland

	Country data	Sub-Saharan Africa group	Lower middle-income group
Population (millions) **1.2** Land area (1,000 sq. km) **17** GDP ($ billions) **3.7**			

	Country data	Sub-Saharan Africa group	Lower middle-income group
GNI per capita, *World Bank Atlas* method ($)	2,860	1,547	1,965
Adjusted net national income per capita ($)	2,392	1,005	1,574
Change in wealth per capita (2010 $)	-421	-273	117
Urban population (% of total)	21.2	36.8	38.9
Agriculture			
Agricultural land (% land area)	71	44	46
Agricultural irrigated land (% of total agricultural land)	..	..	..
Agricultural productivity, value added per worker (2005 $)	*1,373*	765	938
Cereal yield (kg per hectare)	1,083	1,417	3,029
Forests and biodiversity			
Forest area (% land area)	33.0	27.4	26.9
Deforestation (avg. annual %, 2000-2010)	-0.8	0.5	0.3
Terrestrial protected areas (% of total land area)	3.0	16.4	11.9
Threatened species, mammals	6		
Threatened species, birds	11		
Threatened species, fish	4		
Threatened species, higher plants	11		
Oceans			
Total fisheries production (thousand metric tons)	0.22	6,906	43,067
Capture fisheries growth (avg. annual %, 1990-2012)	..	2.1	2.6
Aquaculture growth (avg. annual %, 1990-2012)	7.5	15.9	9.9
Marine protected areas (% of territorial waters)	10.2	11.7	14.7
Coral reef area (sq. km)	..	17,980	124,480
Mangroves area (sq. km)	..	27,808	58,917
Energy and emissions			
Energy use per capita (kg oil equivalent)	*373*	681	687
Energy from biomass products and waste (% of total)	..	57.6	26.8
Electric power consumption per capita (kWh)	..	535	734
Electricity generated using fossil fuel (% of total)	..	65.1	72.3
Electricity generated by hydropower (% of total)	..	20.0	16.9
CO_2 emissions per capita (metric tons)	0.9	0.8	1.6
Water and sanitation			
Internal freshwater resources per capita (cu. m)	2,178	4,391	3,144
Total freshwater withdrawal (% of internal resources)	39.5	3.2	19.6
Agriculture (% of total freshwater withdrawal)	97	84	88
Access to improved water source (% of total population)	74	64	88
Rural (% of rural population)	69	53	85
Urban (% of urban population)	94	85	94
Access to improved sanitation facilities (% of total population)	57	30	48
Rural (% of rural population)	56	23	36
Urban (% of urban population)	63	41	66
Environment and health			
Particulate matter (urban-pop.-weighted avg., µg/cu. m)	52	77	90
Acute resp. infection prevalence (% of children under five)	8	5	..
Diarrhea prevalence (% of children under five)	13	14	..
Under-five mortality rate (per 1,000 live births)	80	98	61
National accounting aggregates—savings, depletion and degradation			
Gross savings (% of GNI)	8.2	26.3	28.6
Consumption of fixed capital (% of GNI)	13.4	13.0	11.1
Education expenditure (% of GNI)	8.8	3.4	3.1
Energy depletion (% of GNI)	0.0	10.3	4.4
Mineral depletion (% of GNI)	0.0	1.8	1.1
Net forest depletion (% of GNI)	1.4	1.8	0.8
CO_2 damage (% of GNI)	0.3	0.6	0.9
Particulate emissions damage (% of GNI)	0.2	1.2	1.4
Adjusted net savings (% of GNI)	*1.4*	0.9	12.0

Sweden

Population (millions)	**9.5**	Land area (1,000 sq. km)	**410**	GDP ($ billions)	**523.9**

	Country data	High-income group
GNI per capita, *World Bank Atlas* method ($)	56,120	38,444
Adjusted net national income per capita ($)	48,812	32,262
Change in wealth per capita (2010 $)	8,008	2,210
Urban population (% of total)	85.4	80.2
Agriculture		
Agricultural land (% land area)	7	29
Agricultural irrigated land (% of total agricultural land)	2.0	..
Agricultural productivity, value added per worker (2005 $)	38,066	25,238
Cereal yield (kg per hectare)	5,097	4,374
Forests and biodiversity		
Forest area (% land area)	68.7	35.0
Deforestation (avg. annual %, 2000–2010)	-0.3	0.0
Terrestrial protected areas (% of total land area)	14.5	13.9
Threatened species, mammals	1	
Threatened species, birds	4	
Threatened species, fish	12	
Threatened species, higher plants	5	
Oceans		
Total fisheries production (thousand metric tons)	165	37,661
Capture fisheries growth (avg. annual %, 1990–2012)	-2.3	-2.0
Aquaculture growth (avg. annual %, 1990–2012)	1.9	2.5
Marine protected areas (% of territorial waters)	5.3	14.4
Coral reef area (sq. km)	..	82,210
Mangroves area (sq. km)	..	15,504
Energy and emissions		
Energy use per capita (kg oil equivalent)	5,190	4,872
Energy from biomass products and waste (% of total)	20.4	4.3
Electric power consumption per capita (kWh)	14,030	8,896
Electricity generated using fossil fuel (% of total)	2.5	61.8
Electricity generated by hydropower (% of total)	44.2	12.2
CO_2 emissions per capita (metric tons)	5.6	11.6
Water and sanitation		
Internal freshwater resources per capita (cu. m)	18,097	11,335
Total freshwater withdrawal (% of internal resources)	1.5	7.0
Agriculture (% of total freshwater withdrawal)	4	40
Access to improved water source (% of total population)	100	99
Rural (% of rural population)	100	98
Urban (% of urban population)	100	100
Access to improved sanitation facilities (% of total population)	100	96
Rural (% of rural population)	100	93
Urban (% of urban population)	100	97
Environment and health		
Particulate matter (urban-pop.-weighted avg., µg/cu. m)	20	27
Acute resp. infection prevalence (% of children under five)	..	..
Diarrhea prevalence (% of children under five)	..	..
Under-five mortality rate (per 1,000 live births)	3	6
National accounting aggregates—savings, depletion and degradation		
Gross savings (% of GNI)	24.8	20.1
Consumption of fixed capital (% of GNI)	13.2	14.2
Education expenditure (% of GNI)	6.5	4.7
Energy depletion (% of GNI)	0.0	1.6
Mineral depletion (% of GNI)	0.4	0.3
Net forest depletion (% of GNI)	0.0	0.0
CO_2 damage (% of GNI)	0.1	0.3
Particulate emissions damage (% of GNI)	0.1	0.3
Adjusted net savings (% of GNI)	17.5	8.1

Switzerland

| | Population (millions) | **8.0** | Land area (1,000 sq. km) | **40** | GDP ($ billions) | **631.2** |

	Country data	High-Income group
GNI per capita, World Bank Atlas method ($)	80,970	38,444
Adjusted net national income per capita ($)	67,578	32,262
Change in wealth per capita (2010 $)	12,239	2,210
Urban population (% of total)	73.8	80.2

Agriculture

Agricultural land (% land area)	38	29
Agricultural irrigated land (% of total agricultural land)	2.4	..
Agricultural productivity, value added per worker (2005 $)	28,132	25,238
Cereal yield (kg per hectare)	6,271	4,374

Forests and biodiversity

Forest area (% land area)	31.1	35.0
Deforestation (avg. annual %, 2000–2010)	-0.4	0.0
Terrestrial protected areas (% of total land area)	26.3	13.9
Threatened species, mammals	2	
Threatened species, birds	3	
Threatened species, fish	9	
Threatened species, higher plants	4	

Oceans

Total fisheries production (thousand metric tons)	3.2	37,661
Capture fisheries growth (avg. annual %, 1990–2012)	-2.1	-2.0
Aquaculture growth (avg. annual %, 1990–2012)	0.8	2.5
Marine protected areas (% of territorial waters)	0.63	14.4
Coral reef area (sq. km)	..	82,210
Mangroves area (sq. km)	..	15,504

Energy and emissions

Energy use per capita (kg oil equivalent)	3,207	4,872
Energy from biomass products and waste (% of total)	9.0	4.3
Electric power consumption per capita (kWh)	7,928	8,896
Electricity generated using fossil fuel (% of total)	1.7	61.8
Electricity generated by hydropower (% of total)	51.5	12.2
CO_2 emissions per capita (metric tons)	5.0	11.6

Water and sanitation

Internal freshwater resources per capita (cu. m)	5,106	11,335
Total freshwater withdrawal (% of internal resources)	6.5	7.0
Agriculture (% of total freshwater withdrawal)	2	40
Access to improved water source (% of total population)	100	99
Rural (% of rural population)	100	98
Urban (% of urban population)	100	100
Access to improved sanitation facilities (% of total population)	100	96
Rural (% of rural population)	100	93
Urban (% of urban population)	100	97

Environment and health

Particulate matter (urban-pop.-weighted avg., µg/cu. m)	21	27
Acute resp. infection prevalence (% of children under five)	..	..
Diarrhea prevalence (% of children under five)	..	..
Under-five mortality rate (per 1,000 live births)	4	6

National accounting aggregates—savings, depletion and degradation

Gross savings (% of GNI)	31.7	20.1
Consumption of fixed capital (% of GNI)	17.2	14.2
Education expenditure (% of GNI)	4.5	4.7
Energy depletion (% of GNI)	0.0	1.6
Mineral depletion (% of GNI)	0.0	0.3
Net forest depletion (% of GNI)	0.0	0.0
CO_2 damage (% of GNI)	0.1	0.3
Particulate emissions damage (% of GNI)	0.1	0.3
Adjusted net savings (% of GNI)	18.9	8.1

Syrian Arab Republic

Population (millions)	**22.4**	Land area (1,000 sq. km)	**184**	GDP ($ billions)	*40.4*

	Country data	Middle East & N. Africa group	Lower middle-income group
GNI per capita, *World Bank Atlas* method ($)	*1,850*	*3,451*	*1,965*
Adjusted net national income per capita ($)	*1,429*	*2,602*	*1,574*
Change in wealth per capita (2010 $)	..	101	117
Urban population (% of total)	56.5	59.5	38.9
Agriculture			
Agricultural land (% land area)	75	23	46
Agricultural irrigated land (% of total agricultural land)	10.1	..	..
Agricultural productivity, value added per worker (2005 $)	..	2,642	938
Cereal yield (kg per hectare)	1,594	2,350	3,029
Forests and biodiversity			
Forest area (% land area)	2.7	2.4	26.9
Deforestation (avg. annual %, 2000–2010)	-1.3	-0.1	0.3
Terrestrial protected areas (% of total land area)	0.7	6.1	11.9
Threatened species, mammals	16		
Threatened species, birds	15		
Threatened species, fish	33		
Threatened species, higher plants	4		
Oceans			
Total fisheries production (thousand metric tons)	10.2	3,976	43,067
Capture fisheries growth (avg. annual %, 1990–2012)	0.2	3.0	2.6
Aquaculture growth (avg. annual %, 1990–2012)	4.4	12.8	9.9
Marine protected areas (% of territorial waters)	*0.63*	9.1	14.7
Coral reef area (sq. km)	..	5,700	124,480
Mangroves area (sq. km)	..	217	58,917
Energy and emissions			
Energy use per capita (kg oil equivalent)	910	1,376	687
Energy from biomass products and waste (% of total)	0.0	0.9	26.8
Electric power consumption per capita (kWh)	1,715	1,696	734
Electricity generated using fossil fuel (% of total)	92.0	91.7	72.3
Electricity generated by hydropower (% of total)	8.0	5.5	16.9
CO_2 emissions per capita (metric tons)	2.9	3.9	1.6
Water and sanitation			
Internal freshwater resources per capita (cu. m)	325	679	3,144
Total freshwater withdrawal (% of internal resources)	235.0	122.1	19.6
Agriculture (% of total freshwater withdrawal)	88	86	88
Access to improved water source (% of total population)	90	90	88
Rural (% of rural population)	87	83	85
Urban (% of urban population)	92	95	94
Access to improved sanitation facilities (% of total population)	96	88	48
Rural (% of rural population)	95	80	36
Urban (% of urban population)	96	94	66
Environment and health			
Particulate matter (urban-pop.-weighted avg., µg/cu. m)	27	79	90
Acute resp. infection prevalence (% of children under five)	..	..	..
Diarrhea prevalence (% of children under five)	..	..	..
Under-five mortality rate (per 1,000 live births)	15	26	61
National accounting aggregates—savings, depletion and degradation			
Gross savings (% of GNI)	*29.4*	25.9	28.6
Consumption of fixed capital (% of GNI)	*12.0*	9.9	11.1
Education expenditure (% of GNI)	*2.6*	4.5	3.1
Energy depletion (% of GNI)	*17.6*	12.9	4.4
Mineral depletion (% of GNI)	*0.0*	0.5	1.1
Net forest depletion (% of GNI)	*0.0*	0.2	0.8
CO_2 damage (% of GNI)	*1.3*	0.7	0.9
Particulate emissions damage (% of GNI)	*0.3*	0.9	1.4
Adjusted net savings (% of GNI)	*0.9*	5.3	12.0

Tajikistan

| | Population (millions) | 8.0 | Land area (1,000 sq. km) | 140 | GDP ($ billions) | 7.6 |

	Country data	Europe & Central Asia group	Low-Income group
GNI per capita, *World Bank Atlas* method ($)	880	6,658	594
Adjusted net national income per capita ($)	830	5,541	495
Change in wealth per capita (2010 $)	-12	263	-39
Urban population (% of total)	26.6	60.2	28.2

Agriculture

Agricultural land (% of land area)	35	66	39
Agricultural irrigated land (% of total agricultural land)	*14.8*	..	..
Agricultural productivity, value added per worker (2005 $)	1,065	4,866	367
Cereal yield (kg per hectare)	2,657	2,519	1,982

Forests and biodiversity

Forest area (% land area)	2.9	10.5	27.4
Deforestation (avg. annual %, 2000-2010)	0.0	-0.5	0.6
Terrestrial protected areas (% of total land area)	4.8	5.1	13.7
Threatened species, mammals	8		
Threatened species, birds	12		
Threatened species, fish	5		
Threatened species, higher plants	13		

Oceans

Total fisheries production (thousand metric tons)	1.4	1,022	11,789
Capture fisheries growth (avg. annual %, 1990-2012)	5.5	-4.0	3.8
Aquaculture growth (avg. annual %, 1990-2012)	-8.7	1.8	5.1
Marine protected areas (% of territorial waters)	5.1	10.4	13.1
Coral reef area (sq. km)	..	..	15,120
Mangroves area (sq. km)	..	..	25,817

Energy and emissions

Energy use per capita (kg oil equivalent)	306	2,078	360
Energy from biomass products and waste (% of total)	0.0	2.9	66.0
Electric power consumption per capita (kWh)	1,714	2,951	233
Electricity generated using fossil fuel (% of total)	1.2	65.8	30.9
Electricity generated by hydropower (% of total)	98.8	17.9	45.5
CO_2 emissions per capita (metric tons)	0.4	5.3	0.3

Water and sanitation

Internal freshwater resources per capita (cu. m)	8,120	2,744	5,121
Total freshwater withdrawal (% of internal resources)	18.1	34.8	4.4
Agriculture (% of total freshwater withdrawal)	91	70	90
Access to improved water source (% of total population)	72	95	69
Rural (% of rural population)	64	89	61
Urban (% of urban population)	93	99	88
Access to improved sanitation facilities (% of total population)	94	94	37
Rural (% of rural population)	95	90	33
Urban (% of urban population)	94	97	46

Environment and health

Particulate matter (urban-pop.-weighted avg., µg/cu. m)	15	48	74
Acute resp. infection prevalence (% of children under five)	1	..	6
Diarrhea prevalence (% of children under five)	15	..	14
Under-five mortality rate (per 1,000 live births)	58	22	82

National accounting aggregates—savings, depletion and degradation

Gross savings (% of GNI)	18.0	18.9	24.6
Consumption of fixed capital (% of GNI)	11.0	12.4	11.8
Education expenditure (% of GNI)	3.7	3.8	3.2
Energy depletion (% of GNI)	0.3	4.4	1.4
Mineral depletion (% of GNI)	1.0	0.6	1.9
Net forest depletion (% of GNI)	0.1	0.0	4.4
CO_2 damage (% of GNI)	0.4	0.8	0.4
Particulate emissions damage (% of GNI)	0.0	1.8	1.0
Adjusted net savings (% of GNI)	9.0	2.8	7.0

Tanzania

Population (millions)	**47.8**	Land area (1,000 sq. km)	**886**	GDP ($ billions)	**28.2**

	Country data	Sub-Saharan Africa group	Low-Income group
GNI per capita, *World Bank Atlas* method ($)	570	1,547	594
Adjusted net national income per capita ($)	473	1,005	495
Change in wealth per capita (2010 $)	-92	-273	-39
Urban population (% of total)	27.2	36.8	28.2
Agriculture			
Agricultural land (% land area)	42	44	39
Agricultural irrigated land (% of total agricultural land)	..	..	
Agricultural productivity, value added per worker (2005 $)	302	765	367
Cereal yield (kg per hectare)	1,314	1,417	1,982
Forests and biodiversity			
Forest area (% land area)	37.3	27.4	27.4
Deforestation (avg. annual %, 2000–2010)	1.1	0.5	0.6
Terrestrial protected areas (% of total land area)	32.2	16.4	13.7
Threatened species, mammals	35		
Threatened species, birds	44		
Threatened species, fish	175		
Threatened species, higher plants	305		
Oceans			
Total fisheries production (thousand metric tons)	383	6,906	11,789
Capture fisheries growth (avg. annual %, 1990–2012)	-0.5	2.1	3.8
Aquaculture growth (avg. annual %, 1990–2012)	9.4	15.9	5.1
Marine protected areas (% of territorial waters)	30.4	11.7	13.1
Coral reef area (sq. km)	3,580	17,980	15,120
Mangroves area (sq. km)	1,287	27,808	25,817
Energy and emissions			
Energy use per capita (kg oil equivalent)	448	681	360
Energy from biomass products and waste (% of total)	88.2	57.6	66.0
Electric power consumption per capita (kWh)	92	535	233
Electricity generated using fossil fuel (% of total)	50.7	65.1	30.9
Electricity generated by hydropower (% of total)	49.3	20.0	45.5
CO_2 emissions per capita (metric tons)	0.2	0.8	0.3
Water and sanitation			
Internal freshwater resources per capita (cu. m)	1,812	4,391	5,121
Total freshwater withdrawal (% of internal resources)	6.2	3.2	4.4
Agriculture (% of total freshwater withdrawal)	89	84	90
Access to improved water source (% of total population)	53	64	69
Rural (% of rural population)	44	53	61
Urban (% of urban population)	78	85	88
Access to improved sanitation facilities (% of total population)	12	30	37
Rural (% of rural population)	7	23	33
Urban (% of urban population)	25	41	46
Environment and health			
Particulate matter (urban-pop.-weighted avg., µg/cu. m)	62	77	74
Acute resp. infection prevalence (% of children under five)	4	5	6
Diarrhea prevalence (% of children under five)	15	14	14
Under-five mortality rate (per 1,000 live births)	54	98	82
National accounting aggregates—savings, depletion and degradation			
Gross savings (% of GNI)	23.7	26.3	24.6
Consumption of fixed capital (% of GNI)	14.2	13.0	11.8
Education expenditure (% of GNI)	4.8	3.4	3.2
Energy depletion (% of GNI)	0.3	10.3	1.4
Mineral depletion (% of GNI)	4.7	1.8	1.9
Net forest depletion (% of GNI)	0.0	1.8	4.4
CO_2 damage (% of GNI)	0.3	0.6	0.4
Particulate emissions damage (% of GNI)	0.4	1.2	1.0
Adjusted net savings (% of GNI)	8.7	0.9	7.0

Thailand

Population (millions)	**66.8** Land area (1,000 sq. km)	**511** GDP ($ billions)	**366.0**

	Country data	East Asia & Pacific group	Upper middle-income group
GNI per capita, *World Bank Atlas* method ($)	5,210	4,884	6,969
Adjusted net national income per capita ($)	4,336	4,305	5,845
Change in wealth per capita (2010 $)	817	1,172	1,039
Urban population (% of total)	34.5	49.6	60.7
Agriculture			
Agricultural land (% land area)	41	48	44
Agricultural irrigated land (% of total agricultural land)	..	..	..
Agricultural productivity, value added per worker (2005 $)	1,136	794	1,131
Cereal yield (kg per hectare)	3,092	5,145	4,255
Forests and biodiversity			
Forest area (% land area)	37.2	29.7	29.1
Deforestation (avg. annual %, 2000–2010)	0.0	-0.4	0.0
Terrestrial protected areas (% of total land area)	18.8	15.1	16.1
Threatened species, mammals	57		
Threatened species, birds	47		
Threatened species, fish	96		
Threatened species, higher plants	131		
Oceans			
Total fisheries production (thousand metric tons)	3,068	108,399	90,024
Capture fisheries growth (avg. annual %, 1990–2012)	-1.4	3.4	1.5
Aquaculture growth (avg. annual %, 1990–2012)	6.8	9.1	9.1
Marine protected areas (% of territorial waters)	4.4	1.4	7.3
Coral reef area (sq. km)	2,130	137,690	52,070
Mangroves area (sq. km)	2,484	56,537	50,160
Energy and emissions			
Energy use per capita (kg oil equivalent)	1,790	1,671	1,893
Energy from biomass products and waste (% of total)	18.3	10.1	8.5
Electric power consumption per capita (kWh)	2,316	2,582	2,932
Electricity generated using fossil fuel (% of total)	92.0	80.9	74.7
Electricity generated by hydropower (% of total)	5.2	14.5	20.0
CO_2 emissions per capita (metric tons)	4.4	4.9	5.4
Water and sanitation			
Internal freshwater resources per capita (cu. m)	3,372	4,438	6,791
Total freshwater withdrawal (% of internal resources)	25.5	10.9	7.4
Agriculture (% of total freshwater withdrawal)	90	73	69
Access to improved water source (% of total population)	96	91	93
Rural (% of rural population)	95	85	85
Urban (% of urban population)	97	97	98
Access to improved sanitation facilities (% of total population)	93	67	74
Rural (% of rural population)	96	58	62
Urban (% of urban population)	89	76	82
Environment and health			
Particulate matter (urban-pop.-weighted avg., µg/cu. m)	45	75	65
Acute resp. infection prevalence (% of children under five)	..	..	..
Diarrhea prevalence (% of children under five)	..	..	..
Under-five mortality rate (per 1,000 live births)	13	21	20
National accounting aggregates—savings, depletion and degradation			
Gross savings (% of GNI)	31.5	47.6	36.4
Consumption of fixed capital (% of GNI)	13.5	12.0	12.5
Education expenditure (% of GNI)	4.1	2.1	3.2
Energy depletion (% of GNI)	3.2	2.7	4.1
Mineral depletion (% of GNI)	0.0	1.4	1.2
Net forest depletion (% of GNI)	0.8	0.1	0.2
CO_2 damage (% of GNI)	0.9	1.0	0.8
Particulate emissions damage (% of GNI)	0.4	1.6	1.3
Adjusted net savings (% of GNI)	16.7	30.9	19.5

Timor-Leste

| | Population (millions) | **1.2** | Land area (1,000 sq. km) | **15** | GDP ($ billions) | **1.3** |

	Country data	East Asia & Pacific group	Lower middle-income group
GNI per capita, *World Bank Atlas* method ($)	3,620	4,884	1,965
Adjusted net national income per capita ($)	..	4,305	1,574
Change in wealth per capita (2010 $)	..	1,172	117
Urban population (% of total)	28.7	49.6	38.9
Agriculture			
Agricultural land (% land area)	24	48	46
Agricultural irrigated land (% of total agricultural land)	..	..	..
Agricultural productivity, value added per worker (2005 $)	*320*	794	938
Cereal yield (kg per hectare)	2,342	5,145	3,029
Forests and biodiversity			
Forest area (% land area)	49.1	29.7	26.9
Deforestation (avg. annual %, 2000–2010)	1.4	−0.4	0.3
Terrestrial protected areas (% of total land area)	8.7	15.1	11.9
Threatened species, mammals	4		
Threatened species, birds	7		
Threatened species, fish	6		
Threatened species, higher plants	1		
Oceans			
Total fisheries production (thousand metric tons)	4.8	108,399	43,067
Capture fisheries growth (avg. annual %, 1990–2012)	..	3.4	2.6
Aquaculture growth (avg. annual %, 1990–2012)	..	9.1	9.9
Marine protected areas (% of territorial waters)	6.7	1.4	14.7
Coral reef area (sq. km)	..	137,690	124,480
Mangroves area (sq. km)	18.0	56,537	58,917
Energy and emissions			
Energy use per capita (kg oil equivalent)	*58*	1,671	687
Energy from biomass products and waste (% of total)	..	10.1	26.8
Electric power consumption per capita (kWh)	..	2,582	734
Electricity generated using fossil fuel (% of total)	..	80.9	72.3
Electricity generated by hydropower (% of total)	..	14.5	16.9
CO_2 emissions per capita (metric tons)	0.2	4.9	1.6
Water and sanitation			
Internal freshwater resources per capita (cu. m)	6,986	4,438	3,144
Total freshwater withdrawal (% of internal resources)	14.3	10.9	19.6
Agriculture (% of total freshwater withdrawal)	91	73	88
Access to improved water source (% of total population)	70	91	88
Rural (% of rural population)	61	85	85
Urban (% of urban population)	95	97	94
Access to improved sanitation facilities (% of total population)	39	67	48
Rural (% of rural population)	27	58	36
Urban (% of urban population)	69	76	66
Environment and health			
Particulate matter (urban-pop.-weighted avg., µg/cu. m)	..	75	90
Acute resp. infection prevalence (% of children under five)	2	..	..
Diarrhea prevalence (% of children under five)	16	..	..
Under-five mortality rate (per 1,000 live births)	57	21	61
National accounting aggregates—savings, depletion and degradation			
Gross savings (% of GNI)	76.7	47.6	28.6
Consumption of fixed capital (% of GNI)	2.9	12.0	11.1
Education expenditure (% of GNI)	2.0	2.1	3.1
Energy depletion (% of GNI)	0.0	2.7	4.4
Mineral depletion (% of GNI)	0.0	1.4	1.1
Net forest depletion (% of GNI)	0.0	0.1	0.8
CO_2 damage (% of GNI)	0.0	1.0	0.9
Particulate emissions damage (% of GNI)	..	1.6	1.4
Adjusted net savings (% of GNI)	..	30.9	12.0

Togo

	Country data	Sub-Saharan Africa group	Low-income group
GNI per capita, *World Bank Atlas* method ($)	500	1,547	594
Adjusted net national income per capita ($)	377	1,005	495
Change in wealth per capita (2010 $)	-165	-273	-39
Urban population (% of total)	38.5	36.8	28.2

Population (millions) 6.6 Land area (1,000 sq. km) 54 GDP ($ billions) 3.8

Agriculture
Agricultural land (% land area)	68	44	39
Agricultural irrigated land (% of total agricultural land)	..	..	..
Agricultural productivity, value added per worker (2005 $)	563	765	367
Cereal yield (kg per hectare)	1,313	1,417	1,982

Forests and biodiversity
Forest area (% land area)	4.9	27.4	27.4
Deforestation (avg. annual %, 2000–2010)	5.1	0.5	0.6
Terrestrial protected areas (% of total land area)	24.7	16.4	13.7
Threatened species, mammals	10		
Threatened species, birds	9		
Threatened species, fish	24		
Threatened species, higher plants	12		

Oceans
Total fisheries production (thousand metric tons)	19.3	6,906	11,789
Capture fisheries growth (avg. annual %, 1990–2012)	0.9	2.1	3.8
Aquaculture growth (avg. annual %, 1990–2012)	-0.4	15.9	5.1
Marine protected areas (% of territorial waters)	0.14	11.7	13.1
Coral reef area (sq. km)	..	17,980	15,120
Mangroves area (sq. km)	10.9	27,808	25,817

Energy and emissions
Energy use per capita (kg oil equivalent)	427	681	360
Energy from biomass products and waste (% of total)	82.1	57.6	66.0
Electric power consumption per capita (kWh)	104	535	233
Electricity generated using fossil fuel (% of total)	24.5	65.1	30.9
Electricity generated by hydropower (% of total)	74.1	20.0	45.5
CO_2 emissions per capita (metric tons)	0.2	0.8	0.3

Water and sanitation
Internal freshwater resources per capita (cu. m)	1,777	4,391	5,121
Total freshwater withdrawal (% of internal resources)	1.5	3.2	4.4
Agriculture (% of total freshwater withdrawal)	45	84	90
Access to improved water source (% of total population)	61	64	69
Rural (% of rural population)	41	53	61
Urban (% of urban population)	92	85	88
Access to improved sanitation facilities (% of total population)	11	30	37
Rural (% of rural population)	2	23	33
Urban (% of urban population)	25	41	46

Environment and health
Particulate matter (urban-pop.-weighted avg., µg/cu. m)	34	77	74
Acute resp. infection prevalence (% of children under five)	..	5	6
Diarrhea prevalence (% of children under five)	..	14	14
Under-five mortality rate (per 1,000 live births)	96	98	82

National accounting aggregates—savings, depletion and degradation
Gross savings (% of GNI)	0.0	26.3	24.6
Consumption of fixed capital (% of GNI)	15.7	13.0	11.8
Education expenditure (% of GNI)	4.8	3.4	3.2
Energy depletion (% of GNI)	0.0	10.3	1.4
Mineral depletion (% of GNI)	2.2	1.8	1.9
Net forest depletion (% of GNI)	6.9	1.8	4.4
CO_2 damage (% of GNI)	0.6	0.6	0.4
Particulate emissions damage (% of GNI)	0.3	1.2	1.0
Adjusted net savings (% of GNI)	-21.3	0.9	7.0

Tonga

| Population (thousands) **105** | Land area (sq. km) | **720** | GDP ($ millions) | **471.6** |

	Country data	East Asia & Pacific group	Upper middle-income group
GNI per capita, *World Bank Atlas* method ($)	4,220	4,884	6,969
Adjusted net national income per capita ($)	4,092	4,305	5,845
Change in wealth per capita (2010 $)	–82	1,172	1,039
Urban population (% of total)	23.6	49.6	60.7
Agriculture			
Agricultural land (% land area)	43	48	44
Agricultural irrigated land (% of total agricultural land)	..	..	..
Agricultural productivity, value added per worker (2005 $)	3,705	794	1,131
Cereal yield (kg per hectare)	..	5,145	4,255
Forests and biodiversity			
Forest area (% land area)	12.5	29.7	29.1
Deforestation (avg. annual %, 2000–2010)	0.0	-0.4	0.0
Terrestrial protected areas (% of total land area)	15.6	15.1	16.1
Threatened species, mammals	2		
Threatened species, birds	5		
Threatened species, fish	12		
Threatened species, higher plants	4		
Oceans			
Total fisheries production (thousand metric tons)	2.6	108,399	90,024
Capture fisheries growth (avg. annual %, 1990–2012)	1.5	3.4	1.5
Aquaculture growth (avg. annual %, 1990–2012)	..	9.1	9.1
Marine protected areas (% of territorial waters)	3.0	1.4	7.3
Coral reef area (sq. km)	1,500	137,690	52,070
Mangroves area (sq. km)	3.4	56,537	50,160
Energy and emissions			
Energy use per capita (kg oil equivalent)	567	1,671	1,893
Energy from biomass products and waste (% of total)	..	10.1	8.5
Electric power consumption per capita (kWh)	..	2,582	2,932
Electricity generated using fossil fuel (% of total)	..	80.9	74.7
Electricity generated by hydropower (% of total)	..	14.5	20.0
CO_2 emissions per capita (metric tons)	1.5	4.9	5.4
Water and sanitation			
Internal freshwater resources per capita (cu. m)	..	4,438	6,791
Total freshwater withdrawal (% of internal resources)	..	10.9	7.4
Agriculture (% of total freshwater withdrawal)	..	73	69
Access to improved water source (% of total population)	99	91	93
Rural (% of rural population)	99	85	85
Urban (% of urban population)	99	97	98
Access to improved sanitation facilities (% of total population)	91	67	74
Rural (% of rural population)	89	58	62
Urban (% of urban population)	99	76	82
Environment and health			
Particulate matter (urban-pop.-weighted avg., µg/cu. m)	..	75	65
Acute resp. infection prevalence (% of children under five)	..	..	..
Diarrhea prevalence (% of children under five)	..	..	..
Under-five mortality rate (per 1,000 live births)	13	21	20
National accounting aggregates—savings, depletion and degradation			
Gross savings (% of GNI)	5.7	47.6	36.4
Consumption of fixed capital (% of GNI)	11.5	12.0	12.5
Education expenditure (% of GNI)	2.9	2.1	3.2
Energy depletion (% of GNI)	0.0	2.7	4.1
Mineral depletion (% of GNI)	0.0	1.4	1.2
Net forest depletion (% of GNI)	0.1	0.1	0.2
CO_2 damage (% of GNI)	0.3	1.0	0.8
Particulate emissions damage (% of GNI)	..	1.6	1.3
Adjusted net savings (% of GNI)	..	30.9	19.5

Trinidad and Tobago

Population (millions)	**1.3**	Land area (1,000 sq. km)	**5.1**	GDP ($ billions)	**23.3**

	Country data	High-income group
GNI per capita, *World Bank Atlas* method ($)	14,710	38,444
Adjusted net national income per capita ($)	8,444	32,262
Change in wealth per capita (2010 $)	-3,111	2,210
Urban population (% of total)	14.0	80.2

Agriculture

Agricultural land (% of land area)	11	29
Agricultural irrigated land (% of total agricultural land)	..	..
Agricultural productivity, value added per worker (2005 $)	1,968	25,238
Cereal yield (kg per hectare)	3,611	4,374

Forests and biodiversity

Forest area (% land area)	44.0	35.0
Deforestation (avg. annual %, 2000–2010)	0.3	0.0
Terrestrial protected areas (% of total land area)	32.6	13.9
Threatened species, mammals	2	
Threatened species, birds	4	
Threatened species, fish	25	
Threatened species, higher plants	1	

Oceans

Total fisheries production (thousand metric tons)	12.0	37,661
Capture fisheries growth (avg. annual %, 1990–2012)	-0.1	-2.0
Aquaculture growth (avg. annual %, 1990–2012)	13.2	2.5
Marine protected areas (% of territorial waters)	2.5	14.4
Coral reef area (sq. km)	<100	82,210
Mangroves area (sq. km)	65.7	15,504

Energy and emissions

Energy use per capita (kg oil equivalent)	15,691	4,872
Energy from biomass products and waste (% of total)	0.1	4.3
Electric power consumption per capita (kWh)	6,332	8,896
Electricity generated using fossil fuel (% of total)	100.0	61.8
Electricity generated by hydropower (% of total)	0.0	12.2
CO_2 emissions per capita (metric tons)	38.2	11.6

Water and sanitation

Internal freshwater resources per capita (cu. m)	2,881	11,335
Total freshwater withdrawal (% of internal resources)	6.0	7.0
Agriculture (% of total freshwater withdrawal)	9	40
Access to improved water source (% of total population)	94	99
Rural (% of rural population)	93	98
Urban (% of urban population)	97	100
Access to improved sanitation facilities (% of total population)	92	96
Rural (% of rural population)	92	93
Urban (% of urban population)	92	97

Environment and health

Particulate matter (urban-pop.-weighted avg., μg/cu. m)	16	27
Acute resp. infection prevalence (% of children under five)	..	..
Diarrhea prevalence (% of children under five)	..	..
Under-five mortality rate (per 1,000 live births)	21	6

National accounting aggregates—savings, depletion and degradation

Gross savings (% of GNI)	44.6	20.1
Consumption of fixed capital (% of GNI)	14.9	14.2
Education expenditure (% of GNI)	2.9	4.7
Energy depletion (% of GNI)	28.8	1.6
Mineral depletion (% of GNI)	0.0	0.3
Net forest depletion (% of GNI)	0.0	0.0
CO_2 damage (% of GNI)	2.8	0.3
Particulate emissions damage (% of GNI)	0.0	0.3
Adjusted net savings (% of GNI)	-17.6	8.1

Tunisia

	Population (millions)	10.8	Land area (1,000 sq. km)	155	GDP ($ billions)	45.7

	Country data	Middle East & N. Africa group	Upper middle-income group
GNI per capita, *World Bank Atlas* method ($)	4,150	3,451	6,969
Adjusted net national income per capita ($)	3,167	2,602	5,845
Change in wealth per capita (2010 $)	68	101	1,039
Urban population (% of total)	66.5	59.5	60.7
Agriculture			
Agricultural land (% land area)	65	23	44
Agricultural irrigated land (% of total agricultural land)	3.8	..	..
Agricultural productivity, value added per worker (2005 $)	4,115	2,642	1,131
Cereal yield (kg per hectare)	1,674	2,350	4,255
Forests and biodiversity			
Forest area (% land area)	6.6	2.4	29.1
Deforestation (avg. annual %, 2000–2010)	-1.9	-0.1	0.0
Terrestrial protected areas (% of total land area)	5.4	6.1	16.1
Threatened species, mammals	13		
Threatened species, birds	7		
Threatened species, fish	35		
Threatened species, higher plants	7		
Oceans			
Total fisheries production (thousand metric tons)	118	3,976	90,024
Capture fisheries growth (avg. annual %, 1990–2012)	1.0	3.0	1.5
Aquaculture growth (avg. annual %, 1990–2012)	10.1	12.8	9.1
Marine protected areas (% of territorial waters)	2.7	9.1	7.3
Coral reef area (sq. km)	..	5,700	52,070
Mangroves area (sq. km)	..	217	50,160
Energy and emissions			
Energy use per capita (kg oil equivalent)	890	1,376	1,893
Energy from biomass products and waste (% of total)	14.6	0.9	8.5
Electric power consumption per capita (kWh)	1,297	1,696	2,932
Electricity generated using fossil fuel (% of total)	99.0	91.7	74.7
Electricity generated by hydropower (% of total)	0.3	5.5	20.0
CO_2 emissions per capita (metric tons)	2.5	3.9	5.4
Water and sanitation			
Internal freshwater resources per capita (cu. m)	393	679	6,791
Total freshwater withdrawal (% of internal resources)	67.9	122.1	7.4
Agriculture (% of total freshwater withdrawal)	76	86	69
Access to improved water source (% of total population)	97	90	93
Rural (% of rural population)	90	83	85
Urban (% of urban population)	100	95	98
Access to improved sanitation facilities (% of total population)	90	88	74
Rural (% of rural population)	77	80	62
Urban (% of urban population)	97	94	82
Environment and health			
Particulate matter (urban-pop.-weighted avg., µg/cu. m)	79	79	65
Acute resp. infection prevalence (% of children under five)	..	..	..
Diarrhea prevalence (% of children under five)	..	..	..
Under-five mortality rate (per 1,000 live births)	16	26	20
National accounting aggregates—savings, depletion and degradation			
Gross savings (% of GNI)	15.2	25.9	36.4
Consumption of fixed capital (% of GNI)	16.4	9.9	12.5
Education expenditure (% of GNI)	5.9	4.5	3.2
Energy depletion (% of GNI)	3.8	12.9	4.1
Mineral depletion (% of GNI)	1.2	0.5	1.2
Net forest depletion (% of GNI)	0.3	0.2	0.2
CO_2 damage (% of GNI)	0.6	0.7	0.8
Particulate emissions damage (% of GNI)	1.9	0.9	1.3
Adjusted net savings (% of GNI)	-3.2	5.3	19.5

Turkey

	Country data	Europe & Central Asia group	Upper middle-income group
Population (millions) **74.0** Land area (1,000 sq. km) **770** GDP ($ billions) **789.3**			
GNI per capita, *World Bank Atlas* method ($)	10,830	6,658	6,969
Adjusted net national income per capita ($)	9,392	5,541	5,845
Change in wealth per capita (2010 $)	220	263	1,039
Urban population (% of total)	72.3	60.2	60.7
Agriculture			
Agricultural land (% land area)	50	66	44
Agricultural irrigated land (% of total agricultural land)	13.6		
Agricultural productivity, value added per worker (2005 $)	6,598	4,866	1,131
Cereal yield (kg per hectare)	2,956	2,519	4,255
Forests and biodiversity			
Forest area (% land area)	14.9	10.5	29.1
Deforestation (avg. annual %, 2000–2010)	-1.1	-0.5	0.0
Terrestrial protected areas (% of total land area)	2.1	5.1	16.1
Threatened species, mammals	17		
Threatened species, birds	16		
Threatened species, fish	70		
Threatened species, higher plants	10		
Oceans			
Total fisheries production (thousand metric tons)	645	1,022	90,024
Capture fisheries growth (avg. annual %, 1990–2012)	0.6	-4.0	1.5
Aquaculture growth (avg. annual %, 1990–2012)	17.8	1.8	9.1
Marine protected areas (% of territorial waters)	2.4	10.4	7.3
Coral reef area (sq. km)	..	..	52,070
Mangroves area (sq. km)	..	..	50,160
Energy and emissions			
Energy use per capita (kg oil equivalent)	1,539	2,078	1,893
Energy from biomass products and waste (% of total)	3.3	2.9	8.5
Electric power consumption per capita (kWh)	2,709	2,951	2,932
Electricity generated using fossil fuel (% of total)	74.6	65.8	74.7
Electricity generated by hydropower (% of total)	22.8	17.9	20.0
CO_2 emissions per capita (metric tons)	4.1	5.3	5.4
Water and sanitation			
Internal freshwater resources per capita (cu. m)	3,107	2,744	6,791
Total freshwater withdrawal (% of internal resources)	17.7	34.8	7.4
Agriculture (% of total freshwater withdrawal)	74	70	69
Access to improved water source (% of total population)	100	95	93
Rural (% of rural population)	99	89	85
Urban (% of urban population)	100	99	98
Access to improved sanitation facilities (% of total population)	91	94	74
Rural (% of rural population)	75	90	62
Urban (% of urban population)	97	97	82
Environment and health			
Particulate matter (urban-pop.-weighted avg., µg/cu. m)	65	48	65
Acute resp. infection prevalence (% of children under five)	..	..	..
Diarrhea prevalence (% of children under five)	..	..	..
Under-five mortality rate (per 1,000 live births)	14	22	20
National accounting aggregates—savings, depletion and degradation			
Gross savings (% of GNI)	14.6	18.9	36.4
Consumption of fixed capital (% of GNI)	10.8	12.4	12.5
Education expenditure (% of GNI)	2.6	3.8	3.2
Energy depletion (% of GNI)	0.2	4.4	4.1
Mineral depletion (% of GNI)	0.2	0.6	1.2
Net forest depletion (% of GNI)	0.0	0.0	0.2
CO_2 damage (% of GNI)	0.4	0.8	0.8
Particulate emissions damage (% of GNI)	2.3	1.8	1.3
Adjusted net savings (% of GNI)	3.3	2.8	19.5

Turkmenistan

	Country data	Europe & Central Asia group	Upper middle-income group
Population (millions) **5.2** Land area (1,000 sq. km) **470** GDP ($ billions) **35.2**			

	Country data	Europe & Central Asia group	Upper middle-income group
GNI per capita, *World Bank Atlas* method ($)	5,410	6,658	6,969
Adjusted net national income per capita ($)	3,323	5,541	5,845
Change in wealth per capita (2010 $)	..	263	1,039
Urban population (% of total)	49.1	60.2	60.7
Agriculture			
Agricultural land (% land area)	69	66	44
Agricultural irrigated land (% of total agricultural land)	..	..	..
Agricultural productivity, value added per worker (2005 $)	..	4,866	1,131
Cereal yield (kg per hectare)	1,778	2,519	4,255
Forests and biodiversity			
Forest area (% land area)	8.8	10.5	29.1
Deforestation (avg. annual %, 2000–2010)	0.0	-0.5	0.0
Terrestrial protected areas (% of total land area)	3.2	5.1	16.1
Threatened species, mammals	9		
Threatened species, birds	16		
Threatened species, fish	11		
Threatened species, higher plants	4		
Oceans			
Total fisheries production (thousand metric tons)	15.0	1,022	90,024
Capture fisheries growth (avg. annual %, 1990–2012)	-4.6	-4.0	1.5
Aquaculture growth (avg. annual %, 1990–2012)	-20.2	1.8	9.1
Marine protected areas (% of territorial waters)	0.95	10.4	7.3
Coral reef area (sq. km)	..	..	52,070
Mangroves area (sq. km)	..	..	50,160
Energy and emissions			
Energy use per capita (kg oil equivalent)	4,839	2,078	1,893
Energy from biomass products and waste (% of total)	0.0	2.9	8.5
Electric power consumption per capita (kWh)	2,444	2,951	2,932
Electricity generated using fossil fuel (% of total)	100.0	65.8	74.7
Electricity generated by hydropower (% of total)	0.0	17.9	20.0
CO_2 emissions per capita (metric tons)	10.5	5.3	5.4
Water and sanitation			
Internal freshwater resources per capita (cu. m)	275	2,744	6,791
Total freshwater withdrawal (% of internal resources)	1,989.3	34.8	7.4
Agriculture (% of total freshwater withdrawal)	94	70	69
Access to improved water source (% of total population)	71	95	93
Rural (% of rural population)	54	89	85
Urban (% of urban population)	89	99	98
Access to improved sanitation facilities (% of total population)	99	94	74
Rural (% of rural population)	98	90	62
Urban (% of urban population)	100	97	82
Environment and health			
Particulate matter (urban-pop.-weighted avg., µg/cu. m)	21	48	65
Acute resp. infection prevalence (% of children under five)	..	..	..
Diarrhea prevalence (% of children under five)	..	..	..
Under-five mortality rate (per 1,000 live births)	53	22	20
National accounting aggregates—savings, depletion and degradation			
Gross savings (% of GNI)	..	18.9	36.4
Consumption of fixed capital (% of GNI)	13.9	12.4	12.5
Education expenditure (% of GNI)	..	3.8	3.2
Energy depletion (% of GNI)	30.0	4.4	4.1
Mineral depletion (% of GNI)	0.0	0.6	1.2
Net forest depletion (% of GNI)	0.0	0.0	0.2
CO_2 damage (% of GNI)	1.8	0.8	0.8
Particulate emissions damage (% of GNI)	0.3	1.8	1.3
Adjusted net savings (% of GNI)	..	2.8	19.5

Turks and Caicos Islands

Population (thousands) **32** Land area (sq. km) **950** GDP ($ millions) ..

	Country data	High-income group
GNI per capita, *World Bank Atlas* method ($)	..	38,444
Adjusted net national income per capita ($)	..	32,262
Change in wealth per capita (2010 $)	..	2,210
Urban population (% of total)	94.1	80.2

Agriculture

Agricultural land (% land area)	1	29
Agricultural irrigated land (% of total agricultural land)	..	..
Agricultural productivity, value added per worker (2005 $)	..	*25,238*
Cereal yield (kg per hectare)	..	4,374

Forests and biodiversity

Forest area (% land area)	36.2	35.0
Deforestation (avg. annual %, 2000–2010)	0.0	0.0
Terrestrial protected areas (% of total land area)	44.4	13.9
Threatened species, mammals	2	
Threatened species, birds	2	
Threatened species, fish	19	
Threatened species, higher plants	7	

Oceans

Total fisheries production (thousand metric tons)	3.8	37,661
Capture fisheries growth (avg. annual %, 1990–2012)	0.1	-2.0
Aquaculture growth (avg. annual %, 1990–2012)	..	2.5
Marine protected areas (% of territorial waters)	0.33	*14.4*
Coral reef area (sq. km)	730	82,210
Mangroves area (sq. km)	236	15,504

Energy and emissions

Energy use per capita (kg oil equivalent)	..	4,872
Energy from biomass products and waste (% of total)	..	4.3
Electric power consumption per capita (kWh)	..	8,896
Electricity generated using fossil fuel (% of total)	..	61.8
Electricity generated by hydropower (% of total)	..	12.2
CO_2 emissions per capita (metric tons)	5.2	11.6

Water and sanitation

Internal freshwater resources per capita (cu. m)	..	11,335
Total freshwater withdrawal (% of internal resources)	..	7.0
Agriculture (% of total freshwater withdrawal)	..	40
Access to improved water source (% of total population)	..	99
Rural (% of rural population)	..	98
Urban (% of urban population)	..	100
Access to improved sanitation facilities (% of total population)	..	96
Rural (% of rural population)	..	93
Urban (% of urban population)	..	97

Environment and health

Particulate matter (urban-pop.-weighted avg., μg/cu. m)	..	27
Acute resp. infection prevalence (% of children under five)	..	..
Diarrhea prevalence (% of children under five)	..	..
Under-five mortality rate (per 1,000 live births)	..	6

National accounting aggregates—savings, depletion and degradation

Gross savings (% of GNI)	..	20.1
Consumption of fixed capital (% of GNI)	..	14.2
Education expenditure (% of GNI)	..	4.7
Energy depletion (% of GNI)	..	1.6
Mineral depletion (% of GNI)	..	0.3
Net forest depletion (% of GNI)	..	0.0
CO_2 damage (% of GNI)	..	0.3
Particulate emissions damage (% of GNI)	..	0.3
Adjusted net savings (% of GNI)	..	8.1

Tuvalu

	Country data	East Asia & Pacific group	Upper middle-income group
Population (thousands) **10** Land area (sq. km) **30** GDP ($ millions) **39.9**			

	Country data	East Asia & Pacific group	Upper middle-income group
GNI per capita, *World Bank Atlas* method ($)	5,650	4,884	6,969
Adjusted net national income per capita ($)	..	4,305	5,845
Change in wealth per capita (2010 $)	..	1,172	1,039
Urban population (% of total)	51.0	49.6	60.7

Agriculture

Agricultural land (% land area)	60	48	44
Agricultural irrigated land (% of total agricultural land)	..	..	..
Agricultural productivity, value added per worker (2005 $)	5,666	794	1,131
Cereal yield (kg per hectare)	..	5,145	4,255

Forests and biodiversity

Forest area (% land area)	33.3	29.7	29.1
Deforestation (avg. annual %, 2000–2010)	0.0	-0.4	0.0
Terrestrial protected areas (% of total land area)	1.9	15.1	16.1
Threatened species, mammals	1		
Threatened species, birds	1		
Threatened species, fish	10		
Threatened species, higher plants	0		

Oceans

Total fisheries production (thousand metric tons)	14.4	108,399	90,024
Capture fisheries growth (avg. annual %, 1990–2012)	16.3	3.4	1.5
Aquaculture growth (avg. annual %, 1990–2012)	..	9.1	9.1
Marine protected areas (% of territorial waters)			
Coral reef area (sq. km)	710	137,690	52,070
Mangroves area (sq. km)	0.40	56,537	50,160

Energy and emissions

Energy use per capita (kg oil equivalent)	..	1,671	1,893
Energy from biomass products and waste (% of total)	..	10.1	8.5
Electric power consumption per capita (kWh)	..	2,582	2,932
Electricity generated using fossil fuel (% of total)	..	80.9	74.7
Electricity generated by hydropower (% of total)	..	14.5	20.0
CO_2 emissions per capita (metric tons)	..	4.9	5.4

Water and sanitation

Internal freshwater resources per capita (cu. m)	..	4,438	6,791
Total freshwater withdrawal (% of internal resources)	..	10.9	7.4
Agriculture (% of total freshwater withdrawal)	..	73	69
Access to improved water source (% of total population)	98	91	93
Rural (% of rural population)	97	85	85
Urban (% of urban population)	98	97	98
Access to improved sanitation facilities (% of total population)	83	67	74
Rural (% of rural population)	80	58	62
Urban (% of urban population)	86	76	82

Environment and health

Particulate matter (urban-pop.-weighted avg., µg/cu. m)	..	75	65
Acute resp. infection prevalence (% of children under five)	..	..	..
Diarrhea prevalence (% of children under five)	..	..	..
Under-five mortality rate (per 1,000 live births)	30	21	20

National accounting aggregates—savings, depletion and degradation

Gross savings (% of GNI)	..	47.6	36.4
Consumption of fixed capital (% of GNI)	7.9	12.0	12.5
Education expenditure (% of GNI)	..	2.1	3.2
Energy depletion (% of GNI)	0.0	2.7	4.1
Mineral depletion (% of GNI)	0.0	1.4	1.2
Net forest depletion (% of GNI)	..	0.1	0.2
CO_2 damage (% of GNI)	..	1.0	0.8
Particulate emissions damage (% of GNI)	..	1.6	1.3
Adjusted net savings (% of GNI)	..	30.9	19.5

Uganda

	Country data	Sub-Saharan Africa group	Low-income group
Population (millions) **36.3** Land area (1,000 sq. km) **200** GDP ($ billions) **20.0**			

	Country data	Sub-Saharan Africa group	Low-income group
GNI per capita, *World Bank Atlas* method ($)	480	1,547	594
Adjusted net national income per capita ($)	392	1,005	495
Change in wealth per capita (2010 $)	-193	-273	-39
Urban population (% of total)	16.0	36.8	28.2
Agriculture			
Agricultural land (% land area)	70	44	39
Agricultural irrigated land (% of total agricultural land)	..	..	..
Agricultural productivity, value added per worker (2005 $)	213	765	367
Cereal yield (kg per hectare)	2,029	1,417	1,982
Forests and biodiversity			
Forest area (% land area)	14.5	27.4	27.4
Deforestation (avg. annual %, 2000–2010)	2.6	0.5	0.6
Terrestrial protected areas (% of total land area)	11.5	16.4	13.7
Threatened species, mammals	22		
Threatened species, birds	22		
Threatened species, fish	61		
Threatened species, higher plants	41		
Oceans			
Total fisheries production (thousand metric tons)	504	6,906	11,789
Capture fisheries growth (avg. annual %, 1990–2012)	2.3	2.1	3.8
Aquaculture growth (avg. annual %, 1990–2012)	40.7	15.9	5.1
Marine protected areas (% of territorial waters)	10.7	11.7	13.1
Coral reef area (sq. km)	..	17,980	15,120
Mangroves area (sq. km)	..	27,808	25,817
Energy and emissions			
Energy use per capita (kg oil equivalent)	..	681	360
Energy from biomass products and waste (% of total)	..	57.6	66.0
Electric power consumption per capita (kWh)	..	535	233
Electricity generated using fossil fuel (% of total)	..	65.1	30.9
Electricity generated by hydropower (% of total)	..	20.0	45.5
CO_2 emissions per capita (metric tons)	0.1	0.8	0.3
Water and sanitation			
Internal freshwater resources per capita (cu. m)	1,110	4,391	5,121
Total freshwater withdrawal (% of internal resources)	0.8	3.2	4.4
Agriculture (% of total freshwater withdrawal)	38	84	90
Access to improved water source (% of total population)	75	64	69
Rural (% of rural population)	71	53	61
Urban (% of urban population)	95	85	88
Access to improved sanitation facilities (% of total population)	34	30	37
Rural (% of rural population)	34	23	33
Urban (% of urban population)	33	41	46
Environment and health			
Particulate matter (urban-pop.-weighted avg., µg/cu. m)	29	77	74
Acute resp. infection prevalence (% of children under five)	15	5	6
Diarrhea prevalence (% of children under five)	23	14	14
Under-five mortality rate (per 1,000 live births)	69	98	82
National accounting aggregates—savings, depletion and degradation			
Gross savings (% of GNI)	13.1	26.3	24.6
Consumption of fixed capital (% of GNI)	14.7	13.0	11.8
Education expenditure (% of GNI)	3.1	3.4	3.2
Energy depletion (% of GNI)	0.0	10.3	1.4
Mineral depletion (% of GNI)	0.0	1.8	1.9
Net forest depletion (% of GNI)	12.4	1.8	4.4
CO_2 damage (% of GNI)	0.2	0.6	0.4
Particulate emissions damage (% of GNI)	0.1	1.2	1.0
Adjusted net savings (% of GNI)	-11.2	0.9	7.0

Ukraine

	Country data	Europe & Central Asia group	Lower middle-income group
Population (millions) **45.6** Land area (1,000 sq. km) **579** GDP ($ billions) **176.3**			
GNI per capita, *World Bank Atlas* method ($)	3,500	6,658	1,965
Adjusted net national income per capita ($)	3,250	5,541	1,574
Change in wealth per capita (2010 $)	352	263	117
Urban population (% of total)	69.1	60.2	38.9
Agriculture			
Agricultural land (% land area)	71	66	46
Agricultural irrigated land (% of total agricultural land)	5.3	..	..
Agricultural productivity, value added per worker (2005 $)	4,375	4,866	938
Cereal yield (kg per hectare)	3,169	2,519	3,029
Forests and biodiversity			
Forest area (% land area)	16.8	10.5	26.9
Deforestation (avg. annual %, 2000–2010)	-0.2	-0.5	0.3
Terrestrial protected areas (% of total land area)	4.0	5.1	11.9
Threatened species, mammals	11		
Threatened species, birds	14		
Threatened species, fish	21		
Threatened species, higher plants	17		
Oceans			
Total fisheries production (thousand metric tons)	178	1,022	43,067
Capture fisheries growth (avg. annual %, 1990–2012)	-7.6	-4.0	2.6
Aquaculture growth (avg. annual %, 1990–2012)	-5.5	1.8	9.9
Marine protected areas (% of territorial waters)	9.2	10.4	14.7
Coral reef area (sq. km)	..	..	124,480
Mangroves area (sq. km)	..	..	58,917
Energy and emissions			
Energy use per capita (kg oil equivalent)	2,766	2,078	687
Energy from biomass products and waste (% of total)	1.2	2.9	26.8
Electric power consumption per capita (kWh)	3,662	2,951	734
Electricity generated using fossil fuel (% of total)	48.0	65.8	72.3
Electricity generated by hydropower (% of total)	5.6	17.9	16.9
CO_2 emissions per capita (metric tons)	6.6	5.3	1.6
Water and sanitation			
Internal freshwater resources per capita (cu. m)	1,162	2,744	3,144
Total freshwater withdrawal (% of internal resources)	72.5	34.8	19.6
Agriculture (% of total freshwater withdrawal)	51	70	88
Access to improved water source (% of total population)	98	95	88
Rural (% of rural population)	98	89	85
Urban (% of urban population)	98	99	94
Access to improved sanitation facilities (% of total population)	94	94	48
Rural (% of rural population)	89	90	36
Urban (% of urban population)	96	97	66
Environment and health			
Particulate matter (urban-pop.-weighted avg., μg/cu. m)	47	48	90
Acute resp. infection prevalence (% of children under five)	..	..	..
Diarrhea prevalence (% of children under five)	..	..	..
Under-five mortality rate (per 1,000 live births)	11	22	61
National accounting aggregates—savings, depletion and degradation			
Gross savings (% of GNI)	9.4	18.9	28.6
Consumption of fixed capital (% of GNI)	11.9	12.4	11.1
Education expenditure (% of GNI)	5.9	3.8	3.1
Energy depletion (% of GNI)	2.6	4.4	4.4
Mineral depletion (% of GNI)	0.0	0.6	1.1
Net forest depletion (% of GNI)	0.1	0.0	0.8
CO_2 damage (% of GNI)	1.8	0.8	0.9
Particulate emissions damage (% of GNI)	2.7	1.8	1.4
Adjusted net savings (% of GNI)	-3.7	2.8	12.0

United Arab Emirates

Population (millions)	**9.2**	Land area (1,000 sq. km)	**84**	GDP ($ billions)	**383.8**

	Country data	High-income group
GNI per capita, *World Bank Atlas* method ($)	38,620	38,444
Adjusted net national income per capita ($)	29,424	32,262
Change in wealth per capita (2010 $)	..	2,210
Urban population (% of total)	84.6	80.2

Agriculture

Agricultural land (% land area)	5	29
Agricultural irrigated land (% of total agricultural land)	19.1	..
Agricultural productivity, value added per worker (2005 $)	12,146	25,238
Cereal yield (kg per hectare)	73,200	4,374

Forests and biodiversity

Forest area (% land area)	3.8	35.0
Deforestation (avg. annual %, 2000–2010)	-0.2	0.0
Terrestrial protected areas (% of total land area)	18.1	13.9
Threatened species, mammals	8	
Threatened species, birds	9	
Threatened species, fish	14	
Threatened species, higher plants	0	

Oceans

Total fisheries production (thousand metric tons)	75.3	37,661
Capture fisheries growth (avg. annual %, 1990–2012)	-1.1	-2.0
Aquaculture growth (avg. annual %, 1990–2012)	..	2.5
Marine protected areas (% of territorial waters)	16.6	14.4
Coral reef area (sq. km)	1,190	82,210
Mangroves area (sq. km)	68.2	15,504

Energy and emissions

Energy use per capita (kg oil equivalent)	7,407	4,872
Energy from biomass products and waste (% of total)	0.1	4.3
Electric power consumption per capita (kWh)	9,389	8,896
Electricity generated using fossil fuel (% of total)	100.0	61.8
Electricity generated by hydropower (% of total)	0.0	12.2
CO_2 emissions per capita (metric tons)	19.9	11.6

Water and sanitation

Internal freshwater resources per capita (cu. m)	17	11,335
Total freshwater withdrawal (% of internal resources)	2,665.3	7.0
Agriculture (% of total freshwater withdrawal)	83	40
Access to improved water source (% of total population)	100	99
Rural (% of rural population)	100	98
Urban (% of urban population)	100	100
Access to improved sanitation facilities (% of total population)	98	96
Rural (% of rural population)	95	93
Urban (% of urban population)	98	97

Environment and health

Particulate matter (urban-pop.-weighted avg., µg/cu. m)	132	27
Acute resp. infection prevalence (% of children under five)	..	..
Diarrhea prevalence (% of children under five)	..	..
Under-five mortality rate (per 1,000 live births)	8	6

National accounting aggregates—savings, depletion and degradation

Gross savings (% of GNI)	..	20.1
Consumption of fixed capital (% of GNI)	14.6	14.2
Education expenditure (% of GNI)	..	4.7
Energy depletion (% of GNI)	14.9	1.6
Mineral depletion (% of GNI)	0.0	0.3
Net forest depletion (% of GNI)	0.0	0.0
CO_2 damage (% of GNI)	0.6	0.3
Particulate emissions damage (% of GNI)	0.6	0.3
Adjusted net savings (% of GNI)	..	8.1

United Kingdom

Population (millions)	**63.6**	Land area (1,000 sq. km)	**242** GDP ($ billions) **2,475.8**

	Country data	High-income group
GNI per capita, *World Bank Atlas* method ($)	38,500	38,444
Adjusted net national income per capita ($)	33,658	32,262
Change in wealth per capita (2010 $)	1,283	2,210
Urban population (% of total)	79.8	80.2
Agriculture		
Agricultural land (% land area)	71	29
Agricultural irrigated land (% of total agricultural land)	..	
Agricultural productivity, value added per worker (2005 $)	28,466	25,238
Cereal yield (kg per hectare)	6,213	4,374
Forests and biodiversity		
Forest area (% land area)	11.9	35.0
Deforestation (avg. annual %, 2000–2010)	-0.3	0.0
Terrestrial protected areas (% of total land area)	27.9	13.9
Threatened species, mammals	5	
Threatened species, birds	4	
Threatened species, fish	43	
Threatened species, higher plants	15	
Oceans		
Total fisheries production (thousand metric tons)	834	37,661
Capture fisheries growth (avg. annual %, 1990–2012)	-0.9	-2.0
Aquaculture growth (avg. annual %, 1990–2012)	6.6	2.5
Marine protected areas (% of territorial waters)	18.2	14.4
Coral reef area (sq. km)	..	82,210
Mangroves area (sq. km)	..	15,504
Energy and emissions		
Energy use per capita (kg oil equivalent)	2,973	4,872
Energy from biomass products and waste (% of total)	3.3	4.3
Electric power consumption per capita (kWh)	5,472	8,896
Electricity generated using fossil fuel (% of total)	71.3	61.8
Electricity generated by hydropower (% of total)	1.6	12.2
CO_2 emissions per capita (metric tons)	7.9	11.6
Water and sanitation		
Internal freshwater resources per capita (cu. m)	2,292	11,335
Total freshwater withdrawal (% of internal resources)	9.0	7.0
Agriculture (% of total freshwater withdrawal)	10	40
Access to improved water source (% of total population)	100	99
Rural (% of rural population)	100	98
Urban (% of urban population)	100	100
Access to improved sanitation facilities (% of total population)	100	96
Rural (% of rural population)	100	93
Urban (% of urban population)	100	97
Environment and health		
Particulate matter (urban-pop.-weighted avg., µg/cu. m)	20	27
Acute resp. infection prevalence (% of children under five)	..	..
Diarrhea prevalence (% of children under five)	..	..
Under-five mortality rate (per 1,000 live births)	5	6
National accounting aggregates—savings, depletion and degradation		
Gross savings (% of GNI)	10.9	20.1
Consumption of fixed capital (% of GNI)	12.3	14.2
Education expenditure (% of GNI)	5.8	4.7
Energy depletion (% of GNI)	1.0	1.6
Mineral depletion (% of GNI)	0.0	0.3
Net forest depletion (% of GNI)	0.0	0.0
CO_2 damage (% of GNI)	0.2	0.3
Particulate emissions damage (% of GNI)	0.2	0.3
Adjusted net savings (% of GNI)	3.0	8.1

United States

Population (millions) **313.9** Land area (1,000 sq. km) **9,147** GDP ($ billions) **16,244.6**

	Country data	High-income group
GNI per capita, *World Bank Atlas* method ($)	52,340	38,444
Adjusted net national income per capita ($)	45,590	32,262
Change in wealth per capita (2010 $)	1,991	2,210
Urban population (% of total)	82.6	80.2

Agriculture

Agricultural land (% land area)	45	29
Agricultural irrigated land (% of total agricultural land)	..	..
Agricultural productivity, value added per worker (2005 $)	*49,817*	*25,238*
Cereal yield (kg per hectare)	5,922	4,374

Forests and biodiversity

Forest area (% land area)	33.3	35.0
Deforestation (avg. annual %, 2000–2010)	–0.1	0.0
Terrestrial protected areas (% of total land area)	13.8	13.9
Threatened species, mammals	36	
Threatened species, birds	78	
Threatened species, fish	236	
Threatened species, higher plants	270	

Oceans

Total fisheries production (thousand metric tons)	5,558	37,661
Capture fisheries growth (avg. annual %, 1990–2012)	–0.4	–2.0
Aquaculture growth (avg. annual %, 1990–2012)	1.3	2.5
Marine protected areas (% of territorial waters)	2.0	*14.4*
Coral reef area (sq. km)	1,250	82,210
Mangroves area (sq. km)	3,030	15,504

Energy and emissions

Energy use per capita (kg oil equivalent)	7,032	4,872
Energy from biomass products and waste (% of total)	4.2	4.3
Electric power consumption per capita (kWh)	13,246	8,896
Electricity generated using fossil fuel (% of total)	68.4	61.8
Electricity generated by hydropower (% of total)	7.4	12.2
CO_2 emissions per capita (metric tons)	17.6	11.6

Water and sanitation

Internal freshwater resources per capita (cu. m)	9,044	11,335
Total freshwater withdrawal (% of internal resources)	17.0	7.0
Agriculture (% of total freshwater withdrawal)	40	40
Access to improved water source (% of total population)	99	99
Rural (% of rural population)	98	98
Urban (% of urban population)	99	100
Access to improved sanitation facilities (% of total population)	100	96
Rural (% of rural population)	100	93
Urban (% of urban population)	100	97

Environment and health

Particulate matter (urban-pop.-weighted avg., µg/cu. m)	18	27
Acute resp. infection prevalence (% of children under five)	..	..
Diarrhea prevalence (% of children under five)	..	..
Under-five mortality rate (per 1,000 live births)	7	6

National accounting aggregates—savings, depletion and degradation

Gross savings (% of GNI)	16.3	20.1
Consumption of fixed capital (% of GNI)	12.5	14.2
Education expenditure (% of GNI)	4.8	4.7
Energy depletion (% of GNI)	0.7	1.6
Mineral depletion (% of GNI)	0.1	0.3
Net forest depletion (% of GNI)	0.0	0.0
CO_2 damage (% of GNI)	0.3	0.3
Particulate emissions damage (% of GNI)	0.1	0.3
Adjusted net savings (% of GNI)	7.2	8.1

Uruguay

	Population (millions)	**3.4**	Land area (1,000 sq. km)	**175**	GDP ($ billions)	**49.9**

	Country data	High-income group
GNI per capita, *World Bank Atlas* method ($)	13,580	38,444
Adjusted net national income per capita ($)	12,101	32,262
Change in wealth per capita (2010 $)	160	2,210
Urban population (% of total)	92.6	80.2
Agriculture		
Agricultural land (% land area)	82	29
Agricultural irrigated land (% of total agricultural land)	1.4	..
Agricultural productivity, value added per worker (2005 $)	9,371	25,238
Cereal yield (kg per hectare)	4,252	4,374
Forests and biodiversity		
Forest area (% land area)	10.2	35.0
Deforestation (avg. annual %, 2000–2010)	-2.1	0.0
Terrestrial protected areas (% of total land area)	2.7	13.9
Threatened species, mammals	10	
Threatened species, birds	24	
Threatened species, fish	38	
Threatened species, higher plants	22	
Oceans		
Total fisheries production (thousand metric tons)	76.3	37,661
Capture fisheries growth (avg. annual %, 1990–2012)	-0.8	-2.0
Aquaculture growth (avg. annual %, 1990–2012)	16.8	2.5
Marine protected areas (% of territorial waters)	0.33	14.4
Coral reef area (sq. km)	..	82,210
Mangroves area (sq. km)	..	15,504
Energy and emissions		
Energy use per capita (kg oil equivalent)	1,309	4,872
Energy from biomass products and waste (% of total)	29.3	4.3
Electric power consumption per capita (kWh)	2,810	8,896
Electricity generated using fossil fuel (% of total)	28.1	61.8
Electricity generated by hydropower (% of total)	62.6	12.2
CO_2 emissions per capita (metric tons)	2.0	11.6
Water and sanitation		
Internal freshwater resources per capita (cu. m)	17,438	11,335
Total freshwater withdrawal (% of internal resources)	6.2	7.0
Agriculture (% of total freshwater withdrawal)	87	40
Access to improved water source (% of total population)	99	99
Rural (% of rural population)	95	98
Urban (% of urban population)	100	100
Access to improved sanitation facilities (% of total population)	96	96
Rural (% of rural population)	96	93
Urban (% of urban population)	96	97
Environment and health		
Particulate matter (urban-pop.-weighted avg., µg/cu. m)	33	27
Acute resp. infection prevalence (% of children under five)	..	..
Diarrhea prevalence (% of children under five)	..	..
Under-five mortality rate (per 1,000 live births)	7	6
National accounting aggregates—savings, depletion and degradation		
Gross savings (% of GNI)	15.5	20.1
Consumption of fixed capital (% of GNI)	13.6	14.2
Education expenditure (% of GNI)	2.3	4.7
Energy depletion (% of GNI)	0.0	1.6
Mineral depletion (% of GNI)	0.1	0.3
Net forest depletion (% of GNI)	1.5	0.0
CO_2 damage (% of GNI)	0.2	0.3
Particulate emissions damage (% of GNI)	0.8	0.3
Adjusted net savings (% of GNI)	1.6	8.1

Uzbekistan

	Country data	Europe & Central Asia group	Lower middle-income group
Population (millions) **29.8** Land area (1,000 sq. km) **425** GDP ($ billions) **51.1**			

	Country data	Europe & Central Asia group	Lower middle-income group
GNI per capita, World Bank Atlas method ($)	1,720	6,658	1,965
Adjusted net national income per capita ($)	1,312	5,541	1,574
Change in wealth per capita (2010 $)	..	263	117
Urban population (% of total)	36.3	60.2	38.9
Agriculture			
Agricultural land (% land area)	63	66	46
Agricultural irrigated land (% of total agricultural land)	..	..	..
Agricultural productivity, value added per worker (2005 $)	2,024	4,866	938
Cereal yield (kg per hectare)	4,435	2,519	3,029
Forests and biodiversity			
Forest area (% land area)	7.7	10.5	26.9
Deforestation (avg. annual %, 2000–2010)	-0.2	-0.5	0.3
Terrestrial protected areas (% of total land area)	3.4	5.1	11.9
Threatened species, mammals	10		
Threatened species, birds	16		
Threatened species, fish	7		
Threatened species, higher plants	17		
Oceans			
Total fisheries production (thousand metric tons)	10.7	1,022	43,067
Capture fisheries growth (avg. annual %, 1990–2012)	-0.8	-4.0	2.6
Aquaculture growth (avg. annual %, 1990–2012)	-5.3	1.8	9.9
Marine protected areas (% of territorial waters)	0.04	10.4	14.7
Coral reef area (sq. km)	..	..	124,480
Mangroves area (sq. km)	..	..	58,917
Energy and emissions			
Energy use per capita (kg oil equivalent)	1,628	2,078	687
Energy from biomass products and waste (% of total)	0.0	2.9	26.8
Electric power consumption per capita (kWh)	1,626	2,951	734
Electricity generated using fossil fuel (% of total)	80.5	65.8	72.3
Electricity generated by hydropower (% of total)	19.5	17.9	16.9
CO_2 emissions per capita (metric tons)	3.7	5.3	1.6
Water and sanitation			
Internal freshwater resources per capita (cu. m)	557	2,744	3,144
Total freshwater withdrawal (% of internal resources)	342.7	34.8	19.6
Agriculture (% of total freshwater withdrawal)	90	70	88
Access to improved water source (% of total population)	87	95	88
Rural (% of rural population)	81	89	85
Urban (% of urban population)	98	99	94
Access to improved sanitation facilities (% of total population)	100	94	48
Rural (% of rural population)	100	90	36
Urban (% of urban population)	100	97	66
Environment and health			
Particulate matter (urban-pop.-weighted avg., µg/cu. m)	35	48	90
Acute resp. infection prevalence (% of children under five)	..	..	..
Diarrhea prevalence (% of children under five)	..	..	..
Under-five mortality rate (per 1,000 live births)	40	22	61
National accounting aggregates—savings, depletion and degradation			
Gross savings (% of GNI)	..	18.9	28.6
Consumption of fixed capital (% of GNI)	12.7	12.4	11.1
Education expenditure (% of GNI)	9.4	3.8	3.1
Energy depletion (% of GNI)	7.7	4.4	4.4
Mineral depletion (% of GNI)	5.8	0.6	1.1
Net forest depletion (% of GNI)	0.0	0.0	0.8
CO_2 damage (% of GNI)	1.9	0.8	0.9
Particulate emissions damage (% of GNI)	0.5	1.8	1.4
Adjusted net savings (% of GNI)	..	2.8	12.0

Vanuatu

	Country data	East Asia & Pacific group	Lower middle-income group
Population (thousands) **247**	Land area (1,000 sq. km) **12**	GDP ($ millions)	**787.1**

	Country data	East Asia & Pacific group	Lower middle-income group
GNI per capita, *World Bank Atlas* method ($)	3,000	4,884	1,965
Adjusted net national income per capita ($)	2,582	4,305	1,574
Change in wealth per capita (2010 $)	78	1,172	117
Urban population (% of total)	25.2	49.6	38.9
Agriculture			
Agricultural land (% land area)	15	48	46
Agricultural irrigated land (% of total agricultural land)	..	..	..
Agricultural productivity, value added per worker (2005 $)	2,775	794	938
Cereal yield (kg per hectare)	571	5,145	3,029
Forests and biodiversity			
Forest area (% land area)	36.1	29.7	26.9
Deforestation (avg. annual %, 2000–2010)	0.0	–0.4	0.3
Terrestrial protected areas (% of total land area)	4.2	15.1	11.9
Threatened species, mammals	7		
Threatened species, birds	9		
Threatened species, fish	15		
Threatened species, higher plants	10		
Oceans			
Total fisheries production (thousand metric tons)	60.3	108,399	43,067
Capture fisheries growth (avg. annual %, 1990–2012)	1.7	3.4	2.6
Aquaculture growth (avg. annual %, 1990–2012)	..	9.1	9.9
Marine protected areas (% of territorial waters)	16.0	1.4	14.7
Coral reef area (sq. km)	4,110	137,690	124,480
Mangroves area (sq. km)	20.5	56,537	58,917
Energy and emissions			
Energy use per capita (kg oil equivalent)	*159*	1,671	687
Energy from biomass products and waste (% of total)	..	10.1	26.8
Electric power consumption per capita (kWh)	..	2,582	734
Electricity generated using fossil fuel (% of total)	..	80.9	72.3
Electricity generated by hydropower (% of total)	..	14.5	16.9
CO_2 emissions per capita (metric tons)	0.5	4.9	1.6
Water and sanitation			
Internal freshwater resources per capita (cu. m)	..	4,438	3,144
Total freshwater withdrawal (% of internal resources)	..	10.9	19.6
Agriculture (% of total freshwater withdrawal)	..	73	88
Access to improved water source (% of total population)	91	91	88
Rural (% of rural population)	88	85	85
Urban (% of urban population)	98	97	94
Access to improved sanitation facilities (% of total population)	58	67	48
Rural (% of rural population)	55	58	36
Urban (% of urban population)	65	76	66
Environment and health			
Particulate matter (urban-pop.-weighted avg., µg/cu. m)	23	75	90
Acute resp. infection prevalence (% of children under five)	..	..	..
Diarrhea prevalence (% of children under five)	..	..	..
Under-five mortality rate (per 1,000 live births)	18	21	61
National accounting aggregates—savings, depletion and degradation			
Gross savings (% of GNI)	*19.8*	47.6	28.6
Consumption of fixed capital (% of GNI)	14.5	12.0	11.1
Education expenditure (% of GNI)	5.0	2.1	3.1
Energy depletion (% of GNI)	0.0	2.7	4.4
Mineral depletion (% of GNI)	0.0	1.4	1.1
Net forest depletion (% of GNI)	0.0	0.1	0.8
CO_2 damage (% of GNI)	0.2	1.0	0.9
Particulate emissions damage (% of GNI)	0.1	1.6	1.4
Adjusted net savings (% of GNI)	*10.5*	30.9	12.0

Venezuela, RB

	Country data	Latin America & Caribbean group	Upper middle-income group
Population (millions) **30.0** Land area (1,000 sq. km) **882** GDP ($ billions) **381.3**			

	Country data	Latin America & Caribbean group	Upper middle-income group
GNI per capita, *World Bank Atlas* method ($)	12,460	9,070	6,969
Adjusted net national income per capita ($)	9,361	7,325	5,845
Change in wealth per capita (2010 $)	456	180	1,039
Urban population (% of total)	93.7	79.0	60.7
Agriculture			
Agricultural land (% land area)	24	37	44
Agricultural irrigated land (% of total agricultural land)	..	..	..
Agricultural productivity, value added per worker (2005 $)	9,210	4,135	1,131
Cereal yield (kg per hectare)	4,074	4,082	4,255
Forests and biodiversity			
Forest area (% land area)	52.1	48.1	29.1
Deforestation (avg. annual %, 2000–2010)	0.6	0.5	0.0
Terrestrial protected areas (% of total land area)	53.0	21.4	16.1
Threatened species, mammals	34		
Threatened species, birds	40		
Threatened species, fish	37		
Threatened species, higher plants	77		
Oceans			
Total fisheries production (thousand metric tons)	239	10,964	90,024
Capture fisheries growth (avg. annual %, 1990–2012)	-2.0	-0.6	1.5
Aquaculture growth (avg. annual %, 1990–2012)	18.4	10.8	9.1
Marine protected areas (% of territorial waters)	1.7	9.0	7.3
Coral reef area (sq. km)	480	14,860	52,070
Mangroves area (sq. km)	3,569	39,988	50,160
Energy and emissions			
Energy use per capita (kg oil equivalent)	2,380	1,292	1,893
Energy from biomass products and waste (% of total)	0.9	16.0	8.5
Electric power consumption per capita (kWh)	3,313	1,985	2,932
Electricity generated using fossil fuel (% of total)	31.5	37.3	74.7
Electricity generated by hydropower (% of total)	68.5	55.1	20.0
CO_2 emissions per capita (metric tons)	6.9	2.7	5.4
Water and sanitation			
Internal freshwater resources per capita (cu. m)	24,488	21,735	6,791
Total freshwater withdrawal (% of internal resources)	1.3	2.0	7.4
Agriculture (% of total freshwater withdrawal)	44	68	69
Access to improved water source (% of total population)	..	94	93
Rural (% of rural population)	..	82	85
Urban (% of urban population)	..	97	98
Access to improved sanitation facilities (% of total population)	..	81	74
Rural (% of rural population)	..	62	62
Urban (% of urban population)	..	86	82
Environment and health			
Particulate matter (urban-pop.-weighted avg., μg/cu. m)	38	43	65
Acute resp. infection prevalence (% of children under five)	..	..	..
Diarrhea prevalence (% of children under five)	..	..	..
Under-five mortality rate (per 1,000 live births)	15	19	20
National accounting aggregates—savings, depletion and degradation			
Gross savings (% of GNI)	26.3	19.0	36.4
Consumption of fixed capital (% of GNI)	6.0	12.2	12.5
Education expenditure (% of GNI)	5.8	5.1	3.2
Energy depletion (% of GNI)	17.9	4.7	4.1
Mineral depletion (% of GNI)	0.5	1.2	1.2
Net forest depletion (% of GNI)	0.0	0.4	0.2
CO_2 damage (% of GNI)	0.6	0.3	0.8
Particulate emissions damage (% of GNI)	0.6	0.8	1.3
Adjusted net savings (% of GNI)	6.5	4.5	19.5

Vietnam

Population (millions)	**88.8**	Land area (1,000 sq. km)	**310**	GDP ($ billions)	**155.8**

	Country data	East Asia & Pacific group	Lower middle-income group
GNI per capita, *World Bank Atlas* method ($)	1,550	4,884	1,965
Adjusted net national income per capita ($)	1,269	4,305	1,574
Change in wealth per capita (2010 $)	54	1,172	117
Urban population (% of total)	31.7	49.6	38.9
Agriculture			
Agricultural land (% land area)	35	48	46
Agricultural irrigated land (% of total agricultural land)	..	..	..
Agricultural productivity, value added per worker (2005 $)	468	794	938
Cereal yield (kg per hectare)	5,462	5,145	3,029
Forests and biodiversity			
Forest area (% land area)	45.0	29.7	26.9
Deforestation (avg. annual %, 2000–2010)	-1.6	-0.4	0.3
Terrestrial protected areas (% of total land area)	6.5	15.1	11.9
Threatened species, mammals	54		
Threatened species, birds	45		
Threatened species, fish	73		
Threatened species, higher plants	170		
Oceans			
Total fisheries production (thousand metric tons)	5,942	108,399	43,067
Capture fisheries growth (avg. annual %, 1990–2012)	5.7	3.4	2.6
Aquaculture growth (avg. annual %, 1990–2012)	14.7	9.1	9.9
Marine protected areas (% of territorial waters)	1.7	1.4	14.7
Coral reef area (sq. km)	1,270	137,690	124,480
Mangroves area (sq. km)	1,056	56,537	58,917
Energy and emissions			
Energy use per capita (kg oil equivalent)	697	1,671	687
Energy from biomass products and waste (% of total)	24.0	10.1	26.8
Electric power consumption per capita (kWh)	1,073	2,582	734
Electricity generated using fossil fuel (% of total)	69.8	80.9	72.3
Electricity generated by hydropower (% of total)	30.1	14.5	16.9
CO_2 emissions per capita (metric tons)	1.7	4.9	1.6
Water and sanitation			
Internal freshwater resources per capita (cu. m)	4,092	4,438	3,144
Total freshwater withdrawal (% of internal resources)	22.8	10.9	19.6
Agriculture (% of total freshwater withdrawal)	95	73	88
Access to improved water source (% of total population)	95	91	88
Rural (% of rural population)	94	85	85
Urban (% of urban population)	98	97	94
Access to improved sanitation facilities (% of total population)	75	67	48
Rural (% of rural population)	67	58	36
Urban (% of urban population)	93	76	66
Environment and health			
Particulate matter (urban-pop.-weighted avg., µg/cu. m)	69	75	90
Acute resp. infection prevalence (% of children under five)	..	..	..
Diarrhea prevalence (% of children under five)	..	..	..
Under-five mortality rate (per 1,000 live births)	23	21	61
National accounting aggregates—savings, depletion and degradation			
Gross savings (% of GNI)	33.1	47.6	28.6
Consumption of fixed capital (% of GNI)	16.5	12.0	11.1
Education expenditure (% of GNI)	5.9	2.1	3.1
Energy depletion (% of GNI)	6.8	2.7	4.4
Mineral depletion (% of GNI)	0.3	1.4	1.1
Net forest depletion (% of GNI)	0.7	0.1	0.8
CO_2 damage (% of GNI)	1.2	1.0	0.9
Particulate emissions damage (% of GNI)	0.7	1.6	1.4
Adjusted net savings (% of GNI)	12.7	30.9	12.0

Virgin Islands (U.S.)

Population (thousands) **105**   Land area (sq. km)   **350**   GDP ($ millions)   ..

	Country data	High-income group
GNI per capita, *World Bank Atlas* method ($)	..	38,444
Adjusted net national income per capita ($)	..	32,262
Change in wealth per capita (2010 $)	..	2,210
Urban population (% of total)	95.6	80.2

Agriculture
Agricultural land (% land area)	11	29
Agricultural irrigated land (% of total agricultural land)	..	
Agricultural productivity, value added per worker (2005 $)	..	25,238
Cereal yield (kg per hectare)	..	4,374

Forests and biodiversity
Forest area (% land area)	57.4	35.0
Deforestation (avg. annual %, 2000–2010)	0.8	0.0
Terrestrial protected areas (% of total land area)	15.3	13.9
Threatened species, mammals	2	
Threatened species, birds	1	
Threatened species, fish	16	
Threatened species, higher plants	12	

Oceans
Total fisheries production (thousand metric tons)	0.53	37,661
Capture fisheries growth (avg. annual %, 1990–2012)	-1.3	-2.0
Aquaculture growth (avg. annual %, 1990–2012)	..	2.5
Marine protected areas (% of territorial waters)	1.7	14.4
Coral reef area (sq. km)	200	82,210
Mangroves area (sq. km)	2.6	15,504

Energy and emissions
Energy use per capita (kg oil equivalent)	..	4,872
Energy from biomass products and waste (% of total)	..	4.3
Electric power consumption per capita (kWh)	..	8,896
Electricity generated using fossil fuel (% of total)	..	61.8
Electricity generated by hydropower (% of total)	..	12.2
CO_2 emissions per capita (metric tons)	..	11.6

Water and sanitation
Internal freshwater resources per capita (cu. m)	..	11,335
Total freshwater withdrawal (% of internal resources)	..	7.0
Agriculture (% of total freshwater withdrawal)	..	40
Access to improved water source (% of total population)	100	99
Rural (% of rural population)	100	98
Urban (% of urban population)	100	100
Access to improved sanitation facilities (% of total population)	96	96
Rural (% of rural population)	96	93
Urban (% of urban population)	96	97

Environment and health
Particulate matter (urban-pop.-weighted avg., µg/cu. m)	..	27
Acute resp. infection prevalence (% of children under five)	..	..
Diarrhea prevalence (% of children under five)	..	..
Under-five mortality rate (per 1,000 live births)	..	6

National accounting aggregates—savings, depletion and degradation
Gross savings (% of GNI)	..	20.1
Consumption of fixed capital (% of GNI)	..	14.2
Education expenditure (% of GNI)	..	4.7
Energy depletion (% of GNI)	..	1.6
Mineral depletion (% of GNI)	..	0.3
Net forest depletion (% of GNI)	..	0.0
CO_2 damage (% of GNI)	..	0.3
Particulate emissions damage (% of GNI)	..	0.3
Adjusted net savings (% of GNI)	..	8.1

West Bank and Gaza

Population (millions)	**4.0**	Land area (1,000 sq. km)	**6.0**	GDP ($ millions)	..

	Country data	Middle East & N. Africa group	Lower middle-income group
GNI per capita, *World Bank Atlas* method ($)	..	3,451	1,965
Adjusted net national income per capita ($)	..	2,602	1,574
Change in wealth per capita (2010 $)	..	101	117
Urban population (% of total)	74.6	59.5	38.9
Agriculture			
Agricultural land (% land area)	43	23	46
Agricultural irrigated land (% of total agricultural land)	4.9	..	..
Agricultural productivity, value added per worker (2005 $)	..	2,642	938
Cereal yield (kg per hectare)	1,498	2,350	3,029
Forests and biodiversity			
Forest area (% land area)	1.5	2.4	26.9
Deforestation (avg. annual %, 2000–2010)	-0.1	-0.1	0.3
Terrestrial protected areas (% of total land area)	0.6	6.1	11.9
Threatened species, mammals	3		
Threatened species, birds	10		
Threatened species, fish	0		
Threatened species, higher plants	0		
Oceans			
Total fisheries production (thousand metric tons)	..	3,976	43,067
Capture fisheries growth (avg. annual %, 1990–2012)	..	3.0	2.6
Aquaculture growth (avg. annual %, 1990–2012)	..	12.8	9.9
Marine protected areas (% of territorial waters)	..	9.1	14.7
Coral reef area (sq. km)	..	5,700	124,480
Mangroves area (sq. km)	..	217	58,917
Energy and emissions			
Energy use per capita (kg oil equivalent)	..	1,376	687
Energy from biomass products and waste (% of total)	..	0.9	26.8
Electric power consumption per capita (kWh)	..	1,696	734
Electricity generated using fossil fuel (% of total)	..	91.7	72.3
Electricity generated by hydropower (% of total)	..	5.5	16.9
CO_2 emissions per capita (metric tons)	0.6	3.9	1.6
Water and sanitation			
Internal freshwater resources per capita (cu. m)	207	679	3,144
Total freshwater withdrawal (% of internal resources)	51.5	122.1	19.6
Agriculture (% of total freshwater withdrawal)	45	86	88
Access to improved water source (% of total population)	82	90	88
Rural (% of rural population)	82	83	85
Urban (% of urban population)	82	95	94
Access to improved sanitation facilities (% of total population)	94	88	48
Rural (% of rural population)	93	80	36
Urban (% of urban population)	95	94	66
Environment and health			
Particulate matter (urban-pop.-weighted avg., µg/cu. m)	..	79	90
Acute resp. infection prevalence (% of children under five)	..	..	..
Diarrhea prevalence (% of children under five)	..	..	..
Under-five mortality rate (per 1,000 live births)	23	26	61
National accounting aggregates—savings, depletion and degradation			
Gross savings (% of GNI)	..	25.9	28.6
Consumption of fixed capital (% of GNI)	..	9.9	11.1
Education expenditure (% of GNI)	..	4.5	3.1
Energy depletion (% of GNI)	..	12.9	4.4
Mineral depletion (% of GNI)	..	0.5	1.1
Net forest depletion (% of GNI)	..	0.2	0.8
CO_2 damage (% of GNI)	..	0.7	0.9
Particulate emissions damage (% of GNI)	..	0.9	1.4
Adjusted net savings (% of GNI)	..	5.3	12.0

Yemen, Rep.

| Population (millions) | **23.9** | Land area (1,000 sq. km) | **528** | GDP ($ billions) | **35.7** |

	Country data	Middle East & N. Africa group	Lower middle-income group
GNI per capita, *World Bank Atlas* method ($)	1,290	3,451	1,965
Adjusted net national income per capita ($)	1,162	2,602	1,574
Change in wealth per capita (2010 $)	-344	101	117
Urban population (% of total)	32.9	59.5	38.9
Agriculture			
Agricultural land (% land area)	44	23	46
Agricultural irrigated land (% of total agricultural land)	3.3	..	..
Agricultural productivity, value added per worker (2005 $)	929	2,642	938
Cereal yield (kg per hectare)	1,057	2,350	3,029
Forests and biodiversity			
Forest area (% land area)	1.0	2.4	26.9
Deforestation (avg. annual %, 2000–2010)	0.0	-0.1	0.3
Terrestrial protected areas (% of total land area)	0.8	6.1	11.9
Threatened species, mammals	9		
Threatened species, birds	15		
Threatened species, fish	24		
Threatened species, higher plants	161		
Oceans			
Total fisheries production (thousand metric tons)	231	3,976	43,067
Capture fisheries growth (avg. annual %, 1990–2012)	5.1	3.0	2.6
Aquaculture growth (avg. annual %, 1990–2012)	..	12.8	9.9
Marine protected areas (% of territorial waters)	1.8	9.1	14.7
Coral reef area (sq. km)	700	5,700	124,480
Mangroves area (sq. km)	9.3	217	58,917
Energy and emissions			
Energy use per capita (kg oil equivalent)	312	1,376	687
Energy from biomass products and waste (% of total)	1.5	0.9	26.8
Electric power consumption per capita (kWh)	193	1,696	734
Electricity generated using fossil fuel (% of total)	100.0	91.7	72.3
Electricity generated by hydropower (% of total)	0.0	5.5	16.9
CO_2 emissions per capita (metric tons)	1.0	3.9	1.6
Water and sanitation			
Internal freshwater resources per capita (cu. m)	90	679	3,144
Total freshwater withdrawal (% of internal resources)	169.8	122.1	19.6
Agriculture (% of total freshwater withdrawal)	91	86	88
Access to improved water source (% of total population)	55	90	88
Rural (% of rural population)	47	83	85
Urban (% of urban population)	72	95	94
Access to improved sanitation facilities (% of total population)	53	88	48
Rural (% of rural population)	34	80	36
Urban (% of urban population)	93	94	66
Environment and health			
Particulate matter (urban-pop.-weighted avg., µg/cu. m)	78	79	90
Acute resp. infection prevalence (% of children under five)	..	..	..
Diarrhea prevalence (% of children under five)	..	..	..
Under-five mortality rate (per 1,000 live births)	60	26	61
National accounting aggregates—savings, depletion and degradation			
Gross savings (% of GNI)	8.6	25.9	28.6
Consumption of fixed capital (% of GNI)	6.9	9.9	11.1
Education expenditure (% of GNI)	4.1	4.5	3.1
Energy depletion (% of GNI)	10.7	12.9	4.4
Mineral depletion (% of GNI)	0.0	0.5	1.1
Net forest depletion (% of GNI)	0.0	0.2	0.8
CO_2 damage (% of GNI)	0.6	0.7	0.9
Particulate emissions damage (% of GNI)	1.3	0.9	1.4
Adjusted net savings (% of GNI)	-10.8	5.3	12.0

Zambia

Population (millions)	**14.1**	Land area (1,000 sq. km)	**743**	GDP ($ billions)	**20.6**

	Country data	Sub-Saharan Africa group	Lower middle-income group
GNI per capita, *World Bank Atlas* method ($)	1,350	1,547	1,965
Adjusted net national income per capita ($)	1,040	1,005	1,574
Change in wealth per capita (2010 $)	-303	-273	117
Urban population (% of total)	39.6	36.8	38.9

Agriculture

Agricultural land (% land area)	32	44	46
Agricultural irrigated land (% of total agricultural land)	..	..	..
Agricultural productivity, value added per worker (2005 $)	619	765	938
Cereal yield (kg per hectare)	2,693	1,417	3,029

Forests and biodiversity

Forest area (% land area)	66.3	27.4	26.9
Deforestation (avg. annual %, 2000–2010)	0.3	0.5	0.3
Terrestrial protected areas (% of total land area)	37.8	16.4	11.9
Threatened species, mammals	9		
Threatened species, birds	15		
Threatened species, fish	20		
Threatened species, higher plants	13		

Oceans

Total fisheries production (thousand metric tons)	89.2	6,906	43,067
Capture fisheries growth (avg. annual %, 1990–2012)	0.7	2.1	2.6
Aquaculture growth (avg. annual %, 1990–2012)	10.4	15.9	9.9
Marine protected areas (% of territorial waters)	..	11.7	14.7
Coral reef area (sq. km)	..	17,980	124,480
Mangroves area (sq. km)	..	27,808	58,917

Energy and emissions

Energy use per capita (kg oil equivalent)	621	681	687
Energy from biomass products and waste (% of total)	80.2	57.6	26.8
Electric power consumption per capita (kWh)	599	535	734
Electricity generated using fossil fuel (% of total)	0.3	65.1	72.3
Electricity generated by hydropower (% of total)	99.7	20.0	16.9
CO_2 emissions per capita (metric tons)	0.2	0.8	1.6

Water and sanitation

Internal freshwater resources per capita (cu. m)	5,882	4,391	3,144
Total freshwater withdrawal (% of internal resources)	2.2	3.2	19.6
Agriculture (% of total freshwater withdrawal)	76	84	88
Access to improved water source (% of total population)	63	64	88
Rural (% of rural population)	49	53	85
Urban (% of urban population)	85	85	94
Access to improved sanitation facilities (% of total population)	43	30	48
Rural (% of rural population)	34	23	36
Urban (% of urban population)	56	41	66

Environment and health

Particulate matter (urban-pop.-weighted avg., μg/cu. m)	46	77	90
Acute resp. infection prevalence (% of children under five)	5	5	..
Diarrhea prevalence (% of children under five)	16	14	..
Under-five mortality rate (per 1,000 live births)	89	98	61

National accounting aggregates—savings, depletion and degradation

Gross savings (% of GNI)	26.1	26.3	28.6
Consumption of fixed capital (% of GNI)	11.5	13.0	11.1
Education expenditure (% of GNI)	1.3	3.4	3.1
Energy depletion (% of GNI)	0.0	10.3	4.4
Mineral depletion (% of GNI)	13.4	1.8	1.1
Net forest depletion (% of GNI)	0.0	1.8	0.8
CO_2 damage (% of GNI)	0.1	0.6	0.9
Particulate emissions damage (% of GNI)	0.7	1.2	1.4
Adjusted net savings (% of GNI)	1.8	0.9	12.0

Zimbabwe

	Country data	Sub-Saharan Africa group	Low-income group
Population (millions) **13.7** Land area (1,000 sq. km) **387** GDP ($ billions) **9.8**			

	Country data	Sub-Saharan Africa group	Low-income group
GNI per capita, *World Bank Atlas* method ($)	650	1,547	594
Adjusted net national income per capita ($)	566	1,005	495
Change in wealth per capita (2010 $)	..	-273	-39
Urban population (% of total)	39.1	36.8	28.2
Agriculture			
Agricultural land (% land area)	42	44	39
Agricultural irrigated land (% of total agricultural land)	..	..	..
Agricultural productivity, value added per worker (2005 $)	239	765	367
Cereal yield (kg per hectare)	855	1,417	1,982
Forests and biodiversity			
Forest area (% land area)	39.5	27.4	27.4
Deforestation (avg. annual %, 2000–2010)	1.9	0.5	0.6
Terrestrial protected areas (% of total land area)	27.2	16.4	13.7
Threatened species, mammals	9		
Threatened species, birds	15		
Threatened species, fish	3		
Threatened species, higher plants	18		
Oceans			
Total fisheries production (thousand metric tons)	18.5	6,906	11,789
Capture fisheries growth (avg. annual %, 1990–2012)	-4.0	2.1	3.8
Aquaculture growth (avg. annual %, 1990–2012)	19.6	15.9	5.1
Marine protected areas (% of territorial waters)	..	11.7	13.1
Coral reef area (sq. km)	..	17,980	15,120
Mangroves area (sq. km)	..	27,808	25,817
Energy and emissions			
Energy use per capita (kg oil equivalent)	697	681	360
Energy from biomass products and waste (% of total)	64.2	57.6	66.0
Electric power consumption per capita (kWh)	757	535	233
Electricity generated using fossil fuel (% of total)	25.6	65.1	30.9
Electricity generated by hydropower (% of total)	73.6	20.0	45.5
CO_2 emissions per capita (metric tons)	0.7	0.8	0.3
Water and sanitation			
Internal freshwater resources per capita (cu. m)	918	4,391	5,121
Total freshwater withdrawal (% of internal resources)	34.3	3.2	4.4
Agriculture (% of total freshwater withdrawal)	79	84	90
Access to improved water source (% of total population)	80	64	69
Rural (% of rural population)	69	53	61
Urban (% of urban population)	97	85	88
Access to improved sanitation facilities (% of total population)	40	30	37
Rural (% of rural population)	32	23	33
Urban (% of urban population)	52	41	46
Environment and health			
Particulate matter (urban-pop.-weighted avg., µg/cu. m)	104	77	74
Acute resp. infection prevalence (% of children under five)	4	5	6
Diarrhea prevalence (% of children under five)	13	14	14
Under-five mortality rate (per 1,000 live births)	90	98	82
National accounting aggregates—savings, depletion and degradation			
Gross savings (% of GNI)	..	26.3	24.6
Consumption of fixed capital (% of GNI)	11.4	13.0	11.8
Education expenditure (% of GNI)	2.5	3.4	3.2
Energy depletion (% of GNI)	1.2	10.3	1.4
Mineral depletion (% of GNI)	5.0	1.8	1.9
Net forest depletion (% of GNI)	0.0	1.8	4.4
CO_2 damage (% of GNI)	1.1	0.6	0.4
Particulate emissions damage (% of GNI)	1.0	1.2	1.0
Adjusted net savings (% of GNI)	..	0.9	7.0

Notes

a. Data series will be calculated upon finalization of the ongoing revisions to official statistics reported by the National Statistics and Censuses Institute of Argentina.

b. Refers to area free from ice.

c. Excludes South Sudan.

Glossary

Access to improved sanitation facilities refers to the percentage of the population using improved sanitation facilities. The improved sanitation facilities include flush/pour flush (to piped sewer system, septic tank, pit latrine), ventilated improved pit (VIP) latrine, pit latrine with slab, and composting toilet. (World Health Organization and United Nations Children's Fund; data are for 2012)

Access to improved water source refers to the percentage of the population using an improved drinking water source. The improved drinking water source includes piped water on premises (piped household water connection located inside the user's dwelling, plot, or yard) and other improved drinking water sources (public taps or standpipes, tube wells or boreholes, protected dug wells, protected springs, and rainwater collection). (World Health Organization and United Nations Children's Fund; data are for 2012)

Acute respiratory infection prevalence is the percentage of children under age five with acute respiratory infection in the two weeks prior to the survey. (United Nations Children's Fund; data are for the most recent year available during 2007–12)

Adjusted net national income per capita equals gross national income minus consumption of fixed capital, energy depletion, mineral depletion, and net forest depletion, divided by midyear population. (World Bank; data are for 2012)

Adjusted net savings equal gross savings minus consumption of fixed capital, plus education expenditures, minus energy depletion, mineral depletion, net forest depletion, and particulate emissions and carbon dioxide damage. (World Bank; data are for 2012)

Agricultural irrigated land refers to agricultural areas purposely provided with water, including land irrigated by controlled flooding. (Food and Agriculture Organization; data are for 2011)

Agricultural land is arable land, land under permanent crops, and permanent pastures. Arable land includes land defined by the Food and Agriculture Organization of the United Nations as land under temporary crops (double-cropped areas are counted once), temporary meadows for mowing or for pasture, land under market or kitchen gardens, and land temporarily fallow. Land abandoned as a result of shifting cultivation is excluded. Land under permanent crops is land cultivated with crops that occupy the land for long periods and need not be replanted after each harvest, such as cocoa, coffee, and rubber. This category includes land under flowering shrubs, fruit trees, nut trees, and vines but excludes land under trees grown for wood or timber. Permanent pasture is land used for five or more years for forage, including natural and cultivated crops. (Food and Agriculture Organization; data are for 2011)

Agricultural productivity is the ratio of agricultural value added, measured in 2005 U.S. dollars, to the number of workers in agriculture. Agricultural productivity is measured by value added per unit of input. Agricultural value

Glossary

added includes that from forestry and fishing. Thus interpretations of land productivity should be made with caution. (Food and Agriculture Organization and World Bank; data are for 2012)

Aquaculture growth is the exponential change in aquaculture fisheries production for the period indicated. Aquaculture is understood to mean the farming of aquatic organisms including fish, molluscs, crustaceans, and aquatic plants. Aquaculture production specifically refers to output from aquaculture activities, which are designated for final harvest for consumption. (Food and Agriculture Organization; data are for 1990–2012)

Capture fisheries growth is the exponential change in capture fisheries production for the period indicated. Capture fisheries production measures the volume of fish catches landed by a country for all commercial, industrial, recreational, and subsistence purposes. (Food and Agriculture Organization; data are for 1990–2012)

Carbon dioxide (CO2) damage is estimated at \$20 per ton of carbon (the unit damage in 1995 U.S. dollars) times the number of tons of carbon emitted. (World Bank estimates; data are for 2012)

Carbon dioxide (CO2) emissions per capita are carbon dioxide emissions divided by midyear population. (Carbon Dioxide Information Analysis Center, World Bank, and United Nations; data are for 2010)

Cereal yield measured as kilograms per hectare of harvested land, includes wheat, rice, maize, barley, oats, rye, millet, sorghum, buckwheat, and mixed grains. Production data on cereals relate to crops harvested for dry grain only. Cereal crops harvested for hay or harvested green for food, feed, or silage and those used for grazing are excluded. The FAO allocates production data to the calendar year in which the bulk of the harvest took place. Most of a crop harvested near the end of a year will be used in the following year. (Food and Agriculture Organization; data are for 2012)

Change in wealth per capita is a measure of sustainability that indicates whether enough assets are saved to sustain the same welfare per capita in the future. It is based on gross national savings adjusted for changes in physical, human, and natural capital and accounting for additional resource needs due to population growth. (World Bank estimates; data are for 2010)

Consumption of fixed capital is the replacement value of capital used up in the process of production. (United Nations; data are extrapolated to 2012 from the most recent year available)

Coral reef area is a country's area of coral reefs, which are shallow marine habitats defined both by a physical structure (corals) and by the organisms found on them. (See *The World Atlas of Coral Reefs* (2001), UNEP-World Conservation Monitoring Centre)

Deforestation is the permanent conversion of natural forest area to other uses, including shifting cultivation, permanent agriculture, ranching, settlements, and infrastructure development. Deforested areas do not include areas logged but intended for regeneration or areas degraded by fuel-wood gathering, acid precipitation, or forest fires. Negative numbers indicate an increase in forest areas. (Food and Agriculture Organization; data are for 2000–10).

Diarrhea prevalence is the percentage of children under age five who had diarrhea in the two weeks prior to the survey. (United Nations Children's Fund; data are for the most recent year available during 2007–12)

Education expenditure is public current operating expenditures in education, including wages and salaries and excluding capital investments in buildings and equipment. (United Nations; data are extrapolated to 2012 from the most recent year available)

Electric power consumption per capita is the production of power plants and combined heat and power plants, minus transmission, distribution, and transformation losses and own use by heat and power plants plus imports minus exports divided by midyear population. (International Energy Agency; data are for 2011)

Electricity generated by hydropower is use of hydropower as a percentage of total inputs to the generation of electricity. (International Energy Agency; data are for 2011)

Electricity generated using fossil fuel is use of coal, oil, and gas as a percentage of total inputs to the generation of electricity. (International Energy Agency; data are for 2011)

Energy depletion is the ratio of the value of the stock of energy resources to the remaining reserve lifetime (capped at 25 years). It covers crude oil, natural gas, and coal. (See World Bank 2011 for details; data are for 2012)

Energy from biomass products and waste is energy from solid biomass, liquid biomass, biogas, industrial waste, and municipal waste as a percentage of total energy use. (International Energy Agency; data are for 2011)

Energy use per capita refers to apparent consumption, which is equal to indigenous production plus imports and stock changes, minus exports and fuels supplied to ships and aircraft engaged in international transport. (International Energy Agency; data are for 2011)

Fisheries production, total, measures the volume of aquatic species caught by a country for all commercial, industrial, recreational, and subsistence purposes. The harvest from mariculture, aquaculture, and other types of fish farming is also included. (Food and Agriculture Organization; data are for 2012)

Forest area is land under natural or planted stands of trees, whether productive or not. (Food and Agriculture Organization; data are for 2011)

Freshwater withdrawal, agriculture, is withdrawals for irrigation and livestock production as a percentage of total freshwater withdrawal. (World Resources

Glossary

data are for various years; for details see *World Development Indicators 2014, Primary data documentation*)

Freshwater withdrawal, total, is total water withdrawal, excluding evaporation losses from storage basins and including water from desalination plants in countries where they are a significant source. Withdrawals can exceed 100 percent of internal renewable resources because river flows from other countries are not included, because extraction from nonrenewable aquifers or desalination plants is considerable, or because there is significant water reuse. (Food and Agriculture Organization and World Resources Institute; data are for various years; for details see *World Development Indicators 2014, Primary data documentation*)

GDP is gross domestic product and measures the total output of goods and services for final use occurring within the domestic territory of a given country, regardless of the allocation to domestic and foreign claims. GDP at purchaser values (market prices) is the sum of gross value added by all resident and nonresident producers in the economy plus any taxes and minus any subsidies not included in the value of the products. It is calculated without deductions for depreciation of fabricated assets or for depletion and degradation of natural resources. (World Bank, Organization for Economic Co-operation and Development, and United Nations; data are for 2012)

GNI is gross domestic product plus net receipts of primary income (employee compensation and property income) from abroad. GNI per capita is in current U.S. dollars, converted using the *World Bank Atlas* method (see *World Development Indicators 2014, Statistical methods*). (World Bank, Organization for Economic Co-operation and Development, and United Nations; data are for 2012)

GNI per capita is gross national income (GNI) divided by midyear population.

Gross savings are calculated as gross national income less total consumption, plus net transfers. (World Bank and Organization for Economic Co-operation and Development; data are for 2012)

Internal freshwater resources per capita are internal renewable resources, which include flows of rivers and groundwater from rainfall in the country but excludes river flows from other countries, divided by midyear population. (Refers to data reported to the Food and Agriculture Organization as of 2011)

Land area is a country's total land area, excluding area under inland water bodies, national claims to continental shelf, and exclusive economic zones. In most cases the definition of inland water bodies includes major rivers and lakes. (Food and Agriculture Organization; data are for 2012)

Mangroves area is a country's total area of mangroves, which are plants of a variety of different species, including trees, shrubs, palms, and ferns, that grow in the tropics and subtropics in saline intertidal coastal habitats, such as estuaries and shorelines. (See *The World Atlas of Mangroves* (2010), International Society for Mangrove Ecosystems, The Nature Conservancy,

Glossary

Food and Agriculture Organization, UNEP-World Conservation Monitoring Centre)

Marine protected areas are areas of intertidal or subtidal terrain—and overlying water and associated flora and fauna and historical and cultural features—that have been reserved by law or other effective means to protect part or all of the enclosed environment. (United Nations Environmental Program and the World Conservation Monitoring Centre, as compiled by the World Resources Institute; data are for 2012)

Mineral depletion is the ratio of the value of the stock of mineral resources to the remaining reserve lifetime (capped at 25 years). It covers bauxite, copper, iron, lead, nickel, phosphate, tin, gold, silver, and zinc. (See World Bank 2011 for details; data are for 2012)

Net forest depletion is the product of unit resource rents and the excess of round-wood harvest over natural growth. If growth exceeds harvest, this figure is zero. (Food and Agriculture Organization and World Bank estimates of natural growth; data are for 2012)

Particulate emissions damage is calculated as the willingness to pay to reduce the risk of illness and death attributable to particulate emissions. (World Bank estimates; data are for 2011)

Particulate matter is fine suspended particulates of less than 10 microns in diameter that are capable of penetrating deep into the respiratory tract and causing damage. The indicator is the population-weighted average of all cities in the country with a population greater than 100,000. (World Bank estimates; data are for 2011)

Population includes all residents who are present regardless of legal status or citizenship except for refugees not permanently settled in the country of asylum, who are generally considered part of the population of their country of origin. (United Nations; data are midyear estimates for 2012)

Terrestrial protected areas are totally or partially protected areas of at least 1,000 hectares that are designated as national parks, natural monuments, nature reserves, or wildlife sanctuaries; protected landscapes and seascapes; and scientific reserves. It includes World Conservation Union–protected area categories I–VI. (United Nations Environmental Program and the World Conservation Monitoring Centre, as compiled by the World Resources Institute; data are for 2012)

Threatened species, birds, are the number of species of birds classified by the International Union for Conservation of Nature (IUCN) as endangered, vulnerable, rare, indeterminate, out of danger, or insufficiently known. Birds are listed for countries included within their breeding or wintering ranges. (World Conservation Monitoring Centre and IUCN; data are for 2013)

Threatened species, fish, are the number of species of fish—cold-blooded aquatic vertebrates of the superclass Pisces—classified by the IUCN as

Glossary

endangered, vulnerable, rare, indeterminate, out of danger, or insufficiently known. (World Conservation Monitoring Centre and IUCN; data are for 2013)

Threatened species, higher plants, are the number of native vascular plant species classified by the IUCN as endangered, vulnerable, rare, indeterminate, out of danger, or insufficiently known. (World Conservation Monitoring Centre and IUCN; data are for 2013)

Threatened species, mammals, are the number of species of mammals—excluding whales and porpoises—classified by the IUCN as endangered, vulnerable, rare, indeterminate, out of danger, or insufficiently known. (World Conservation Monitoring Centre and IUCN; data are for 2013)

Under-five mortality rate is the probability that a newborn baby will die before reaching age five if subject to current age-specific mortality rates. (United Nations and United Nations Children's Fund; data are for 2012)

Urban population is the share of the midyear population living in areas defined as urban in each country. (United Nations; data are for 2012)

References

World Bank. 2011. *The Changing Wealth of Nations: Measuring Sustainable Development in the New Millennium*. Washington, D.C.: World Bank.

———2014. *World Development Indicators 2014*. Washington, D.C.: World Bank.